I0188339

LIVING IN REALITY

EVERYTHING I NEEDED TO KNOW
I LEARNED IN PRISON

A True Story by:
David W. Jones

C P

Cadmus Publishing
www.cadmuspublishing.com

Copyright © 2021 David W. Jones
Published by Cadmus Publishing
www.cadmuspublishing.com
Port Angeles, WA

ISBN: 978-1-63751-094-0
Library of Congress Control Number: 2021921565

All rights reserved. Copyright under Berne Copyright Convention, Universal Copyright Convention, and Pan-American Copyright Convention. No part of this book may be reproduced, stored in a retrieval system, or transmitted in any form, or by any means, electronic, mechanical, photocopying, recording or otherwise, without prior permission of the author.

When necessary, names have been changed to protect others' identities. This book expresses the Author's thoughts and recollections of his life, before and during prison. The Author believes that change is possible – even in the worst of society.
He would like to know what you think:
71davidjones@gmail.com
Or go to Jpay.com and send a line: (TDCJ # 1476876)

davidwjones71.com

This book is dedicated to:
My Mom
I Love You.
"Promise, Promise."
"Always, Always."

IT'S ALL IN THE MIND

It's all in the mind—you either go crazy, or you don't. Doing time takes a lot of mind manipulation. When I entered Texas Prison, I was twenty years old. As the door slammed shut behind me, I told myself, "I can leave anytime I want, I just don't want to."

And that is how it all started. The lies, the fantasies, the assimilation. Not that I didn't lie to myself on the outside. I've come to find out that's *where* it all started, that my whole life was a lie, and sadly I believed those lies. And the fantasies; well, everyone knows that we fantasize to make ourselves feel better. Right?

How many of us have comforted ourselves with thoughts of revenge when somebody has done us wrong? Fantasies are just a string of thoughts where you can make everything go your way. Sexual fantasies also bring comfort. I fantasized my way to prison.

A mind that goes unchecked is very dangerous. A fantasy can ignore all boundaries and proper etiquette, and even the respectful treatment of others. Because no one knows, and there is no one to confront the thought as it crosses the line and keeps on going. That is, except the person *thinking* the thought. But if that person has never been taught those boundaries, etiquette and respect, then be careful, because you never know what a person may be thinking.

When I came to prison my first concern, being a sex offender, was survival. But I also wanted comfort. Don't we all, in bad situations? Prison is a really bad situation. All the lies that I had believed out there came with me, and I reinforced them by living in a made-up world in my mind. Music, books, and movies all aided in my escape, but I continued to fantasize about the men I was attracted to around me. In psychology they say that our thoughts cause our feelings, and then we act upon our feelings.

Well, I *acted* very promiscuously. Survival and comfort were my motivations. That, and I hated being alone. Prison is a very lonely place, and since I was gay and living around my sexual preference, I decided to have a ball—or two, so to speak.

Along the way several things happened. I learned to have compatible relationships with adults, I had a turning point that made me question my whole belief system, and as Dr. Phil says, "You must get to your core belief, what you truly believe about yourself, and change it." That is what I did. I changed my thought patterns, which had kept me in an ever-unending cycle of bad decisions. I changed my beliefs about myself, and my perception of reality, and I found my identity.

No more mind manipulation, no more lies. I choose every day to live in the sobriety of reality.

"Imagine the difficulty of listening to, and then accepting, a truth that overturns everything you believe about the world.
And not merely that, but a truth that informs you that 'the world is not what you think it is. And, by the way, neither are you.'
How many of us have the intellectual courage to consider, let alone accept, the truth when it demands so much?"
-Osha Gray Davidson

"What is real isn't necessarily true."
"The past is obdurate."
-Stephen King

"You know nothing, Jon Snow."
-George R. R. Martin

INTRODUCTION BY THE AUTHOR

"If it makes sense, don't do it."

Motto for Texas Prison

-Unofficial

I've been in prison for thirty years. I came down at the age of twenty. I've spent more time behind bars than I have out in the free world. We, the locked-up, call living out there "the free world". A strange concept. Because the only thing "free" out there is that you may do what you want, when you want to. In here, I am locked in a cell that is about 12' by 9', and may go to the dayroom when the officers open the cell door. I go to chow when *they* call it, and can go to recreation a possible two times a day—when *they* call it. On each unit it varies, but dayroom time is generally between 6 a.m. and 10:30 p.m., on weekdays; and on weekends it closes at 1 a.m.

The Texas Department of Criminal Justice (TDCJ) is a very strange world-within-a-world. There are real people in here: they go to work, they come "home," shower, sit in the dayroom and watch TV, play board games, go to rec., play basketball, handball or exercise. They either throw food items from the commissary together to make a "spread," or go down to the chow hall and eat the food there. We are offered, throughout the day, what is called "ingress and egress," or what we call "in and outs." This is where the correctional officer (CO) comes into the wing and opens our cell doors, and allows us to go in, either stay or grab something (a cup of coffee, a snack, or a book) and return to the dayroom. In theory, in and outs are to be given "every hour on the hour." But you learn that in here nothing ever happens as it's "supposed" to. It's a common saying among both the inmates and the COs that "the only thing that is constant about TDCJ is its inconsistency."

You may be asking yourself, "Why is he telling us all of this?" And the answer is that out of all the movies and books that I've read that portray the prison life, well, they fall short of the reality of it. Granted, I have not exhausted every prison book or movie, and I am writing this from my cell, but I wanted to write this book to give you a look into the Texas Prison System, through one person's eyes. Maybe by the end you can judge if our prisons are doing their job.

Although that's not the only reason that I'm writing this book. I'm writing to tell you my life story. How does one go to prison right after he "grew up?" I hope to give you a deep insight into how someone can become a sex offender. I'll go into the (dark, irrational) thoughts and beliefs that correspond to sexual offending—I hope that this will help you or others to be aware how *not* to be, or even raise, a sex offender. I hope it will inspire you to examine yourself and be a better person.

This book will expose the Texas Prison System, and the delusion that is mass incarceration. This book will *not* glorify my crimes. I won't delve into all that. I will tell you that the Dallas Police labeled me the "most prolific child molester" in Dallas history. I'm not proud of that. No, when they said it at first, I was angry. Now it disgusts me that I earned that label. You hear in the news, practically every day, about some form of sex offenses, whether its harassment, or up the scale to rape; it has reached every class of people, from poverty to the POTUS. The media the pomp and the person getting punished and going to prison. But I don't know of that many people who've overcome this and opened up their deep secrets, put out their shame and guilt for everybody to see.

This book is about survival, not only in prison, but of childhood also. This is about rehabilitation and overcoming big obstacles and even the lowest depths. Do you have that 'intellectual courage' to go on this journey with me? This is about love, acceptance, relationship, power, control, rejection, pain, and hurt. I guess you could say that it's about life. This book may just show how you and I are more alike than different. Are you ready to be assimilated? Welcome to Texas Prison, where resistance just may save your life and sanity. Do you think that you can spot the truth from reality? Feeling lucky? We'll leave the count lights on for you.

This is a journey that you don't want to miss.

Come on, let's turn back time.

CONTENTS

PROLOGUE

MY ASSESSMENT OF CIVIL COMMITMENT

—◦〜◦—

"He that would make his own liberty secure, must guard even his enemy from oppression: for if he violates this duty, he establishes a precedent that will reach to himself."
-Thomas Paine

"Government is instituted for the common good; for the protection, safety, property, and happiness of the people; and not for profit, honor, or private interest of any one man, family, or class of men."
-John Adams

"The liberties of our county, the freedom of our civil constitution, are worth defending against all hazards: And it is our duty to defend them against all attacks."
-Sam Adams

Texas Civil Commitment began in 1999. When it started the men that had been placed on civil commitment lived at their own homes in the community; they had an ankle monitor and a GPS box. Do you remember the "cell phones" from early 1990? A phone on top of a big battery. That was what the GPS box looked like, sans the phone. The ankle monitor told the box, which told the satellite where the person was.

This was called outpatient civil commitment. The men were checked up on by a case manager, and they were required to go to group therapy twice a week. Did I mention that all this was done after you'd completed your prison sentence?

It was 2003 and my fifteen years would end in 2006. They began the assessment early then, while you are still in prison; they interviewed you and got one outside evaluation. If all that determined that you had a behavioral abnormality—which is *not* a legal term, but a psychological one—but Texas Legislature had redefined it. If you run red lights, get angry when someone cuts in front of your car, or overeat, you have a behavior abnormality.

Texas Legislature defined it as, "Behavioral Abnormality (B.A. herein,) means a congenital or acquired condition that, by affecting a person's emotional or volitional capacity, predisposes the person to commit a sexual violent offense, to the extent that the person becomes a menace to the health and safety of another person."

Lawmakers can do what they want and call it legal. The courts have upheld them so far in civil commitment laws. These are ex post facto laws. In 1991, I pled guilty in the understanding that I was receiving fifteen years. Now, I have finished my sentence, having paid my debt to society, and had to go to another prison? In the 2003 legislature the civil commitment laws were amended. Now all civilly committed men were forced to live in a locked residential facility—namely halfway houses. Whilst keeping the term "outpatient." Legislature has now made the law unconstitutional. It's contradictory to order someone to "outpatient civil commitment", and in the same order require them to live in a locked residential facility.

The law looked pretty on paper to the Supreme Court, but in application this law is unconstitutional. It violates the civil liberty rights of the men who are committed. Yeah, they were given a, cough, uh, civil commitment, cough, trial. But has anyone in all of history ever stopped the horse from getting out of the barn by shutting the door after he got out? And all these trials are held in Conroe, Texas and heard by a retired Judge, (Conroe—very conservative, very white) or a jury of your, cough cough, peers. You are judged solely on your past convictions, which, they say, indicate that you will repeat them. But the statute says, "Repeat offenders," which means that you have had to have got out of prison and reoffended. That is one of the two requirements to be civilly committed. The other is to have the behavioral abnormality.

I want to point out a couple of contradictions. First, in my original trial in 1991, the law, statues, the court, the DA, were all in agreement—that I had broken the laws, and that I would have a trial to be held accountable for my actions. The very fact that I was first arrested, then prosecuted, then found guilty and sentenced to prison says that I, David Wayne Jones, am indeed responsible for my actions.

While I was doing my prison sentence, more laws came out to further imprison me, but here is the contradiction (even though I can't find in the constitution where it's legal to keep me past my original sentence especially when I was not told that this would happen to me in 1991). The civil commitment statute and definition of the behavioral abnormality state that "I was either born this way or have acquired a condition that affects my emotions or volitional (my choice) capacity and that I am predisposed (without control) to commit sex offenses." (paraphrased)

At the first trial I was responsible. At the civil commitment trial, I have some condition and I cannot make a choice, I have no control over the matter and that makes me commit sex crimes. Thus, I'm not responsible to get out and not commit anymore crimes. Therefore, I must be further confined, and get this—treated for the behavioral abnormality. How are you gonna treat someone, who can't make a choice, to change?

The second contradiction concerns a provision placed in the civil commitment laws when they began in 1999. Since the men were living in the community in their own homes, the statute provided a penalty for breaking rules. Just having a penal code inside a civil law is a travesty. But let's look at it. Texas Health and Safety Code 841.085 provides for a felony to be charged against these men for breaking any of the hundred rules for the program. They have been enhanced to a third degree felony for the civilly committed men in the interest of "protecting the community." It's right there in the statute. This is an element of the law.

But here is what it's saying in reality: "We civilly committed you for a behavioral abnormality. We are treating you for this B/A. But if you break a rule, we *think* this is an indicator that you *may* reoffend in the community so to protect them we give you a felony, send you to prison, oh and we can't *treat* your B/A, because you broke a rule."

Has anyone read *1984* by George Orwell lately? I'm just wondering if that sounds a little too much like Big Brother and the thinking crimes?

Okay, so you may say, "Yeah, that's a little extreme, but they are out in the community and they need protection. And now that they are in a locked residential facility there is no more felony for rule violations, correct? It's moot, right?"

Which I will respond: "The law sets a precedent. If they can have a Big Brother law for one class of people, what makes you *think* that one day they won't enact another law for you saying, "Since you bend over to pick up the newspaper in your yard instead of squatting this indicates you are planning a bank heist." And for the 'No more felony for violations,' I say, we are in Texas. Of course they left this provision in place and it is used as a vehicle to send SOs back to prison. Yes. I know that they are *not* in the community anymore, yes, I understand they are civilly committed to be treated not punished, but it is still there in the statutes and all the amendments after that have never repealed it.

Can you imagine that you have a child who is suicidal. You have to have them committed to a psychiatric facility because they might hurt themselves. Then the doctor calls you up and says, "We sent your child to prison. Why? Well, they were showing symptoms of depression, not eating, not showering, and so for their protection we sent them to prison."

This is what Civ. Comm. laws do. Civilly committed to treat a BA, but if you break a rule we can no longer treat you and to protect the community that you *don't* live in, we are sending you to prison.

Please tell me you see the injustice in the law? The law makers make this out to be ideal for those sex offenders but what's really going on is the precedents it sets. We must take this box down and destroy it. It's not okay just because these people are sex offenders.

Do you know what Thomas Paine said? "He that would make his own liberty secure, *must guard even his enemy from oppression; for* if he violates this duty, he establishes a precedent that will reach even to himself."

And again, Martin Luthor King said it like this: "Injustice for one is injustice for all."

There has been no one released from civil commitment since its enactment.

In 2015 Texas thought they were doing the right thing. Sen. John Whitmire said, "We are bringing the Civ. Comm. laws into constitutional compliance. The [Civ. Comm.] program is a total failure."

That legislative session they omitted the term "outpatient" from the statue, they removed the felony provision, in part, and they designed a tiered program that would allow people the hope of working their way off of Civ. Comm. And they moved all the civilly committed men to an old juvenile prison in Littlefield, TX. But the guys committed are told, "Don't call this a prison and that's not a cell you are in it's a room, you are not a prisoner, you are a resident."

And the cherry on top is that the changes made to the law in 2015 are *not* retroactive. So, in 2015 there were about two hundred men back in prison for violating Civ. Comm. rules (and that was about half of the civilly committed men at the time). The men in prison were the ones harmed by the unconstitutional laws and they were *not* given relief. *They remain in prison* for a crime that has been decriminalized and should never have been a crime in the first place.

"Don't mess with Texas" —I think they got the point.

I ask for reader participation. Google Texas Civil Commitment. My sources are the Texas Observer article "A prison by any other name."

Prison Legal News, *Houston Chronicle*, Personal experience.

*   *   *

Also, you are paying thirty million a year in taxes for this debunked program. Research the company that is over security and treatment: Texas Civil Commitment Center, 2600 South Sunset Blvd, Littlefield, TX. And if you come to the conclusion that this is a waste of time, tax payers' money and a civil rights violation to a class of people, and that it sets a precedent for Big Brother laws, if you see that they (the legislature) never declared the old law unconstitutional, that they just changed the law, and this leaves the precedent in place for the next class of people, then please go to www.texas.gov and tell the governor about it. Demand that this law be abolished. It's the humane thing to do.And in support of the above, I offer the following- My story. I have been locked up for thirty years on a fifteen-year sentence. But it feels like I've been locked up my whole life.

As you read, you may not believe that all this could've happened to one man, yours truly. But I guarantee you that what I tell you is not only true, but will open your eyes to what's really going on in the prisons, the criminal justice system, and what lurks inside people's minds.

PRISON BEFORE PRISON

―――⊸o◠◡◠o⊷―――

"Welcome to the real world. It sucks. You're gonna love it."
-Monica on Friends

Some prisons we go to ourselves, some prisons, others put us there.

Before I was in prison, I was in prison. I was in the free world for the first twenty years of my life, but I went to prison at age five. The memory of the night that my life was shattered has always been clear. And for a long time, I let that memory empower me to garner pity and to feed my identity as a victim. Looking back, I used many external things as my identity. But I also used my perception of life, and my thoughts about it, to tell me who I was. This made me as unstable as that proverbial man who has built his house on the sand. My foundation was taken from me before it could ever solidify. And as I grew and added onto that foundation, I was always sinking. I never learned the basics in life. I believed that everything was normal, that I was normal.

When I reached age five my mother remarried, and I remember thinking, "I got a daddy." When I was born, my biological father was in

Vietnam. He came home in 1973 on leave, and before he went back for his second tour, he got my mother pregnant with my brother. I have a couple of memories from my biological father in 1973, but it was this step-father who was here now. When my brother and I first met the guy who would become our step-dad, he rode up on a motorcycle and gave us a ride on it. My brother was three and I don't know what he thought of this guy. He was not a replacement because there was no one there before him. We lived with my grandparents (maternal).

Before my mom began dating this guy, she dated a different guy named Sonny. I found out later that my grandmother had advised my mom not to marry Sonny because at the time he didn't have a job. It's weird, but I remember Sonny. Two very distinct memories come to mind. The first one is my Mom driving her father's Chevy Nova and I was lying in her lap. I was telling her to "find my song" on the radio. It was *New Kid in Town* by the Eagles. I can't explain why I liked that song at age four, but I did. I probably liked it because my mom liked it—she is the one who gave me a love for music. Then she pulled over to the side of the road and we got out. Someone had pulled over behind her. It was Sonny. He was so tall to me; I remember grabbing his leg and he reached down and picked me up and held me high in the air. I remember the sense of feeling that he cared for me. I never felt that with the guy who became "Daddy"; I never felt love from or special to him.

In the second memory of Sonny, we were at White Rock Lake. We had a picnic and Sonny brought a kite and he flew it so high that I didn't know how we would ever get it down. Those are my two memories of Sonny. But as it became custom in my young life, men came and then they went.

When my mom married "Daddy," all of a sudden we had an instant family. We moved into the Lochwood Apartments in Dallas off of Garland Road. My brother and I shared a room and we had a bunk bed. We even fought over who got the top bunk.

Everything seemed normal and safe. He told us to call him Daddy. We had another set of grandparents, and uncles and aunts. My mom had three brothers and two sisters. "Daddy" had two brothers and three sisters. They both came from a big family. And ironically, my mom's parents' telephone number was 327-7122, and his parents' number was

327-7112. They'd both gone to Bryan Adams High School, but my mom had had to drop out when she became pregnant with me.

Like I said, it seemed like a normal family. Then one night that illusion was shattered. Before that happened, I don't remember much of it. I just know that I went to sleep safe, secure and maybe would have grown up normal. I still don't know for sure what caused it. Was it the alcohol? Was it his inner demons? You see, before they dated, he used to be friends with one of my mom's brothers, who was in the same class as him. One night they were out drinking and driving. They wrecked the car and my mom's brother died. But he survived. Could it have been something as simple as survivors' guilt that plagued him, and was the ever-present presence over the next nine years that fueled his terror?

That is how I see those nine years of my life: a terror. But on that first night, of many to come, I was awoken by loud voices and my mom screaming. I came out of my room to the scene of my new daddy chasing my eight-month pregnant mom around the pool table that was in the living room.

Every sense of normalcy, safety and security fled that night. A new normal began. And deep down, on a deeper subconscious level, other thoughts began to form. They didn't solidify that night, but they sure began. They were solidified, nurtured, affirmed, and reinforced over the next nine years. Thoughts that it was my fault, and there must be something wrong with me. That's the night that I met my new best companion, *Fear*, who became my constant standard in which to live and act out.

They stopped when they saw me and my brother coming out of our room. My mom grabbed our hands and we left the apartment. We walked about a hundred yards and sat on the curb across from the apartments. My mom said, "Look," and she pointed back the way we had come. We saw him come out of the apartment, go to the car and lift the hood. She said that he'd taken the wire from the distributor cap so that we could not take the car. I was too young to know what that meant, but we ended up walking about a quarter of a mile to a motel.

It really seems, in my memory, that this happened every weekend for the next nine years. We had to leave, then we would go back—a never-ending cycle. One with a lot of emotional and mental abuse and neglect along the way, from him and even his family. And love and being doted on from my mom and her family.

A horrible combination of terror and love, rejection and acceptance—never feeling safe and never feeling secure. This became my norm, my definition of life, and the constitutional right to the pursuit of happiness.

Real world, here I come.

FERGUSON UNIT

1994

"If you really wanna see what people are, all you have to do is look."
-Auggie in the movie Wonder

"I Will Survive" by Gloria Gainor

"I Want to Get Away" by Lennie Kravitz

In January 1994, three years into my prison sentence, I was sent to the Ferguson Unit, which was named after a governor who was very generous with pardons. All units have a reputation, and I had been hearing about this place ever since county jail. They called it the Gladiator Unit.

Terrifying horror stories, that are not exaggerated, are told about this unit. Stories that instill fear in the toughest of men. I was twenty-three years old, coming from a small, "friendly" unit to this place. I was very scared. I had only heard of the term, "riding" with someone, in an abstract way. It meant that you paid for protection to another inmate with either commissary or sex. In the unit I'd just come from there was no extortion, no coercing you into doing things. Being bi-sexual, I chose whom I had sex with, and whom I didn't. I have found that a majority of people hold the irrational belief that a gay person will have sex with any guy, just because, well, he's gay, but gay people have preferences also. Ask yourself, "Would just any of the opposite sex suit you?" It works both ways.

Prison can be so many things, but the main thing it will do is reveal who you are. On the friendly unit, I was very promiscuous with many different sexual partners. At this time in my life, I had neither morals nor values to live by. I had no standards for myself. I did not value myself as a person.

Now I found myself on this Blue Bird headed to this gladiator unit, handcuffed to another inmate. It was still dark outside and the only light was the beam from the headlights of passing cars shining temporarily though the bus's windows, so that I could see the other guys around me. But not well enough to tell if they were as scared as I was.

The prison is a small world in itself, which imitates real life. People out there in the free world get on a bus to get to their destination. In prison we are handcuffed to another person and made to get on this bus, in which we are locked, then told which "stop" to get off at. Maybe some of you feel the same way going to your job. The officer driving our bus doesn't regard his passengers as he speeds down back roads. I think that I can speak for all inmates everywhere when I say, "We are all scared of having a wreck while on this bus." Did you see the movie *48 Hours*? If this bus flipped over once, much less fifty-six times, we would be seriously hurt or killed. But this is the only way a prison can transport inmates. I can't wait for technology to create teleporters.

On any bus there is conversation, but on a prison bus there is a group conversation. One guy will say something and another will respond and anyone can put their two cents in. This morning all I hear is horror stories from the guys who had been to Ferguson before. These stories terrified me.

"This young n___ went up there one time with brand new Jordans on. He acted like he belonged. Well, when he woke up in the infirmary, he didn't have no shoes. The lieutenant kept asking him, 'Where are your shoes?' He responded, 'Shoes?'"

Everyone laughed at this story. As if it were a joke or okay to do that to someone. Or maybe their laughter was to cover up their own fear.

Well, my fear was in full force, my heart beating fast, and I had to use the restroom—that type of fear. I was glad for the darkness because no one could see my fear. I looked down the next time a beam of light came through the window. I had on a pair of commissary-bought Converse shoes. I would make sure that I wore my state-issued brogans while I was in the dayroom. They were steel-toed.

The talk continued around me. "Yeah, 'F__, fight, or bust a $60'; that's all they'll ask when you walk into the dayroom."

In 1994, we were allowed to purchase items from the commissary, but only $60 every two weeks. When you entered into the dayroom on the Ferguson unit, one of the regulars would approach you with those three options and they were your only ones. The fourth option was to tell an officer—which was not a healthy option, not there, not ever. You found out pretty quick that the COs let this system run itself. The COs were mostly men, but were human and enjoyed a good fight also.

This was still the early '90s and the Ruiz lawsuit was not final, as the Federal Court was still supervising the change from a convict-run and -controlled prison to a correctional officer-controlled prison. But with the loss of building tenders, Texas Prison had an uprising of gangs. And on the cell block, at least at Ferguson, the cons still controlled what went on.

The ranking officers at this time had begun when there were building tenders, so they were not bothered by a con-controlled cell block. It was less work for them. Their view of prison compared to society's, is a total opposite. I remember seeing the warden and major look in the dayroom window one time; they could tell by where you were sitting if you were riding or fighting.

The three options are self-evident, and *usually* the first option, "F___," is not a willing one. "Fight" means that you have to fight another person anywhere from three to six times. This gains respect for yourself, and shows that you will "stay down" for yourself. Sometimes, though, three or four people will clique on you at once, give you a good ass-kicking and then you don't have to "Ride." "Bust a $60" means that you agree to pay commissary to your protector. They will give you hygiene products, and maybe some coffee and cigarettes, if you get a nice protector. But the rest of your mother's money goes to this guy who won't let anyone else bother you. Then you sit on the back bench where all the guys who are "riding" sit. Ironic, huh, the back bench? I even heard a black regular tell the "white boy" who was riding with him say, "That's for making my ancestors sit in the back of the bus," and then he slapped him.

The Blue Bird chain bus pulled up to the back gate. Two officers stepped off and delivered up their weapons to the tower; then the driver was let in through the gate. An officer had been assigned to work the back gate and he searched the bus to make sure that nothing was being smuggled in. Names were called and the inmates getting off grabbed their property bags, and still handcuffed to each other made their way to the front of the bus. My heart was beating so fast that I was sure the others could hear it as I walked by.

When we got off the bus, we were uncuffed and corralled into a holding area. Then later we were called into a separate room one at a time and strip searched; they also went through our property. The CO looked at me and said, "Have you been doing your push-ups?" I guess the fear was palpable on my face. Or he took one look at me and just knew that I was not going to make it. Either way, having this unit's rep confirmed by an officer in such a way drove it home for me. *This is real. I'm in prison. How am I going to survive?*

After everyone was finished, we were brought into the prison. We walked down the long hallway towards the end of it, but when we entered the hall the sounds of the prison hit us. It was just a loud white noise, interspersed with the occasional yell. Maybe it was just my fear that made me hear screaming.

At the end of the hallway there were double doors that opened into a big room. Around the walls of this room were offices, and there were dividers put up to make other, temporary offices. But straight ahead there were those hard plastic chairs lined up in rows for us to sit on and wait to be called. There was a sign on the wall that stated: "Remain seated, face forward, and keep quiet, or you will receive a disciplinary."

When you get to a unit for the first time, you are interviewed by different departments: medical, education, and classification. Then you go before the Unit Classification Committee or UCC, which consists of a classification counselor, the warden, or his designee (sometimes a major or captain), and one other person from a different department of the prison. This committee determines everything: your job, housing, education, and so on. When my name was called and I was alone in this room with the people who had the power to do anything in the prison, I shot my shot.

The first thing I noticed is the sign attached to the front of the desk that said, "Yes, sir, no, sir, or yes, ma'am, no, ma'am, ONLY." I already knew that if I were asking for something and I wanted things to go in my favor that I would have to adhere to these rules.

"Jones, initial here," a lady said.

"Yes ma'am," I said as I initialed where she indicated.

"Have a seat," a man said, who by his very demeanor you could tell was the warden. Plus, it was how everyone was kowtowing towards him. He introduced himself and the others, then opened up my file, read it and passed it to the others. My face reddened in embarrassment because I knew that they were reading about my crimes. I had multiple cases of sex offenses against children. Nobody likes a sex offender, but especially not those who hurt children. I already felt defeated and ashamed. They were not going to want to help me. I was dead before I even opened my mouth. But I felt that if I could just begin to talk that I could get the ladies on my side and vote for what I was needing; the problem was that I was not allowed to just speak without permission.

The status I wanted to be classified under was "safekeeping" (S/K). There are different custody statuses in TDCJ. General Population (GP) is the base custody that is automatic, unless circumstances call for a different custody. Safekeeping is just like GP except that S/K is kept separate, for the most part, on a separate wing or block. But they go to chow, work or school with GP. The safekeeping block is made up mostly of homosexuals and effeminate men who cannot defend themselves. There are also a lot of sex offenders, ex-cops, COs and judges. I was not about that life, the one in GP; I needed S/K.

When I came down to prison, in 1991, I was automatically classified as S/K status. Personally, I hated living in that environment; men pretending to be feminine and acting like women (or their perception of one). In 1993, they were called queens. In my own life I had never wanted to be a girl, or thought that I was. I just identified as gay. I requested to get off of S/K status in 1993, because I was on a friendly unit. Now I was on a gladiator unit and I need back on S/K. After everyone had looked at my file the Warden took charge. "Place him in the hoe squad," he began, barely glancing over the file to look at me. "Make sure that his visitation restrictions have 'No contact with children'. He's not in any education classes right now." Then looking at me he says, "You can submit a request for further education. Any questions?"

Here I go. "Sir, I used to be on safekeeping, and at this time I am requesting to be placed back on it."

"Why?" He glared at me to intimidate me into giving up this endeavor.

But I am very resilient in my survival. In this game I have experience. "Because, uh, sir, I can't fight these guys and if they find out my case, well…"

"Don't tell them. Request denied." Looking at the classification lady he said, "GP." Then to the CO standing behind me, "Next." I was dismissed.

I was returned to the chair that I'd vacated earlier in the big room. I was sitting between a black guy and a Hispanic. I was somber and quiet, pondering how I was going to survive this. I thought of turning to God, but I had turned to God when I first came to jail (like most inmates) and I'd never got any tangible answers to my prayers. I had left Him when I didn't get my first parole (like most inmates). I did not see Him coming to rescue me here after I had left Him to live the way that I wanted. I really didn't know God at all.

My thoughts turned to the advantages of being gay in prison. But I was very picky who I would mess with and who I wouldn't. Just like Julia Roberts in *Pretty Woman*, "I say who, I say when, I say where!" I know that sounds weird, but I am talking about attraction. I couldn't have intimate relations with someone that I was not attracted to.

I had heard that if you were gay and with a Hispanic, that they would put you "on the street," something I dreadfully feared. This term "out on the street" means that the person "riding" would have to "catch cells" with anyone that was willing to pay. This was part of the "protection."

So, basically, prostitution. I was not down with that at all. I had to avoid the Hispanics. The problem was that I had to "deal" with the first person to approach me. I couldn't just go in searching for an attractive guy. It was crazy, but my survival depended on it.

On top of all this was my problem of being in prison for sex crimes against children. Normally a person would make up a crime to tell people, and I had a story ready, but in order to "sell that hog" you have to not just lie with your words but with your body language. I had not had practice with this because in the first unit where I was everyone found out, and in the last unit, it hadn't mattered. And to keep this up over time took a lot of energy.

I'd had a high-profile case in Dallas not even three years ago. And even when I was found out on Beto One unit in 1991, I was on S/K status and still had some problems behind it. It was mostly other sex offenders glad that the spotlight wasn't on them, and they relished my bad fortune.

It's crazy, all I was thinking in order to survive, but our minds are amazing. I remembered meeting other people with nicknames, who went by them rather than their last names. I decided to give myself a nickname; that way if someone addressed me by my true name, I would know that they knew my case. Then I could be ready for either fight or flight. But I was determined to survive.

I came up with DJ, my initials. Something simple but easy for people to remember, and it had character. I would just introduce myself as "DJ." Now I just had to figure out how I was going to pick the person that I wanted to be with.

I knew the blaring irony here, that "the molester doesn't want to get raped," but the irony is even deeper, because in therapy I discovered that I basically molested or misused sex to soothe myself from negative emotions, experiences, or painful times. (As if an orgasm can make it all okay again.) Yet, here I was, planning on using my sexuality to protect me from being raped in prison. It is what it is, though, but aside from suicide, I had to keep myself safe. At this time I was very selfish, I hadn't developed empathy yet, to be remorseful for my crimes. I only wanted to make sure that I survived, and to try to be comfortable while doing so.

Now ask yourself: what is the purpose of prison? Is it the loss of freedom? To separate you from the community so you don't repeat your crime? Maybe rehabilitation? Or do you want the criminal to suffer every moment of his fifteen-, twenty-, fifty-year or life sentence? Do we want to correct the problem or exacerbate it? Careful how you answer—you might just reveal yourself.

* * *

"Psst, psst, psst, psst." I heard someone making this noise a couple rows behind me. Made like that it is a sexual come on, usually a guy will do it to a female to see if she will answer. "Hey Wera," he calls, the Spanish name for a white girl. Number 1 rule in prison: mind your own business. Guess I still haven't learned it. But they never mind their own business, they're always trying to make someone ride.

I turned to see who he was talking to, and it turned out that he was directing it to me. I said earlier that I'd never wanted to be a girl, and I didn't look like a girl nor did I wear my clothes tight the way the queens do. But on the other hand, I didn't look like a hardened criminal either. No tattoos, and I still had my boy softness, and exhibited some female characteristics, which stemmed from identifying with my mother, since I did not have a good male role model to look up to. But just then I was at least wishing that my step-dad would have beat me into a fighter or at least taught me how to defend myself. No, instead he'd verbally and emotionally abused me into a fearful coward, seeking others' approval. I did not like confrontation.

Cardinal rule #2: don't make eye contact—unless you can back it up. I looked right at him. He said something in Spanish to the guy sitting next to me and they switched seats. Where was the officer when you needed him to enforce the rule to remain seated? It was posted right there on the wall.

"You new, Wera?" He asked me when he sat down next to me.

"Yeah," I said. Going for confidence, it came out sounding scared. "To this unit. I've been down for three years." These guys were seasoned veterans. My three years was a cake walk to them. They could see right through a new boot.

"They put all the new boots on my block. So when they move you over there, go to the dayroom after the noon count. Ya understand me?"

he said.

I wasn't expecting this until I got back to the block and I wasn't prepared. They hadn't even given me a chance to pick someone that I wanted. There really ought to be a rulebook about this so that we can all get on the same page. Come on, people.

"What for?" I asked him, hoping that he just wanted to play dominoes or something.

"I'll talk to you then." He went back to his seat.

Everyone, from county jail to prison, always told me that when I got down to prison to stick with my own race. I was told, "You don't have to join a gang, but there is a group of white guys that just stick together. Find them." I did not want to join a gang; it had never appealed to me. At school and the places that I worked I'd had black and Hispanic friends. My grandfather had taught me at a young age to not hate anyone just because they were different from me. And he told me to never say the N-word. My baby's mama is a beautiful black woman. I met her when I was working at McDonalds. I've never understood racism and prejudices against a whole race. Growing up I felt rejected by my white peers, more than anyone else. In my naiveté I did not understand why it had to be different in prison.

Later, when I got to the cell block the dayroom was completely empty. There were three tiers with thirty-two cells on each tier. The dayroom was to the left as you entered the block. When he saw me, the hallway boss let me in, the Rover made his way over to put me in my cell. The cell doors all roll together, unless the picket boss pins the cells that he does not want open. "Let him in 1-11 cell," the rover told the picket. I heard the clanking of the machinery as he pinned all the cell doors but mine. I walked down toward my cell as he opened it. I looked inside and let out a deep breath. It was empty—no cellie. I carried my personal property and the state-issued property into the cell, and the door rolled closed behind me. I will always keep my personal property, but the state-issued, i.e. mattress, sheets, blanket, the state clothes, and so on, will stay on each unit and the next unit will reissue it over there. The state also provides toilet paper, soap, tooth brushes, and baking powder to use to brush our teeth. (But you can get Colgate in the commissary.)

The cell had three walls with the bars at the front. To the left stood two bunks in bunk bed fashion, but they were bolted to the wall. In the left corner there was a porcelain sink, and directly across from the cell door on the back wall was a porcelain toilet. The cell was 6' by 9'. I put my property in my locker, which was right above me as I stepped in the door. I made my bed. You were supposed to sleep with your feet toward the bars, otherwise someone could reach in and slit your throat while you were asleep and you woke up dead.

Our state uniforms are white. The shirt is a pullover V-neck made out of heavy cotton. The pants are the same material with an elastic waistband. Before the 1993 budget cuts our pants were button fly, and had pockets in the front and back. I still had pockets on the pants I was wearing when I caught chain to come over here.

When the doors opened after count cleared this was what I was wearing. The commissary sold combination locks so we could lock our lockers to prevent stealing. But they had an unintended purpose also; I'd heard the stories. So I put the lock in my pocket and went to the dayroom.

I was determined not to "ride" with anyone, or be forced to be with someone that I did not want to be with. I most certainly feared being put out on the street. Is it coincidental that I created DJ at this time? I don't think so. I think DJ had always been inside me, that he emerged when I was five years old. I believe that on the night that little David's life got shattered, that DJ was the one who took control and began to protect David. I am not suggesting a multiple personality or anything so sinister. But a dual mind, if I can use that term to describe it. Maybe there are different parts of us in our psyche: the protector, the proud, the angry, the sad, the lover, the hater, the happy, the survivor and so on. And maybe abuse will bring one out to be dominant at the times it is needed. Again, I've had no blackouts nor periods of time that I cannot remember, which means that this protector was in me always. I just didn't name him until 1994.

Abuse will cause a person to compartmentalize like this, because when life is not cohesive in a young child, he has to do something to make it make sense. In the Bible, James writes about double-minded people, and Jesus was always talking about overcoming and being "one" with Him and the Father. What if He meant to not be dual in ourselves but to overcome that, overcome having to protect yourself? And to serve God in singleness of mind and heart and be one with Him, by trusting Him? But in 1994 DJ was far away from any of those types of thoughts.

Right now, DJ came out of that cell and was ready to defend himself, even unto serious bodily damage to that other person. It's crazy what fear can drive a person to do. It also takes psyching yourself up to be ready to fight.

I stood next to this brick half-wall, by the fountain with my back to the wall. It appeared that the blacks sat on one side of the dayroom and the Hispanics got the other side: six benches and a TV for each. The one bench in the middle against the wall, not facing the TV but facing the dayroom, was for the "peckerwoods"—the white guys who'd chosen to fight and garnered their respect.

I looked around the dayroom and saw a few black guys on their side of the dayroom; there were a couple of Hispanics sitting down watching TV. The only white guy besides me was a chubby, young, bespectacled guy sitting on the back bench on the black guy's side.

The guy who'd accosted me in the big waiting room was nowhere to be seen. Yet I did not relax. I still wasn't in Kansas. C-Block on Ferguson unit was just as foreign to me as Munchkin Land was to Dorothy and Toto.

I had all this adrenaline pumping through me and no one was paying me any attention. I had my hands in my pocket with the "u" of the lock around my middle finger.

Once the officer finished the out, he locked the dayroom and left the block and went to the other one across the hall. I was surprised to see an inmate coming down the stairs outside the dayroom. He was pulling on his state shirt. When he got to the bottom of the stairs, he tucked in his shirt then pulled a palm brush out of his back pocket and began to brush his waves. He was about 5'7", chocolate-bar-colored skin, with an athletic build and a small gap between his two front teeth. He noticed me looking at him.

He approached the bars of the dayroom and nodded to me and said, "You new?"

Ah, here we go. "Yeah," I replied.

"Watcha gonna do?" he asked, skipping the phrase.

"I guess I'm gonna fight," I said. Real smooth DJ, 'I guess', really?

"Hard way to do your time," he said. As if that were a good enough reason to get raped and give your mother's money away.

"These ain't my rules, these are ya'll's rules." It felt like we were playing a verbal chess game, where the goal was not to get the king, but to be king of your own destiny.

Then I made a quick decision, because I thought that I had to hurry and get this done and over with. And he was not bad-looking at all.

He was saying, "Look, I got to get to medical. I'll talk to you when I get back. Go sit on that back bench until I get back."

"Look, I'll be with you but I'm not going to ride with you," I told him.

"What?" he asked. I thought it was very clear, but obviously not.

"I said, I'll be with you but I won't ride with you."

The hall boss opened the outer door to let him out. "I gotta go to medical; if anyone asks you just say that you talked to Scott. And go sit on that back bench until I get back." The boss told him to go and he left.

I wasn't about to go sit on that back bench as if I was riding. One of the black guys that were in the dayroom came over to me and the other one went to the dayroom window and put his ear to the window as if listening to someone. But I was focused on this guy that came up to me.

"So have you been situated?" he said to me. As if this were a business and he was checking to see if I was satisfied. I had an urge to just hit him with the lock for asking such a stupid question.

But I just played dumb. "Huh?" Real sophisticated, DJ.

"You know, F___..." he was interrupted by his homeboy, the one who'd gone to the window.

"Hey, Scott said to go sit over there 'til he gets back." Pointing to the back bench. I guess that had been Scott talking through the window. I decided to just go sit down and I'd straighten it out with Scott when he got back.

The chubby white guy was sitting on the end of the bench so I went to the other side and sat about half way down the bench. The chubby guy turned to me with a happy expression on his face and said, "So, are you riding?" Just smiling away.

* * *

A little while later Scott came back from medical. He sat down next to me but we didn't discuss what I had meant about not riding with him. We talked about what unit I came from and how long I had been locked up. Then on to where I was from. It turned out that he was from Dallas also.

I came to learn that it is prison etiquette that you do not ask people what they are in prison for. I already lived by that because I did not want them to ask me. But at this time, a lot of convicts were still here and living by the convict code. And that question fell under 'mind your own biz.' There are tacit rules and there are verbal rules, that over time came to be *overstood*. A prison slang term that means one understands, the rule or topic of discussion, so much that it does not need to be said.

I do not have a point of reference anymore on the origins of certain slang or sayings, whether it started in prison or not. I just know that I have only heard certain phrases or words in prison. And when prisoners get a new phrase, we use it so much that we wear it out. Maybe to be a part of something, maybe because it's new. But have you ever noticed how that there really is not anything new? I was reading a book by a retired warden, called *Texas Prisons: The Longest Hotel Chain in Texas,* by Lon Bennett. And reading the stories about the prisoners from when he first started out as a CO I came to realize that we are not doing anything new. Whatever we are doing in prison right now, even down to the nicknames that we use, it's all been done and said before. We are not original, even at the base of society—prisons—we are all alike.

* * *

I figured that Scott had known what I meant when I told him that I'd 'be with him', because he never asked me to clarify what I meant. I was just going to wait for him to make the first move. And almost everyone knew that I was considered to be under 'his protection.' However, after last chow, when I got back to the dayroom I was once again standing by that brick wall—I just had an aversion to that back bench. Some black guy approached me and said the three options, calmly as if he were selling me options for the car I'd just bought. But before I could respond another guy overheard him and told him that I was with Scott.

That day drew to an end and I had thought that I had seen every guy who lived on this block. And I was thinking that out of all the choices that I had that I did pretty good getting with Scott. I had not noticed anyone that was better looking or bigger or even better connected. In the prison hierarchy there were soldiers and leaders. The two big factions at this time were the Bloods and the Crips. The majority on this cell block were the soldiers. I instinctively knew that they would not be the type to have a relationship with. Not the kind that would save me. I had to outsmart the fierce brutality of the way the prison structured its caste system. I was no match for these guys, and I did not want to, after being delegated to being a number by the courts, prisons, and so on, be further debilitated by paying protection and being forced to have sex with many partners. I believed that if I could get a guy that I liked, then I could make him fall in love with me and he wouldn't hurt me.

The next evening, I was sitting on the back bench at the end. I told myself that people knew that I was different, that they knew that I was not riding. (The lies we tell ourselves.) I heard the dayroom door open and looked over to see who was coming in. Have you ever been so affected by someone's appearance that you cannot control your facial expressions, or even feel that you could control them? This goes the same for men as it does for women. You know, when a drop dead gorgeous, beautiful man or woman, enters a room and your mouth goes slack and people can see the lust in your eyes?

Yeah, that's what happened here. The guy who walked into the dayroom had smooth, lighter colored skin, was very good-looking, and I could see his muscles though his shirt. He saw me looking at him and walked straight towards me.

His first words were, "Who you with?"

"Scott," I said, and tried very hard to inflect in my voice that I had made a big mistake and that I wanted to take it back and to just choose him.

But he just nodded his head and walked away. These guys are very respectful to each other. They won't talk to someone else's piece of game (POG); of course, once it is established that he is somebody else's POG.

This guy went by the nickname Geechi Dan. People gave him a lot of respect. He was the speaker for the block that we lived on. Well, for the blacks. But the speakers from the other races would let him know what was about to go down, such as a fight or whatever else. I have never seen the level of respect that people gave him in such a way since then. But he earned every bit of it with his fists.

I found out later, from Geechi, that when he walked away from me that day he went to Scott and said, "You got you one."

To which Scott replied, "Nah, he ain't no boy."

"Yeah, you got you one," Geechi said and left it at that.

A "boy" is a gay boy. The phrase, "You got you one," is the way a con recognizes another con's come-up. In the '90s it was another notch on your belt to not just have someone pay protection, but to have a 'boy' for sex.

Scott didn't come and confirm it or anything. After a few days went by and we were talking, I worked up the nerve to say, "After chow can you come to my cell to kick it for a while?"

"I didn't know you got down like that," he said.

"Well, that's what I meant when I said, 'I would be with you but not ride with you.'"

*   *   *

I was on Ferguson unit from January to August in that year, 1994. This eight month period was one of the pivotal moments of my incarceration. As I said before, I had been on a friendly unit before I came there, and my well-being had not been in jeopardy. I have come to believe that if I had remained there I would never have taken prison seriously. Had I remained there my mind probably would not have made the connection that there were grave consequences to my past behavior. Life is cumulative, and it would take all these experiences, put together, to cause me to desire to be a different person than who I was.

In prison one either gets assimilated (resistance is futile) to the way things are, or one walks just outside that line of institutionalization. I speak here of the system put in place by the convicts, and in one aspect of that there are two groups: one, those who prey on others for sex and money, and two, those who are the prey. Not everyone in here gets involved in this, but it is so prevalent that it's all you see. And this was how it was right there, right then, in the environment that I was in.

I told myself that I was resisting this mentality of either predator or prey. I had never been taught how to fight. These guys had been fighting and preying on others since they'd been young. I couldn't fight them to protect myself, and I could not be a predator. I had too much pride to say that I was the prey. I fell back on what I knew from my childhood: survive in my mind and with my mind. I had to grow up fast, and take care of my mom and siblings, and little David.

It may have looked like I was prey, but in my mind I believed that I was in control. I believed that I had outsmarted their 'system.' I appeared to have fallen into the prey category. But I was using their system against them: I was already gay so I wanted to pick who I was going to be with and be with just him. And I got the benefit of being protected, and I wasn't lonely because I got someone to do my time with. But could living this lifestyle hurt me later? We will find out in later chapters.

There is a saying among the group of people in prison who seek relationships with others while in prison to stave off that loneliness: "You can't find true love in prison." And you cannot. Not when the majority of the men in here only have homosexual relationships while in prison. You cannot expect them to commit the rest of their life to you.

But in the moment when you are together with someone, it is you and him against time, the Man, and others. One person alone has to deal with everything alone. When you are with someone and go through the travails of prison, and the worries of the free world, facing years and all that "doing time" entails, you bond and become very close. True love? Maybe not. But in this moment, I'll take it.

*   *   *

I never got that far with Scott. He came to my cell a couple of times. And he didn't take all my commissary, as happens with the guys who were riding. Then two things happened. Geechi Dan became my new cellmate (cellie). I don't know if he got this done (he had pull with his boss), or if it was just one of those strange coincidences.

Don't get me wrong, I was happy, Geechi was happy, but Scott wasn't. But Scott never accused me of doing anything, and did not appear to have any beef with Geechi. I already told you who I would rather have been with, and I don't think that I need to clarify that the Las Vegas rule applies here, too: what happens in the cell stays in the cell.

The second thing that happened was that a few weeks later, Scott told me that he had caught a disciplinary. He worked as a janitor at night, and sometimes he cleaned up on the safekeeping block. Supposedly he was seen by a bosslady putting his penis through the bars of a cell door down the tier. There are a lot of homosexuals on that cell block, the implication being that he was receiving oral sex through the bars.

Scott denied this, and in all of my three years of incarcerated wisdom I believed him. I figured that since he had me why would he go elsewhere? Later, when I became more wise in the way of prisons, I saw just how naive that was.

Scott got "rolled." That's what we call going to court for the disciplinary and then UCC placing you on medium custody. This meant he was going to be moved to a different block. But before he left, we had a talk in the dayroom. It was a sad moment. Just because we hadn't bonded in the way that I described earlier does not mean that we did not have some feelings for each other.

"Code says that I leave you with my homeboy."

"I want to be with Geechi Dan," I told him bravely.

"You like him, huh?"

"Yeah, I already know him and he won't put me on the streets." I had already told Scott about my fears. He tried to keep a stoic face, but I could see that he was struggling with his own fears—that I had been cheating on him with Geechi. Before he could flesh that out, I continued, "Look, Scott, you are leaving, and I wish that you weren't, but why should I have to be with someone that I don't want to be with? Let me be with who I want, okay?"

He let me. Because no matter what the code says, guys like Scott and Geechi, who are well respected, can override it; they are the 'last say.' And no one questioned it. Done deal.

Geechi and I bonded beyond what I have ever experienced in my life. He taught me how to be a convict. He showed me the little things that make you a convict, and explained why. He said that a convict never puts the cell block's mop and broom in their cell—those things are nasty. What you do is hold your shirt from the neck in your fist, and starting from the back of your cell whip it around like a fan and this creates a wind that blows the dust and dirt out. You fan it right out of the cell and onto the run where the janitor will sweep it up. The only cleaning agent that the prison issues is called 'Bippy.' It is similar to Ajax. It's an abrasive powder and cleans the porcelain and stainless steel sinks and toilets. You may have heard that a prisoner keeps his toilet so clean that you could eat out of it; well, he taught me how to clean it that good but we never ate out of it.

If you are in prison reading this then I must tell you this next tidbit of info: when brushing your teeth never spit in the sink that you have to share with your cellie. Spit in the toilet. It is considered real disrespectful to spit the germs from your mouth into that sink. So just don't.

The way we "mop" our cell is we use commissary soap (the good stuff—Zest or Ivory) or shampoo, or some stolen bleach from the state, and suds up the water in the toilet bowl, soak that water into a rag, then wring the rag out onto the cell floor. You have to get on your hands and knees to use that rag to scrub every part of your floor. Then you keep wringing the water in the rag back into the toilet, using the rag to sop up the water on the floor.

We could buy T-shirts and gym shorts off of the commissary; they are white, as are all of our clothes. He taught me how to wash these clothes in that same toilet. During the winter the toilet water is ice cold, and we can put our soda pops in there to get icy.

He taught me what to look for in people's body language, if they were about to fight, and how to carry myself confidently in a way that told people to leave me alone.

The bonding that I told you about, well—while we were alone in the cell, this big, muscular, hard, possible gangster, the speaker for the blacks on C-Block, would share with me his feelings and fears. This was important, because for someone of his status to open up like this to a gay boy, or at all, shows how he felt about me. Now, I do not want you to get the idea that I was a cold, manipulating person who planned to make someone fall in love with me just for protection. I was not that calculating. I did this instinctively, knowing that if a guy developed feelings for me he would not want to send me to some other guy for money. Yes, my number one motive was to survive, but I wanted comfort at the same time. Like in *Pretty Woman*, she (Julia) wanted it all—the prince, the castle, and the rescue—she wanted the whole fairy tale. And this was my 'reality' and I wanted it all—this, Geechi, and what we gave each other. I took their system of paying for protection, and took it further, into a relationship, and in that premise, I left the status of being a 'boy who pays for protection,' and I got the fairy tale. At least in my mind.

On the outside Geechi appeared fearless. But on the inside, he was the same human that we all are. I think that we tend to forget that because we seem to believe the 'outward' mask that people wear. When he came down, prison had been a lot worse. He'd had to fight constantly to keep the predators off, and now he had that well-earned respect. It would be a better world if we automatically gave that type of respect first, that instead of having to earn it it would be a given, and then step in if someone lost that respect. The real world sucks, but it is what we make it.

At this time, he was not in a gang, but he had some connection to the Bloods and did a lot of fighting with and for them.

I didn't know about the connection then, but as always seems to happen in prison, later down the years, you'd run across a person who was on the same unit you were, but later. You begin talking, and you realize that you know the same people, and they tell you things about them. It's weird how that happens. They say that it's a small world out there, but it's even smaller in here.

*   *   *

In the 1990s the TDCJ produced their own food. And this was done through the hard labor of inmates working in the hoe squad. Over the years I have picked okra, cantaloupes, broccoli, and even cotton.

A loud voice penetrated my sleeping brain: "All that hoe squad get up! Get ready!"

I looked out through the bars of my cell to the windows and saw that it was still dark outside.

Geechi had recently been moved a couple of cells down from me, and I yelled out of my cell to him, "Geechi, what…"

"Get ready, we are going to work," he replied.

I have always kept my shoes, clothes, and ID by the cell door. The doors are on a track controlled by a picket boss and when he opens, he gives it a couple minutes then he shuts them. The important thing is to get yourself through, then you can get the rest of your things by reaching through the bars. But there is no second chance to come out. They open one time, and if you miss it then you are what they call, "stuck out." You will miss work and receive a disciplinary for not going.

I hurried up and brushed my teeth; I did not have any hot water so I used the cold sink water on a face towel to wash my face. I finished just in time, because I heard the boss yell, "Stand clear! Opening One row. If you are in the hoe squad fall out!"

Policy states that the COs give us fifteen minutes to get ready before they let us out, and that they yell out to the whole block "Get ready." They also have to yell for us to stand clear when they open the doors, so that no one gets an arm or hand caught in the door.

But it's not always fifteen minutes. I stepped outside my cell and saw others step out not dressed or ready. I heard the clanking of keys, and the tinkling of spurs, as the COs that were over the hoe squad entered the block. They added to the clamor, and started yelling at us for not being ready, then yelled up at Two and Three row that they better do a better job than One row.

The rover yelled, "Clear, closing One row." After the doors had shut, I reached through and grabbed my clothes and my brogans to get dressed. The brogans are state-issued boots. They are steel-toed and have no arch support and are very uncomfortable (as is everything that is state-issued).

*　　*　　*

The medical squad that I was "working" in was not too far from Geechi's squad. I could see and hear what they were doing and saying. Geechi was "lead row" and as lead row he set the pace of the squad. The job today was to till the furrows between the rows of whatever produce that was planted in this section. Geechi would stand just inside the first furrow sideways and the squad would line up behind him in their own rows. They held the hoe in their fists, the left fist down by their hip and their right fist up by the shoulder. The metal edge of the hoe lifted in the air, and Geechi would count off, "A one and a two and a three and a four step." Every hoe would drop down in sync, breaking up the ground, particles of dirt exploding in the air. As the hoes came back up as one, the sun shone off the metal. The tail row was experienced also, and helped keep the end of the line in sync. The boss said that it should look like a machine moving down the row. If the Olympics ever get synchronized hoeing, these guys should represent America.

Deterrence. As Texas prisons have progressed into the future, they've left behind vital components that would deter people from coming back to prison. A lot of the practices that went on, especially in the '90s, taught me responsibility and other things that I will describe later. Prison was a father to me in a lot of ways that the men in my early life never were.

At the end of the work day, we turned back toward the prison and walked back. The field sergeant stood at the back gate and called out our names one at a time, and we would call out our TDCJ number to him as he compared our face to the picture in his hand. At the back dock we had to strip out of our dirty clothes and line up to go to the showers. Yeah, we had to stand in a line outside naked as we waited to go in in groups to shower.

In the shower area there was a half wall and the top half is all chicken wire with openings in it to pass our clothes through and receive clean clothes. The rest of this room was some benches and showers. There were shower heads all along the wall, and several posts dispersed throughout the area with four shower heads around the top of each post. When you got your clean clothes you placed them on an open space on the bench, provided for that reason. Then you went to find a shower head and get under it.

One of the bosses yelled, "You got two minutes. Get it on while you get it off." Water burst out of the head, and we had to endure the cold that came out first because we only had two minutes.

The boss controlled the water on this unit. He turned it on, then exactly two minutes later it would cut off. "Get it on" meant the soap. "Get it off" is the rinse. We had to rinse off practically as we lathered up. After the two minutes is up you have to leave, dry off, get dressed. The next group was coming in to shower, so even if you still had soap on you, you had to leave. There was no discussion, your shower was over. Ferguson Unit is infamous for this.

The bosses always wanted us to hurry up. When the inmates wanted to do something, it never went fast or came fast. It was always wait. When it was time to eat or shower, we were rushed through it. And such is prison; we have the time, but the COs get to structure it.

*   *   *

Besides books, music was an escape for me. 1994 did not disappoint. I loved the Counting Crows' "'Round Here," and "Mr. Jones and Me," and Sheryl Crow with "All I Wanna Do". Tom Petty's "Last Dance." Toni Braxton's "Unbreak My Heart." But I really related to Lenny Kravitz's "I Want to Get Away." Because I really wanted to get away from that place. I was comfortable with Geechi and everything, but this is one prison I could leave and never look back. Nothing is ever secure; anything could happen at any moment.

And being with Geechi had its privileges. I no longer had to sit on the back bench. One night, when a lot of people were in the dayroom, Geechi stood at the bench that was the third back from the front, and he said, "This is DJ's bench." And no one sat on that bench. I mean, literally, no one. Sometimes he would sit with me, and sometimes he would sit on the front bench, with the other 'regulars.' But no one would sit by me and no one bothered me.

The administration would send all the new boots to our block—C-Block. For whatever reason, all the new guys coming in would come to C-Block. It probably had to do with the fact that all the new boots were assigned to work in the hoe squads. Everyone on C-Block was assigned to the hoe squad, so that when the bosses came to get their workers, they would only have to go to that one block.

With a lot of new boots coming in all the regulars would approach them to see if they would fight or pick the other options. If you chose to fight you had to wait for an opportune time to fight when it was cool and you wouldn't get caught. Tonight was one of those times when it was cool. Which meant that all the bosses that were working in this four-block section—the picket, the turnkey and the rovers—were okay with the cons conducting 'heart-checks.' There was a new black guy who had not been approached when he'd come in, and hadn't settled up with anyone. He entered the dayroom that evening and sat on "my" bench, at the opposite end from me. He didn't appear to be a gangsta'. Just some new boot who did not know the rules of the game. Somebody had missed him when he'd gotten here earlier that day and he'd slipped through their net. But he messed up by sitting down on the bench, (it could have been any bench) without first establishing what he was about or going to represent. You could not just come in and sit down, as if you were a regular, when you had not earned it. Hadn't this guy paid attention to the stories on the bus on the way over here?

I noticed two things. The rover went up to Three row (I didn't know that it was a prearranged thing until later), and everyone on all the benches on the black side began to go to the back, and find a space on the wall to keep their back against. I heard someone say, "DJ," and I looked behind me, and one of Geechi's homeboys motioned me back there with him. I went over to him and sat next to him. Then I saw one of the regulars go up to the new boot and steal off of him from behind. He got up to fight. Then there were two separate fights on the Hispanic side, as they conducted their own cora-checks—heart-checks. Then two more fights right in front of me, as two regulars fought two different white guys, who'd both chosen to fight.

The guy who motioned me back leaned towards me and whispered, "The boss man is cool and he knows what's going on. He went upstairs so we all could handle up. Geechi wants you to just sit here and chill."

"But what did that guy do that was sitting on the bench?" I asked.

"He sat down like he's a regular. He didn't check in with anyone. There are no free passes in here. You gotta fight or ride. You earn everything you get."

I just nodded and watched the fights. It's hard to watch several fights at once but it was kind of exciting. There was a guy watching out the door to the hallway holding jiggers. He yelled, "5-0 5-0."

Two guys went to help break up the fights, and get everyone seated. A guy whistled and the rover came back downstairs. It was like a very coordinated dance. Another couple of guys was ready to divert attention, one yelled something and pointed towards the TV and the other guy began to laugh and clap. Then everyone began to laugh and clap. The boss that was walking by and had caused the 5-0 may have been suspicious that something was going on, but he did not see anything. And he was not about to make his co-worker look bad by calling rank. He just called the turnkey boss and told him something. Probably, "Keep an eye out, I think they were fighting." The turnkey boss was an old convict boss and he knew what was up. He was purposely staying away so the fight could happen. He knew that this practice, the "heart-check," kept things under control. It was a part of the process.

In a perfect world everyone would come in and be respectful and never get in fights. But this was prison, where society throws their worst all together in one place. And, God bless us, we are as dysfunctional as they come. All up and down the scale of disorders. And the majority has created this system. The COs, for the most part, love it. The strong and the smart survive, the rest—well, it makes a bad situation a worse one.

The interfering boss left and the turnkey went back to the other block and spoke to the rover over there. Our boss went back upstairs, and it was like someone had rung a bell, and the fighting resumed.

One of the white guys got hit, and stumbled backward and tripped over Geechi's foot. He told me later that he wanted to hit him but did not see that as fair, since he was already getting whipped. And winning was not the objective. You only had to prove that you would fight for yourself. With all the stopping and starting you ended up fighting about seven or eight times. There were a few more stops and starts this night. The next time the fight started the other white guy who was fighting a regular, he was 6' but a little pudgy, said, "Alright, I'll ride. I'll ride." That was crazy. That would have been his last fight and he gave up; he broke weak.

When the fighting ended, the pudgy white guy and the black guy who'd sat on the bench were now riding and they sat on the back bench. The other white guy had earned himself a seat on the "woods" bench. He was labeled a down-wood. The guy I was sitting by whispered in my ear again, "We really letting them woods make it. Look at them. There are only two or three on each block. We outnumber them."

I just took it all in, thankful that I didn't have to live like them. I wasn't built like that. But these guys chose to live like this. This was their world. I didn't pay much attention to the disposition of the Hispanics. They had their own little world. But the leader would confer sometimes with

Geechi. Geechi was on the front bench and he called me up there to sit by him. He put his arm around me. I pulled two Kool cigarettes from my pack and lit them both and gave one to Geechi. He told me a lot of the same stuff that his homeboy had told me, but he told me other things that I didn't know.

*   *   *

The minimum amount of time a person works in the fields is ninety days. If you are a good, hard worker the field captain will give you a job inside the prison-laundry, kitchen, and so on.

Geechi had already stayed past the time, and the last time he'd refused so he could stay in the same block and job as me. He came and told me that they were making him leave the fields this time. They'd given him a job in the laundry, and he would be moved to the north side of the unit. The field force could only have so many inmates assigned to it, and they had to get rid of the ones who have been there the longest.

"I'm going to leave you with Skyblue," he told me.

"No, Geechi, let me get with Ty," I pleaded.

"It's only temporary. I'll be right back and you will be back with me."

"I don't want to be with Skyblue." I said.

"Sky is just going to watch you until I get back. If you get with Ty he won't let you go. Do you want that?" he asked.

"No, but are you sure you will be back?" I asked, and he nodded. "And I won't have to do anything with Sky?"

"I'll tell him, 'No sex.' Just ask him what he needs when you go to the store."

Skyblue lived in the cell next to mine. He would hold his mirror out the bars and we talked through the bars. We could see each other in the mirror as we talked.

One night, before we went to sleep, he asked me if I was going to breakfast. Geechi had been gone about three days now, and I was still used to going to breakfast with him. "Yeah," I told Skyblue, "Can't miss a meal." Working in that heat, I needed all the energy I could get.

"After breakfast, instead of going back to your cell, fall into mine. Then you can leave out at 5 a.m. when they call education and library," he told me.

"Geechi said no sex," I told him.

"What he don't know won't hurt him. And I just want some head. That's not sex." And it was only 1994, Bill Clinton had not set that trend yet. There must have been a universal redefining of terms and no one had notified Webster.

"Alright," I told him. And after breakfast I went to his cell. He didn't have a cellie. And the officers weren't due to count until after 6 a.m. They wouldn't notice me going into a cell that was not mine. The rover stayed up by the first cell, the picket opened the cells and then shut them. It was 3:45 a.m. when they racked up our block after breakfast. The rover left the wing.

In Sky's cell I did what he asked me to do. Now I had to wait until 5 a.m. For the out for education and library. He lay down on his bunk and I climbed up on the top bunk. It was just hard steel, no mattress, no sheets. But I'd rather lie up here than sit and talk to him down there. I was mad because this had not been supposed to happen.

After about thirty minutes he got up and looked at me. He said "Look." I looked at what he was indicating and saw that he had an erection. He said, "Get down."

I climbed off the top bunk and sat on the bottom bunk by the bars. I assumed that he wanted a repeat of the earlier act. But he didn't want oral sex this time. I don't know what had been going through his mind the last thirty minutes, but it wasn't that we were through. No wham-bam tonight. He reached into the locker above him and pulled out a small plastic container of Vaseline, and showed it to me.

I began shaking my head, saying, "But Geechi…"

He cut me off, saying, "You're with me now and this is what it's come down to."

"But I don't...uh, I can't…" I stammered.

His hand was up by the locker and I guess his hand fell on the combination lock and maybe the idea hit him then, or he had been planning it in the last thirty minutes. But he grabbed the lock and showed it to me and said, "We can do this the easy way or the hard way."

I've seen the movies and read the books. This is where the underdog usually gets the upper hand somehow. Either biting off his penis, or grabbing the lock and turning the tables on him. Oh yeah, that's great entertainment. And maybe in real life that happens one out of a hundred times, and then usually on the hundredth time.

But cowardice and fear were my two closest friends. And I was raped that night. If "DJ" had had time to think things through, he could have outsmarted the situation, but it came upon him pretty quickly. (I had gotten too used to thinking I was protected.) But rather than getting beat up with the lock and then raped anyway, I chose just the rape. Why suffer twice and physically at that? I wasn't built like that.

Now I was lying on the cell floor and holding the mirror on the run outside the bars to watch for the boss. I so wished the boss would come over just then. I would let them walk up on us. But usually when you need one, they are never around. I instead kept my mind on planning to go out when they called education and report to the lieutenant that I'd been raped.

*   *   *

I didn't associate this rape with my crimes and develop empathy. At the time I was still deep in victim-stance and very selfish. And this just added to the injustice of 'everything' that was being done to me. When a woman is raped, it is reported that there are people who say that "she was asking for it," or "she led him on." This is ludicrous and stems from an irrational belief system. I think that the people who say these things use it as a defense mechanism. They don't want to feel the emotions that "someone being raped" evokes, and they blame the victim. Maybe they themselves have continued after their partner said no. Rationalization is not exclusive to criminals; everyone has some form of rationalization in their cognitive armory.

To put in perspective what this was like for me or anyone else inside these prison walls, you must understand that when we are behind bars this is our world, our reality. The free world is just a phantom memory. Prison life had become my reality, and in this reality I, first of all, had to survive.

I felt violated, scared that this would be repeated, scared that I'd be beat up, shame, guilt, and out of control. I feared that I would have to sit on the back bench. There was a complex myriad of emotions and thoughts going through me. And now, I can trace it back to that five-year-old boy that night our lives were shattered. I felt that this was my fault, that bad things always happen to me. That there was something wrong with me. This was what, at my deepest level, I felt and thought about myself. This was my core identity. And Dr. Phil always says, "We generate, in life, the results that we believe we deserve." I believed that I deserved all this because there was something wrong with me. My step-dad knew it, and now these guys knew it.

(In my later prison years, when I couldn't get treatment from the prison, I had to con the guys in the dayroom to put the TV on ABC so I could watch Dr. Phil. It was the only way I could get any type of cognitive-behavior therapy.)

Criminals, sex offenders and even everyday John Q. Public—we all compartmentalize. Some compartmentalization is very detrimental, some is harmless. I compartmentalized everything and, of course, mine was very destructive. I do not like painful feelings, and anything that happened that was painful I put into a nice little compartment. As I did this rape, as I did in the world when I was offending, and as I did every time my step-dad got drunk and began to beat up my mom. I'm a pro at the art of compartmentalizing, and have been since I was five years old. When any bad feelings persisted, I used my favorite drug, sex, to deal with it.

Now, as I went out of Sky's cell and out of the block, I put the rape in its compartment, and pulled survival out of its compartment. That's what I focused on as I went to the lieutenant and told him, "I was just raped."

GROWING UP TOO FAST

"If he gets up, we'll all get up.
It will be anarchy."
-Line from *The Breakfast Club*

At the young age of five I didn't know what drove my step-dad to act the way that he did. My mother always said that it was the alcohol, and I believed that alcohol was the bad guy. I blamed and hated him also. Yet, at the same time I wanted his love and acceptance. I wanted a Daddy.

I grew up thinking that my family was the norm. I didn't know anything else. All I knew was rejection, fear, trying to get him to love me, rejection, fear, trying to get him to love me, wash, rinse, repeat, ad nauseam. Talk about the definition of insanity. And to top it all off I believed that it was my fault, that there was something wrong with me.

(Please go tell your children right now that it's not their fault—wash, rinse, repeat—yeah, it's that serious.)

One night I woke up terrified. Not by the yelling this time; that was commonplace. But by *what* he was yelling: "I'll kill David Jones if he walks in here right now." I was seven or eight and I was the only David Jones that I knew. We had moved to a house on Laprada Drive, about three houses down from the Dallas/Mesquite City line. The bathroom that my brother and I would normally use was not working, and that meant that we would have to enter our parents' bedroom to get to the only working bathroom. I just sat there holding it in, trembling. They continued their yelling at each other. I didn't know if he would come in here to kill me or not. Then my little brother, three years younger than me, woke up and started to get out of the bed that we shared. In my mind I realized real quick that he'd slept through all that yelling and that he was headed to the restroom, and that he did not know that he may be mistaken for me and be killed. Right then, there was a lull in the yelling from the other room. I broke out of my paralysis and grabbed for my brother. I whispered, "Don't go in there. Stop." We wrestled as he said that he had to go to the restroom. He slipped out of my grasp, took two steps into the hall and our step-dad began yelling again. He ran back into the room and jumped up into his bed.

"I tried to tell you," I whispered. "He said he would kill me if I walked in there." I told him as I held him.

We heard a slap, a scream, and scuffling coming from their bedroom. Then suddenly he was in our room.

'Why are y'all awake?" he yelled. "Get out here!"

In the hallway he first picked me up and held me against the wall. He had a belt in one hand and he swung it at me but missed. He let go of me and I dropped to the floor, scared but uninjured.

My brother, who was smaller than me, he picked up and held against the wall. He swung the belt and it hit his bottom and leg. By then my mother was there.

"Let him go! What are you doing?" she screamed, as she began hitting him with her fists against his back. He let go of my brother and dropped him to the floor, then turned to my mom and hit her with his fist and belt.

I did not know it at the time, but the reason my mom wasn't there when my step-dad first held me against the wall was because she'd called her brother to come pick us up. I grabbed my little brother and we went back to our room.

"Get dressed. We will probably have to sneak out again." I told him, pulling on some jeans.

The window in our room faced the front of the house. And it was on this window that my uncle knocked. He still lived with his parents, two and a quarter miles away; not that far. I ran to the front door and let him in, telling him that they were in the den.

He ran in there and freed my mom. I remember seeing him hold my step-dad back from going after my mom. She ran to get our baby sister and we met her in the hallway and went to my uncle's car.

I still don't know to this day if my uncle and step-dad fought or not. But my uncle came out of the house and before he could get into the car a police car pulled up behind his car. My uncle talked to them, then a cop came to the passenger side window where my mother was and knocked on the window. She rolled down the window and I heard him ask her if she would like to press charges.

I got really excited. Yes, finally he would go to jail and be out of our lives.

"No, it will be alright," she told them.

What? I could not believe my ears. I was deflated. An opportunity to be free—gone.

My uncle got into the car and drove us to our grandparents' home, mom's and his parents'. When we got in the house my brother and I ran to our grandmother and hugged her and began to cry. And what happened next, I will never forget and still do not understand, but my mother told both of us, "Come over here. Stop crying, you will just worry her."

But it was enough to damage an already damaged childhood. It was the lesson learned that "You don't talk about it, you don't cry about it, you just push your feelings deep down, and don't let anyone know our personal business."

I learned in therapy, years later, that I experienced a different type of abuse from my mother. She inadvertently used me as a husband-surrogate, *not* sexually, but emotionally. After that first fight that they had I had to grow up and be a man and take care of her. That was the result anyway. I felt that I had to and she certainly depended on me.

As I stated before, at the age of five my life was shattered. Everything that happened afterward became my perception of reality. But there is one significant memory (perception) that happened before I was five. I was three years old. I remember a big house and there were a lot of people there that night. My biological father was back from Vietnam on leave. I was opening the doors looking for my mom. When I finally found the room they were in, I walked in on my mother performing oral sex on my dad. They yelled at me and I went back out, shutting the door behind me. That is the end of that memory.

I mention this because I've come to believe that this made a considerable impression upon my young mind. I think it influenced decisions that I made later in life.

Another memory, this time back at the house on Laprada. I was eight or nine. The den was across from our bedroom. The den did not have a door, but over the years there was sometimes no door, and at other times, over the years they put up different things that acted as a "door". Once they even put up stringed beads, but this night in my memory there was a curtain, nailed at the top. I remember my mom wanting something up there blocking us from seeing in there while my step-dad watched his pornos.

I was coming back from using the restroom this night, and on the way back I heard strange noises coming from the den. I peeked through the curtain and saw my step-dad and mother having sex on the couch. The couch folded out to a bed. They did not see me, and I ran back to my room.

At age eleven I was left home alone a lot. And as children do all over the world when left in this position, I went exploring. In my parents' room I checked out their dresser. In one drawer I found my step-dad's gun. That didn't interest me. But two drawers down I struck gold. But it was fool's gold that I wish that I had never found. In that drawer were Playboy and Hustler magazines, and some VCR tapes of porn flicks.

At age eleven, a sexual orgasm became the drug that soothed me anytime I experienced negative emotions; fear, pain, and terror. Don't let any sex offender tell you that "it just happened," or that "it was a one-time event." It starts young. It is a slow fade, but it starts making ruts in the cognitive process. And I am not saying that at age eleven I began to think of offending. I am saying that at age eleven I learned to use sex to make myself feel better. It's not normal for an eleven-year-old to masturbate, but that's when I began. Masturbation, though, is never enough.

Looking back, it appears that my life was cursed with some type of sexual affliction. At least outwardly. But what was going on mentally and, more than that, emotionally?

When I was nineteen years old, months before I was arrested, I had racked up some late fees at a video store. I got a call from the lawyers of the store threatening me that if I did not pay them, that I would be brought to court, sued, and have to pay not only the late fees, and my lawyer fees, but that I would have to pay the store owner's lawyer fees and court costs. I laughed at him on the phone and told him that he was crazy. "Why would I have to pay their lawyer fees when they are the ones suing me?" I asked him.

Now it was his turn to laugh: "Where have you been for the last twenty years?" he asked me incredulously.

I yelled into the phone, *"Growing up!"* and hung up on him.

This question, though, has haunted me while I've been in prison. I have come across so many things that I did not know that I should have learned growing up, or at least absorbed by osmosis or something.

I began to ask myself, "Did I grow up? Was my family normal?" Just to be able to live with myself I had been justifying everything, and had rationalized the contradictions. I tried to harmonize the outward with the anguish of the inward. And life did not stop on the outside; when I was stunted on the inside, it kept going. I did not have a pause button. I had to try to keep up with the proverbial "Joneses," pushing down the negative, and trying to stay on top of the mountain. Anytime I got too close to the valley I would sexualize my way to the top again.

My whole view of life became sexualized: "How can I make *myself* feel good?" I did not have those conscious thoughts, but looking back, I see that this is what I trained myself to do. This had become my perception of reality. What goes on inside a boy to the point where he gets of age to make his own decisions, and that he draws upon during his 'growing up,' so that he pulls out sexual offending against children?

The book you are holding in your hands will reveal all this as never before. But don't judge too quickly, as you just might find something out about yourself.

* * *

At elementary school, I was the first one in second grade to get sent to the principal's office. Actually, the teacher made me wait in the hall outside of our classroom, and the principal came to me. I do not remember what I had done, but the principal brought his paddle with him. I was scared. He told me to turn and face the wall and to place my hands on the wall. I did as he told me but I kept turning my head back to watch the paddle. He had to sternly tell me to stay faced forward. He struck twice really quick making loud slapping sounds. I remember turning real quick, and as I did, I noticed heads popping out of the doorways all down the hallway. I looked up at the principal in surprise.

He said, "Next time I'll spank you for real. Go back in and behave." He must have struck his leg but he didn't spank me. But the fear of it worked. At least until I got to fourth grade.

In the school office there was a pencil machine that cost two quarters. You would get a pencil with an NFL team logo and colors on it. But you never knew what you would get. I hoped for a Dallas Cowboys pencil, but never got it. On my eighth birthday I had some change and went to the office to get a Cowboys pencil. What came out was a Pittsburgh Steeler pencil. I immediately thought, "I'll give this to my step-dad." Thinking that *this* would make him like me, because it was something that he didn't have, and it was the team that he liked. (I wasn't aware of the rivalry between the Steelers and the Cowboys—my step-dad never explained sports to me—I just knew that my mom's side of the family were all Cowboys fans, and my step-dad liked the Steelers.)

I did not have a big party with lots of friends. After school when our little family was there, my brother, baby sister, mom and step-dad, they all sang "Happy Birthday" to me. I blew out the candle to make a wish, (*please let my step-daddy stop drinking and like us*), and I opened up my presents. I got a Huffy bike (used—my step-dad's mom always encouraged my mom to buy used when it came to my brother and I), and some other things. I was waiting for just the right time to give him the pencil. We always called him "Daddy," from the beginning, because that is what we thought he was. Now, the name had stuck.

"Daddy, here, I got this for you," I told him, handing him the pencil. His next words crumpled my whole world.

"Huh, I know who I can give this to," he said, and walked out of the room.

I was speechless. I guess my mother knew something was wrong, because she came and put her fingers through my hair. I turned and hugged her.

This was a rare moment when our family wasn't fighting, and he wasn't drinking yet. So, I didn't bring it up, I just thanked her for the presents. But even when he wasn't drunk, he was able to cut me deep in my heart by his rejection of me.

LEW STERRETT

Dallas County Jail

"Are you happy? Uncle Bob always wanted you to be happy."
-Line from the movie *Urban Cowboy*

"The Sweetest Gift" by Linda Ronstadt

On June 11, 1991, after a plea bargain was agreed upon by the DA and my attorney, I turned myself in to the Dallas police station in downtown Dallas. I had been out on bail since March 7, the day before my twentieth birthday. I remember, a few weeks before this, at my grandmother's house, where I had been living since I was seventeen, my mom and sister had come over to go swimming. She was standing in the shallow end and I was standing on the sidewalk that girded the pool dressed in my usual summer garb: T-shirt, shorts and tennis shoes. My mom asked me why I wasn't swimming.

She knew that I loved swimming and that usually she couldn't get me out of the pool. She was there when my grandfather first got the pool, and my cousin and brother and I had all sat at the bottom as the pool filled up. She saw my grandfather later throw me in the deep end and teach me how to swim. She was there when I made the swim team in 7th grade, and she came to all my swim meets. No one ever had to ask me to get in the pool.

I don't remember the excuse that I gave her that day, but the real reason I was not swimming was that I had an irrational fear that if I relaxed and had any fun, then they would come and arrest me. Looking back, it was like I was thinking that if I punished myself enough then this would all go away, as if I was trying to appease some god, and as soon as he saw that I was aptly punished, he would get me out of this bind. It goes to show my true belief in who/what I thought God was.

My mom worked at Southwestern Bell. She worked the night shift, and her job was to deliver mail and supplies to different Southwestern Bells around Dallas. The night before I was to turn myself in, I went to work with my mom. We wanted to spend my last night of freedom together. We did not know the amount of years (sentence) that I would get in the plea bargain, as that wasn't decided yet. We were hoping for a small sentence, but just in case, we were going to spend this last night together before I went to jail.

From my mom I got my love for music, dance, and movies. She always played with us and tried to make us happy. She started a sort of tradition between us kids and her: she would quote lines from the movies that we watched, and we would laugh. Our favorite one was from *Urban Cowboy*, after his uncle died and he was talking to his aunt, and she asked, "Are you happy? Uncle Bob always wanted you to be happy." She was the kind of mom who always sacrificed herself so that we would have. In 1 Corinthians in the Bible where it defines love, her name should be there.

Linda Ronstadt, Carole King and Carly Simon were a few of her favorite singers. And on weekends or in the car (especially when we would drive away from him), she would turn up the volume, put in the tapes, and we would escape through songs. She would dance as she sang the songs. She could just make a bad situation fun.

One of our favorite songs, that we always sang together, was called "The Sweetest Gift" by Linda Ronstadt, on her *Prisoner in Disguise* album. Looking back, it seems strange that we always sang this song together as I was growing up. When I got to prison it seemed very fitting for my whole life. It's like even then, as a child, I was in prison, and she always brought me the sweetest gift to help me get through. And it became our inside code between me and her in the letters that I would write her from prison: "I need the sweetest gift." She would always show up the next weekend after I wrote that in a letter. That song talks about a mother's love for her son and that whwen she visits him in prison, she brought only a mother's smile, that being the sweetest gift.

*   *   *

That night in her Southwestern Bell van we played many of our favorite songs but we played "The Sweetest Gift" several times. We talked. She wanted to drive me to somewhere and hide me from the police and from everyone. She blamed herself for how I turned out, she didn't think prison was the answer, she said I should be getting therapy not prison. We cried.

I assured her that night and in many letters and all throughout my prison sentence, that she was the best mom ever. I told her that it wasn't her fault. I never did blame her. She was a victim also, that is how I saw it. She told me in later letters that she never spanked us because she felt sorry for us due to the abuse from her husband. At this time, and for many years later, I always blamed my step-dad. I garnered pity and felt sorry for myself by blaming him for my actions.

The memory of this night with my mom and seeing that she felt that she was to blame, haunts me on those nights when I am alone in my prison cell, and the past overrides the present. Every distraction has run out, all the justifications are gone. I'm alone with me and the past creeps in. Time does this to you. In prison it happens a lot. Everything just drops down at once—the past, the people I've hurt, the careless words that I've said, the painful acts I have done, the prison, the denied parole, the sense of never getting out, the feelings of helplessness. Time slows down. My thoughts become more tortuous; I mentally beat myself up.

How could I have hurt anyone, especially children? I've screwed up their whole lives. How could I be so selfish? Then I think of how much I hurt my mom and my family, and the girlfriend who I was with at the time. I hurt her so much that she would not even talk to me after my arrest. So much hurt, so much pain—all at my hands.

If I wasn't such a coward, I'd take the easy way out. But that is selfish too.

I go to sleep, putting those thoughts back into their compartments. When I wake up, I continue to distract myself from reality.

These moments weren't without purpose. Right then, they bordered between false and true remorse. I wanted to change but it wasn't there yet; I hadn't been all the way broken yet. But it was coming. By God, it was coming. I wanted to do it all for my mom.

*   *   *

Dallas County Jail, Lew Sterrett, 1991.

After processing I was escorted to an eight-man tank, carrying my mattress and bed linen and a clean pair of pink boxers and a pair of socks. Even though it was an eight-man tank, I was the fourteenth man living in this tank. Some guys shared a one-man cell, a mattress on the bunk and one on the floor. The rest of the guys had a mattress lined up around the wall of the dayroom.

I did not know that they had tanks designated for particular crimes when I got there. Everyone was in this tank either had sex cases or abuse cases against children or the elderly. But it makes sense to do that. Nobody was looking at me strangely or made any threatening moves. Everyone seemed all nice. One guy pointed to a spot on the floor where I could place my mat.

"First timer?" he asked.

"What's that?" I responded.

"Yeah, you's a new boot. First time in jail, is what I was saying," he explained.

"Oh, yeah," hoping that he wouldn't ask me what I was in for.

And he didn't. He began to give me a few helpful tips. The shoes that the county jail gave us to wear were bright orange, opened-toed sandals.

+ 49 +

This guy told me to wear those when I took a shower.

"You don't want to put your bare foot on that shower floor. You'll catch fungus and a few things that haven't been discovered yet."

Then other guys came around and introduced themselves, and offered some tips also.

"Sleep late, lose weight," a skinny guy said with a smile.

At my look of confusion, a black guy said, "What he means is make sure you get up and grab your food tray or someone else will eat it for you. You make the fourteenth person in this tank. In the morning—that's 3 a.m.—they serve fourteen breakfast trays. If you sleep through it there are no do overs. It'll be gone."

A Mexican guy told me, "We all get along in here. We keep it clean. Everyone helps out."

Dinner came and afterward I helped clean the tables and then I mopped. I took a shower, and I could see mold and fungus growing on the shower floor. At 10 o'clock the night news was coming on. I did not know the TV etiquette in here. But I was told that the media may report about my case, and I did not want people to see it, so I asked out loud, "Do ya'll ever watch *Hunter*?"

It must not have been offensive to them for a new guy to request to watch something. A few of them claimed that they loved that show, a black guy reached up and turned the TV to *Hunter*.

The next day I met Randy. His cell was the back corner cell, out of direct view of the picket, and was the most desired cell. He got it by moving in when it became available, and by seniority—he had been here the longest. He mainly stayed in his cell but was sociable at times.

He motioned me back to his cell. The first thing that I noticed was a stack of paperback novels in the corner. There were at least fifteen or twenty. He noticed me looking and asked, "You like to read?"

"I haven't read a book since I read Dr. Seuss in kindergarten," I told him. "I always just watched movies."

"Really? What about book reports in school?"

"I cheated or just didn't do it."

"How much time are you looking at?" he asked.

"Well, I got a plea bargain, but I don't know the years yet."

"Well, anyway, I recommend that you begin to read, it will help pass your time. Try this one and this one," he said, handing me a Dean Koontz and some other lesser-known authors. "So did you do it?"

"Do what?" I asked.

"Your crime. You're pleading guilty."

"How do you know that I'm pleading guilty?"

"You just said that you had a plea bargain. What was it boys or girls?" he asked.

"What? How can… What?" I stuttered.

"Look, I've been down for twelve years, and I'm back on a parole violation right now. I've seen it all. So…?"

I felt comfortable enough to tell him, he seemed to already know. "Boys," I confessed. "What's going to happen to me in prison?"

"It was girls for me. Texas prison is better than this. You don't have to stay in one tank all day. You go to work. You walk to chow hall. You get in and outs, where you can go to your cell or go to the dayroom. Trust me, it's better. It's a world within a world. You'll be fine. Don't tell anyone what you are in for. Get a convincing story ready and stick to it. Mind your own business," he told me.

We talked a lot. He prepped me for doing prison time. And, I'll always be grateful, he gave me my first book to read. I was hooked. A book is a thousand times better than a movie; the rollercoaster of emotions that a book evokes. Books became my best friend in prison—it was a great escape.

On Friday, three days after I got to jail, I was called out to court. My lawyer came out to meet me and said, "The DA is offering fifteen years on all cases to run concurrent. Today you'll go before the judge, plead guilty and be sentenced. There are three cases today. They are going to milk this for the media."

"Can't you get less than fifteen?" I asked, numb.

"No, David. This is a high-profile case. This is a big deal," he said.

And so it began. Fifteen years; 2006 looked so far away. It's now 2021 as I'm writing this. Why am I still in prison?

* * *

I wrote earlier that at age five I was in a prison. It was made by my step-dad. It was a prison of fear. The first five years we had mostly lived with my grandparents, and the impression I got from them was love and acceptance. I didn't feel rejected or not wanted. But after that first fight between my mother and step-dad, it seemed like he hated or resented me. I felt rejected, and always at fault. He didn't do the things you see a loving father do. He didn't spend time with me or teach me sports, how to fight or the many other things that a man is supposed to teach a child.

That feeling of rejection was a tangible feeling. And it wasn't just him; it was his family too. I remember a time when I was about seven and we were in the car headed to his parents' house. When we pulled up, my brother and I got out of the car and ran up the driveway and around to the back of the house. His parents, a couple of his sisters, and one of his brothers was sitting out on the patio. We, as kids, were running up as if we were part of this family, like we were going to be hugged or something. My brother doesn't remember this but I heard an audible groan, as we rounded the corner and they saw us. As if to say, "Not these two."

I heard it and just came to a stop. My brother, being four, stopped with me, until our mom and step-dad came up behind us. I walked my brother over to the swing set and didn't say anything to them.

The combination of love from my mom and her family, with the hate and rejection from him and his family, was not good for my sense of self-worth and self-esteem. How was I to build a secure identity with this type of environment? Inside I was bankrupt, confused and very scared and alone. The love wasn't enough to heal the constant fear that there was something wrong with me and that no one, especially men, did not like me. It translated over to school, where the other boys, kids my age, did not like me. I always got along with the girls, though. It had something to do with how I viewed the dominant male and female in my life. I guess you can say that I generated that result because that is what I believed that I deserved from each sex.

After school, my brother and I would have to be at home with him until Mom got home from work. We didn't want to be in the same room with him. He would sit on the couch in the den and play solitaire with a deck of cards, and watch TV shows that only he liked. He'd take turns calling one of our names to "Get me a beer."

These are the times I'd stay in my room with fear permeating my soul. I felt all alone, even with my brother there. And this lasted the whole nine years they were married. I used to read John 14:1-3. They are my favorite verses and I had them memorized; they gave me comfort. In these verses Jesus promised to come get me and to bring me to a room in heaven. It had to be better than here. Other times I'd sit at the front window in my room that faced the driveway. Every time I would see a car, I would hope that it was my mom. She was working at Southwestern Bell as a 411 operator at this time.

A prison of fear and loneliness. This is how it was in my childhood. Can you imagine being brought up this way? This is the '70s and '80s. The needs of a child were not as well-known as they are now. My mother's family knew what was going on but I don't' think anyone knew the long-term effects that this type of abuse would have on me.

Her family loved us and they were always there to help. My mother loved me but she depended on me as if I were an adult. She never disciplined us because she didn't want to hurt us more than we had been already. She was seventeen when she had me. There were times as I got older that I made her so angry that she would slap me and spank me, for as long as she could keep me in front of her to be able to reach me. We argued a lot, and especially once I became a teenager. I think that as I got older and after she left him, she wanted to be the mother again, and I wanted to keep going the way things were. From age five to fourteen she depended on me and that was too much for a kid that had no foundation in himself of who he was. I wasn't emotionally capable of dealing with it all.

There was the constant fear and rejection from him that completely overwhelmed me. He put me down all the time, called me a momma's boy, and made fun of things that I did wrong as a kid rather than teach me the right way as a father should.

My brother and I were just slaves to him.

I used to blame my crimes on him, and everything else that was wrong in my life; I used to hate him. I no longer blame or hate him. And I do not tell you this to place blame for my crimes on my childhood. I tell you this because a big part of this book is to show you what goes on inside a person (and outside), who grows up and sexually offends against children. I did not grow up thinking, "I'll be a child molester when I grow up."

I grew up in fear and loneliness. I was empty of the things on the inside that made for a healthy and whole human being. And yet I kept seeking his love and approval, like with the pencil. And was continuously rejected over and over

I grew up mimicking the types of behavior that was considered good: helping the elderly, mowing the lawn, being respectful, polite and courteous, saying the right thing. But I didn't have these in my foundation to be able to live by it as if it were natural, or a part of my character. It was outward behavior that I knew was not only good and accepted but also gave the impression that I was a good person.

Inside there was pain, hurt, fear, rejection, and feeling unloved, unworthy. Outside I conformed to the image of what made me look good. Then when masturbation entered the picture, it twisted what sex was about, and while it soothed me, it gave me the sense that getting the feeling of an orgasm equaled having control over my out-of-control emotions and life.

A child needs a father to instill things in him that he will use for the rest of his life. I never had positive things from a father. I never got the sense of him loving me for me. Instead, I was criticized during my developmental years. My foundation was sand with a few rocks. The rocks' names were fear, rejection, loneliness, and worthlessness.

I'd be standing on the sand and those rocks were the only thing I had to grab onto when life got hectic, and it was always hectic (that's what I deserved). I would live my life out of fear, trying to please people so they wouldn't be mad at me and hope that they would accept me. I didn't want to disagree with anyone because I thought that would make them not like me. And you, dear reader, you are exactly right about what you are thinking right now, I was a mess, I agree with you. The old adage is true: "If you don't stand for something, then you will fall for anything."

*　　*　　*

By the time that I left county jail I had a total of sixteen counts of Indecency With a Child. I got fifteen years on each case but they ran concurrent. I had also received ten years deferred adjudicated probation each for two counts of aggravated sexual assault of a child under fourteen. This also ran simultaneously with my prison sentence. It was a great plea bargain and it was all based on my cooperation with the investigators and telling them everything that I'd ever done, crime-wise.

And my attorney had been correct; they milked it for the media. The reason it was such a high-profile case was because I'd worked at a child care facility whose name was reduced to just initials, familiarly. I'd worked there for twenty-two months. It stayed out of the media the whole time I was out on bail. But the police couldn't pass up the chance to look good for catching the bad guy. It was a six-month investigation and some of the parents had put their child up to accuse me of some horrible things that I did not do. The newspaper later said that those accusations were for them to gain more leverage in their lawsuits against the place that I worked at. In the same article the investigating lieutenant stated, "There was *no* evidence that he [Jones] did anything other than fondling, at ... [the place where I worked]." (Dallas Morning News, Feb. 6, 2000 "Prosecutors." byline Brooks Egerton)

I was labeled the most prolific child molester in Dallas history. I was labeled a monster. I, sadly, earned those labels. The two aggravated cases were not in connection with the place where I'd worked. And I was sixteen and seventeen at the time and the boy was twelve, he was the brother of a friend of mine from school.

I do not minimize what I did. I know, now, how much I hurt and confused my victims. I only bring up my offenses to show that I got caught at a very young age, and to tell the truth about what I did. I haven't escalated to worse acts. What I did was bad enough, but I did not do the things that I was accused of. I remember reading in those early articles about me that some psychologist stated that it was a good thing that I was caught at my young age, before the patterns were cemented in my mind. I didn't understand that then, but I totally get it now. And I am grateful for that child who was brave enough to turn me in and got this whole investigation started. Thank-you—you saved a lot of others and myself also.

Later, in 1993, I was bench warranted back to Dallas County jail for three more cases. When I asked my lawyer where these cases came from, he said that they were a part of the original confessions, and that they needed to be on the record so the parents could sue the place where I'd worked. When I looked at the indictments, I noticed there was one that I did not confess to, and I knew that I didn't do anything to him. I mentioned this to my lawyer and he said that it's too late to rock the boat. In essence, what's one more case in the midst of so many? So, I plead guilty to all three just to get it over with, and to "not rock the boat." I got the same time and my lawyer assured me that the cases were backdated to begin on June 11, 1991, the same as the others.

During the investigation the police and the DAs gave me a polygraph test on specific accusations, and as a whole to determine if I was telling the truth, and telling them everything. I passed each polygraph and according to my attorney, they were completely satisfied. That is why the lieutenant said what he said to the newspaper and why I did not get any more cases that were aggravated—because I did not do the things that I was accused of. And for the parents to put their children up to saying that, when I didn't do it, hurt their children even worse. I had no reason to lie *then* or *now*. So, for a parent to do that is very much akin to them victimizing their own children.

I sometimes wonder about them. I can only come to the conclusion that either they are just plain lying, for the lawsuit, or someone molested them and they put it on me as to protect that other person. I don't know. Maybe we will never find out. But I still categorically deny doing anything other than what I did confess to doing in writing to the police. I have no reason to lie.

JUST A THOUGHT

"... How many of us have the intellectual courage to consider, let alone accept, the truth when it demands so much?"
-Osha Gray Davidson

"...Get Wisdom, and whatever you get, get Insight."
-Proverbs 4:7

"A man is commended according to his good sense, but one of twisted mind is despised."
-Proverbs 12:8

"The essence of Government is power; and power, lodged as it must be in human hands, will ever be liable to abuse."
-James Madison

"It's a slow fade…"
-Casting Crowns

"Laws are made for men of ordinary understanding and should, therefore, be construed by the ordinary rules of common sense." -Thomas Jefferson.

"He who is void of virtuous attachments in private life is, or very soon will be, void of all regard for his country. There is seldom an instance of a man guilty of betraying his country, who has not before lost the feeling of moral obligations in his private connections." -Sam Adams

In the movie *National Treasure*, the character played by Nicholas Cage, after reading the Declaration of Independence, stated: "People don't talk this way anymore." That got me interested in our Founding Fathers. In county jail I came across a book that depicted how they brought, or shall I say wrought, America to become a nation. Did you know that in the early 1770s Sam Adams and a few others fasted and prayed that the thirteen Colonies would become a nation? That's astounding: he prayed and fasted that this country would become America—the US of A.

Our forefathers were astounding and amazing men. The way they thought, spoke and wrote. They were Christian men and they incorporated God's moral law into the Constitution, schools and government. Not to force a religion on anyone, but because mostly everyone was a Christian. But teaching and governing from God's moral standard instills a virtuous and moral lifestyle. John Adams put it this way: "Our constitution was made for a moral and religious people. It is wholly inadequate to the government of any other."

When I read the Sam Adams quote above, I realized how important it is to learn these things in every aspect of life growing up. But I was void of these virtuous attachments in my private life, so it is no wonder that I betrayed the people who trusted me. I betrayed my city, state and country.

In the book about our forefathers, there was a chart and it showed the contrast of certain statistics before and after the Supreme Court made the decision to stop prayer and reading the Bible in schools. Schools showed an increase in teenage pregnancy, school dropouts, and crime.

I wonder, sometimes, what America would be like if that decision had never been handed down. Would we see less crime? Less of the #MeToo movement? Have you ever noticed that some form of sexual harassment, all the way to sexual assault, has permeated every class of people, from the homeless to the military to the White House? From major businesses to schools, and to everyday people? I watch the news and there is a report every day of some form or manner of sexual offenses. And the media is part of the problem. The people we grew up being entertained by, from Bill Cosby and Michael Jackson, to Jared, who did the subway commercials. It has permeated every walk of life as we know it. When will it all stop?

I think that that is the wrong question. In order to stop something, you cannot attack the symptoms. You must get to the root and start there. From my objective—with a slight bias—viewpoint from prison, America is trying to attack this beast from the wrong end: the symptoms. The symptoms come after the virus has invaded our bodies. No, we must start at the beginning.

"Criminals cause crime. Crime resides within the minds of human beings and is not caused by social conditions. "

Stanton E Samenow

Inside the Criminal Mind I agree with this quote. I do *not*, in any way, blame my childhood or abuse for my crimes. I chose to do what I did. I take full responsibility for my sex offenses and the harm that I caused to my victims.

In writing this I would like to bring understanding to all who read this that, and I speak specifically for me, but generally for other sex offenders, that there is something more going on here than just a person being a sex offender. And the response from society should not be, "Lock them up and throw away the key." There is a big misconception about sex offenders out there. It goes deeper than the offending and it transcends the modern response to it.

And again, I say this without minimizing the heinousness of what I did. There is *no excuse* for what I did, it cannot make sense, and it is horrible to hurt a child in any way.

And people will believe what they want to believe. There are enough facts available but they only believe what will keep them in their comfort zone. They don't want to leave their ordered lives and deal with anything outside the box. And we are all guilty of this to some degree. We are blind to explanations that lie outside our perception of reality. And we are all guilty of having our own perception of reality.

In the book *Texas Prisons: The Longest Hotel Chain in Texas,* the retired warden Lon Bennet put it this way:

"The difference between Reason and Excuse:

A reason is a persuasive basis for an action;

An excuse is a basis that is not persuasive."

What I am trying to get to is the *reason* for sexual offending. Anyone can label it and place it in a box and not deal with it. But the pandemic is now so great that we need to pull this box back down and come at this a different way.

I used to weigh 186. Now I am 213. But to my eyes I don't look any different. That's because I slowly grew into this weight so that I didn't notice it. Yet, someone who has not been with me over the years, since I weighed 186, has recently told me that I have gotten bigger. The same thing applies to the people making decisions on how to deal with sex offenders. They have been doing this over time and cannot see things, i.e. ex post facto laws, that are not helping matters at all. And the definition of insanity being what it is.

There is a lot of 'junk science' out there that is reporting that the recidivism rate for sex offenders is high. There is a study that has been released from the U.S. Justice Department in 2003 that counters that. It shows the child molester rearrest rate for *new* sex crime against a child is 3.3%. All sex offenders rearrest rate for *new* sex crime against a child is 2.2%. Sex offenders were less likely than non-sex offenders to be rearrested for any offense—43% of sex offenders verses 68% of non-sex offenders (U.S. Dept. of Justice Bureau of Statics, Recidivism of Sex Offenders Released from Prison in 1994, November 2003, NCJ 198281).

The laws and requirements on sex offenders after they have completed their time are redundant and have become more than just punishment—they are pure revenge. But for the lawmaker they are a vehicle for reelection, saying, "Look how tough I am on sex crimes." While they violate their very oath of that office—the defense of the Constitution; and the last time I checked the US Constitution protects the civil rights of its people. There is nothing in the Sixth Amendment, or any Amendment, that allows for ex post facto laws, that keeps humans beyond their prison sentences—what happened to the whole "paying your debt to society"? Thomas Jefferson said, "The care of human life and happiness, *and not their destruction,* is the first and only legitimate object of a good government."

But it's like there is a frenzy stemming from the media's reporting of the junk science, and the widespread reports of sexual assault that come from every walk of life. And without thinking, or thinking from revenge, those unconstitutional laws are being made. And this is not the answer. The answer lies at the beginning.

What is being done to make sure the next generation does not grow up void of these virtuous and moral attachments? Look at what is going on in today's society: caller ID to screen calls, a person can 'unfriend' you on Facebook, texting, period—what's up with that? Breaking up with someone through a text, instant chat, mail, pictures, orders, and so on. All these take away the human aspect. It also takes away the process. When a person has to wait for something, or face a live person when breaking up, it's a learning experience, you take away something from that, and you develop empathy and responsibility. But if I can break up with you in a text then I don't see how that affects you and I become immune to how others feel.

I see the current generation in both young officers and young inmates that are entering the prisons today. The officers get hired, work until they accrue comp time and sick time, then they call in from work. Texas prisons are full of this type of officer. The inmates argue and get upset when things don't go their way, then blame everyone else for their problems. Texas prisons are full of this type of inmate also. Neither group wants to take responsibility. And there was a time that this prison instilled that value in both its employees and inmates just by how the prison was run. Now it is a joke.

Back to the 'reason.' Social conditions *do not* cause crime. They do, however, have everything to do with the reason people grow up and make the choices that they do. Sam Adams said: "... he who is void of virtuous attachments..." How does he become void of them? It has to tie into how he is raised and the social conditions.

I did not just wake up one day and say, "I want to be a child molester."

I was not born this way. But just like the song it was a "Slow Fade." And now society has labeled me a monster, put me in that box, and does not care about any injustice done to me because I have offended sexually against children. But when Martin Luther King said, "Injustice for one is injustice for all," he wasn't only referring to racism. But that truism encompasses all injustices.

In this prison world there are a lot of messed-up people, dysfunctional people, and you can see why they are here. I sometimes wonder who invented the concept of prison. I can see the town leaders of that society in a time long, long, ago saying, "Let us build a place for all the people who break the law and put them all together and we will lock them in." Then over time it was defined and redefined, until we have what we got today. But no one on the outside really understands what really goes on in prison. No one knows what it does to a person to sit around others who have no virtue or morals, and encourage that person to negative behavior, for years. This is called 'mass incarceration.' It's easier to assume that we deserve what we get. It is easier to believe that criminals and sex offenders are all just monsters and that its okay to treat them the way we are being treated: worthless, unredeemable. But the same messed-up and dysfunctional people can be fixed. (I hope that you can see that in the people that I write of in this book.) If people outside these walls would see us as people, then maybe they would snap out of that frenzied mentality of revenge and reelection, and approach this subject outside of the box and come to a better, less expensive, and more humane rehabilitation and prevention. It's like everyone has the 'Don't ask, don't tell' mentality, but please ask me: I will tell you.

As I said I was not born as this monster. There is a reason, not an excuse, of how I came to be the type of person who makes these types of decisions. There are a lot of things that contributed to the choices that I have made. Again, I do not blame those things for my crimes; but they need to be considered in context, possibly understood before you judge me worthless and throw me away. With a monster there is no reasoning. There are human monsters who set out to destroy other people's lives. Those people need to be cut off from society. I am not a monster. I am a human being. I grew up in an abusive house, developing an immoral, non-virtuous foundation built on sand. No security—just a few rocks:

fear, loneliness, rejection and feelings of worthlessness. Hey, there is a new rock over there, let's go see what it is. 'Sexualizing'. Makes sense. I was using sex (masturbation) to stave off fear. Masturbation, mixed with sexual fantasies, soothed my negative emotions. At first, my fantasies were of the women in the magazines. As I got older, approximately twelve or thirteen, I would notice other boys in the locker room at school. In my mind I would compare, then wonder what they had that I didn't. Why did other guys like them and not me? It was as if everyone got the memo on "how to be liked and influence people," except me. I was missing something. The true definition of sex had been twisted inside me, I was sinking in my foundation and the only rock in my foundation that ever gave me pleasure was the sexualizing one. I grabbed a hold of it. I wanted a connection with other boys, to be liked and accepted, validated even. In my mind I sexualized that true need. I didn't know how to be normal on the inside. What is normal?

Even as I grew up on the outside, my thoughts, emotions, and sexualizing didn't grow up. They didn't develop normally, didn't go through a process. And no one knew my inner thoughts or fantasies. Which means there were no barriers put in place. I grew up with no boundaries in my mind. If someone knew, I am sure they would have confronted me and that would have been the start of a process. But instead, those patterns of thoughts became well grooved into my neurons' synapses.

As you are reading this it probably terrifies you to think that people grow up like this. And to think that it is not just me; there are thousands of people who grow up like this—maybe someone you know? Watching the news, hundreds more are found all the time. And at times it all seems so overwhelming. I mean that, I get the box, I do. I am a pro with compartmentalizing. But in my experience putting things that are uncomfortable in a box is just as detrimental as committing crimes.

Let's not forget that I am still a human being. I did not go wholly over to the dark side. Getting caught early while I was still young helped. Prison was a deterrent, and a crucible that revealed how void I was on the inside. Then there was my resolve to do something about it; I developed empathy in therapy, and in encountering the human beings behind these prison walls. And I set out to build a better foundation not built on sand—but one of virtue and good morals. Cement. Good, old fashioned, American cement.

DO AS I SAY, NOT AS I DO

"Let them revere nothing but religion, morality and liberty."
-John Adams (in reference to his children)

I was precocious as a child, and intuitive. I picked up on things easily. As soon as VCRs came out, my step-dad bought one and I hooked it right up. It was effortless for me. But a couple of weeks later we were over at his parents' house and he was helping his brother hook up their VCR to their TV. When he got behind the TV and looked at the cables, he called me over and asked me which cable went where. I froze. I stupidly repeated the words of his question. Then I shrugged. He called me a stupid mutt.

The reason I did not answer wasn't because I did not know. I wasn't able to answer because I was scared. I didn't have the confidence to tell him how to do it. He had already cowed me into fearing him and I didn't want to get it wrong. But if he would have just told me to do it from the beginning, I could have done it no problem. It seemed that I was always like this around men; I could do anything, but if a man asked me a question about it, I could not give an answer.

In third grade I had a male teacher named Mr. Thomas. If you ask me what a child learns in third grade, I couldn't tell you. But Mr. Thomas gave me something I have never received from a man in nine years of living; he gave me praise. I remember that he asked the class who wanted to read out loud from the textbook. I was sitting close by and I raised my hand. He let me sit on the table and he sat next to me as I read the passage out loud. When I was finished, he gushed with praise at how good I had read. And I could sense his sincerity, that he really meant it. He wasn't condescending at all. It meant a lot to me and because he did that, I became real good at reading and spelling. Which gave me a good comprehension and a love for words.

This was the first time I had been told that I was good at something from a man. Looking back, it seems crazy that that one bit of praise could give me something valuable on the inside, even if everything else was not. It makes me believe that children need this type of praise and validation until they get it deep down into their foundation. There were men on my mother's side of the family, my grandpa, two uncles, that I learned from but never put it in perspective, with the exception of the moral my grandpa taught me about not judging or hating people because they are different or because of the color of their skin, and to never say the N-word. The other things they may have conveyed to me were too few and far between to make a difference. Those were given in small increments, whereas what my step-dad was doing was full time and on full blast. Those lessons were prevalent and took the right of way. And I do not believe that the men on my mother's side knew what was going on inside, that what I was learning at home would have lasting effects. And they also pitied us because of our home life, and they did not want to be strict with us. No one, at this time, knew how growing up in an abusive home would affect young children. After the divorce they tried to teach me things but my core was developed and it was wrought with fear and pain. It would have taken something to break that core to "learn" me something new.

*   *   *

Tonight it was a really bad fight. I woke up to him chasing her through the hallway into the den. She was trapped. I went to the den door and she yelled for me to get help, I was ten years old. I grabbed my clothes and told my brother to come with me.

Outside in the front yard I told my brother to get in mom's car and wait. I went to the next-door neighbor and asked if I could use their phone. They said that they did not want to get involved. I just looked up at this guy incredulously then took off running. I was barefoot and in blue jeans only, but I ran all the way to the 7-11, about a mile down the road. I called my grandpa collect and asked him to come and get us. I hung up and ran all the way back to the house.

There was a median in the middle of Laprada Drive, a wide patch of grass. When I got back my brother was standing in the middle of this patch of grass. He had the clothes that I had grabbed when leaving the house in his hands. I took these from him and we watched as our step-dad stood holding a gun by his side, facing my mom who was on the curb of our driveway holding our baby sister. He suddenly grabbed my sister with his free hand and they wrestled for her. He pushed my mom down with the gun hand and wrenched my sister from her hands. My sister started crying, not knowing what was going on.

When my mom hit the ground, I dropped my clothes and stepped toward her. But my step-dad noticed this and said, "C'mon you little punk. Whatcha gonna do?"

I was struck with fear and just stood there staring at him.

"That's what I thought. You're a pussy momma's boy. You're a cocksucker." he said as he laughed and took my sister into the house with him.

My brother and I went to my mom and of course, she said that she was alright. (God forbid that we feel anything or help her.) But we three sat on the curb and I told her that I called her father. He was there several minutes later.

My mother told him that she wasn't leaving without her daughter. My grandpa told us to get in the car, and he went to the door with my mom. He came to the door with his gun, but tried to hide it when he saw our grandpa. My grandpa asked for my sister and my step-dad said, "No." I guessed my mom felt emboldened with her father there and she pushed past him in the door and went into the house. My grandpa called her name and said, "No," to her. But my step-dad stayed in the door and didn't go after her. She came back out with my sister and got into the car and we went to my grandparents'.

*   *   *

These nights stand out in the hall of shame in my memories. There are more than just the ones that I've written about. It truly seemed that we had to leave the house every weekend and go to motels or be rescued by my grandpa or uncle. But the abuse wasn't only when he was drunk. He put me down the most when he was sober. There was never a time that I can remember when I felt safe, peaceful or loved in his presence. I didn't want to be in the same room with him. I only felt safe if my mom was in the room also.

When she was not there, he would give us hard chores. One time he told us to go to the alley and clear off all the foliage that had grown and intertwined in the fence. The whole fence was covered in vines and has been since we moved into this house. I was nine and my brother was seven. We had to use our bare hands. Another time he hired some company to reroof the house. They threw the old shingles onto the ground all the way around the house. He told the company supervisor that his two brats would pick them up and put them in the back of the truck; we were just kids.

For a while I thought my name was, "Get me a beer." I was glad when he bought a new refrigerator and put the old one in the garage, which had a connecting door to the den. But he still couldn't get up and walk the ten feet to get his own beer. He should have just put a tap in the wall behind the couch where he sat.

Can you imagine growing up scared? Scared all the time. At the time when a child is supposed to be able to run to both parents and feel safe, secure and loved, all I felt was fear. Waking up to fear, going to sleep in fear. There were small rays of love interspersed here and there from my mom and her family. But the constant was fear. Constantly feeding off of fear. This damages a child. It damaged every aspect of my life.

I would read the Bible to get comfort, and I had these small rays of love, but that conditioned me in the opposite way of what is normal. A normal, healthy, functional child feels love as the norm, with the occasional negative emotions or events in his/her life. But fear, feelings of worthlessness and rejection was my norm, with an occasional feeling of love or peace. This ruined me. It damaged my belief in God and it distorted how I viewed women, children and men, and the world. It taught me that I can go to the women in my life and use them, take them for granted and manipulate them to get my way. I learned that I had no hope with a man ever loving me (unless I did something). And my peers, other boys, did not seem to like me, but the girls did. Then in junior high school, I was accepted by the blacks and Hispanics. They more readily accepted me than my own race.

My definition of love was what I saw outwardly between my mom and step-dad. Although I never treated the girls I went out with in high school and later badly other than to take them for granted. By "badly" I mean physical abuse. You see, I didn't think women should be treated that way because I didn't like my mom being treated that way. I never related to him the way a child relates to a father figure. I did not want to be anything like him. I related to my mother. I didn't want to be a girl, or a female, however I still related to her. In relationships I identified as the female emotionally. Love was about being hurt, then going back for more. This was the meaning of love that I inferred, and it set into my own "operating system." It wasn't a conscious thought.

And as I said earlier, I began to wonder about other boys in the locker room. Then I sexualized it. I would wonder what was different between us. Then I'd fantasize about it, the fantasies consisting of the other kids liking me. Then they became masturbatory fantasies of a sexual nature, because masturbation had soothed me before. And when you pair the intense feelings of an orgasm with whatever you fantasize about it makes a powerful connection in your brain. Our brains "learn" to pair pleasure with the thought of a child, it connected the two together. And as I got older my emotions didn't mature and what made me feel good, out of all that evil, didn't develop normally. Throughout my teen years, my sexual development years, puberty and sexual identity, children stayed in my mind, and there was no one to counter that pattern as it developed, and to me I couldn't see an error in my thinking. I was just going by what made me feel good. And it was reinforced over and over, not just becoming my preference, but became like a drug that I would use when

I felt fear or any negative emotion.

I remember seeing a news segment, when I was fifteen, on the TV show *A Current Affair*, about some old man who'd molested children. The story enraged me, that he would hurt children in that way. But my next thought illustrates my belief system: "He's not loving them the way I am." I, of course, had not molested anyone yet, but I knew what was going on in my mind. I knew that it was against the law but I justified it in my conscience that "I was loving them." I had to have this belief so I could live with myself and enable myself to be able to do it. "Human reasoning can excuse any evil. That is why it is so important that we don't rely on it." (Tris said this in the book *Divergent* by V. Roth.) But it is true. I reasoned and rationalized away my behavior. And my thoughts were private and secret. I didn't tell anyone. The Bible says, "Whoever isolates himself seeks his own desire; he breaks out against all sound judgment." (Prov. 18:1)

I remember thinking that I was different and unique. I thought I had it all figured out and that no one else did. I would go to school and do just enough to pass, but I never applied myself. I remember in sixth grade one time we were doing math problems and the girl in front of me turned around and asked me, "What did you get for number three?"

And I wanted to be a part of that world. A world where I was equal, and I would have answered her, "I got the answer 142 with a remainder of 5, and I got it by..." but I wasn't wired like that.

I just shrugged and shook my head, thinking, "I was hoping to get the answer from you." I can still see the look of disappointment mingled with disgust on her face.

I practically grew up in church. My grandmother and great grandmother always brought me to church. My mother got saved in the early 80s and then she would take us to church. I didn't have a true picture of God. They said that He is our Father, but if He was anything like my step-dad then I didn't see a point. But this Jesus guy, He promised peace and always showed love; and he died for my sins. But I didn't truly know Jesus either. So, the Bible became something that I could grab to get a verse to comfort me, and being a "Christian" and going to church became a way to build that false image that I was a good person. But not just to others; I believed that lie too. I had too. On the inside I was lacking anything and everything good. So I had to have the outward 'conformity' to being good. But again, these were not conscious thoughts; no, nothing so diabolical. It was a learned behavior. I had an outward conforming to the norm, while deviancy lurked within. All along the way searing my conscience and justifying my behavior to the point that I believed I was okay.

PRISON TERMS - TIME

"I have sworn upon the alter of God, eternal hostility against every
form of tyranny over the mind of man."
-Thomas Jefferson

"Almighty God hath created the mind free, and manifested
His supreme will that free it shall remain by making it altogether
Insusceptible of restraint; ..."
-Thomas Jefferson

"Time...you ain't no friend of mine."
-Hooty and the Blowfish

The word "chain" is a prison term for being transferred from one unit to the next, either for a medical appointment, or being reassigned to a different unit. Back in the day, when transporting prisoners, each inmate was connected to a long chain that was locked around their neck. Over time the prison had improved on this policy and now they placed a handcuff on one guy's wrist and the other side of the same handcuff would be on another guy's wrist, and the two would sit together on the bus—thus making it harder for an escape. But the term "chain" was still being used to tell us that we were being shipped or transferred.

There are a lot of terms and phrases that are used in prison every day that dehumanize the process, and desensitize everyone to the fact that we, the prisoner, are indeed human.

I fight against this in my mind because I refuse to let them defeat *me* by *me*. I resist the sentiment that I am less than human. Maybe the prison system did not purposely set out to use these terms that dehumanize, but they have developed in here and over time it can take a toll. The sad thing is that most people don't realize it is happening to them, then wonder why they can never seem to overcome their issues and problems. Here is a small sample of prison speak:

The supervisor over the radio to a pod or wing: "E-wing, send me a shot of chow." A 'shot' is a group of inmates, usually twenty-five humans going to eat 'chow': lunch, dinner, or whatever.

An officer says over the intercom on the wing: "Pill window all the way out."

This means if the doctor prescribed you medication that is not OTC, then you have to go stand in a line that leads to a window at medical and the nurse in the window will dispense your meds to you. An officer will watch you to make sure that you take it. When we are called out for mail, an appointment, or to visit, they use our cell and bunk number: "H1-08T you have a visit."

The "H" is the letter used to identify the pod or wing you live on. And the 1-08 is the cell number (1 row 08 cell) and the "T" is for top bunk, a "B" is used for bottom bunk.

"In and out," "Hey, inmate...you in the white," (we all wear white.) The radio code for an inmate is 95 and for a boss it is 86. These codes are still used if a boss is escorting inmates toward the fence to clean up or work: "I have three 95s and one 86 heading to the back gate." The COs get away with calling us names and cussing us out, using profanity towards us, but will write a disciplinary case on us if we say "damn." There are so many other ways our humanity is dehumanized, that we have become inured to it. If I recognize it, I resist it and have self-talk that reinforces my humanness. Can you imagine living in an environment where you hear, speak, live and are treated like this for years, for decades, day in and day out? It takes a toll. It desensitizes and gives both the inmate and the officer a non-real sense of who we are. But what is politically correct, and what is a better way? In our language, out there and in here, we are getting lazy. We want to speak fast and get a response faster. Texting and emojis are an example of this and are equivalent to the prison's 'send me a shot.' I couldn't imagine the prison speaking correctly over the radio: "Lieutenant Bates to Officer Smit, would you please send me twenty-five people to eat their lunch meal?" Or an officer saying to me: "Mr. Jones, I am affording you an opportunity to go into your living quarters and get something, or you may stay in there for the next hour until I come back and open the door. Or better yet, just send someone to get me when you are ready to come out." The prison almost has to operate in a dehumanizing way.

We are not people in here, we are numbers, or a product in this human warehousing. And our property, practically all that we own in this world, has been reduced to "s___." Word association is a serious thing. Can you imagine having to hear these terms over and over for years and decades? I try to resist it but sometimes, when I am dealing with other things, it is so prevalent that it seeps in. And it matters, it builds up. It matters when you are young, it matters when you are old, and it especially matters when you are in prison. Do you see the cycle? The words you hear growing up are associated with the value of not just property, "s___," but with life—yours and others'. And you grow up always having that "value" associated with life. Then in prison that same sentiment is spoken and we are treated like that. Nothing changes, the TDCJ says that their mission is to integrate offenders back into society. But over years the above is what we are indoctrinated with. That is TDCJ's true mission. Then when we get out of prison with these "values," maybe in a neighborhood near you, and you wonder why people commit another crime.

Dr. Phil talks about the core belief that we hold about our self, and he says that you are never to reward negative behavior. The TDCJ reinforces our low self-esteem (core belief that we are bad, and unworthy) and they reward negative behavior all the time.

Just the everyday terms: cell, prisoner, inmate, offender, dayroom, rack time, chowtime, one row, Two row, shower time, work time, boss man, warden, major, CO; they all blur into a constant mantra that takes away the fact that we are people. We hear these voices in our sleep, as time just keeps slipping us into the monotonous collective that we are being assimilated into.

"NOW YOU ARE BUD"

"Are you a real cowboy?"
"Depends… on what you think a real cowboy is."
-Sissy and Bud, *Urban Cowboy*

I was eleven years old the first time I met my biological father. I had memories of him from when I was three, but now I could talk in whole sentences. In my mind I never thought badly of him; he was my father. He had to be better than the one my mother was married to (my first step-dad). I ignored the glaring fact that if he was so good, then where had he been for the last eleven years? I didn't see that because my mom had always said that she left him, and I guess that I held onto that as proof that it wasn't his decision to be absent.

My grandparents had lived in the same house since my mother was born, and they'd kept the same number. That is how my father got in touch; he called my grandparents and they called my mom and asked if I wanted to meet my father. I got very excited and told her yes.

He called my mom and made plans to pick me up at noon on the coming Saturday. By 11 a.m. I was on the trunk of our car in the driveway waiting for him. Noon came and went—no sign of him. I kept on waiting.

My mom would keep coming out to check on me, and asked if I wanted to come in. I said no. She told me, "This is what he does." But I didn't want to believe that. I felt that if I stayed out there, he would show up, as if my will could empower it. She came out every fifteen minutes but I didn't want to leave from that spot. I lay back against the rear window and held my vigil.

At 1:30 p.m., my resolve broke. Why did men and fathers always reject me?

The next time my mom came out she said, "Come inside with me, we can watch *Urban Cowboy*." I went in with her. *Urban Cowboy* was my favorite movie and we had recorded it off of Cable. We'd all loved John Travolta since *Grease* and *Welcome Back Kotter*. But movies were a two-hour distraction from reality and misery.

The den was our living room, and we had a TV, VCR, and a cable box. Cable in the '80s was called "Preview." Our den had a sliding glass door to the backyard. There was a gaudy orange colored curtain over it to block out the sun. But we could see the shadow of anyone who was out there.

I sat on the sofa and my mom sat by me with her arm around me as we watched the movie. About forty-five minutes into the movie, we saw a shadow through the curtains. The shadow had on a cowboy hat, and I looked from the movie, where John Travolta had on a cowboy hat, back to the shadow, and for one moment I had a strong feeling that John Travolta was out there. The shadow knocked and my mom got up, parted the curtain to see who it was and she looked at me and said, "It's your dad."

I got up and ran to her as she pulled the curtain back and opened up the glass door. "I knocked on your front door and pushed the doorbell but no one answered," he said.

My mom explained that the doorbell didn't work, and that we couldn't hear the knock from the den. He had dark hair that came down to his shoulders from under the hat, he had the same Kirk Douglas chin that I had, and his skin was smooth. He looked to me and said, "Are you ready to go?"

"Yes," I said looking at my mom.

"Why are you late?" She asked him. I didn't care. He was here now.

"I had trouble finding a ride, and I finally got one. We are going to White Rock Lake," he told her. We went through the back yard and to the front and got in the car that had brought him. I knew right away that the guy was drunk. Then my dad started talking to me and I forgot all about the driver. I told my dad that we were watching *Urban Cowboy* and how I thought he was Bud when he came up to the door.

He took off his hat and put it on me and said, "Now you are Bud." I was elated. This is what I'd always wanted, a father who loved me and told me things like "You are Bud." That's all boys need in life, a father to tell them that they can be somebody.

We pulled up to White Rock Lake in the lot by the spillway. My father and I got out and the guy who drove said he would wait right there. We walked to the edge of the lake and he told me the story of the "Lady of the Lake." He said that on the "Lady's" wedding night that her husband cut off her head and threw it in the lake. He said, "At night you can see her ghost walking in the lake."

"Really?" I asked, looking up at him in wonder.

"It's true. Now no one is allowed to go swimming in the lake."

We walked over to an area where there were some picnic tables and there were people cooking out on a grill and they had a cooler of beer. A lady noticed me and asked my father, "Is this your son? Ya'll look so much alike." I was so proud. My dad then struck up a conversation, and soon we were invited to eat with them and they gave my dad a beer. The lady had a horse and she let me pet it. Back at the table she doted on me as my dad talked with the others as if he had always known them. I admired his ability to be able to do that. I wished I could do it.

My dad asked me, "Do you want a beer?" (Now he was offering me their stuff?)

I made an 'ooh gross' face and said "No." The lady commented that I was only eleven. But my dad said, "Here, taste it," handing me his beer. At least it was not the same brand that my step-dad drank. I wanted to please my dad so I took a drink. It was bitter, and I didn't know how people could drink this stuff. I smiled at my dad and he told me to drink it and he got him another one.

While we were eating, we heard a car start up and we looked and it was the guy who brought us. He was leaving, and I asked my dad how he would get home. He said that he would come back.

I believed him. Why would he lie? The lady let me ride her horse sitting behind her. And then they left, she said that they lived close by. She hugged me and told me to hug the horse, and I reached up and hugged his neck. My dad and I walked to another parking area and we found the guy who'd brought us there. He was passed out in the front seat. My dad took me out to the spillway and I asked him if I could come live with him. He said that he didn't have his own home that he was living with an army buddy. I wanted to tell him how bad my step-dad was but I held back right then.

When we got back to the parking lot the guy was gone again. But my dad talked some guy into giving us a ride home. Since my grandmother's house was closest, he had him drop me off there. He hugged me and said he loved me and he would see me soon. I didn't see him again until I was fourteen.

RAMSEY 2 UNIT

1992-1996

"When this baby hits 88, you're going to see some serious stuff."
-Doc from *Back to the Future*

"I want your sex." by George Michael

In June 1992, I found myself on the chain bus leaving Beto One and going to Ramsey 2. I stayed the night at the Walls unit and the next morning I was on the bus. As the bus pulled up to the back of the unit I saw an old concrete building, and attached to it as an afterthought, a red brick one. There was an old door in the front of that building that had been paved over with concrete and was not used anymore. Above that concrete arch the year 1936 was etched into it. I said to myself that this is an old unit, and that the red brick part must have been added later.

There was a gun tower by the back gate, and the officers sent up their guns and the bus pulled into the sallyport of the back gate. Everyone who was assigned to Ramsey 2 got off as the bus driver called our names. After the bus left an officer took us through a gate that led to a recreation yard. In the red brick there was a door that led into the building. The door opened to a hallway that was similar to the Ferguson unit, just not as long. Like a stunted telephone pole. We walked all the way to the end of the hallway where there was a caged area that had a couple of benches affixed to the wall and which acted as a holdover for us to sit in and wait for UCC. There was a different feel to this unit. Inmates were walking here and there, all on the right side of the yellow line. They must have been going to work, a medical appointment, or school. There were a lot of officers in the hallway also. Next to the turnout door there was a big wooden desk. Not your typical teacher's desk. This one sat on a raised platform, and was made of wood. The front of the desk stood at least six feet high and had a flat surface on top for a phone and paperwork. There was a Texas state seal on the front of it that had the words, "Department of Corrections," curving around the top of the seal and, "State of Texas," curving along the bottom. It looked like an inmate had made it in the craft shop—very good work.

Normally a CO and a Sergeant were assigned to work this desk, to control traffic, open doors to the departments you might need access to, and to do an occasional pat search. I could see inmates casually talking to the CO and the sergeant at the desk. Most of the officers and rank that I'd seen so far were black. There was not the tension that I'd felt on the other unit. I sensed no anger or fear. At Beto One, especially in general population, it is a rough unit and the tension was something you could feel. And on the safekeeping wing we could always smell the gas that was constantly being sprayed over there.

This was weird. Was I still in prison? There were inmates and bosses laughing together. Why weren't they angry? Why weren't they yelling? On Beto I'd been so focused on my survival that I hadn't gotten a chance to observe the nuances of the prison and the COs. It had just seemed that they were all against me.

A lady in free-world clothes came out of the Classification office and called our names as a sort of roll call to see if everyone was there. She asked the desk boss to unlock the holdover and we were led into the small office. There was a small lobby with a couple of benches, and whoever didn't get a seat just stood up or sat on the floor. Three doors around the lobby were offices and there was also a bathroom.

In the early 90s, when the TDC still had money because they grew their own food and made their own clothes, they had plenty of staff and administration. Every inmate had a classification counselor who would bring us before the UCC and help us get jobs or into school, or promotions in our good time, earning status. We would be called into their office once every quarter to check on us. But as always happens when Texas needs to do budget cuts, they hit the prisons first and usually they take away the things that help us or that are a privilege.

The Chief of Classification introduced herself and told us the names of our counselors: "If your last name begins with letters from A-G, your counsel is Mr. Davis. H-N Mr. Woods and O-Z Ms. Saenz. Just write an I-60 if you need anything," she told us.

As you can imagine, if you were running a prison that held over a hundred and forty thousand people, and all these people needed something, there had to be paperwork in order to process the requests. And every paper or form had its own number to identify it. An I-60 is the number of the form labeled "Inmate's request to official." It is the most-requested form because with it we ask for any and every thing, and we call it an I-60 for short.

I had not heard an official so freely say, "Just write an I-60," before or since. Usually no one wanted us to write for anything because it meant work for them. But there was something strange going on here. Where was Alice, because I think I fell down that hole with her.

The chief continued to tell us other things: "I have to tell you the following: It is against TDC policy and rules for you to have sex with each other, but we also know that it happens. I ask you to be aware that this unit has 85% of the population that are HIV positive. So be careful out there."

"Alright, when the warden gets here, we will start UCC. We will call you in one at a time."

And with that she went into her office and a nurse came in to talk to us. "Does anyone have any emergency illness that needs attention right now?"

No one spoke up. "Who is the President of the United States?"

We all said, "Bush."

"Does anyone want to inflict harm on themselves?" Everyone looked around but no one said anything, and she asked one more question. "Without looking at the clock, what time do you think it is right now?"

These questions are designed to find the crazy or just ill. I guess that if you do not know what time is you are not grounded in reality. I don't know. Hey TDC, here's a hint, we do not want to live in reality, prison sucks! We want to (*Place E-word here*). [I still can't say that word out loud, yet, it's just like saying the B-word on a plane. It's taboo, but I'll get over it.]

She handed us a medical orientation packet, and instructed us to write a sick call if we needed medical attention. The form to get medical attention was always called just a 'sick call.' Then the front door opened and three black men walked in, one had on what we call free world clothes (no uniform) the other two had on TDC uniforms, but on their lapels, one had the insignia of a captain and on the other was that of a major. Someone said that the first guy was a warden, and that all the top rank was black. I thought to myself, "This will be a laid-back unit." Because in my experience black people do not get all out of whack when things go wrong. They just deal with it, I've never seen a black person panic, it's like they have an innate ability to handle adversity.

They began calling people into UCC, and then I heard my name. There was a genial mood in the room. "Jones, initial here and have a seat."

"TDC policy states that you have to go to the field squad for ninety days, but after that you can put in an I-60 to request a job and we will give you one then." The warden said. My file was open before him but he was not reading it nor was he passing it around. "We got a good unit here. I think that you'll like it. Let me know if you have any problems. Do you have any questions?" he asked me.

I was in shock. There was no shaming me for my offense, no wishing bad things to me. I wanted to ask him when I would wake up, but I only asked about college classes.

"Yes, we have that here, but you will need to write an I-60 to the Education counselor."

"Yes, sir," I said.

"Alright, we are through. We will try to get y'all moved after the count.

Go back out there and wait."

Back in the lobby I was asked by the others what job I'd been given. "Fields," I told them.

"That's easy on this unit," a guy said.

*   *   *

The Sex Offender Treatment Program, or SOTP, as it is familiarly called by everyone on the unit: I do not know the history or how the program came to be in the TDC, but I have come to believe that this program is one of the best things that the TDC has ever done. It is a cognitive-behavioral therapy which is a fancy term that means that your thoughts cause your behavior, and if you change your thoughts, beliefs, and so on, then your behavior will change. Also, the program confronts irrational thoughts and beliefs, and this is something that has never happened to a sex offender, who usually keeps their thought life a secret.

In the early '90s the program was still in its beginning stage, so it was only being tried out on a couple of units. It was a voluntary program which made it more of a serious program. Later, it would be made into a carrot and stick program, meaning that parole will tell you, "If you take this eighteen-month program we will give you parole," which hurts the integrity of the program.

When I was still at Beto unit I had seen parole. That was within months of getting there. But the parole guidelines were different back then. I spoke with a voting member after he told me that he did not think that I was ready to get out and he gave me a two-year set off.

Although I believe that SOTP being voluntary made it better program, I think that for me I did want to stop being who I was. I knew that it was wrong on an intellectual level. And I saw this program as a way to help me, but looking back on my twenty-year-old self, I see that I was lost in a cycle of thought and belief patterns that overruled my intellect. Have you ever met a person who seemed sincere about changing, but then they went and did the same thing? It was an inner struggle of feeling versus logic. And my feelings were winning every time.

In county jail and at the beginning of my prison sentence I had 'turned back' to God. I wanted comfort from the big bad feeling of being taken out of my comfort zone. I believe that if I showed that I could 'conform' to His rules then He would get me out of prison. I clearly didn't know God at all. But our human errors do not deter a big God who hears the cries of our heart. Deep down I did not want to hurt anyone, and I think that He heard that, even when I did not know how to tell Him. In 1992 while still on Beto unit I had a dream, and this dream had to be from God because to this day I still remember it so clearly and vividly.

I dreamed:

I saw my mother and some children running. They were in a forest and I saw a tornado behind them and they were scared. The tornado tore up the forest and pursued them. Then I came out of the tornado and I ran to catch up with my mother and those children. We ran and then came to a clearing where there was a fence and a house. We all ran into the house and we were safe from that tornado.

After that dream I prayed that God would help me interpret or understand it. I believed that he was telling me that my life was such a destructive force that it was like a tornado. I had hurt my mother and also children in the fashion of what a tornado does. But God never leaves it at that. He, through the dream, showed that He would deliver me from being destructive like a tornado, and would bring me to a safe place.

* ·*   *

While we waited in the cage the laundry boss came by to issue us linen, a mattress, and a pillow, and asked our clothing size. When count had cleared the move boss handed us our move tickets and told us to go to our assigned wing.

They had assigned me to C-15 wing, 104 cell. There was not a bunk assignment, we went to the open bunk in that cell, which was always the top bunk. We could move to the bottom only when our cellie left, or medical said that we needed it for medical reasons. When I was a kid, I remember fighting with my little brother for the top bunk, but in prison it is the bottom bunk that is highly coveted.

My cellie was an older replica of the character "Piggy" on Lord of the Flies. Though not flamboyant, he was very gay.

"Are you here for the Trailer?" was his first question to me.

"What is a trailer?"

"Oh, I mean SOTP. They have it in a trailer on the grounds of the prison, so everyone just calls it the Trailer. They give us a blue folder to put our paperwork in and everyone knows that you are a sex offender," he said.

"Does anyone try to do something to you, since they know?" I ask.

He gave me a crazy look. "On this unit? Are you kidding? The only fights on this unit are between the drag queens. They should call them drama queens," he said.

"Wow. I just came from Beto and there is always a fight over there. Not on S/K mind you, but it is a bad unit."

He asked again.

"Yeah," I told him. "What's it like?"

"They use Cognitive-Behavioral Therapy. They want us to use words like rape or force when describing our offenses, not 'touch' or 'sex' or 'they let me.' This is to drive into our brains that our offenses were *not* consensual. We do worksheets about our offenses then present them in group, and the guys in the group and the therapist confront the irrational beliefs behind your thinking. We learn the thirty-six thinking errors. It is pretty intense. A friend and I are trying to get the legislature to allow us to get castrated. So, what did you do?"

I told him and then asked when he thought that I would start group.

"You go for your initial interview and evaluation in a couple of days. They put you in the fields?" he asked.

"Yeah, what do they do in the fields?" I asked.

"I am unassigned so I could not tell you. But there are guys cutting the tendon in their pinky finger so they don't have to go," he told me.

"Well, I am not doing that. How else can I get out of the fields?"

"What about school? If you go to school, you can miss half a day in the fields," he said.

"I want to take college classes; I already have my GED."

"College is at night. But put in an I-60 to take college prep classes, that's during the day," he said.

The dayroom was smaller than the one on Beto. There were three rows of benches facing the wall, where a TV on a stand was fixed to the wall. There were three tables behind these benches. Another three benches were on either side of the center three.

It was cramped and crowded and loud as I entered the dayroom. It was probably because the dayroom was smaller that the flamboyant queens really stood out and were the majority. But the difference between here and Beto was that I do not feel that immediate sense of rejection. When a new person comes to a unit everyone wants to find out about them, and meet them. It breaks up the monotony of the norm of prison life. But once they find out what you are all about, they label you and put you in a box (just like out in the world).

I was eager to be accepted, especially after how I'd been treated on Beto. A lot of people came up to me to introduce themselves. Everyone seemed real nice. I heard my cellie call me, and I looked around and he was over by the dayroom bars talking to another guy on the other side. He had a push broom in his hands which made him a janitor.

"This is J. Him and a few others have been in SOTP the longest. D. lives over there," pointing to the wing across the hall. "We are all real good friends."

"Nice to meet you." I said to J.

"Have you met H?" he asked, pointing to a tall guy sitting on a bench on the right side of the dayroom.

"No, not yet." I replied.

He looked at my cellie, L., and said, "Go introduce him to H."

That's how I met H. I had not met D. yet, but my cellie, L., H., D. and me, over the next few years would become best friends. But J. was not a part of the bond that the four of us had made.

The four of us all had male victims. Three of us identified as gay, but D. was different. He sought out young-looking men for his sexual gratification, but always as a top or pitcher, never as a bottom. We'd always wanted love and acceptance and, as we learned the program, we would half-joking half-seriously point out each other's behavior and confront each other about it.

H. and I claimed to be Christians. We grew really close because we were in the same groups and liked the same things. We went to church together and didn't have any secrets from each other.

I finally met D. and I didn't like him at first. He was very condescending and was a know-it-all. He spent a lot of time in the craft shop. This is a privilege for inmates where they could work on their craft, i.e. leather, art, wood, or metalwork, and sell it at visitation or to the officers. D. did metalwork.

L. and D. were campaigning hard to get the state to castrate them. I personally thought that it was crazy. I believed the problem was in the mind and not the testicles. All three of us had a lot to learn though, going forward.

My first interview came and I found myself in the lobby of the Trailer with H. and others, waiting our turn to talk to a therapist. The other guys who came out there with us went into other rooms for their group therapy. In the lobby there were chairs around the room. And in one wall a window had been cut out, but the glass was opaque and you could not see through it.

The window opened and a secretary handed me a blue folder and told me to fill out the form and that a therapist would be with me shortly. A little later a lady called my name and I was led to her office. I remember that I wanted to impress upon her that I was a really good person and that I knew that I did something wrong but I was more than ready to correct that.

My cellie had already laced me up on the terminology used and what the therapist liked to see in us, so when she asked her questions, I already knew how to answer. I admitted my crimes to her and took responsibility. When she began to explain to me about the terminology that they used in group, I told her that someone had explained it to me and that I agreed with it because, "I wasn't 'touching' them I forced my hand on them."

I told her this in my first interview.

I would later realize that I was very 'superoptimistic.' Superoptimism is one of the thirty-six thinking errors that are taught to us in SOTP. In using this thinking error, I truly believed that I had it all together, that I could get things to go my way, and I could persuade others to go along with me.

I really believed that I could convince this program of licensed therapists that I had changed and I was a normal person. I would come to learn that they saw through me from the beginning. Words and actions always give it away. But eventually, everything that I did learn so I could be able to spit back at them to show 'change,' would become a lifeline to me when I would most need it. When I would have my turning point, it would all be sitting there waiting to be internalized.

I left her office that day feeling confident that I had convinced her of my sincere wish to change, and that I was practically there. She gave me some work to do in preparation for group. I would like for you to understand that in my situation, again this was not a diabolical intent to manipulate. There are many layers of denial, and self defense mechanisms that were all in use here. I believed my own lies, I had to in order to live with myself, so I believed the BS that I was telling myself.

I constantly had to make others think that I was a good and decent person. It was like I was on some inner program to do so. I had to make myself think that I was conforming on the outside; I was always telling my conscience that it was not as bad as it was making it out to be. It seemed that I was always fighting something, fighting feeling bad all the time, and I did not know where it was coming from. I was empty and void of 'good' things on the inside, but I did not know it because I was always telling myself that I was okay.

I did not know all that was going on on a deep level, but I would learn. But all this raises the question, "Can a sex offender really change?" I sure hope so, because I think my life depends on it. Everything depends on it.

It was refreshing to be on Ramsey 2. Just being around others that had sex offenses and the fact that everyone else knew about us abated the ostracization and rejection. We were in the majority and it was liberating to not have to worry about being attacked, verbally or otherwise. I found out that three out of every five inmates on Ramsey 2 had sex offenses, and had chosen not to go to SOTP.

The thing that I did not like was safekeeping. The small dayrooms and men pretending to be women, dramatically, making scenes to be seen, made living there uncomfortable. Someone told me that I could write an I-60 and request to be taken off of safekeeping status. They didn't have to tell me twice.

I spent six months on safekeeping, and that was six months too long. In January of 1993, the UCC approved my removal from S/K status, and I was moved to the other side of the unit, past the stairs and chow hall. And into freedom. It was a different world beyond the chow hall. All the general population wings were dormitory-like settings. There were ten dorms; some had thirty cubicles, others had sixty. The best part of living in a dorm was that there were not any cells. The cubicles were made out of a metal that partitioned off each individual bunk. The metal came up to my sternum and enclosed around the bunk with an opening to enter in. Each bunk had a locker underneath and a table affixed to the head of the bed. There was a small aisle to walk alongside your bunk. When you lay down no one could see you unless they walked by.

I was moved to 3 dorm, a thirty-man dorm. It was quiet. There were two TVs, one at the front and one in the back. And in between there were cubicles—a row on both outer walls and a row going down the middle. Behind the back TV there was a bathroom area. Four porcelain sinks that actually ran hot water. There was a four-foot cinderblock wall that blocked three toilets and a urinal for privacy. Having been in locked cells since county jail, sometimes with another person, this was true freedom. Just the ability to be able to go to your bunk or to the TV whenever you wanted, and not to have to wait on an in and out, was very liberating. Anyway, it did not feel like prison living in the dorms; I hope that the officials don't find out about this, or they might take it away.

$$* \quad * \quad *$$

At this point of my incarceration, I do not know whether or not it was just this unit or men being locked up, that made them lower their standards and choose to have sex with a man. But here on Ramsey 2 there were non-gay and non-sex-offender, straight men who would seek out a gay person for sexual relations. In *Orange is the New Black*, Piper called it "Gay for the stay," we just said "he messes around." Or if they were in denial and we wanted to tease them about it we would parody the old commercials, "I'm not really homosexual, I just play one in the penitentiary." Or we would say to them, "Oh, you're not gay but your boyfriend is."

Most movies portray that all inmates are determined to rape all weaker men. That everyone in here is just champing at the bit to have sex. I just have not found that to be the case. Most people just use their imagination and their hand. I am not saying that rape does not happen, it does, but it's not as bad as the movies make it out to be. Guys that want to have sex while incarcerated seek out those that are willing. Others might persuade someone who is not gay into doing it. As in the world out there, there are mitigating circumstances in here, and most rapes occur in medium and close custody. And the unit has a lot to do with it; there are very strict units and there are lax units, and there are corrupt units. All this will either enable or inhibit a predator.

Ramsey 2 wasn't strict or corrupt, it was lax. It's like everyone came to an unspoken agreement to just do their time and be comfortable. You did not have to fight on this unit to be accepted, but you did have to have a basketball game. In my assessment the ratio between gay/straight was 50/50, but if you counted the non-gay gays then it went up to 75/25.

I was entering a free, relaxed environment with a sexually charged atmosphere, in my third year of incarceration. I was in a program that was geared to help me gain control over my deviant sexual lifestyle. And in fact, it was a rule that we did not engage in any sexual activity while in the program. I even signed a paper agreeing that I would abstain. This was an agreement that I would fail to keep.

I was not yet twenty-two when I moved to the dorms in GP. A lot of older guys started talking to me to "help" me or to teach me the ropes. I was still too green to know that they had ulterior motives. But I was strong enough to say no to the things that I was not interested in doing. I was big on attraction, and I couldn't have sex with someone unless I was attracted to them.

I met an older, effeminate homosexual man, who gave me a lot of pointers that helped me along the way. He did not have any ulterior motives; he just helped me because I was young. All through my incarceration I did meet that type of people, who would help without wanting anything back. And in time I was able to tell when somebody was true or wanting something back. They would give you crumbs and want a whole loaf back. Insight came quick when it might have cost me something that I wasn't willing to do.

I was on Ramsey 2 from 1992 to the end of 1995, with the exception of the eight-month period on Ferguson unit. I believe that these were the pivotal years in my incarceration that crushed me in the crucible that is prison, and set up the foundation for my turning point in 1996.

Some people in prison find themselves a "prison daddy" that will take care of them in return for sexual favors. Being on Ramsey 2 saved me from that. But on the opposite side of that I became very promiscuous. And then something else happened; prison itself became my "daddy." And it wasn't your traditional, *Leave it to Beaver* type of dad. No, nothing so tidy. But I can say that everything that I needed to know I learned in prison. Prison has its own underlying way of thinking. If "this" happens it means "that." This way of thinking was already set in motion, hard to resist and a lot of it was needed for survival.

As I began to talk to and hang out with people, I was able to pick up on it. There were things that you did not do or say, or it could be perceived as disrespect. There were things that were accepted to say, and when to say them. But on a friendly unit like Ramsey 2, and even in the worst of units, an openly gay person will always be treated as a second-class person. That is the nice term; the "men" considered us as hoes. Even a man that messed around.

The front TV was considered the sports TV and I had saved myself a seat to watch a game. There weren't many seats and when I got up some "man" moved my stuff and said that he was sitting there. I had started to feel confident in this new environment, but the cowardice in me that had been long tempered from my step-dad, rose up in me and I was very fearful, and quick to believe the worst about myself. I felt a righteous anger and the sting of rejection, but deep down this is what I believed that I deserved, and I just walked away.

I didn't grow up watching sports or learning them. Who was going to teach me? During those family get-togethers at my grandparents, my uncles and their kids would play street football and basketball games. They would need my brother and I to complete a team. They assumed that we knew how to play, then they just assumed that we were bad at it. But for a lack of anything else we had to get out there and make a fool of ourselves.

I would usually watch the movie TV while everyone else was watching sports. That day when that guy took my seat, I was going to try to watch a basketball game, just to try to fit in, but that didn't work out. In January 1993 the sports fans put the Superbowl on both TVs—, it was the Cowboys' first Superbowl since the 70s. I just lay down in my bunk to read a book, only rising to watch MJ at halftime.

I'd signed up for the college prep class and went to the three-hour class from noon till 3 p.m. I had to go to the fields in the morning, and when we came in for lunch at 11 a.m., I did not go back out during the second half. Like everyone else I dreaded this. The field squad at this time did hard labor and provided the food that we ate. I remember that my first job was that we had to pick broccoli. A trustee handed us burlap bags that were longer than I was tall. We each had our own row and we were told to fill up our bags. I looked at this guy in the row next to me and chuckled, "He's joking, right?"

He looked at me and laughed. "Yeah, right," he said, as he ate the head off a broccoli sprout.

I got on my knees and began to pick the sprouts and throw them in my bag. When I thought no one was looking I lifted a sprout to my nose and sniffed it then took a bite. It wasn't so bad.

In school the first thing that we were given was a test similar to the GED test to determine what area we needed to be "prepped" in. This test was called the Education Assessment test or E.A. test for short. To me the test was very easy but I failed it on purpose, because the reason I got into this class was to get out of the fields.

By the time the next football season—the 1993 season—came around I was in one of the sixty-man dorms. I met a guy who was called "DeathRow". He had this name because he used to be on death row, but his sentence had been commuted to life. He had been locked up for longer than I had been alive (twenty-two years). DeathRow was a convict in the truest form of the word. I have never seen someone generate respect the way that he did, most of it deriving just from having been on death row.

As you can imagine, a man in his position did mess around, but he wanted a relationship. Not just sex. His interest in me, while I liked the attention—I just wasn't attracted to him. I told him this up front, because I had enough sense to not play with people's emotions in here. It's better to be a little disappointed now, then to raise your expectations and be hurt worse later on.

We remained friends. People in here really need that emotional connection; others sexualize it as a substitute. Some people were able to keep it separate, and DeathRow was one of those guys. I was nowhere near trying to be tied down in a relationship. We spent time together and he knew not to expect sex, or anything long term. But he got some sort of emotional connection and he taught me things.

I didn't know that the things that I was learning were working on the inside and that that would help me later. I was too self-absorbed to notice it then, but in retrospect this is what happened.

DeathRow was a big sports fan, and a Cowboy fan. I was sitting on the bench with him one Sunday and a guy came up to him and handed him a paper and asked him if he wanted to get on the quarter board. DeathRow bought a couple of squares and asked if I wanted to get on it also. I said that I don't know anything about it. He told me to write my name in two different squares, and I did so. It cost two ramen noodle soups per square (we purchased the soups off of the commissary for 25¢ each and that was their street value).

The guy used some dominoes to pull the numbers and we paid him the soups and he gave us our numbers that corresponded to the squares that we bought. DeathRow told me that it was a game of chance and that it paid either $1.25 or $1.50 each quarter, and if your numbers matched the score at the end of the quarter then you won. This board was on the Dallas/Arizona game.

When the game began something else began to transpire inside me. We sat there and watched the game and these two teams lined up facing each other, one trying to get the ball down the field and the other team trying to stop them. This generated in me a thrill of excitement that I didn't know existed, at least not coming from sports. Then the ref. would throw a yellow flag before the start and I would ask what happened, and DeathRow would patiently explain, "False start. If the offense moves before the snap, they are penalized five yards."

I forgot about the numbers as I was learning something new. I hadn't known that football could be this exciting. Every Sunday the sports TV was overcrowded with guys watching football. I was always assured a seat because of DeathRow. I began to feel like a regular guy. It was like this was something that I'd been missing growing up. This was why I couldn't relate to other guys. Because I didn't have the inner knowledge of football. This was the memo that I hadn't gotten. Now, I knew football, I needed to tell Bo Jackson that *I* knew football. It was very exciting, to be able to sit with a group of men and be accepted and just know guy stuff like football. And someone had taken the time to explain it to me, without taking something from me. I was receiving the things that I hadn't gotten from a "father" growing up. What kind of place is prison that this could happen?

I am not claiming to have changed overnight. This was just a beginning. It was giving me normal things to be interested in. Just like in the *Karate Kid*, when Mr. Miagi-San taught Daniel to wax on and wax off, he didn't know that that was a skill for fighting, but when it came time to fight, Mr. Miagi told him to wax on and wax off and he was able to utilize that skill. That is what learning football was like for me. It will become clear later on when all this junk is gone, and the good stuff remains. God does work in mysterious ways. It's the little things that add up to a new thing. It's a process when you didn't even know you are a part of the mix. As much as I wanted to, I couldn't bypass the process. But I did try.

*   *   *

In group therapy there were between eight and ten guys in the group with two therapists. One of the therapists was my primary therapist and the other was a second therapist. At the start of group somebody would nominate a peer leader. The peer leader's job would be to coordinate the group, and ask questions about the paperwork that was being presented. Being a peer leader taught skills that most sex offenders lacked: being assertive, leading in an appropriate way, talking to others appropriately.

In the early stages of SOTP everyone would say a 'layout.' A layout is a very short synopsis of our offenses, using the correct terminology, the word rape, force, and so on. This got us used to using those terms to describe our offenses. If someone used the terms "I only touched," or said, "we had sex," then we knew that this was their true belief behind their offenses. And the peer leader would confront this belief, and the therapists would weigh in also. But the layouts started to take up too much group time and they limited them to two or three a group.

Then a person would be chosen to present their paperwork. The peer leader would ask questions, but the rest of us in group would also, because we were in the same position as the presenter and we could spot lies quicker. Some guys did not ask questions, or confront people because they did not want anyone to confront them. But once I picked up on the "your language conveys your beliefs," theory, I would use it to confront others. I was trying to impress the therapist, but that insight did go a long way to help me identify my true beliefs. And as much as I thought that I was impressing the therapist that way, I had a whole bunch of other body language, and way of speaking that showed the therapist that I was only intellectualizing, and not internalizing. I got tired of being confronted about not internalizing, because I believed my own lies, that I was improving by just changing certain terminology.

Besides group we also had education classes, where we learned the Thirty-Six Thinking Errors which were identified by two criminal psychologists named Yochelson and Samenow, after they interviewed hundreds of the worst criminals. We were also taught the "Criminal Offense Cycle." This is a module that breaks down the identification of our thoughts and the beliefs behind our behavior. The human brain is just like a computer's operating system, and it absorbs the information that we feed it all our lives, and if certain thoughts are repeated our brain will create shortcuts to get there faster when we need to find that info. It's kind of like an APP. But we develop a pattern of thought that becomes our belief, and we teach our brain that when certain things happen, such as a negative emotion, then we have to do a certain thing, such as fantasize about somebody, in order to get rid of the negative emotion. And it's just like GIGO: garbage in, garbage out. I had conditioned my own brain to think in this way automatically, on a subconscious level. It's because some event or thought just happened, and you have conditioned your brain to interpret that event or thought in a certain way, and you process this without being aware of your thoughts about it.

The Criminal Offense Cycle broke down these steps and then I was able to see that I really did have a lot of beliefs about a lot of things that happen every day, and since our thoughts cause feelings, I was feeling bad or negatively all the time, and I would associate it with the event that someone else had caused. These thoughts or beliefs were irrational, based off of lies and therefore the things that I was feeling were not true. They were real feelings, but they were not true feelings. This was the cycle of my life, a lot of lies—how was I to break free?

I have a friend who found a small field mouse, and this mouse was as long as his middle finger. My friend cleaned out a peanut butter jar and this mouse, which he named Buddy, lived in this jar. He had poked breathing holes in the plastic, and Buddy ate better than the homeless. He laid that jar on its side and Buddy would start running just like in a hamster wheel. And the jar rolled all over the dayroom. He went everywhere in the dayroom, but he was still stuck in that jar. I wonder if Buddy thought that he was free but in reality he was still stuck in a constant cycle that made him think that he was getting somewhere but in reality, he hadn't ever left. That is what it's like to develop a destructive thinking cycle; when I start feeling bad or down, I spend all my energy trying to make myself feel better but I am still stuck in that same rut of thoughts, just spinning my wheels.

Later, the name of this module was changed to the Addictive Offense Cycle, because it wasn't just criminals who used it. I understood the cycle real good, because I love learning new things. They stimulate my brain. But at this time, I didn't internalize it; I did the same thing that I did with the new terms, I told myself that just learning it was helping me.

The educational classes also taught us the "Tactics Used to Obstruct Effective Therapy." There were nineteen tactics, which Yochelson and Samenow came up with. I am sure that I was not the only one getting tired of Yochelson and Samenow, because they seemed to have all the bases covered, and we couldn't get anything past the therapist.

It was very effective for me to be taught these things, because it pushed me further to try to think deeper to try to outsmart them, but there was nowhere else to go. This was a part of the crucible that crushed me. I was very fortunate to have this therapy at the beginning of my prison sentence. I was able to learn it, retain it, and then when I had my turning point, I was able to apply it and finally internalize it.

In the 1990s the Texas Prisons were better staffed than they are at the time that I am writing this. There were enough officers on one unit to staff another unit. One of the perks for us inmates was that outside recreation was run all day. Just as there was an in and out for the dayroom, there was an in and out for rec.

Ramsey 2 was a laid-back unit. To be able to play basketball was the determining factor if you were accepted or not (if you were a man). I was not considered a man because I was gay, so it didn't matter if I could play or not. But it was fun to be a spectator on the yard and watch the games. The warden allowed a live inmate band to play music for us on the rec. yard. Any inmate that could play an instrument or sing could be in the band. There was a country band, a rock and roll band, and a Spanish band. It was a thing to go to rec. and watch a game of B-ball and listen to the band. There was a volleyball net, a handball court and a weight set. Sometimes I would meet with friends and we would walk around the rec. yard, following the well-grooved path made by the thousands of inmates who had walked there before us.

There were times that there was not a full-court B-ball game going on and this gave the rest of us non-athletic people a chance to shoot hoops or play horse. There was a guy named Marvin. Marvin was shaped like a pear, bald and seemingly very effeminate. I assumed at first that he was gay, but I was wrong. He was just one of those guys who had soft characteristics. We always played horse, and sometimes 21. Marvin told me that he was teaching himself new things so that his time would go faster.

One day in the middle of our horse game two guys approached us and asked if we would play a two-on-two game with them. Marvin looked at me for my answer.

"I don't know how to play," I exclaimed.

"I don't know either, not that good, so this is the perfect time to learn," he said.

"Let's make this even, one of you will be on my team and the other will be on his." The guy who had asked us to play said, pointing first at himself then his friend.

"Alright. But don't expect me to play like Michael Jackson," I said.

"Jordan. It's Michael Jordan," Marvin replied.

"Proves my point," I responded. I was nervous because I knew that I could not play. And I made a fool of myself. I did not make one bucket. I fouled everyone, even my own teammate, and we lost. Marvin had already been teaching himself so he was better coordinated than I was.

Heading back to the dorms Marvin said, "How do you feel?"

"Besides embarrassed, I feel strangely exhilarated. Why is that?"

"Endorphins. When you exercise it releases endorphins in your brain."

he said.

"What is an endorphin?" I asked.

"Oh, well, that is a God-made chemical, it's a natural high," he said.

"We have a chemical that is already in us that is released by exercise?" I asked in wonder.

And just like that I wanted to play every day. Later, years from then, I would look back to this and make the connection that when we either pair the natural chemical that our brain releases with an activity, or an outside pleasure with certain thoughts or patterns of thought then it can become a cycle that we repeat over and over. And the only way to break the cycle is to pair that activity, thought or behavior with a negative connotation. (If those cycle patterns are harmful.)

Marvin and I began playing as much as we could. One-on-one, and he gave me helpful tips, and I got better. More coordinated, and when I concentrated, I had a good set shot. But this activity gave me something that I barely had growing up. Here was a guy spending time with me, teaching me, and he didn't want anything in return. My uncles only assumed that I knew how to play and that I was not a good player. They didn't teach me, and my cousins made fun of me. But here was a guy in prison doing what my family had never done. It was moments like these and the not-so-good moments that helped me grow up in prison. Looking back, I can see all these things as if they were choreographed. Things that happened, to prepare me, to shape me to be able to make the important changes when the time came. I can only attribute that to God. I believe that He is Sovereign and He knows those who belong to Him, and even in my sin He began to build the ladder that would help me climb out of the pit I was in.

The negative side of this pseudo-freedom that living in the dorms gave me was I became very promiscuous. As much as I could I practiced safe sex. But the fear of HIV was always prevalent, especially since there was a high rate of HIV-positive people on this unit. Every six months I would request an HIV test, through medical. When the results came in a nurse would call us down and show us the results. To this day I do not know how I made it through these thirty years without getting sick. But my test always read, "Negative by ELISA." I would always tell my friends, "I don't know Elisa, but I really like her." (I didn't know that ELISA was the name of the test.)

One time when I went in there for my results the nurse said, "You know that getting a test is not a preventive measure?"

"What does that mean?" I asked.

"It means that you can't go have sex and think that you're okay because you got tested every six months." She said looking at me with a mixture of hope of getting through to me and a feeling that it was a lost cause.

"Oh," I responded. I did think just that. "I practice safe sex." I told her. She just shook her head as I left her office.

There was a couple that stand out from that time. They were a black couple. The "man" of the relationship went by the name Sugar Hill. (I think that a whole book could be written about the nicknames that people go by in prison.) And the "girl" went by Bubbles. This was before LGBT, and all the "girls" were considered drag queens. Bubbles was a tall and slim, pretty queen. Everyone loved Sugar Hill. He was a very attractive man, well built. But the main reason that everyone loved him was because he "married" Bubbles knowing that "she" was in an advanced stage of AIDS. He did not have HIV. But he did not want Bubbles to be alone during the last days of his life.

The day that Bubbles passed away, you could feel the sadness over the whole unit. And I don't think that it was just because someone that we all knew and loved had died, but it was a stark reminder of what was in store for a lot of people on the unit. (85% of the population was HIV-positive.) It was a weird feeling, that sadness, that emanated from the whole unit. After about three days it went back to normal. Our defenses went back up from the reality of death; we got back to distracting ourselves. It was something that we were all good at doing.

*　　*　　*

Before I had gone to general population, D., L., H., and I had spent a lot of time on the rec. yard talking about everything. When H. and I were alone we studied the criminal thinking errors. We had made flashcards and one of us would read the definition and the other would see if he could identify the error. H. and I were in the same group and educational classes, since we started around the same time. D. and L. would help to prep us for the types of questions that we would be asked if we presented our paperwork.

I heard this from my therapist my first few years:

"Mr. Jones, when you talk about your offenses you seem to be bragging. Do you not realize that you terrorized a whole [name of the place I worked]?"

"Mr. Jones, you did not *touch* your victim, you forced your hand on them. Your vocabulary shows what you believe about your offending behavior. You are still in denial that you hurt anyone. Stop minimizing your offenses." (When I was in the hot seat presenting my paperwork and being confronted, I could not help but let slip my true beliefs by the words I used. And they saw this.)

"A person who remains in victim stance, Mr. Jones, will never change. If you continue to blame your offenses on your step-dad or on your childhood, you will never change."

"In life there are mountains and valleys. To think otherwise is irrational."

"You can come in here and tell us what we want to hear but you only hurt yourself. You volunteered and if you did not want to change then quit, so the people who do can get into the program."

These statements were made towards me by the therapist in group, in class or in individual therapy, for the first few years. I did think that I was better and unique. Both of those are thinking errors:

Thinking Error #11 - Uniqueness - "I considered myself to be special, one of a kind, and totally different from others, especially other unhealthy individuals. I want to be above the rest and stress my unique set of circumstances. I think that my circumstances and/or situation are different from others. This thinking enables me to ignore all outside input."

#30 - Pretentiousness - "I have tremendously overrated ideas about myself. I think that I am the best, I will be the best, but not that I will be my best. I may like to... appear superior to others, feeling that I do not need to put forth the same effort as others to be a success or get what I want. I set unrealistic goals but I am not willing to follow through with the real work involved in honest achievement."

[You can google all Thirty-Six Thinking Errors - Yochelson, Samenow]

I knew that my offenses were wrong. And that the things that I was being taught made good sense. I agreed with them. Even in the world I'd known that what I was doing was wrong and against the law; I had not wanted to get caught. I was not playing with my therapy, so much as the beliefs that I had developed over time overrode what the program was teaching. I know now that the point of the program was to override what I believed, to internalize it and not intellectualize it. I did not know how to do that, yet. As sick as it is, I had paired a powerful, pleasurable connotation, with the fantasies of children. And it was going to take something just as powerful in the negative sense to change that.

And we were taught that it's the powerful feeling that sex offenders seek. For me the powerful feeling was being in control, feeling loved and secure and accepted. But I had been telling myself that that was what it meant since I first used masturbation to soothe my scared and hurt feelings. At that young age I felt so unloved and insecure and out of control that the feeling of an orgasm, when it soothed me, I interpreted as being back in control and loved, and so forth.

When the therapist taught us the Criminal Offense Cycle module it gave me some insight into my offending behavior. But although I understood it very well, it has turned out to be even deeper, because it just keeps on giving, even today.

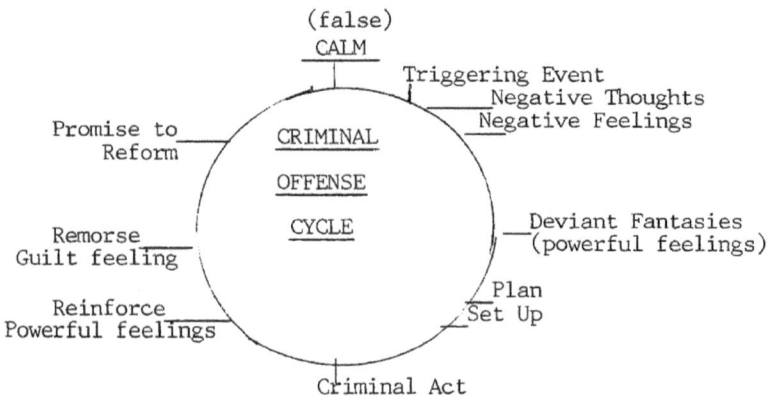

The above is the chart. I will explain each phase:

Calm – this is when everything in your life seems to be okay. It's not a true calm, it's more like at this time you believe your own lies that you are in control. It is a false calm. [* It is important to note that during this time we still have needs, which is normal in any human being, but in a criminal who does not know how to meet their needs in an appropriate way, we are always trying to meet these needs. They taught us that when a person's needs are unmet they become "issues". During the "calm" phase these issues are not clamoring to be resolved.]

Triggering Event - Or TE, is any neutral event that happens in life, but in your self-talk you tell yourself that it was a personal thing, and you perceive it to be against you. It could be another car that pulled out in front of you, a boss getting on to you, or an argument with someone. And it could be something personal, but we allow the event to trigger those issues.

Negative Thoughts - Everything starts in your thoughts—or your self-talk. You begin to think about the event in a negative way, and then you turn it to yourself: "This event, person or situation is putting *me* down. I must not be a good person, no one likes me." (This activates your core belief about yourself.)

*Cognitive Behavioral Therapy teaches that: "Your thoughts cause your feelings and you act off of your feelings."

Negative Feelings - Those negative thoughts caused negative feelings, and reinforces how we already deep down felt/thought about our self. (As we become more familiar with each step, it became easier to recognize it when it was happening and to stop it by changing our self-talk)

*Nobody wants to feel those negative feelings, so we continue in the cycle and begin to fantasize.

Deviant Sexual Fantasies - When a person fantasizes, he/she imagines the subject of the fantasy doing good and pleasurable things to you. These thoughts or fantasies make you feel better; they raise you from that negative state to a seemingly feel-good state. For a sex offender this is the most important phase of the cycle, important as in pivotal. When you fantasize about someone sexually you are fantasizing about this person meeting your needs, wanting you, telling you the things that you want to hear. These thoughts cause powerful feelings and a majority of the time they are masturbatory fantasies, and when you pair the pleasure of an orgasm to the deviant fantasy of a child, it makes a very powerful connection. And now there is the sick association of normal things like the needs of love, acceptance, security and being in control with the sexual assault of a child. And it is very dangerous, that after you got this powerful feeling from such fantasies, then it makes you think or believe that it will actually meet that need if you do the *act*.

Plan - Once again in your mind you think of how you would 'plan' this out.

Set-up - this is the physical part of the planning, where you 'set-up' the conditions, to be in the right place, and so on.

Then you commit the Act or offense, and this ushers in the next phase:

Reinforced Powerful Feelings - After the act, feelings you had during the deviant fantasy are reinforced.

Remorse - Guilt - It's not a true remorse or true guilt, but more of a fear of getting caught. Your conscience tells you that you did something wrong. This could happen immediately or in a few days.

Promise to Reform - Since your conscience is bothering you, you tell yourself, or promise to not do it again, you might pray, pay penance, or say whatever is needed to fool your conscience and get you back to the Calm state.

*All these steps are rooted in our thoughts (except triggering event, set-up, and act). And like I said over time we were able to monitor our self-talk and catch ourselves in a cycle. But we could also hear other people's words and tell them, "Hey, you are in a cycle." The cycle is simple but so deeply complex. I wish I would have internalized it then.

Before the explosion of prisons in the mid-'90s, mostly all the prisons were in the red brick, telephone-style buildings. And the shower area was either a fifty-man shower or a hundred-man shower. When they called building showers, we had to leave our wings and go to the shower area. In prison if you had any complex about being naked in front of others you got over it pretty quick.

On Ramsey 2, the desk boss called for a shot of showers and about twenty-five of us walked to the door and the boss opened the door and let us in. There were benches to place our clothes on. And to the right there was a wooden deck that came up three feet off of the floor, and then a six-foot cinder block wall that separated the shower area. A boss usually stood on the deck to monitor the shower area. But it mostly stood empty. The bosses let the unit run itself.

There was a line on the back wall that we were to get into that led to the clothing exchange window. We turned in the dirty clothes that we were wearing and got clean ones in return. We remained naked from this line until we dried off after our shower. We placed our clothes on an open spot on the bench, and walked into the shower area and looked for an open shower head. The stream from the hot water would obscure the area with a fog. There would be couples standing behind the stream of water in their shower and engaged in sexual activity. There were people who did not mess around and showered quickly and left.

I had participated in a shower session with a friend. I was very promiscuous, and I engaged in voyeurism. One time me and a guy were the last of the people showering and we were messing around. The hall boss got on the deck to see how many people were left in the shower and he caught us in the act. He yelled for us to get out of the shower, then he went back to the hallway. We could not sneak out because he had the keys, and he would be the one to open the door.

We waited at the door to be let out. We were sure that he would write us a case. When he opened the door and saw us, he shook his head and came in and pointed to the other door and said, "That way." This door entered into the turn out area. He let us in and said, "You two wait here until I get a chance to talk to you."

When he left, I turned to my friend and said, "What do you think he's going to do?"

"I don't know. I thought he was cool but let's see how it plays out."

My heart was beating fast and I didn't know what was going to happen. I did know that getting caught having sex is a major case and that was not good.

After about fifteen minutes the boss came back in and started saying, "I am not stupid, I seen what I saw, right?" We had already claimed innocence when he caught us. He looked at my friend first.

"Yes, sir, you're right." he said.

He looked at me, and I said, "Yes, you are right"

"Alright then. Don't let me catch you doing that again. Not when I'm working." He looked at each of us.

"Yes, sir," we said at the same time.

"Get out of here," he said, opening the door.

A lot of male bosses did not want to write up any sex cases. Mostly because their coworkers would never let them live it down. Other bosses just wanted you to admit to doing what he accused you of, and since no one knew he could let it go. Every boss was different, and you soon learned what you could do and get away with by which boss was working.

The prison had rules for everything and the officers were required to enforce them by writing disciplinary cases. When an officer writes a case, he/she turns it in to the shift sergeant, and the sergeant "investigates" it by calling the inmate out and asking for his statement. Not his story, just his statement. It does not matter what he says, he will get that case. The boss is always right and would never lie. (That is the rank's take on that.) If you are alright with the sergeant then sometimes you could get the case informally resolved—thrown away. From there the case goes to the Disciplinary office and it is graded a major or minor case, depending on the severity, and your case history, then it's entered into the computer. Then the inmate will get called out a few days later and served the printed-out copy of the case. If it's a minor case then a lieutenant will preside over it. He will find you guilty, and assess the punishment: a verbal reprimand, commissary restriction, recreation or cell restriction, but usually a combo of all. A major case is heard by a captain and after the punishment you have to go to UCC and that could result in a custody charge.

* * *

Besides group therapy and individual therapy and the educational classes, the SOTP had a Treatment Team. This is where you go in before all the therapists and sit in the hot seat and get feedback for some behavior or not progressing fast enough. They also will bring you in to affirm that you are doing a good job and encourage you. I've never had that happen, though.

If they get enough reports from others of rule breaking, they will call you in to confront you about that. And this is where I found myself in

November 1993.

In my super-optimistic way of thinking I wasn't worried. I always brought a book with me whenever I had to sit and wait anywhere. John Grisham was a very popular author at this time and he always resonated in the prison because we all wished we had one of his skillful lawyers to get us out. I read all the time; it was a great escape from reality. I don't think that I spent much time in reality, between fantasies, books, watching TV, and sports; I distracted myself a lot.

I had to come back down to reality real quick when they called me in to the Treatment Team room. I wasn't prepared.

"Mr. Jones, we have been getting reports that you are engaging in sexual activity. This is in violation of the contract that you signed when you began this treatment. We have been very clear that you should abstain from sex and relationships while in this program. Not only is it against prison rules, but while you are in a program that addresses the irrational beliefs and unhealthy thought patterns surrounding sex relationships and even rape, you can't be reinforcing them at the same time." One of the therapists said.

"But I'm not. Who told you that?" I replied.

"See, you won't even admit to it and seek help. How do you ever plan on not reoffending if you won't even be truthful in this?" Then he looked at the other therapist and said, "I recommend terminating Mr. Jones from the program."

"But you can't do that," I cried, looking to my therapist for help.

She said, "You have exhibited this behavior over and over, Mr. Jones. You do not take your therapy seriously. I second your termination."

"But I will take this serious. I won't have sex anymore I promise. Don't kick me out." I was grasping at straws.

"It's too late to backtrack now. I think it's official, you are being terminated. You are dismissed," he said.

I left the room and the trailer in a daze. I was stunned. I knew that I would be transferred to another unit. Fear settled in, an old companion that I had not had in a while. This sent me into a cycle for real. I just didn't know that I would be at Ferguson unit in two months.

IS THIS THE END?

———————⟨⟩———————

Doing the same thing over and over and expecting different results.
-Definition of insanity

Growing up in a big family on my mother's side—she had two sisters and two brothers, and they all had children—we celebrated holidays before the actual day. On Christmas Eve we would go to either an uncle's home or our grandparents'. Thanksgiving and Christmas were the time that the whole family would be together. It felt good to be around the people who always accepted you.

But I seemed to be missing something. It seemed that as I saw everyone having fun, that they did not have any problems. My life was not like that and at these events I was aware of this. I would watch them all talk, open presents and eat. It looked as if they did this without a care in the world. As if all were okay in their world. I wished that I had that type of life at home and everywhere. I longed for those family get-togethers because I could live vicariously through them. I wanted to be free of the invisible restraints that were holding me back.

And as I look back now, I realize that I lived vicariously through a lot of things in life. When a game show contestant would win, I would feel happy, during a funny scene at the movies I would wait for the audience to laugh and then I would join in. I felt normal for a few moments, I felt a connection. It's like I was saying, "Hey, I found that funny also—please accept me."

When I got older, I would go to the movies alone. Now I see why I did that—so I could feel part of a group, of what I had seen as normal. I knew that something was wrong with me but I kept staying in denial, always rationalizing, and convincing myself that I was normal, that I was alright. I never knew that it was alright to not be alright, to feel down sometimes, or that there was help that I could get. In order to live with myself I had to constantly conform on the outside to what the world accepted, and on the inside, I had a lot of delusion going on. It was the only way it could be. It was Sex Offender 101.

*   *   *

At home it was a routine. We had periods of calm then out of nowhere he'd get drunk, and we'd scramble to leave in the middle of the night.

During the calm times we would all watch movies together in the den. But if my mom left the room for some reason, my brother and I would follow her out of the room. We did not want to be in the same room with him. And sure enough he would put us down.

"Two little puppy dogs following their bitch Mommy."

Yeah, I lived in fear of him. Have you ever seen people that are mentally if not spiritually beat down? That is what you would have seen if you could have seen the three of us. My mother was working at Southwestern Bell as a 411 operator. Then when she came home from work, she would attend to us. I can't remember her buying herself new clothes; she would always sacrifice for us.

Towards the end of my twelfth year, something changed in her. My mom had a TV in her bedroom and one day she called me in there and I remember seeing the *700 Club* on that TV. My mom told me that she was saved, that Jesus had come into her heart. She was so excited and I could see a difference in her, there was a glow on her face that can visibly be seen when someone is truly saved. And there was a sense that the usual dejection, the feeling of being cowed, if not gone was somewhat abated.

And it was this change, I believe, that led to a culmination of things. She invited him to church and he would go. I saw him go down at the altar call one time, to give his life to the Lord. He knelt down on the carpeted steps that led to the platform of our small Baptist church, and prayed with a deacon. When he got up, he left his pack of cigarettes on the steps. I remember thinking, "Is he giving it all up? Can the Lord change him that fast?" I really hoped so.

It only lasted till that night, and then he was smoking and drinking again. I was the one he told to go get a beer for him. I couldn't understand that. I mean, didn't he fear God? At this age I did not have a lot of correct beliefs about God but I knew enough to be too scared to go back on a vow so quickly. But reflecting back I now see that I was placing on God my own definition of what a Father was. All I'd ever had as an example had been my alcoholic, abusive stepfather. And as much as I love the Baptist church, they did not teach a lot of things that were pertinent to the Gospel; it's like they assumed that they were tacit. (This is not all Baptist churches—only the one I went to.) It must have been taboo to speak about sexual matters, because they didn't. I knew that you were not supposed to have sex before marriage. This gave the impression that sex is bad. And avoiding speaking about the homosexual issue left it open to going by your feelings. And the sex part felt good. But I grew up with no direct teaching about this and learned by experience and feeling. Experiences are strong and can override knowledge, especially when I did not have knowledge. I had impressions and feelings and no supervision to tell me that what I was feeling was wrong, or to even help me examine those feelings.

I somehow passed the sixth grade. Where we lived on Laprada we were in one school district, and my grandmother lived in a different one. If something bad happened to me at one school I would beg my mother to take me out of that school and enroll me in the other using my grandmother's address. In the fourth, fifth and sixth grade I switched back and forth between the two schools. In the fourth grade the teacher would not let me go to the restrooms and I ended up wetting my pants in the classroom. I pleaded with my mom to let me go to the other school. In fifth grade, I do not remember any one incident but just an overall sense of rejection. I don't remember having any friends or any one person that I called *my* friend. I wasn't a recluse or anything, I spoke with others. I just didn't have the self-confidence to be able to hold up under the scrutiny of other boys. I wanted what other boys had, that close friendship that I saw them have. But on the inside, I was void, so instinctively I didn't get too close to anyone. I think that, subconsciously, I was protecting myself.

In the sixth grade I had a male teacher for English class. One time he told me to look up a word in the dictionary. He handed me the dictionary and stood over me. He was over 6 feet. I felt intimidated. I cracked open the dictionary to the 'P's, but the word I was looking up began with an 'L'. As I was flipping through the 'P's he grabbed the dictionary out of my hand and said real loud, "The word begins with an 'L', not a 'P'. You have to have a brain to be able to look things up." I felt embarrassed and stupid. And don't tell me that stupid is not a feeling because I felt it a lot growing up, especially at the hands (words) of men.

I said before that Dr. Phil always teaches that "We generate, in life, the results that we believe that we deserve." Even at age twelve I was already generating this type of treatment. I had incorporated an aura that told people, "I'm no good, it's okay to abuse me, I deserve it."

But through it all I passed sixth grade. I suppose that the principal wanted to get rid of me, since I was always being sent to the office. On to the seventh grade. Junior high here I come. For better or worse.

The next big fight after I turned thirteen was a bad one. But this is where the difference in my mom came into play. We stayed away longer and this drove him to check himself into rehab. It was an inpatient twelve-step AA program. And since he was not there we moved back home. I don't remember how long the program was, but towards the end they had what is called 'Family Week.' The family would go and stay a week and go to group and tell how they felt about the drinking and abuse.

Only my mom and I went to this family week. I brought my Walkman and my favorite cassette tapes. On the way down there my mom and I wore out my Cyndi Lauper tape; our favorite song that year was "Time After Time" and we played it over and over.

There was a wing designed for families to stay in. It was a separate building, a rectangular wing. When you enter in the door there are tables and a mini kitchen to the left, and a TV/living room on the right. Then through another door where the hospital-like bedrooms were, two beds and a bathroom with a shower. They provided our meals for us, and when they found out that I liked chocolate milk they filled out one whole shelf with those pint-sized boxes of chocolate milk, in the fridge.

I was put in the room with another teenager, and we talked about everything. There was an older lady there who reminded me of my grandmother, and I latched on to her. She didn't seem to mind, though. I would brag to her about myself and she doted on me. One day she tried to trade me her cup of coffee for my chocolate milk. I made an 'Ooh gross' face, and she said, "You don't like coffee?" I told her that I'd never had any, and she had me try hers. But I didn't like it. She told me it was an acquired taste.

My mom and I would talk to one of the therapists together and then alone. We did this a few times, then came the time for the big group therapy. All the families and patients sat in a big circle in chairs. The therapist started around the group asking questions. First to a family then the patient. When they came to my mom and me, she said some things then I spoke. I do not remember any exact words but I expressed how I felt about him getting drunk, fighting my mom, and us always leaving.

Then one of the therapists said that my step-dad had a question that he wanted to ask us. He nodded at my step-dad, and he said, "I wanted to ask ya'll if you'll let me come back home and live with ya'll?" I wanted my mother to say "No, that this was the end." But she didn't say that, she told him that he would have to give up drinking completely. I think that she wanted to please the therapist, and I wanted to please my mom. The therapist looked at me and said, "David, what do you think?"

I looked at the floor between my feet, "Well, I don't want him to get drunk no more. And I don't want to call you 'Daddy' no more." We had always called him Daddy, even though he did not live up to the meaning of the word.

Everyone turned to him to hear his response. He said, "That's fine. I won't drink anymore, and you can call me whatever you like." I should have asked for a Porsche; he would have agreed to it. My mom said, "One more beer and I will leave for good." He said, "Okay." At least she had the presence of mind to say that. I don't know if she was happy with my acquiescence or not. But the therapist was happy. At least somebody got something out of it.

My mother had recently been promoted to work at the main southwestern Bell in downtown Dallas. She sorted mail and supplies to go out to the different SWB locations around Dallas. It seemed that she had never had friends before and now she started having some. Ever since she got saved, she was breaking out of that shell.

We had been back from Family Week for a week and he had not drunk any beer. I thought that maybe the program had worked. For the first time in her life my mom went out with some friends from work. My brother came running into our bedroom and said, "He's drinking. He's drinking." I went to see for myself wondering where he got the beer from.

My brother and I sat in the window in our room, looking out the window and waiting for our mom to come home. A soon as she came home, we ran outside and told her that he started drinking. There was no drunken fight that night. The next morning my mom told us to pack some clothes and we went to stay at my grandmothers for a while.

On Tuesday the following week my mom took me to one of our favorite restaurants, El Fenix. It was just us. After we ordered she showed me her left-hand sans the wedding ring. She said, "I filed to divorce him today." Later, she told me that my eyes lit up like a child on Christmas morning. Even though El Fenix was always good, that was the best meal ever.

I was very happy that she was finally leaving him. But the damage had already been done.

I'M NOT GAY

—◆◦〰◦◆—

Denial… It's not just a river in Egypt.

"Calm Down" by Taylor Swift

When I began seventh grade—junior high—I brought with me my elementary mindset, and my world view. I had always assumed that I was normal and that every family was the same. But in junior high divisions and distinctions began to set in that I would carry with me into adulthood.

In elementary school, when I would wonder how to be like other boys, I never saw the different groups that were in school: the cool, the nerds, the preps, and so on. But I saw them in middle school. Again, it was like everyone had been notified but me. I started seventh grade a nerd, but began to notice the distinctions. I wanted to be accepted and to be in the cool group. I still hated myself on the inside but I wasn't aware of it; I had a strong desire to be cool. So I began to conform to what others deemed was cool.

My mom made more sacrifices to get me the cool clothes, and I would imitate others and the things that they did. I combed my hair differently. And I do not remember having thoughts regarding this, but my relationship with God changed. I didn't pray as much or read my Bible as much. The pull of the world was calling me, the instant gratification of sensuality, of being accepted on sight, of fitting in with a group of people. I began to feel like people liked me. On the inside I truly believed that no guy would ever really like me. But there were guys in our group that were amiable, but I felt more of being in a competition with them, which hurt me and stopped me from being one of the guys.

And there was the sense that the girls liked me but the guys did not. And this was just like my family life, and proved Dr. Phil's precept that we generate the results that we believe that we deserve. The men in my family had seemingly rejected me, and the women all loved me.

Then I met my first love. Wendy had long brown hair with henna highlights. To my thirteen-year-old self she was beautiful. She was fourteen but very mature for her age. She already had plans for after high school.

We had a few classes together. But the times when we didn't, we would meet in the hallway after that class and hug and kiss. My seventh-grade year flew by. (This was the year that my mom and I went to Family Week, and then the divorce happened.) At school Wendy drew me out of being an introvert. I became outspoken and got in trouble a lot. We always ended up in the principal's office together. But Wendy would cry and cry, until the principal just let us go. He fell for it every time.

I passed seventh grade. I kept in touch with Wendy over the summer. We were living with my grandparents until my mom found some apartments on Buckner and Johnwest, in Dallas. It was right down the street from Gaston Middle School where I attended.

Ever since I was five years old and my mom and step-dad had had that first fight, it was like I'd had to grow up and start taking care of my mom. She had depended on me for most of everything. Now that she was no longer with him it was like she wanted to be the parent again, and tell me what to do. But I was used to running my own life, and I did not want to relinquish that control.

A child should grow up and rest secure in that parental supervision, and have his fears allayed by a rational mom or dad. But I'd had an abusive and neglectful step-dad, and an emotionally dependent mom, who taught me to try to control my life and what happened to me. But I couldn't, and fear was my constant companion, which I tried to outrun, but I kept bumping into that wall. And the result of what my mom had done gave me a false sense that I was in control and I was secure.

When my mom tried to exert her parental control I resisted and rebelled. We had big arguments where there was loud yelling and doors slamming. It was like a personal attack, as if she was taking my security and pulling it out from under me. Even though it was not true security it was *my* security, and I fought to keep that control. You just can't take a person's security.

Being divorced from him and being a born-again Christian, she was doing what she was supposed to do as a parent. But she did not know of the damage already done, of the sandy foundation that had already been laid. I didn't know anything either, I just felt like I was being attacked by the only one who was supposed to love me.

Our fighting didn't happen all the time. We still had times of peace. But I needed constant validation that I mattered, that she loved me. And that honed my manipulation skills. I didn't know that what I was doing was manipulating, I just knew that I felt that I was missing something and I needed it badly. And how I went about getting it—getting my way with her—was manipulative.

I ended up failing the eighth grade. My mom had been dating a guy from her work and they got married a year and a half after the divorce. Step-dad number two was cool when they were dating, but when they got married he wanted to be a father, with authority over me. I rebelled against him, too. He moved us to Mesquite, Texas. I had to change schools, and lose friends. I already had enough things that I had to fight, now I had to go to a new school, too? I failed the eighth grade a second time. My step-dad number two grounded me, indefinitely, until I brought home a passing report card. That did the trick. I was finally going to high school.

*   *   *

Teenage years are complicated enough without all the added stuff that comes from abuse. Modern psychology says that it is in our teenage years that we learn our sexual identity. I struggled with who I was as a person, my sexual identity, and the overwhelming feelings that were going on inside of me.

The overt sentiment of rejection and worthlessness from my first step-dad caused me to seek what love I could, where I could find it. These thoughts were not deliberate, but developed as I grew. It was a cry of the heart that needed and craved a father's love, acceptance and security. It drove me to slake my thirsty heart.

There were two girls whom I hung out with a lot growing up. They were the daughters of my grandfather's coworker. One was my age and the other was a few years older. My grandmother would pick them up to go to church with us sometimes. (This was before my mom was saved.)

I was hanging out at their house one time and I overheard the older girl talking with her friend about another friend that went to school with them named Jose. I wasn't paying attention until she said something about Jose being gay. I turned to her and said, "Jose is gay?"

"Yes, you didn't know? He has the hots for you," she said.

I turned back to the TV. I didn't know because he didn't fit into my presuppositions about gays anyway.

About two months later the two girls, Jose, another friend, and I went to the movies. Jose was in his 20s and he had the car so he drove. On the way back he dropped everyone off before me. The older girl had told him, without asking me, that I wanted to find out about being gay.

Going towards my house in Mesquite, he pulled into a motel. He asked me if I wanted to go in the room with him. I was curious so I went in.

By the time I got home late I didn't know what I was going to say. There were a million things going through my brain right then. My mom followed me to my room and we were arguing about me being late. She was screaming at me, I was evasive, then defensive. I felt real weird inside and guilty. Besides that, I couldn't sort out what else I was feeling. Then she also threatened to not let me go out with them anymore. I was in turmoil on the inside and I just screamed, "I'm not gay!"

She looked at me with confusion, like what does that have to do with anything. And I didn't know if I wanted her to confirm that or get me help. She didn't know the inner turmoil I was feeling. The shame, the guilt, the confusion. This was my cry for help. Because I, as a teenager, after everything else that I have been through, was not capable of dealing with being molested too.

Yes, I call it being molested. For years I burned with guilt and shame thinking that I was a willing partner in that. I consented to go in that motel room, after all. In prison therapy, one of my therapist noticed my language about certain topics and she assigned me to do a "Victim Impact Worksheet", using my own victimization as the subject. And when I presented it in group, I gained the insight that I was a victim in this event. All these years I was holding on to the shame and guilt, and the fear.

Then in a pivotal moment in group my therapist led me to a deeper insight, and helped me to correlate what I felt with how my victims felt. And what they must be left feeling and thinking, all these years later.

* * *

I wish that I could have had that insight before I had any victims. I wish that my mom would have seen the signs. I wish that I would never have hurt anyone.

A few weeks later after the incident at the motel, something else happened. I don't know how to explain it. It was not supernatural, no visions or anything like that. But I got this sense of something or Someone that I had not thought of in a while. It was like my defenses were dismantled for a moment. It was the Lord bringing me to a remembrance of Him. During the seventh grade I was always going to church, reading the Bible, talking about Him, praying.

But when I started to get popular in school, my relationship with God wasn't the same. As if the two could not coincide. I chose to go along with the cool crowd and be accepted rather than be what I thought a Christian was supposed to be.

Walking to school in the morning I knew it was the Lord, and He was asking me, "Where are you?" I told him that I missed Him, and I felt that familiar warmth that He'd given me before. But once I got to school the defenses came back up and I had to keep up my image. Even in the years after this, I claimed to be a Christian. I went to church, but on the inside, it was like all my emotions, needs, issues, problems and peer pressure were all clustered up and I couldn't sort it all out. On the outside I put up an image that I was okay, but on the inside, it was like a tornado. Sexual fantasies and masturbation were what soothed me and gave me any respite.

You may wonder why God didn't just deliver me then, and I wish that He had. But God is love and love does not force or go against a person's will. God knocks and He speaks the truth into our hearts. I was not ready at age fifteen to hear it. I was living by my feelings and what the world was giving out. It choked the truth.

FRESHMAN

—◦⊂⟋⟍⊃◦—

"Religion is the only solid basis of good morals; therefore, education should teach the precepts of religion and the duties of man toward God."
-Gouveneur Morris

"It is better to offer no excuse than a bad one."
-George Washington

Although I rebelled against any type of authority over me, my second step-dad grounding me until I brought home passing grades did help me to make it to the ninth grade. But no one knew about the darkness growing in my heart. Like the song says, "It's a slow fade." I did not just wake up and decide to molest children. But when I was checking out the other boys in the locker room to see what was different about them that made other people like them, I started to sexualize it, and then to fantasize about them. It was as if, somehow, I could have "sex" with these boys, then I would be on the same level as them and other people would like me. Irrational? Yes! But that is what my mind perceived. As if sex equaled equality with the person I had sex with. But as I got older, my "attractions", and fantasy stayed on those boys, because in my mind it was *that* that would make me okay, loved, accepted. This became a pattern in my brain, then a belief and then it got reinforced.

There was already the shame from feeling that I was gay, and the stigma that came with it. Being molested reinforced the sex-equals-love-and-acceptance belief, because Jose was an older man and he "accepted" me. But with the way the world viewed gay people I guarded this secret for fear of more rejection. It was crazy how one thing could mean two different things. Being molested, then attracted to the same sex, and even young boys, I equated with love and acceptance, yet at the same time I had to hide it from the rest of the world for fear of being alienated even more. It was like there was always a duality in my life: in my family I was rejected by the father figure and loved by my mother. And now this demented and crazy perception of love, sex and men and boys. And I was in denial, even with myself, because I didn't know how to deal with all this.

I kept building and projecting the image that I was normal, just like everyone else. And now I was starting high school, oh, no pressure there. Since I did not know how to deal with this it all became compounded. All these issues were just under the surface, clustered and rolling, as I tried to control every aspect of my life. I wasn't hiding it so I could revel in it, and grow up to be a pedophile. I hid it because how do you even go and talk about this with someone? I was embarrassed and plagued with guilt and shame, and worried about rejection. And at the same time the things that I was ashamed of gave me relief and soothed me. But the fear of abandonment kept me from seeking help. And I had to keep up the image that I was okay.

And do you know how I dealt with this dragon? I lied to myself. I did not know how to comprehend what I was doing, but this type of stuff cannot lie around in our minds without a disguise. I began to rationalize, justify, deny—lie upon lie. I did not know how to deal with this appropriately so I had to be able to live with myself, and I minimized it all in my mind and that too became a pattern. I believed the lies. I believed that I was a good and decent person. I did not know how to not be this way. I believed that this is how I was. I did not realize that all the mitigating circumstances that contributed to "how I was" could be changed by therapy, or by developing good morals and beliefs.

As I convey the inner turmoil and what was going on in my mind as I was growing up, I hope that you can see what child abuse can do to a person. No one should have to grow up like this. I hate that I caused anyone to go through what I have described. Our brains cannot stay in turmoil; the brain will always seek harmony. And when a child or an adult is going through any type of abuse, if he/she has never learned how to deal with it then their brain will provide the justifications, the rationalizations, the lies, in order to get the brain back to calm.

This is what was happening to me. I had not wanted to grow up to be like this, but I felt that I couldn't tell anyone so my brain sought relief, and thus began my lies to myself. How does acceptance have this strong of a motivation, to drive me to this depth? All of that got pushed down so I wouldn't know, and no one else would either. But Carl Jung said, "What you resist, persists."

If you are a parent and you are reading this, then let this be your sign. If your child begins to act funny, blows up at the slightest provocation, tries too hard to impress an image that he/she is good, if they can't deal with pressure or they act out for attention, are overly defensive, display racing thoughts, then there is something wrong. Ask your children how they are feeling, every day. Help them to understand their feelings in light of what they are thinking. And tell them that sometimes our feelings do lie to us. Help them sort it out, lead them to the connection between our thoughts and feelings. Teach them boundaries, especially boundaries in the mind. Tell them that they have control over what they think and fantasize about, and that we must respect other people's boundaries (even in our minds).

I have said it over and over, ex post facto laws will not stop sexual offenses. It has to start at home in the family. I wish that I'd been asked the above questions growing up. I might have believed that someone cared, and told them. But no one asked and I did not tell. It didn't work in the army, and it's not a good policy for raising children, either.

*   *   *

For my ninth-grade year I attended Poteet high school in Mesquite, Texas. It was a brand-new school and although I was supposed to go to North Mesquite high school, MISD made us go to Poteet for our freshman year. And in tenth grade the ones who lived on the north side of LBJ freeway would go to North Mesquite.

I joined the swim team. We met at Eastfield Community College at 6 a.m., and didn't have to show up to school until second period. Since I was sixteen, I already had my driver's license and I was given my mother's Toyota Celica when she got a new car. But during the summer, I went to see my old girlfriend Wendy and I let her drive it and she hit a tree. It was totaled. I had to take the blame because I wasn't supposed to let her drive it. That was a punishment in itself because now they would think that I was a bad driver. I had been driving since I was eleven. When no one was home one day when I stayed home from school, I took my step-dad's truck for a drive around the block.

My biological father came to see me and my brother when I was fourteen. He was living with an army buddy, and we stayed the weekend at his home. But my father took me out barhopping one Saturday night. When we left the first bar, he told me to drive. I drove us from bar to bar up and down Greenville Avenue. I tried to be exceptionally good at external things to keep up the image. But I had to take a hit with Wendy wrecking my car to avoid getting in trouble.

My second stepfather let me drive his Toyota pickup to swim practice and then to school, but he worked the same place as my mom and they took her car. I was the only one driving to school at the beginning of the year. At my high school there were different groups: preps, punk rockers, the stoners. And at this age I wanted to resist labels and stereotypes. This was because I wanted to avoid rejection, and I didn't have an identity. So, one day I would dress like a prep, the next day like a stoner, and then a punk rocker. I created my own style so I would not be put in a box. It bothered me if I sensed any rejection, and I even tried to control that. Talk about unrealistic.

I was a class clown. Always making a joke or smart remarks. I had a math teacher who was of Cuban descent and she had an accent when she spoke. And when she was mad, she would not finish her sentences. One day she was trying to say, "I am getting tired of all this talking." But what came out was, "I am getting tired." You don't expect me to just let that go, do you? I said, "Well, maybe you should sit down." And that kicked off my revolving door to the principal's office. I told the principal that she might as well put my name on the door as I was so much in there.

My history teacher was almost begging for a class clown. His name was Mr. J. and he would drone on and on for an hour about the same subject. He seemed oblivious to this and just told the same story over and over.

One day I came in late and he asked me why I was late. I said, "Well, I was coming up the stairs, and I was going to be on time, but then Humpty Dumpty fell off the wall, and he had a great fall. Then when all the king's men and horses came to put him back together, I got stuck in the middle of it."

The class burst out laughing. Mr. J. said to the class, "Quiet down, this is between Mr. Jones and me. Have a seat Mr. Jones." Then he resumed telling his story.

Another time I got to class early as Mr. J. stood outside the classroom to monitor the hallway. Being a new school there were sensors for the lights to come on and they would stay on as long as they sensed movement. I climbed the shelf below the sensor and put the sensor into the ceiling and covered the ceiling tile back up. When class began and Mr. J started up a story, a few minutes later the lights went off. Everyone began hollering and making noise. Mr. J. opened up the door to get the light from the hall, and he sent a student to get one of the principals. When he came, he brought a step ladder with him. He pulled the sensor back out and then told me to come with him.

"What for?" I exclaimed, very innocently.

"Come," he said, in a voice that meant he was serious.

I went with him and vehemently denied doing this. Both principals were in there and were saying the same things that they'd said before. I told them that anyone could have done that and I didn't, and that there was no proof. I got detention. They knew it was me.

My English teacher was different; she would just give it right back. She had us reading out loud and when it was my turn, I would change the dialogue and make everyone laugh. *The Breakfast Club* was one of my favorite movies, (anything with Molly Ringwald), and I used a lot of that material. One time during a quiet time in class, I began to whistle like they did in the movie. Then the teacher surprised me. She quoted a line from the movie:

"You think he's funny?" She asked the class. "You just look at him in five years, he'll be in prison. Then you'll think he's funny."

The scary thing was this "joke" turned into a prophecy. It was 1987 and in 1991, I went to prison.

But I drew the line with her one day. I found a screw on the floor, and I went to her desk with the screw on my palm and said, "Do you want a screw?" With the implication in my tone. More detention. Which is where I met Bobby.

Bobby was the same age as me. And he already had his driver's license, too. We would write notes back and forth during detention. In one of his notes, I got the impression that he might be gay. We started hanging out and then began messing around. He was the first same-age boy that I messed with. Then I met another guy named Bishop, and we became best friends. Turns out that he was gay also. We all liked girls too. But the common denominator that we all had—no father figure.

I know that there is so much controversy today concerning nature versus nurture, being born gay or choosing to be. I have met plenty of gay people who had both parents growing up and were never abused. And while I personally don't think that I was born that way, I do not believe that there is a gay gene, I think there is a fine line here that not everyone has been able to traverse. This issue is not so dichotomous. We cannot say, "*This* is the reason for this, or *this* is the reason for that." Our brains want to have a reason to be able to harmonize and compartmentalize, but this is not one of those issues that we can so easily box up. And maybe people do need to calm down and stop hating the things that are different, and the things that they do not understand. Because like what was said in the movie *Wonder*, this is a good precept to live by: "Be kind, everyone is fighting a hard battle." And to hate and bully people makes what is a hard life already that much harder. Maybe if people did not have to spend so much time defending themselves they could discover more about themselves, and the whys and the hows would be self-evident to them. In prison I was able to search myself and I dug deep to find the motives behind why I did certain behaviors. And you will have to keep reading to find out.

Later that school year I talked my mom into letting me quit school. As I was in the principal's office telling her that I was quitting, she changed her tone and acted all concerned and didn't want me to quit. I just let her talk, but I was thinking, "You never seemed to care before," because in my mind when she would punish me for acting up in class, I perceived that as rejection. All authority figures were against me, right? I couldn't figure out why they hated me. Now this concern confused me. So, I drowned her out.

On the way out the door a friend saw me leaving and asked where I was going and I told him that I quit. He said, "See you at McDonalds in five years." This also came true. While I was out on bail, I worked at McDonalds for a few months in 1991, and he came in and saw me.

My step-dad was angry. My quitting school caused arguments at home. He and my mom got into a big argument. My mom defended me and I don't know why. But this was causing too many problems. The next week I went back and the school accepted me back. Do not ask me how but I passed the ninth grade.

FERGUSON - RAMSEY 2

The morning that I was raped on Ferguson, when I came off the wing, I reported to the lieutenant that I had been raped. I said that going to the officers was never an option, but when it came to activity towards me that I did not want to happen, then I had to draw a line.

The lieutenant took me to the infirmary for an examination. Besides the nurses and the lieutenant being in there was also a couple of sergeants asking me questions. When they discovered that I went into his cell after breakfast their focus went from seeing me as a victim to "a punk making them do paperwork". As if going into his cell made it consensual and okay. This was before, "*No* means *no*." Before they made a distinction, or exactly what rape is. For all intents and purposes, I was "riding" with this guy for protection, and I had to do what he told me. I did not want to have anal sex.

Later, that morning I was given a direct order to go back to my cell. I refused and they locked me up. It's called PHD - prehearing detention, a solitary cell that I stayed in until my court date. I received two disciplinary cases: one for refusing a housing assignment, and the other for sexual misconduct.

I also had to see the prison's internal affairs. When I refused to press charges the lady investigator asked me how I expected them to believe me about the rape, when I wouldn't press charges.

I told her, "He raped me because I was unwilling to have anal sex. But I'm not going to make him get more time behind it." The SOTP had taught us the true definition of rape. But it seemed that the world didn't hold the same definition.

Ever since June I had been seeing the unit psychologist. Through her I had requested to get back in the SOTP program. When I was terminated, I was told that I could reapply in six months. It was now August. When a rape occurs, it is policy to see the psychologist. I talked to her about it and she made a report.

A few days later I went to court for the sexual misconduct case. The captain found me guilty and gave me forty-five days cell and recreation and commissary restriction. He took 150 days good time and put me in solitary for fifteen days. Then I got the exact same punishment for the refusing of housing case. After the fifteen days they offered me another cell to move into but I refused that also. I went back to PHD. In PHD we had our property with us, but in solitary we were only allowed a Bible and legal work, and a toothbrush and toothpaste.

On some units you can see other cells and talk to those guys, but on Ferguson the cells were in a row and you could still talk to neighbors, but if you got too loud the CO would shut your door. None of us wanted our door shut. But people have stories and you can just lie back and listen to the stories. When there was a cool boss some guys would sing, and if they sang good, we would make requests. The most popular requests were "Hotel California," "Under the Bridge," or "Friends in Low Places." If a black guy was singing, we would request, "Man in the Mirror," by Michael Jackson.

PHD, lockup, solitary, it was the same all over. With nothing else to do we turned to each other for the necessary distractions from reality. Some guys would even argue from their cells with each other. It could be funny at times but then it got old fast. We called those guys cell warriors.

Distractions. I tried to always stay distracted because when they were gone and all the fantasies were worn out, I was left with myself, and I did not like myself. I did not like reality. But on those nights when the distractions were gone thoughts of people that I'd hurt and all the stupid, horrible things that I had done would plague me. I dreaded these nights, because I had not come to terms with them yet, and my conscience gave me hell behind it. I would be glad when sleep finally arrived, then I could wake up with all my defenses in place.

A few nights later a boss came to my cell and told me to pack up. That I was on the chain. The next morning, I was handcuffed and put on the bus. When the driver told me that I was going to Ramsey 2, I was glad. I never saw Geechi Dan again. I met someone years later who knew him though. This world in prison will bring someone into your life and then take them away, never to be seen again. Did they exist? The things that did and gave, still exist to this day. So, yeah, they existed.

A couple of days later I was back at Ramsey 2, sitting in that cage waiting to be assigned to a bunk in the dorms. Everyone I knew came to the cage to say hi. L., D., and H. all came by. I couldn't wait to tell them my story. I bummed a cigarette from someone that I knew. I'd begun smoking on Ferguson and I didn't want to stop.

The rule still applied, "When you get to a unit, you have to work in the fields for ninety days." And I was placed in the medical squad. We were allowed to bring our cigarettes with us and since the medical squad worked at their own leisure, we would just hide in the tall corn stalks and smoke. But when the boss needed to do a headcount, we would pretend to work.

By the time 1995 came around I had finished my ninety days and I was working in the clothing issue room. I got tired of that and then requested to work in the kitchen. I worked the morning shift and we had to go in at 2 a.m. In there I met a real attractive guy. Have you ever met someone who could make you laugh even when telling a true story? That was this guy; he was the head baker and he had the whole kitchen laughing. He was shorter than me but had a running back's body, and was very cute. I worked real hard for the sergeant and he didn't mind me hanging out in the bakery.

Lil' Mike taught me how to bake for five hundred men, how to make biscuits from scratch, and how to keep cookies and brownies from getting hard when they were served. The sergeant finally recommended me to the kitchen captain and I got assigned to the bakery.

In the '90s before the budget cuts we had dessert at lunch and dinner every day. Then with the cuts, at first, they scaled back to desserts twice a week, and now just once a week. But when we got to work, we had to make two desserts for that day and whatever bread was going to be given that day—sometimes it was cornbread, sometimes it was rolls or biscuits. Every time there is a budget cut they always take away something from us inmates first.

I learned how to make hooch and where to hide it while it "cooked". I learned how to requisition the supplies and ingredients for the whole week. How to pad the requests so that we could have extra ingredients to make peanut brittle, or cookies that we could smuggle out, to "eat all that we could and sell the rest."

In March 1995, the prison posted notices that the prison would be going smoke-free. The commissary would no longer sell tobacco or its products, and that we had four months to use up what tobacco we had.

What?!?

A smoke-free prison? That was unheard of, and un-American. We had got a heads up about it and we had been buying it and stockpiling it. The COs were mad and a lot of people quit because of it. We had heard that there was a class action lawsuit against TDCJ, for second-hand smoke causing cancer. The prison and tobacco companies lost millions behind this ruling.

And this created another item for the black market. Once cigarettes started becoming scarce, the guys who kept it for this reason began selling seven cigarettes for $1.50. We used the code word "square" for a cigarette. As more time went by it was five squares for $1.50. And now today as I'm writing this it is $1.50 for one square. But the word has changed also, to thugs. "Hey you got any thugs?" And a K-2 cigarette is called a stick. And the main way to get these into the prison is through a dirty boss who needs money.

The only unit that rioted behind TDCJ going smoke-free was the Dolph Briscoe unit down in Dilley, Texas. We heard that the National Guard was called to go in and take back control of the unit. But rumors said it was a real bad riot behind the white and black inmates.

Towards the end of 1995 we were told that the administration of SOTP had implemented changes in the program. That it was being divided between three different units.: Ramsey 2, Goree, and the Walls unit. I was told that I would be going to the Walls unit. That was too good to be true; it's the best unit in the system.

In January 1996, I was on the chain. But as I told the bus driver my TDCJ number he said that I was headed to Briscoe unit. I stopped and said, "I'm supposed to go to the Walls unit. There must have been a mistake."

"Yeah,' he said, "I'm supposed to make a million dollars. You can't choose what unit you want to go to. Get on the bus."

I tried to explain to him, but there wasn't anything that could be done. If the paperwork said Briscoe, then I was going to Briscoe.

HIGH SCHOOL - BYE SCHOOL

"Let us tenderly and kindly cherish therefore, the means of knowledge. Let us dare to read, think, speak, and write."
-John Adams

In between the ninth and tenth grade my grandfather gave me a late sixteenth birthday gift. It was a 1977 Mustang Ghia II. I had a cousin who was six months older than me, and he got the Nova. We were the two oldest grandkids, and he knew that our parents couldn't get us a car.

I fell in love with the car. It was a two-door and all black inside and out. I drove it around the block and it was a stick shift and had that kick once you put it in gear. Every guy's dream. I followed my parents home in my car. My step-dad (number two) helped me put in a stereo system and speakers. Now I could jam as I drove.

In 1986 I had worked at McDonalds for a while. But this summer I had gotten a lifeguard's license and I worked at a daycare that was a five-minute walk from my house in Mesquite, as a lifeguard. There was a flood during the summer and it came into the daycare. My step-dad came up there and told me not to start my car or drive it home. The water went up past the wheel. Then he left once I told him that I wouldn't drive home.

We watched the water rise, first in the street and then it started coming into the daycare. Before it got really high on the street, we saw a small red car still in front of the daycare. We thought it looked like one of the parents' cars. The lady driving just sat there, so I went out there and the first thing I noticed was that she was not a parent. But I told her that she needed to get out of the car. She stepped out into the shin deep water and stumbled towards me. I picked her up and carried her across the parking lot and before I got half way the water came up higher and then took the car. It flipped it over onto the roof and floated down to the flooded creek across from the daycare.

"Oh my gosh, you saved my life. I could have been in that car," the lady I was carrying said. My boss and co-workers came out and we were all stunned. We went into the daycare and the lady went to the back with a couple of the women that worked with me to dry off. After about an hour the water abated and it left a line of dirt and trash against the cars in the parking lot, from the debris that was in the water.

After the parents had come to pick up their children, I went to my car and tried to start it. I was sure that my step dad didn't mean not to start the car now that the water went down. But it didn't start, so I walked home. When I got there, he asked me if I tried to start it and I told him that I did. He got mad and began to yell at me. I yelled back and went to my room and slammed the door. I felt stupid, and angry. It was like I could never do anything right, or please anyone, especially a man. Now I felt rejected by the only father who seemed to care about me.

The next day he tried to start the car and it didn't start. "Water must have been in the gas tank and when you tried to start it yesterday it put the water into the engine. Now it will need a whole new engine."

"I didn't know," I exclaimed.

I'd barely had my car for two months and now it needed a new engine. He told me that we would fix it together. Which meant he would do it and I would watch and learn. For the beginning of my tenth-grade year, I rode the bus to school.

* * *

The North Mesquite High School Stallions, tenth grade, 1987. I was sixteen years old. I began the year on the swim team, but soon lost interest. By the end of October, I quit the team, and was placed in study hall during first period. I had to take the bus to school because my car was still out of commission.

I met Annie in study hall, and we shared two other classes together, but we became good friends when I got to study hall. She had a Nissan Sentra and she offered to pick me up for school in the mornings. We had biology class right before lunch, and home ec. for the last class of the day.

In the mornings when Annie picked me up, she would hand me her baggie of weed and I would roll us a joint. We got high most mornings on the way to school, and that made study hall more fun. I was still a class clown. The teacher in study hall came in one day and wrote the date on the chalkboard. Annie and I watched through stoned eyes, and I realized what it was and I blurted out, "Hey, that's the date."

"Mr. Jones, I can't get much past you," the teacher deadpanned.

In sixth period the home ec. teacher talked a lot, and one day she told us that she could tell the difference between "sick" eyes and "stoned" eyes. I leaned towards Annie and whispered, "Thank God that we have her in sixth period." But my whisper wasn't as quiet as I'd thought and everyone laughed, including the teacher.

Annie was a good friend, and we grew tight. I could always copy the answers on class homework assignments and tests. She would tell me to be sure to get a couple wrong so that it wouldn't look copied.

Being sophomores, we would give the freshmen a hard time. In the lunchroom there was a table that they were sitting at and as Annie and I walked by she told them to get up, and made them find another table. She was real good at playing the hard role. But those freshmen were good sports about it and we all became friends and sat at the same table.

I had signed up for Theater Arts class. Ever since a friend and I had snuck into the movies to see *Beverly Hills Cop* back when it came out, I'd had a desire to be a comedian and actor. I loved the way Eddie Murphy could talk himself into any place and get away with it. And he was so funny while he did it, his humor came naturally. I wanted to be funny and make people laugh. I started with being a class clown.

Theater Arts was my favorite class. I learned how to do makeup and all the things that pertain to stage acting. When our teacher announced the play for that year: *Fiddler on the Roof*, I decided to audition for it. I had never seen the movie or read the book. Everyone else seemed to know the characters already. When I read the script, I decided to try out for 'Motel.'

Who was I kidding? I couldn't carry a tune to save my life. I ended up getting the role of the Tailor, who had a few lines. But the stage play had dancing, and we had a choreographer who taught us the steps, and I fell in love with dance, and choreography. It had order, it was fun, it was something put together that spoke to me and it had a sequence, and it had a final outcome. Maybe, on the inside I craved something that made sense, that was sure, and could go step by step and come out the way it was expected to. Because in reality on the inside I was a mess, and there was not any consistency or certainty in my life.

But I struggled with confidence and worried about what people were thinking about me. I would miss my step and turn my head a second too soon, and I could hear the others groan. The instructor told the person next to me to squeeze my hand to give me my cue when to turn or take the step, et cetera. That helped me get my timing right. I knew I could do it, but lacking self-confidence can be debilitating.

During the dress rehearsal I messed up only once, but the next time and in the three performances, we rocked. The last performance was the best in my opinion. We got a standing ovation, and the adulation was addictive. I wanted that all the time. Even though I didn't have big roles, I was a part of the whole, and it felt good. Now I knew how Sally Fields felt that night at the Oscars: "You like me, you like me, you really like me."

My very first job was at McDonalds. Not having any type of work ethic, I quit a couple of months later, and that was in 1986. In the summer of 1987, I got the lifeguard job, and worked there until October. Then the guy who'd had the lead in the *Fiddler* play told me that his boss was looking for someone. He worked at a Tex-Mex place in Mesquite, as an entertainer. He dressed up as a clown and passed out balloons. He told me that this was a good way to build up the portfolio that actors need.

I interviewed with the boss and got the job. He suggested that I pick a different character than a clown. At a costume shop, I found a Bugs

Bunny suit but I didn't want to be Bugs, so I used the suit and the ears and became Oswald the Rabbit. I used glue and glitter and put the name "Oswald" on the cap I used, and some people said that the kids would think of Lee Harvey, who killed Kennedy. But I said kids didn't know that stuff, I barely knew it.

My first night I was in our little closet of a dressing room, using the helium canister to blow up balloons. My co-worker the "clown" was getting off of work and he wished me luck.

When the dining hall began to fill with families, I entered the room with my bouquet of balloons, and got in character and went to my first table. As I gave a balloon to a seven-year-old, he looked up at my cap and read my name and said, "Hey, you killed Kennedy."

Thinking quickly I said, "No, that wasn't me. I'm Oswald the Rabbit, and I only pass out balloons." I tied the balloon to the chair and moved on. The job paid $5 an hour, which was good pay, then, but I only worked Friday evening, and during the rush on Saturdays and Sundays. It wasn't really enough hours and I ended up quitting in January 1988. I was going to miss being able to have all the chips, tortillas and picante sauce that I could eat before each shift.

During the play I met this guy who was on the crew; they were setting up the props, the different sets, and the lighting. He was openly gay, which was a very hard thing to be in the 1980s. We talked a lot about being gay and all the struggles that come with it. It wasn't sexual between us, but there were things that I was curious about and he saw in me my denial and struggle, so we were friends. I did not understand my feelings or why it was so taboo and unaccepted by everyone as a rule. He knew and after rehearsal we were in his car in the school parking lot, and I admitted to him that I thought I was bi-sexual because I liked guys and girls.

"You can't do that," he told me.

"Why?" I asked.

"Because you can't be split on your identity, it will drive you crazy. You got to pick one and stick with it," he explained. This was before LGBT and all that stuff. "How can you be with a guy and still want a girl? You have to be true to yourself."

"Let's eschew all labels," I told him. "If labels and stereotypes come with pre-existing conditions that we have to adhere to, then let's do away with them."

"Yeah, and which reality is going to let you do that? The world hates us," he said.

"Why can't I just be David, and David does who and what he wants? 'I thought I was clever.

He looked at me in a way that I'd never seen before, shook his head and said, "You're not gay. This isn't what that's about at all. It sounds like you are just trying to have your cake and eat it, too. You don't understand and probably never will."

He started up the car and drove off. There was a silence between us as he drove me home. When he pulled up to my house I said, "Are we okay?"

"Yeah, it's just, well, it's a lonely existence when no one understands you, no one gets you, ya know?" he said.

I went inside my house, and just buried all those issues. I always buried anything that made me not feel good. I just embraced my theory on "No labels." I convinced myself that it was a very genius way of thinking and that it was unique because no one else thought on this type of level. Sadly, I kept thinking like this, and I didn't ask anyone for advice because I didn't need it, and no one would understand. Besides, I had it all figured out.

But of course, not having a label was akin to not having an identity, and a person without an identity does not have a foundation. I did not like the damage that labels cause, but I believed that it is important to know who you are and to have an identity.

*   *   *

Whenever Annie didn't go to school I would stay home too. I would transfer my phone to her phone, so that when the school called about my absence, she could answer as if she were my mom.

And if Annie was leaving school early for a doctor's appointment, she would get to one of the payphones in the school and "call" the school and have me excused for the rest of the day, "for a doctor's appointment." It always worked. Before I got my car fixed, we would always get in her car and leave. But then my car finally got fixed, and I had to wait to get a decal to put on my car so I could park in the school lot. I would park at a nearby parking lot and she would take me there.

I passed the tenth grade. Everything except English. In eleventh grade I would have to repeat tenth grade English. I thought that spelling and being able to read was all that I needed; I didn't want to learn all the other stuff.

I was living with my grandparents, because my mom and stepdad had moved out to Farmersville and I didn't want to move out there. We had the usual arguments but, in the end, they let me go live with my grandparents.

I was seventeen at the beginning of eleventh grade. I drove my car to school and went through the motions. Annie and I didn't have any classes together, but we remained friends. She set me up with one of her friends and we dated a few times. I was in Theatre Arts again, and that was the only class that I looked forward to. This year's play was going to be *Death of a Salesman*. But my grades were not going to let me be in it. I was angry about that, and told them, "The one thing that I love you're taking away from me."

That was probably the seed that began my descent. In March of 1989, I turned eighteen and I was in a class and got into an argument with the teacher. And then I realized that I didn't have to stay here. I was an adult now and I could do what I wanted. That's what being 18 meant, right? I was tired of being told what to do. I walked out of the classroom and into the principal's office and told him that I was quitting.

He tried to persuade me to stay, telling me that I needed an education, that I wouldn't have any type of future without one, but when he saw that I was determined he made me to go around to have each teacher sign off on me quitting. The only teacher who put up an argument was my English teacher. And if my resolve hadn't been as strong as it was, she may have convinced me to stay.

Back in his office he asked what my plans were. I told him that I would get my GED and then go to college. He said that 95% of drop-outs never go to college.

"I'll be the first." I declared.

"When you bring me that degree, I'll buy you a steak dinner," he replied.

The next morning, I was rudely awoken around 9 a.m. by my grandpa. He had worked hard all his life and was now retired from a job that he'd had for thirty years. Now he had his own real estate business.

"Why are you still in bed and not at school?" he bellowed. He had already been at work since 6 a.m. and had just stopped by the house to grab something. My grandma told him that I'd quit school.

I squinted into the bedroom light and then he opened the curtain. "Huh, what?"

"Why aren't you at school?"

"I quit."

"How are you going to support yourself? Because you are not going to live here for free if you are not going to school." Already my "being an adult" excuse was looking weak. My grandmother was telling him to leave me alone; she just didn't want there to be an argument. But the women always defended me.

"No, I won't leave him alone. You need to get up and go back to school, or get a job. You cannot sleep in; you need to get up at 6 a.m. every morning and look for a job or you cannot live here."

"Yes, sir," I told him. (In 1990 we had another scene like this but that one was about getting my GED, which I got in October of 1990.)

But that morning I got up and left the house. I didn't have any plans or goals; I didn't even have a purpose. I was just adrift, pulled along by my emotions. I didn't have an anchor. I went from port to port, seeking a good feeling. I thought my feelings were the truth, because I felt them. And I let them guide me; I was restless, had racing thoughts and rampant sex. I never once thought that my feelings could mislead me and lie to me.

I found a McDonalds by my grandparents' house. It was easy work, I knew it already and they didn't much care about an education. The owner was a woman and she assigned me to the drive thru, because I had experience. You had to be fast during rush hour. All the managers liked me because I could fit in at any job, and I was a hard worker. When they needed a cook, they would call me in for that or to wash the dishes, pots, and pans, and so on.

On Tuesdays was when the truck came, and the two guys who unloaded it asked me to give them a hand one day. After they'd taught me the ropes it was us three that were assigned to unload the truck. We had a system and we were fast. We rotated the stock and we had it all ready to go. Then we would go out to eat together.

Those guys liked to exercise and they would ride their bikes for five miles the afternoon of the truck. They invited me and I went with them and rode my bike almost 2.5 miles before I had to stop. But it took getting used to, and we got in the routine of doing it every Tuesday, before the truck. I felt included and like I had friends.

I also met the mother of my son while I was working there. She was a beautiful black woman. And it started out with giving her a ride home from work. About the third time I brought her home, she asked me if I liked to kiss. And I asked her why. She said because when I dropped her off, I never kissed her.

Well, that led to going up to her room, and in her room, we did a little more than kissing. We had sex three times that summer, and she got pregnant one of those times. She didn't find that out until later, though. And told me even later.

An assistant manager's position came open and a lot of us applied for it. But she and another person got it. I was very disappointed. I was still working the night shift.

One night a guy came in wearing a black T-shirt with white letters on it—which were the initials of the place that he worked at. I was big into wearing T-shirts, and I liked the design on this one, the contrast of the colors. On an impulse I asked him if they were hiring. He said that with summer coming up that they would be hiring for summer camp counselors. He gave me a number and a name and I thanked him.

This would be the worst decision of my life. I got hired at this place of initials, and quit McDonalds. It was May 1989, and for almost two years I would work there with my horrible secrets, shame and guilt, and demented thought and belief patterns. Then I would be headed to prison, on a fifteen-year sentence. So why am I still here thirty years later?

TURNING POINT

—◦◦◦—

Walls Unit, 1996

"'But,' say the puling, pusillanimous cowards, 'we shall be subject to a long and bloody war if we declare independence.' On the contrary, I affirm it the only step that can bring the contest to a speedy and happy issue."

-Sam Adams

The world of the survivalist. It takes a lot of energy. And you always have to be watchful and be able to see what's going on, or what might come your way.

I wasn't living in reality and hadn't been for a while. Maybe since I was five years old. Besides the physical survival in prison, I had to survive in my mind. In order to be locked up in prison it takes some mind manipulation: I told myself, "I can leave anytime I want, but I just don't want to leave." That way I thought that I was in control.

I kept myself distracted so I wouldn't feel the negative emotions, the boredom and the reality of what I had done. And I was running from the emptiness inside. I had music, books, and boyfriends—sex. And I had my elaborate (non-sexual) fantasy life.

Fantasies of the governor or the president coming to the unit and presenting me with a pardon. Another fantasy would consist of winning hundreds of millions, or billions, of dollars and I would bribe the warden to give me my own cell with a TV and free world food. And I would buy things for the prison to make it a better place. Wait, I would just buy a pardon and then fix the prison from out there. And of course, I would take care of my family. Sometimes I would just fade out while reading a book and fantasize these things.

Then I would have my musical Glee-like fantasies. I was the star of these fantasies, and mostly they were directed towards whichever guy I was with at the moment. I'd sing, and dance in my cell, a love song if we were going along, but a break-up song if we were fighting. Music is life, and in here it could be used for more than a distraction. It could be used to express your feelings. And, "We can dance—for inspiration." Madonna said that in one of her songs. I wish the people would offer us an opportunity to go to the gym and dance to music. We all need to be able to express ourselves and this is one of the things that being in prison deprives us of. You can only dance so much in a small cell tethered to the radio by headphones.

Fantasies are a powerful thing, but they are dangerous to continue to indulge in and not fulfill. I continued to fantasize because it gave me a sense of control and made me feel good. Being in prison made me feel powerless and helpless, but I felt that out there also. I thought that prison just exacerbated how I already felt on the inside.

There is a prison hierarchy and it starts from the warden and trickles down to the inmate. When the warden gets on to the major, the major then gets on to the captain, the captain to the lieutenant, then to the sergeants, and the sergeant takes it out on the COs. Then the only one left for the CO to take it out on is the inmate. Inmates will take it out on the weaker inmate or they will give it right back to the CO. It is an ongoing cycle. And the cycle has no point, it does not teach the inmate how to integrate into society. It does not promote positive change in our behavior.

We obviously have dysfunctions in a social setting, or we would not be here. Coming here we have these problems, and we need help. But all we get is an authoritarian type of rule over us. We get thrown into mass incarceration, where the weak are eaten up and the ones "guarding" us are just as dysfunctional as we are—and some are criminal, they just haven't been caught yet. There is racism, from all races. There is "white privilege," and the black and Hispanic officers look out for their race also.

But over all, there is the sentiment that comes down the line and is permeated throughout the prison. It's palpable, and it says to us inmates: "You're a piece of shit and you don't deserve to live. You are worthless, and we can treat you however we want to, and get away with it because *nobody cares.*"

Thus, the prison becomes a crucible, and it crushes those who come behind its walls. Most get assimilated into the Borg known as mass incarceration. Because when they see that they are empty, they let the acceptance from the masses fill the void. When I saw my emptiness inside, I resisted the sentiment and the masses, in part because the masses had already rejected me. I was on the bottom of the prison caste system. I was a sex offender and gay. That is two out of the bottom five of hated inmates.

This is the bottom five:

5. Gays

4. Mixing of races

3. An inmate who steals from another inmate

2. Sex offender*

1. Snitch*

*These two are tied for first

And I did mix races too. As much as I would have wanted to be included in the safety, protection and identity of the masses, as most inmates do, I couldn't be. And once I noticed what the masses offered, I didn't want it. I set out resisting institutionalization, and when I became aware of the sentiment, I resisted that too.

The officers wore gray, and the inmates wore white. I lived on the line. I couldn't be with the grays, and the whites didn't want me. This put me in a unique existence. I was able to walk chameleon-like amongst the inmates, the masses, but the whole time I resisted the subliminal sentiment, not just the one within the masses but the one given to the masses from the whole prison system. Once again, just like in the world,

I appeared to be a part of it, while on the inside other things were going on—but this time they were not dark or devious things.

This being the case made all the difference when I had my *turning point*. It was so much easier to change my beliefs to what the turning point implemented, and live by them.

So many people have lost their identity by becoming one with the masses. When one loses his identity, he loses his purpose. And a person without a purpose is not even going to be aware that they have a problem, much less change it.

Coming to prison, I did not have a purpose, and my identity was based in sexuality. But I wasn't lost in the system. I just needed to push to be able to see higher than myself. My turning point provided this.

*   *   *

Ironies. I didn't even know what an irony was before Alanis Morissette came out with her song. Then I started seeing them everywhere. It's like my whole life was ironic. But I believe now that when you go through life trying to manipulate and control every outcome, that you force the irony. It's like Dr. Phil says, "We generate, in life, the results that we believe we deserve."

I didn't believe that I deserved ironic events but living the lifestyle that I was living, always trying to get ahead and feel good all the time, it was like reality spits it back at you and then you end up missing out.

I don't think that I missed out by taking the detour to the Briscoe Unit. By all appearances, it looks as if the timing was just right. I stayed on Briscoe for 2 ½ months and when TDJC administration figured out their mistake, I was transferred to the correct unit. But I kept wondering what if I got to go to the Walls Unit in January? I might not have ever met Elijah.

That night on Briscoe when the officer came to tell me that I was on the chain, I was very excited. I was going to the Walls unit. I think that if they did give us a choice then everyone would choose to be assigned to the Walls unit.

I left, and was escorted to the back gate. The next day was my twenty-fifth birthday and I would spend it on a bus and in transient.

The bus got there and I was handcuffed to someone; of course it was a fat person. With the seats on the bus, I would either be squashed against the window, or have to ride on the edge of the seat and be uncomfortable the whole way. But when we got on the bus, the driver told us that it would only be us fifteen all the way to Darrington. The bus seated forty, so the guy that I was cuffed to sat in one seat and I sat in the seat behind him. We sat with our backs to the window and our hands rested on the seatback between us.

We spent the night at the roach- and rat-infested Darrington, and were back on the road the next morning. The driver on this bus said it was almost two hours to get to the Walls unit.

Finally, we pulled up to the Walls unit. It was in the middle of a neighborhood in Huntsville, not even half a mile from the I-45. It seemed that all the other TDCJ units were way out in a rural area, far away from civilization. But when we pulled off the service road we entered an old neighborhood; cars parked at the curb, people doing what free people do, it was a very lived-in neighborhood.

Then we pulled up around the south east side of the prison and saw a long slab of concrete wall that had an opening and it looked like a stadium. On any Blue Bird bus in prison, you do not even have to ask; some guy will just offer the information.

"The Texas Prison Rodeo, defunct now," a guy started saying. "That place there was in a lot of movies. And back in the day inmates from all units would come here to be in the rodeo or to watch it. They drove them over on a bus."

The memory of my favorite movie, *Urban Cowboy*, came to mind. They'd showed this rodeo in it. It made me wish that the rodeo was still happening here, but as things go in TDCJ, the prison rodeo was cut.

The Walls unit is the Disneyland of prisons, or the state's version of Club Fed. They feed really well and they have TVs in the cells. It doesn't get any better than this. It is a minimum custody unit, but part of it is used as transient also. But even spending one night here you can tell a difference.

We got off the bus and out of the cuffs. The back gate boss took us into the small building to search us and our property. Then we were all led to a transient cell. When I noticed this, I began to ask the boss why, but he interrupted me and said, "Tomorrow you will see UCC, but tonight you will stay in transient."

I was put in a cell that didn't have someone in there already. I unpacked and made my bed, then lay down and was dozing off when I heard an officer yell, "Clear doors are rolling. Come out for chow."

I stepped out of my cell and looked down the run. There were about thirty-five to forty inmates stepping out of them at the same time. We were all in transient, some heading to other units across the state, maybe some were going home, or they could have been someone like me, being assigned here. We all just congregated around the door and waited for them to let us out for chow. Some guys were talking to each other but some were quiet and kept to themselves, like me.

A big part of my life was fantasizing. It made me feel better. And in times like these I felt very alone and there was always apprehension in coming to a new unit. And having a low self-esteem I always felt bad, so lusting and fantasizing made me feel good and in control. There are no boundaries in our fantasies, and I would fantasize about guys that were around me that I found attractive, and in my fantasies they would like me and accept me.

I didn't know anyone so I stood alone looking around, and fantasizing. My eyesight had worsened over the years, nearsightedness, and I had been provided glasses from the state. Thick black frames, like Buddy Holly glasses, sat hard on my nose. The glasses did not help my self-esteem.

I saw two black guys standing close together talking. One was taller than me, and the other one was my height, 5'8". They were both good-looking but the one who was my height had smooth dark skin and a face that grabbed you and made you look. The lust must have been evident in my eyes because the tall one noticed me looking and then the other guy did too.

In my experience the ones who notice 'the look' are in the game themselves. They walked over toward me, keeping eye contact as they came.

"What's your name?" the tall one asked.

"DJ," I answered.

"I'm Tre, this is Elijah. Where are you headed?" Tre, the tall one, said.

"I am headed here. I'll see UCC tomorrow," I told them.

"We saw UCC this morning; we are assigned here, too," Elijah said. "We are waiting to be moved now. You only have to stay one night on transient."

"That's good. Maybe we will be on the same wing." I said, smiling at them.

In the chow hall I ate with Tre and Elijah. The meal was good, but the flirting was exciting. When we got back to the wing we were locked into our cells. Then a short while later they were moved. I waved at them as they passed my cell.

The next day I saw UCC. And they were professional about their job; they didn't make me feel like scum because of my charges. They assigned me to the kitchen, and I left. I was starting to see that the bosses and administration that worked in Huntsville were more professional in their job than when you went to a unit far away.

Back in my cell I packed up and waited to be moved. When I moved, I ended up on the same wing as Elijah and Tre. The wing that I'd moved to had only two rows, labeled 33 and 34 row. The bottom row was 33 and I was assigned to the top row in 22 cell. A boss opened up the door to the wing and I began placing my mattress and property inside the door so that he could shut the door. Elijah and Tre saw me and came to give me a hand.

As I passed by the benches there were some inmates watching TV, but they had on headphones that were plugged into a box at the end of the bench. Besides the sound of dominoes being shuffled it was quiet for a prison. Whoever had thought of using headphones in the dayroom for inmates to hear the TV had been a genius. I wish that they did that on every unit.

When we got to my cell, I noticed that all the cell doors were open. I asked Tre and he told me the doors stay open all day except for count time and rack time (bedtime). With the TVs in our cells and the open-door policy, the great food, and quiet dayrooms it couldn't get any better.

"The boss only comes in here to count, and if you want to go anywhere you don't need a pass, you just go to the door and they will let you out," Tre said.

They told me once I got my property situated to bench next to them and I sat there and plugged my headphone jack into the box. Wow, I could hear the TV. I don't think you understand: on other units we can never hear the TVs because prison dayrooms are very noisy, each noise competing with the others to be heard. It truly was the little things.

When I sat down MTV was on, and I saw my three current favorite videos: Mariah Carey's "Always Be My Baby," Tony Rich Project's "Nobody Knows," and TLC's "Waterfalls."

The videos went off and Tre, Elijah and I moved to an empty table. Tre had been sent to the unit to take a vocational trade. Elijah was here for the SOTP program just as I was. He didn't look like he would be a sex offender but that's what he was here for. Actually, he said that in high school he'd led another student into the locker room and some guy from the football team had raped that student. But Elijah hadn't participated in the rape.

At one point Tre went up to his cell and then Elijah told me, "My homeboy likes you. He wants you to go to his cell while not that many people are here."

"You gonna hold jiggers?" I asked him.

"Yeah, go on up."

So, I went to Tre's cell. We did what we did and came down back to the dayroom. The three of us became good friends and were inseparable. But Elijah never asked me to his cell or to the janitor's closet at the end of Two row. Tre and I frequented there a lot. We also went out to the courtyard for rec. and the gym.

Elijah and I got lay-ins to SOTP. The infirmary building had about four or five floors and we went to the infirmary and took an elevator to the fourth floor, and it had offices and rooms for group therapy. Elijah and I had the same primary therapist, Ms. E. She was brand new, just starting in her career. Not only did she say this but you can tell because when I talked to her she gave you all her attention as if you were all that mattered in the moment. She seemed genuinely interested in me and my progress in therapy. I was sure that after being a sex offender therapist for a few years that she'd lose that.

Elijah and I both had our individual interviews with her and we were both placed in the same group therapy, which would meet later in the week. We went back to the wing and chilled. Tre was at vocation. After lunch we went to the gym and played one-on-one basketball. I was pretty good at one-on-one but I was no match for someone who had been playing a lot longer than the two years that I had.

My mother and grandmother came to see me. Contact visitation was in a small building that was on the rodeo grounds. I loved these visits but they were only two hours long and then I had to go back to my reality. We were allowed to hug at the beginning of the visit and at the end. We sat at a square table, the visitors on one side and the prisoner on the other. I held one of their hands in each one of mine. We talked about this new prison that I was at, and they brought me up to date with family matters. There were vending machines and I'd always get the chocolate candy bars that they didn't sell on commissary such as Reeses and Nestlé Crunch.

"When I get home, I'm going to make you some cookies and mail it to you," my grandmother would say.

I would have to tell her again, "Granny, you can't mail me food."

"Why?"

"Because they think there may be drugs in them."

"But I'd never do that. Don't they know that I wouldn't do that?" she'd ask, really offended.

"Yeah, well some people will do that so to solve the matter they don't allow anyone to do it." I'd tell her.

"That's preposterous!" She would eye the guards on the front door.

Then we'd just reminisce about old times. All too soon the two hours would be up and we would hug and say goodbye. These were the hardest times of my incarceration, walking back into prison after two hours of feeling a sense of family belonging and love.

The unit wasn't anything like the others where you had to stay on guard 24/7. It was better than Ramsey 2 because of the TVs and freedom. I caught a few frowns from older white guys, not just because I was gay, but because I was messing with a black guy. But I didn't care. I didn't owe them anything. But no one was gang-related and no one was going to risk a fight; they didn't want to get kicked off this unit. It was a live-and-let-live type of atmosphere.

Kitchen duty was okay; Elijah and I had the night shift. I was glad because now I could eat all the pancakes and peanut butter that I wanted. Don't ask me! It's a prison thing, putting peanut butter on your pancakes, but it's delicious. IHOP, don't get any ideas now. If you steal this you got to pay me for giving it to you.

Sometimes we would be on the serving line, other days we could work the scullery or the pot room. The kitchen sergeant wanted to rotate where we worked so we knew how to do it all. We had to stay in there the whole eight hours, from 9 p.m. to 4 a.m. During the times when there was no work to be done, we would sit and talk with the other co-workers.

Back on the wing we would get a couple hours of sleep and on Thursdays we would go to group therapy. One time in group it was my turn to present. I was doing the synopsis worksheet, where I talk about my initial victim that got me arrested. I had to describe the offense and the thoughts and events leading up to it.

Walking back to the wing that day I sensed Elijah act different towards me, but back in the wing I soon got distracted and didn't think much of it. He went to his cell to take a nap so I watched TV in my cell. *The Coal Miner's Daughter* was on TBS and I remembered watching it with my mom when I was little. It's weird how when you are apart from someone you love that you can feel a connection to them by watching something that they liked or hearing a song they liked. That happened to me a lot in here with my mom.

A couple days later Eli asked me to go to the gym to play some one-on-one. After a few games we sat down at one of the tables to talk.

"DJ, you gotta make a decision. Tre wants you to be with him only."

"I pretty much am, *we* don't do nothing, and there isn't anyone else," I said.

"But do you want to be with him?"

"That depends," I said, looking into his eyes. "I want to be with you."

His face lit up in that way people have when they find out that someone likes them. "For real?" he asked.

"Yeah, you are the one I wanted from the first day I saw you."

"Alright, it's me and you then. I'll tell Tre you chose me."

"Okay. Why have you never asked for sex?"

"It will come. I just like spontaneity. Planned things don't feel real to me," he explained. "The mood just has to be right."

I just kept falling for this guy. I was attracted to laid-back, and he was laid-back, and he was so cute. We were both twenty-five years old; his birthday was July 5th so he still had a couple months until he actually turned twenty-five, but it didn't matter. "You are so cute," I told him. He just smiled and we walked back to our wing. My only problem was that I thought I had to please him sexually to make him love me.

But over the next several weeks we grew close. I wanted to just be with him 24/7. And I know that sounds weird since we already worked the same hours, went to group together, and lived on the same wing. But now that we'd decided to be together, I felt that I needed to be with him constantly. I placed my self-worth in to him and his acceptance of me. I had expectations in my mind for him without telling him. And when he didn't meet those expectations, I took it as an insult to my self-worth. I had intense, strong feelings for Elijah that I called love, but it was really co-dependency. I was selfish. I felt these feelings for him as long as he made me feel loved. When he didn't make me feel loved I had to "fix" it but I always made it worse. Instead of giving him space I became more clingy.

I think that my clinginess is what caused us to never have any sex. It was a turn-off for him. I believe he had some feelings for me but I never gave him a chance to show it spontaneously. But he didn't tell me to get away from him and every moment possible I was with him. And I equate my feelings for him being what, in the end, gave me the greatest gift in my life—my turning point.

We were in group therapy, and that day we had been given a question by the therapists and we went around the group and everyone gave their point of view. That day Ms. E. asked us, "How do you think that a victim feels after they have been assaulted?" The answer revealed if there had been an internal change of our belief system.

Later, after group we walked back to the wing and went to Eli's cell. During the day the wing was practically deserted with the others at work, school, and so on. I would hang out in his cell until count time. He put it on VH1 and put the headphones on but I could hear the song he was jamming through the headphones. It was Coolio's "1, 2, 3, 4."

He took the headphones off and I said to him, "Your answer to the question was wrong, ya know. You didn't know how a victim feels." I was sitting on his bed and he was standing in front of the toilet in the small 6' by 9' cell. I'd become great at reading body language in prison but even a blind man could have sensed his response. He went rigid and I felt the tension and ambience change. He reacted like a child being scared and recalling being hurt. He looked at me and asked, rhetorically, "I don't know how a victim feels?"

Then he went on to tell me that from age seven to fourteen his cousin had molested him. How it started with 'touching' and then escalated to oral sex and then penetration. He told me that after his cousin would leave that he would bathe in ammonia and put ammonia in his mouth to get the feeling of his abuse off and out of him. "Don't ever tell me that I don't know how a victim feels."

I was panicking on the inside. I heard the count horn which meant the doors were about to shut and I couldn't get counted in here. But I had to fix this. I stood up with my hands out to hug him but he put his hands up in a "*stop*" motion, still standing rigid. I heard the boss yell, "Clear, closing One row."

I looked in Eli's eyes and I said, "I'm sorry." And I slid out the closing cell door with barely inches to spare.

I had enough time to run up to my cell before the officer got there to shut Two row. As the door slammed shut, I sat down on the floor just staring at the wall. There were millions of thoughts going through my mind, but the greatest of them was that instead of thinking, "Poor me, how will I get him to love me?" I made an instant correlation: the way he had just described how he felt at being molested was exactly how my victims must have felt. Is how my victims feel. It was not love. It was sick, disgusting and torture. I was just like his cousin and if I didn't change, I would escalate also. Those past therapists had been right. Oh my God! All the stuff I had learned and had been taught came back to me. It all fell into place. I saw myself in a true light and I didn't like myself at all. How could I have hurt all those children and "believed" that that was love? I was sick. What was wrong with me?

I could see how dangerous it was to fantasize without having boundaries, because I shut off any inhibitions that I had by focusing on the fantasy. And over time the result was that I could engage in such destructive behavior because I conditioned my conscience to *not* alert me to such behavior. I drowned it out with my misplaced focus.

And how could I use normal English words to describe such a tragic, harmful, heinous act against other humans? I was sure this was just the tip of the iceberg because I remember a therapist saying one time, "If you knew the truth about your actions then you would kill yourself." I had barely scratched the surfaced. But that was a start. This was a big slap in the face. Now I was resolved in heart and mind to change the horrendous belief system I had.

I did a 180° turn around. Two things that SOTP taught and that were now my life line was: "Word Association" (new terminology) and "Fear Hierarchy." Before, I had never stopped my mind from thinking whatever it wanted. There were not any boundaries in my mind and those deviant fantasies were a well-grooved and often-used pattern in my brain. I learned that our thoughts are transmitted like an impulse, passing from one neuron to another through a process called the synapse. And there were not any stop signs on my synaptic avenue. It was like I had trained or programmed my mind to fantasize about children. So I had to yell "*Stop!*" in my mind every time a fantasy came and then immediately use the new words: rape, torture, pain, force, and so on, and use the fear hierarchy where I would pair, in my mind, what used to give pleasure with something that I feared. This process will begin to train my mind to associate those new words with the deviant fantasy, rather than with the pleasure I used to pair with it.

All of our lives we develop patterns of thought that become our belief system and you don't "think" it anymore; you just act upon it. For example, if someone enters the room you are in and begins shooting a gun, are you going to think, "I'd better get down so the bullet won't hit me"? No, you already have in your belief system that a bullet will hurt you so as soon as the gunman enters and begins to shoot you get down and hide behind something.

It's crazy because we can, over time, make ourselves believe things that are *not* true. "Oh, he loves me," says the woman whose husband beats her, as she keeps going back to him. And, over time, her definition of love becomes a husband who beats her up. We see it on the news or in movies but we don't understand why she keeps going back. It's because her belief system has been corrupted. I equate our beliefs system to an operating system. A lot of us are still running on MSDos. Hey, the world is at Windows 10 now! Time to upgrade.

Ask yourself, when you watch a movie, who do you root for? The majority of us—even in prison—are rooting for the good guys, the hero, the cop, to win, to defeat the bad guy. And all those bad guys have corrupted their belief system in some way. Art imitates life. And we want the good, we want the world to be better, we want to correct those bad beliefs.

At the end of *Divergent*, the book, the main character says "The human conscience can excuse away any evil, that's why it's so important that we do not rely on it." (paraphrased). But I say that if we examine our consciences daily and feed it the truth, that we can rely on it.

This is what I was up against. Every time that gunman entered the room, I had to force myself to go against the grain and stop believing that the bullet would kill. I was tenacious with this. I kept getting shot, but my goal was to get to the gunman before he could pull that trigger. In reality I was that gunman and my life was a destructive force with potential to kill. And I had to put that gunman down.

I was constantly upgrading my definition of what love is, and this was like trying to teach myself not to breathe, as the bad definition was so ingrained. And I knew that I was the bad guy and that I was all alone, fighting insurmountable odds. I was empty inside, but in that emptiness, I saw that I didn't want to be the person that I was—I didn't want to hurt anyone anymore. And in that I had hope, and I knew that on the inside I had a smidgeon of a 'good guy' to root for, and I so wanted him to win. My very life depended on it.

I began to internalize, right away, the things that I had intellectualized before. I began to feed my conscience the truth; it was like GIGO—"Garbage In, Garbage Out." I used to feed my conscience garbage and lies. Now I was feeding it empathy, morals and values—the truth.

In an earlier chapter I described the Criminal Offense Cycle and I explained that the Deviant Fantasy Phase is the most important part of the cycle. It is the fantasies that drive a person to commit the act (criminal offense). The therapists told us that 98% of a sex offender's life is sexual fantasy, and that a lot of the time they are masturbatory fantasies, and when you pair the pleasures of the orgasm to the deviant fantasy of a child, that is a very powerful connection. And for the sex offender, in his fantasy he is "receiving" love, acceptance and everything is going his way so he feels powerful and in control. This creates the delusion that the fulfillment of his fantasy is the only way to meet his needs. There is no one to confront this irrational belief because no one knows about it.

It made sense then to stop my fantasies and associate pain, fear and torture with them. That's where I started. I didn't completely understand that at the moment when I was sitting in my cell staring at the wall. I just came out of a small part of my denial and knew enough that I didn't want to be that person anymore, and I had to change the association of my fantasies. I had always known, but now I was highly motivated to do so. The insight came later after continuous hard work, never letting up. Every time a fantasy arose, I would stop it and use word association and fear hierarchy; I didn't care how many times an hour that I had to do it, I stuck to it. It began to work. I would put a negative connotation with the fantasy and soon, over a period of time, the deviant fantasies began to abate.

A therapist told me that there is a difference between an "impulse thought" and a fantasy. Everyone has impulsive thoughts, but a fantasy is when you "go along" with that impulse and began to put your thoughts with it. This helped me immensely. I went from overwhelmed to being able to differentiate between the two. And now I have control over what I choose to think. I can stop the impulse when it comes. I have trained my mind to stop it and my corresponding feelings to the impulse is now "disgust." I have changed my beliefs about it; I no longer believe that it is a pleasure or love to molest a child. That old synaptic route in my brain now has "*No Through Traffic*" and "*Dead End*" signs on it (emphasis on dead). It's just not used anymore, that old thought pattern and belief.

* * *

When the cell doors rolled back open when count had cleared, I went back downstairs and to the door of Eli's cell. He was lying in his bed staring at the wall. "Are you okay?" I asked him, still not going in.

"DJ, let's take a break. Just give me some space, okay?"

"Okay," I said in a small voice, walking away. I couldn't contemplate what horrors he was re-living. What I reminded him of. How was he gonna get space when our schedules were the same? I was the exact opposite. I needed (wanted) to be with him 24/7. I was still battling the definition of love.

At work I attempted to stay away from him. My life, my self-worth was shattered because it was all placed into him and he wasn't there. I would walk over by him occasionally in hopes that he would call me. I was devastated. I needed him to validate me as a person.

A couple of days later, at work, I spoke to Elijah, asking how he was doing, but he didn't speak back. I stayed out of his way on the wing, and when everyone saw that we were not together all the guys started coming onto me. I was surprised. I talked to them and hung around them to get my mind off of Elijah. I told them that right now I was too heartbroken to think of being with anyone else. And Tre still talked to both of us, he just stayed neutral.

But that day at work when I was talking to Elijah, one of the kitchen sergeants came to us and he said that he had a prophecy for us. We already knew that he was a Christian minister, but today he had a word for us from the Lord. He said, "Which one of you likes choreography?"

Caught by surprise, I raised my hand; ever since I'd been in that play I'd fallen in love with dance and choreography. "The Lord knows what you like and what you think, don't ever doubt that. But God is calling you to him. He hasn't forgot about you. He loves you." I don't remember his "word" for Elijah, because I was floored with what he told me.

I was living in sin and I knew enough to know that God didn't hear sinners. But could he, in the midst of my sickness and sin, have choreographed the meeting of Elijah knowing how I would feel about him and how because of that feeling I would gain true empathy—and connect it to my victims—when he revealed his abuse?

At the time, I didn't remember that when I first came to prison, I had prayed for Him to deliver me of this sickness, and that a while later I had that dream about me being the tornado and I how I came out of it and went to a safe place. I didn't make that connection at this time. But maybe God did hear the cries of our heart and He answered them. But right now, this was a part of the process, and it would all come to fruition later when I got more pieces to fill in the whole (or hole in my heart).

*   *   *

I kept busy and tried to keep my mind off him. I was tenaciously working on changing my beliefs, thought patterns and associating disgust with those fantasies. I kept waiting for him to call me. He had told me he would call me when he had had enough space.

I ate alone at work. He sat with some friend of his. And then it happened. He called me. I looked up and he waved me over. I practically ran. I approached his table and then he turned to the guy sitting there and pointing at me, said, "You see, that's obsessed." Then turned to me and said, "Okay, you can go. I just was showing him what obsessed was."

"No, Elijah, you can't just do that and just tell me to go," I cried.

The sergeant yelled for us to get ready to go to work and everyone began taking their trays to the scullery. I pulled Eli's sleeve to keep him back so I could talk to him.

"Let me go, DJ," he said.

"But you can't just play with my feelings like that. Calling me when you know that I've been waiting for you to call me and you were just playing games," I told him and he began walking to the scullery.

"DJ, you're just making it worse," he said, walking closer to the scullery.

I pulled his shirt sleeve again to stop him and began to say, "It's al—"

The next thing I knew I was on the floor. I don't remember being hit but the side of my head was pulsing and hot. I looked up and he was standing at my feet and he lunged towards me and I just kicked him in the chest to stop him from attacking me when I was down. I kicked him a couple more times, and then all the officers and rank ran in.

"Break it up. Break it up!" they yelled. One officer pulled him one way and another jerked me up. They placed us against the wall and put handcuffs on us.

As they escorted us out of the kitchen there was a lieutenant and a captain was coming towards us. The lieutenant looked at me and asked, "What's the fight about?"

I had the presence of mind to say, "It's just horseplay that got out of hand." Because if they found out it was "crazy ex-boyfriend is obsessed with lover and won't leave him alone," that was a straight kick off this unit. We might barely make it if it was just horse play that got out of hand. Just barely.

They escorted us to the infirmary to get checked out. He went to one room and I was in the other. The lieutenant went to him first. Then he came and asked me again: "What was the fight about?"

"Sir, it's just horseplay that got out of hand. It will be okay."

"He says that you were in a relationship and that you broke up and that you won't leave him alone," he yelled.

"It was horseplay that got out of hand," I continued to say, looking down at the floor.

"Let me find out it's some gay s____, I will bury you under this prison where God can't find you," he yelled. "Lock them both up."

*   *   *

In lockup he was two cells down from me. I was in 1-03 and he was in 1-05. We got locked up just after 3 a.m. and we'd already eaten breakfast so we went to sleep. I was woken up the next morning by someone yelling, "It's Cinco de Mayo celebration!" Yes, we got locked up on the morning of May 5th. The guy yelling was some Hispanic in his cell down the run. Even though we were in our cells we knew when they were bringing the meals. A boss came by opening the bean slots, another boss brought a tray carrier with the trays of food in it. A janitor brought a Cambryo with juice in it. All this made distinct noises and everyone knew when it was chow time in lockup.

"It's a Cinco de Mayo celebration," the Hispanic kept yelling.

"Yeah, yeah shut up!" someone else yelled.

Even in lockup we still got the same food as everyone else. And every holiday the food is always good. They gave us each enchiladas, Spanish rice, and refried beans, a piece of cake and a pineapple empanada.

After they picked up the trays and shut the bean slots, I heard Elijah call my name. "DJ," he said it quietly so as to not put everyone in our business.

"Yeah, what's up?"

"I didn't want to do that to you but you pushed me," he said.

I didn't care that it wasn't exactly a "take responsibility apology," I was just glad that he talked to me at all. "It's okay. I wouldn't leave you alone. But why did you tell them the truth, I tried to tell them it was horseplaying and…"

"I know, I know but at the moment I was mad and I just told them why. Sorry."

"We are for sure going to be shipped off the farm, unless the program saves us." I said.

The next day we were both escorted, in handcuffs, to the SOTP offices and we talked to Ms. E. separately.

"Mr. Jones, what happened?" she asked me.

"Ms. E., Elijah and I are or were in a relationship but we never had sex or anything. But when he told me about his own victimization, that really helped me see the truth of what I did and I really don't want to do that anymore."

"That sounds like ya'll had a good relationship. But from my understanding they are going to transfer both of ya'll to different units."

"Can't you keep us here? I mean the program," I begged.

"I'll talk to Mr. M. to see but I'm not sure. If security says you have to go, our hands will be tied."

*   *   *

Disciplinary cases are graded either major or minor depending on the severity of the rule infraction. Our cases were graded major. Any fights would garner a major case, but it's the scuttlebutt behind it that would cause the captain and the UCC to either go light or strict.

This was 1996 and overall the TDCJ officials were antigay and they had to prove it by being hard on those who were revealed. Besides the standard cell, commissary, and rec. restrictions the captain dropped my line class to a line 1 (this effects how much good time I earn a month) and he took 380 days off good time that I already earned.

When I went to UCC they demoted me to medium custody. I was moved to a cell where the unit had medium custody inmates waiting to be transferred but we still worked and did the same things until we caught the chain.

Elijah went to a different building and was placed in transient status. Then he got into another altercation and went back to lockup. This time UCC put him on close custody. I still was assigned to the kitchen and got to see Elijah when he came to chow. He was civil towards me but I could sense a difference. I no longer had his heart. Then I was sent to another unit.

PACK 2 UNIT

—◇○◌◌○◇—

1996-1998

"Thank-you, Thank-you, Disillusionment."
-Alanis Morissette

Pack 2 unit, Nacogdoches, TX. Renamed O.L. Luthor unit after somebody important. Units are named after former Governors. I think they ran out of Governors so they started naming them after former directors of the prisons, because there are so many prisons in Texas. I heard someone say that they should just put a fence with concertina wire around Texas.

It's hard to call a unit something new when you've been calling it Pack 2 for so long. When I got there even the officers said Pack 2, so I called it Pack 2.

This was a telephone-pole-styled unit. One long hallway with dorms on both sides. There were twenty dorms, numbered 1 – 20. I would spend two years and one month there. If I'd had to leave the Disneyland of prisons and come here, this would be like Six Flags. There were no cells. It really takes a toll on a person to go willingly into a locked cell. But being in a cubicle dormitory it was freedom. And I freely gave myself over to adult homosexual encounters.

But first the inevitable UCC. The captain looked up from reading my file and asked the Chief of Classification, "He's in medium custody? Why did they send him here? This is a minimum custody unit."

All rhetorical questions but she answered, "I don't know. Why do they do anything? Just give him back his minimum. You're not gonna fight anymore, are you, Jones?" she directed at me.

"Uh… no, ma'am, I won't."

"Put him in the kitchen. Next!" the captain bellowed.

And I was back on minimum custody. Crazy. That was all they had to do back on Walls, but this unit seemed okay. I got assigned to dorm 6 bunk 6. I wrote my mother and told her what unit I was in and gave her my new address. Usually when you get off of work your boss will bring you to the showers. But for people who did not work they have a shower time set aside for them. I heard them say to get ready and I asked my neighbor what that was for and he told me. I went to the showers because people watch to make sure that you keep good hygiene. And a hot shower just felt good after a long day and a long bus ride.

There were several benches, locker-room style, where you got undressed and put on your shower shoes, got in a queue to exchange dirty clothes for clean ones, then went to shower. There was a boss stationed in there to monitor and to let workers out the backdoor.

The shower area was on the left at the back, in an open area with six rows of shower heads, eight heads on each row. I found an opening and showered. There was no rush. I still had those Buddy Holly glasses and I had to take them off to shower but my nearsightedness wasn't so bad yet that I couldn't engage in some voyeurism. I didn't want to let others see me doing this because I didn't know how this unit was towards gays yet. I just kept my head down and discreetly gazed around. There were so many fine guys there. The song that came to mind was "It's Raining Men."

I was still determined to stop each and every impulse and fantasy of a child. I was resolved in my mind to do this with every bit of energy that I had. But I also decided that I was going to totally reinforce and cultivate my adult relationships.

I've shared with you my preference for black guys, and this unit had them in abundance. But a lot of them were in gangs—Crips, Bloods and Gangsta Disciples—there was even a big group of an Islamic faith, a lot of gang members could get cut out of the gang by converting to Islam.

I tell you of the gangs because a typical gangsta was cut-up, muscular, tattooed all over, and there was just something about them that was so sexy. I was turned on by that gangsta look, and what is totally opposite of young boys? Exactly, a gangsta. I delved in and made myself at home.

I met a guy named Lil' D who messed around with gays. He was in a gang, but they didn't know his business.

Lil'D would help me get down and around on the down-low.

And the DL is needed. I was the only gay person that I could find right away. And by "gay" I mean my type. Not the straight guys who messed around while they were in here. But those straight guys I would soon find, and more than you would think.

*   *   *

I put in a request to see the unit psychologist. Although they weren't allowed to give SO treatment, I figured they could help me. I shouldn't try to renew my thoughts all by myself.

"Jones, come on back." The officer said, unlocking the holdover cage that acted as a waiting room for the infirmary. "Down that way second door on the left."

"I'm Ms. Sherman. You requested to come in to talk?" She was young, between twenty-five and thirty, black and had an approachable demeanor.

"Uh yes, ma'am." I began and told her my SOTP history and then told her about Elijah and the wonderful gift he gave me, "But of course I know that it was co-dependency but it felt like love, at least what I believe love is or was, but now he's gone and I know that I got a lot of work to do and I don't have no one to talk to about it, which is why I'm just rattling on now so I'll shut up."

She actually began laughing but it wasn't at me so much as, as she put it, "I've never had a client who so expertly diagnosed himself and knew that he needs help."

"I've been in a lot of therapy and group. Very intense and confrontational feedback. But when Elijah told me about that it shattered my defenses and it all became so clear what I needed to do." I told her.

"Well, Mr. Jones, It will be a delight to work with you. You can write an I-60 request when you want to talk. Our department doesn't do full time one-on-one. But as much as you request, so much I will lay you in, okay?"

"Thank you."

*   *   *

Everyone assigned to the kitchen is at first on 72-hour kitchen temp. I was called out on my second day to the kitchen. I signed the safety papers and was told to receive a job change that evening assigning me to a specific kitchen duty and shift.

That evening I got the job ticket saying I would be a line server on breakfast shift. I loved breakfast, not just the pancakes and peanut butter but biscuits and gravy and scrambled eggs too. I worked for two nights then got a job ticket changing me to first shift. I was upset.

I had decided to not hide that I was gay. It would come up in a conversation and I would say "I'm bi." This unit wasn't a gladiator farm like Ferguson. I didn't seem feminine, and only if you were looking for it could you tell that I had some "gay characteristics." (Even though I hated labels and stereotypes to convey things.) But there was not an overwhelming negative sentiment against me. The bosses didn't know. It seemed to be a best kept secret amongst the inmates.

Being in an open dorm where you walk by other cubicles to get to the front and back, the unspoken rule that you don't look in another man's cell or cubicle was highly respected. And if a guy was getting his "roll out" —a term for jacking off—if the boss lady was known for walking the aisles and watching, he would put his boot on the corner of his bunk and if you saw the boot, you would avoid going that way especially if the boss lady was in the wing. But I would walk up and down the aisle after she left just to see who would cover up or leave it out and let me watch. One guy left a kite to come over after everyone went to sleep.

Reporting to first shift, I soon found out why my shift had been changed. His name was Sam and he was the kitchen clerk. A clerk does all the paperwork for the kitchen captain. Sam had found out that I was gay and he switched me to first shift so that he could have access to me. Yeah, without asking or knowing me.

I was headed to the restroom and he must have seen me go in there because he followed me. Most white guys might get scared to look behind them and see a tall, bald, smooth mocha-color-skinned black guy behind them. I could tell he worked out because I could see the outline of his muscles beneath his shirt.

I smiled and he walked straight up to me and put his hand under my chin to angle my head up to him. "Let's do something," he said, with pretty white teeth.

"I just met you. Is it even cool in here? Someone might come in," I said.

"If I set something up that's cool, will you be willing?"

"Sure," and he left and I took a piss washed my hands and went back to the serving line.

After the lunch meal was over Sam and I were talking and he told me that he'd seen me on the rec. yard the other day and that he could tell that I was gay by the way that I was standing, "A lot of punks stand that way." he said.

"First of all, I'm not a punk. A punk is a turnout and I was already this way. And what way was I standing?" I asked him then it clicked. "Wait a minute, you're the clerk, right?" He nodded. "How did my shift get changed?"

"I was telling you that I saw you standing like this," and he stood and crossed his arms in front of his chest and walked back and forth, "so I knew you were gay, and I put you on this shift so I could talk to you."

"What? Don't you know I wanted to work breakfast shift, you didn't even know if I would mess around with you. Why did you do that? Don't just stand there with that smile on your face that makes it hard to be mad at you."

"Do you want me to change you back?" he asked.

"It depends," I said.

"On what?"

"You said you were gonna set something up?" Looking at him, he was looking at my arms which had become crossed, and I uncrossed them real quick.

"I'll tell you when it's cool." And he went back to work, smiling.

*   *   *

Lil'D was cute. He had the tattoos and I had never been with a red-skinned brother. The D. stood for his first name but he was also from Dallas. I loved my brothers from D-town.

"Oh, okay, I see. I am janitor in the Gym. On the days that I tell you that it's cool you just come down to the gym," he said, after we first met.

"How do I just get down there?"

"Just tell them that you are going to the craft shop. They don't know who all's assigned in there."

I told him okay. And he and I regularly would meet up in the gym. But it was cool because it was understood that it was just sex and no relationship, no feelings—just sex.

*   *   *

"Hey, I talked to one of the kitchen sergeants about you. There is an opening in the ODR. It's washing pots but it's a foot in," Sam told me one day. The ODR is the officers' dining room, where the food is prepared better and tastes better. The officers are supposed to eat the same meal that inmates eat, and for the most part they do, but the cooks always have some extra food that they have requisitioned and have on hand for certain officers.

"Jones," yelled a tall older kitchen sergeant. He was coming from the back into the IDR (Inmate Dining Room) where we sat before meal times.

"Yes, sir," I said, getting up from the table that I was sitting at with Sam.

"C'mon, follow me," he said as he stopped at a locked door that led to the ODR. "I need a pot washer in here. I'm placing you in here as your new job. Don't mess it up. Rodriguez, tell him his duties." He then left and locked us in.

The ODR is a privileged job. They don't trust just anyone with the COs' food. There was a waiter, cook, dishwasher and a pot washer. The ODR resembled a small diner. There were tables in the dining area, a cafeteria-styled counter, behind the counter a grill and oven and deep fryer, and to the left of that a small alcove for the dishwasher. Behind the oven was a wall separating the cooking area from the deep sinks; that was the pot washing area. Three sinks, the first soapy water, then bleach water to sanitize, and clean water in the third sink to rinse. All four of us were locked in the ODR. The front door was not locked, but we were not allowed to use it. There was a phone on the wall by the grill and one out in the dining area. During count time the lieutenant would call us and we would tell him our housing then step out into the hallway so he could put his eyes on us from the sergeant's desk down the hall where the lieutenant did his count from. Other than that, we were not allowed to call anyone. If it rang, we could answer by saying "Inmate Jones ODR."

Rodriguez was the cook, but he told me what my duties were. I met the other guys and they offered me some food that they had prepared for the workers. Privilege. The type of people who work in the ODR are clean-cut; no gang affiliation. They couldn't exclude people with tattoos or they wouldn't have much of a selection to choose from. But you had to be clean and have good hygiene.

This was 1996, and if they, meaning any of the bosses, had known that I was gay I most certainly would not have been allowed to work in there. But right then, they didn't know. And because of that, if I went to the bathroom they didn't get suspicious of anyone going to the back at the same time. Sam took advantage of this.

The thing between Sam and I was, in my eyes, a work thing. I am glad I didn't live on the wing with him. He was obsessive. I know; very ironic considering how I'd acted with Eli. That was different, as he'd started it without asking me, kinda, if you get my drift—the whole breakfast shift to first shift thing. Being the kitchen clerk, Sam was allowed in the ODR and he would come in and talk with me as I worked.

He appeared as a strong person and he was big and muscular, but there is more to strength than just the physical side. I thought he was strong on the inside, because in prison you have to learn to give off that impression—the masks we wear—or you would be run over. Sam was hurting inside, and he was alone and lonely. Having lost his mother a long time ago he'd depended on his grandparents, who came to see him regularly. When Sam first came up for parole his grandparents were even more excited that he may be coming home. The visits increased and they had everything ready for Sam at home.

When Sam got the answer from his parole board his grandfather came to visit the next weekend. After hugging him and then sitting down at the table his grandfather asked if he got the answer yet.

"Yeah, papa, I got a ten-year setoff," Sam informed him.

The smile faded from his grandfather's face. He stood up and walked out and Sam never heard from them again.

"Oh my gosh, how do you deal with that?" I asked him.

"Day by day," he replied.

"I don't know what I'd do without my mom, or if she ever died while I was in here, I think I'd go crazy," I said.

Maybe, that was why he is obsessive when he was with someone; he wanted to make sure that they didn't leave.

*   *   *

Mail call is easy, on the dorms. An officer would bring in the mail and place it on a table and begin calling out bunk numbers. In the pile of mail we could see magazines, newspapers, letters and so on. The mags like *Playboy* and *Penthouse* were sleeved in black plastic, which is what the company did to respect your privacy. But in prison we all knew who received these magazines and the guys would always tell the ones that got them, "Hey, let me see that after you." A lot of people got these magazines.

The officer pulled a magazine out of the pile that was sleeved in a gray plastic, and called my bunk number. "Right here sir, #594835."

He handed it to me. "Hey DJ, let me see that after ..." This one guy began. As I looked at him, he clicked and then said, "Oh, never mind. I don't want to see that."

I wasn't even sure yet, because I didn't know. This was the first time I'd received a magazine at all. I went to my bunk and opened it. It was the gay magazine *The Advocate*. After the boss left a lot of the guys came to my bunk. Curiosity will burn if you don't satisfy it.

"They let you get a gay magazine? For real? What's on the cover?" one guy asked.

"Just flip through the pages, DJ, but don't stop on nothing."

"I guess gays can do what us guys do with a *Penthouse*."

"Man, that's a trip."

"Hey ya'll I only get this for the articles," I quipped. They all burst out laughing as they walked away. But a few later asked me to let them see the mag, "But way way on the down-low, DJ. And if you tell anyone I'll beat you up." Joking but serious.

*   *   *

Prison goes on. Day after day, week after week. I read in a book by one of my favorite authors—he had his main character in prison and had him say, "I don't know why there are clocks and calendars in a prison counting days and months when these guys got years and decades." That was in a Jack Reacher book by Lee Child.

This unit was great in the overall rating system. Time went by fast. When you are on a unit that has cells, once you go in that cell it's like time slows down. You have to constantly distract yourself so reality doesn't set in. Some guys go crazy. They can't handle it. But in an open dormitory there are constant stimuli that your eyes and ears take in and your brain ponders. There is a constant noise that permeates the atmosphere. At rack time that white noise is dampened just a little, but it's there. Awake, in our sleep, always buzzing into our brains. But days were just going fast. Fast is good. I had mandatory Supervision Parole in October 1997. Which meant that when my flat time and good time equaled my sentence (fifteen years) then by state law they had to let me go. It was mandatory. On a fifteen-year sentence I would end up doing a little over six years. The thought kept me going, well, that and the sex.

"Where is the cook?" the kitchen sergeant came in with a bag in his hand.

"He had a medical lay-in, Sergeant," I told him.

"You're up. The Warden wants fried green tomatoes," he said.

"The movie?" I asked. Why was she coming to the ODR for a movie?

"No, she wants us to make her some fried green tomatoes. She brought the tomatoes," he said lifting up the bag.

"You mean it's a real food that you eat? I always thought it was a movie."

"Oh my gosh. So you can't cook?" he asked, exasperated.

"No, I got this. I can do it." *How hard can it be?* I thought.

"Here, get it all prepped and I'll go get a knife to cut the tomatoes with."

We had to check out the sharp objects. We couldn't just leave those in a drawer.

As soon as he went to the back to get the knife, I grabbed a couple of cookbooks that were in the ODR and found one on vegetables. I opened up to the contents page and there was a section on tomatoes. Thank God it wasn't long and complicated. It was similar to making chicken-fried steak. *I got this.* I grabbed two shallow small pans and into one I broke eggs and into the other I poured some flour. I measured some salt and pepper and stirred it into the flour. I turned on the deep fryer.

When I heard the keys in the backdoor, I replaced the cookbook back on the shelf. I grabbed the tomatoes out of the bag and put them in a bowl and took it to a sink to rinse them off. The sergeant was looking at my preparation and he said, "We might just get this done."

"Oh, you didn't have any faith in me?"

"Well, you thought it was a movie," he said.

"I was pulling your leg, sir. I can cook, bake and wash the dishes." And I could, but I'd always thought it was a movie. I'd never seen actual green tomatoes before. But I was glad I could build his trust in me. I sliced the tomatoes and he grabbed one, put it in the eggs, then the flour, and put it in the grease.

"I'm checking if we should double dip or not," he said when I looked at him.

"I'm a fan of the double dip, sir; chicken-fried steak, chocolate-covered peanuts and these."

He used a pair of tongs to retrieve the lone tomato and put it on a plate to cool. "Yeah, the crust looks a little thin, we will double dip," he said, then using the tongs he cut the tomato in half and ate one of them, and pointed at the other and then to me.

"That's delicious. I like this, I hope she brought enough so we have extra," I said. We'd just got a new head warden, a woman. But she hardly made appearances, so I never saw her. She would have others come get her a plate of food from the ODR, or send in something for us to cook. Some wardens were hands-on, others remained out of sight and let the rank run the prison.

I had always seen the cook call a laundry boss on the phone and ask what he wanted for lunch. I assumed that it was okay for all of us to do. I did not realize that it was just something between them, that the cook had built up the trust.

I had written to my grandmother and asked her the recipe for chocolate peanut-butter oatmeal cookies. They were a favorite of mine from the free world. So I had got the cook to requisition the ingredients for me. One Saturday I had made them and I put them on a cookie sheet and let them get hard in the fridge.

The cook and another guy had visits and it was me and the waiter doing all four jobs. Before lunch I called the laundry boss and asked him what he wanted for lunch today. I told him about my chocolate oatmeal cookies. He acted strange and then told me he was going to eat whatever was on the menu.

I didn't think too much about it but several minutes later the kitchen sergeant came in and asked me if I'd used the phone.

"Did you call the laundry boss?"

"Yeah, just like we do every day, to ask what he wants to eat," I defended myself.

"Well, he called to report it. Now you can't work in here anymore."

The kitchen bosses had recently found out that I was gay and they had regretted placing me in the ODR. Now I had given them a reason to fire me. I got assigned to the scullery. Which to some is the worst job, but I like it. When inmates are finished eating, they deposit their tray, spoon, and cup through a slot in the wall. There are different positions in the scullery but the main one was the washer. It's a fast-paced job and if you are not fast the trays pile up on you. We had to grab the tray, bang it on the slop barrel to get rid of the leftover food, spray the tray off (which sometimes required scrubbing) then place it in a tray carrier to run through the machine that washed and sanitized them.

Once they saw that I was fast, they paired me and this twenty-six-year-old black guy named Terry on the washer. Terry was straight, he didn't mess around, and he didn't have a complex about talking to me. I soon found out he loved '80s music as much as I did. We began to play a kind of trivia as we worked.

"Name eight songs that have the word 'Love' in the title," he would challenge me.

"Name six songs with the word 'boy' in the song lyrics," I'd ask him after I answered his correctly.

Sometimes we'd just sing Prince's songs as we worked. If you didn't know Prince's songs then there was just something wrong with you.

"What do you think he meant to 'masturbate with a magazine'?" I asked Terry.

"I'm not going there with you, DJ," he said, laughing.

Some guy who was cool with the laundry boss came to tell me that the laundry boss thought that he was being set up so he'd been forced to report the call. But I had already retaliated in the only way I could—through the inmate grievance system. I wrote a grievance against the boss for requesting food from the ODR that was not on the menu. Which was a violation of rules for officers.

Surprisingly, he admitted to doing that on the grievance. I found out later through mutual friends that the reason he did that was because he figured if he pled guilty to the first grievance then they will believe him on later grievances when he denied them.

Looking back, I think this guy was a dirty boss but I don't know for sure.

I continued every day to *stop* any fantasies of children. I was steadily working on the inside. And I knew that I had always been promiscuous, but my aim in doing it now was to reinforce being with an adult. On this unit I was truly free in that no one knew of my charge. I was received as if I had a respectable crime. And even being openly gay, I was not overtly rejected. I hung around black guys and I would always say things that were risqué or suggestive and everyone pretty much just tripped on me, but in a good way. I was wild and blunt and I tried to make people laugh. I would shoot a slug towards the real straight guys, and we would all laugh at that.

That became part of the excitement, to flirt with someone who would never give in. But there were guys who did not join in the banter or even talk to me. This one guy was so hot to me that I had no words to say, I actually got nervous if he walked by. He was a Crip and his body was like it had been sculpted, and was tatted up. His demeanor and body language told me he did not mess around. He stayed true to the Crips constitution. He walked by one time without a shirt on and he saw me looking and he said, "Two soups to look," and kept walking. Soups were ramen noodle soups, which were a quarter apiece. I wanted to go get a whole case (twenty-four—$6.00) and give it to him, but he might have taken that disrespectfully.

Then there are those guys who might not be good-looking, fine or built, but have sex appeal. Such was this guy named 'South Dallas.' He would talk to me and I would flirt with him shamelessly but he just didn't mess around that way. But I was accepted by all these guys, and I had sex with some of them.

There are stories behind tattoos and I got real good at identifying people by their tats. I could tell where a guy was from by how he acted and I could tell what gang he was in by his tats. Brothers from Dallas and Houston just acted different.

I favored Crips over Bloods, but I described myself as an equal opportunity gay person. I hung around Crips and they shared with me the history of the Crips and how it got started and I liked the color blue better than red.

These guys would discuss everything with me. Later on, even that guy who told me that it cost two soups to look at him—we became close. The two years I was on that unit were very pivotal in my rehabilitation. I had good days and bad days, but overall, for these two years, everything seemed to click and go a certain way that drove home my ability to relate to other men.

I'm not saying that I became normal because of this. I still had thoughts and irrational beliefs relating to men. And having multiple sex partners was not helping in that area. I was motivated by acceptance and comfort but also to reinforce that I could have adult relations that met my needs but not harm others.

And don't think of me as one of those white guys who try to act black and talk slang. I was still as White Texas as they get, but I became fascinated by this culture. I listened to rap so I could be relevant, and I subscribed to *Vibe* and *The Source* magazines. And the fact that I did *not* grow up being taught prejudice helped.

At first I was the only openly gay person. I think, too, a lot of guys liked that I wasn't all girlie, but I had some feminine characteristics that balanced things. Other gays started arriving at the unit.

There were two gay bosses. One was an overweight white guy who was very strict because all the inmates made fun of him. The other was a black boss that worked in the shower area.

On my dorm I told the guys that I was going to pull the white guy. He worked 6 a.m. to 2 p.m., and there aren't that many people on the dorm in the morning. He would always go cubicle to cubicle inspecting the empty ones, taking contraband and so on. I waited until he was on the row across from my row and I held the magazine in front of my face, like I didn't see him, and exposed myself to him with the other hand.

He came to my cubicle to pretend to "inspect" it but he just watched, the first time. After that he was never strict with me and he would let me do things that he normally would never do. But we never talked about the things we did. I think that was his defense, so a person couldn't blackmail him. The other gay boss in the shower area was alright, but we never did anything with each other. He'd overhear me flirting with a guy and later he'd tell me, "You are brazen with it, Jones."

"It's the only way to get what you want," I'd reply.

Mostly, we would talk about different guys. And if there were hardly anyone in the shower area, I'd tell him that me and this guy were going to do something at the back of the showers. He would hold jiggers for us. Ironic, a guard holding jiggers. Then he told me that there was a job opening for the back dock position. He told me to send an I-60 to the captain. Every time I saw the captain at the desk I stopped and asked for the job. He told me that he would give it to me. I kept waiting. One week. Two weeks. Three weeks. I finally saw the captain again at the desk and reminded him about the job.

"You didn't get the job?" he asked.

"No, sir."

"Give me your ID," he said, getting on the phone. "Assign this guy to the back dock job: Jones #594815." Handing me my ID card back he said, "You should get it tonight."

"Thank you, sir." Persistence, patience and P's and Q's is what it takes. I'd gotten another job that was a privilege. There was no direct supervision. My boss was the guy who worked in the shower area. It couldn't have been a better job. I kept the back dock clean and did everything that was required so as to keep the heat off from the rank. My boss would let different guys out the back dock that I had told him about beforehand, so we could mess around. There were blind spots where even the towers could not see.

The Crip who told me "two soups"—he worked in the kitchen back dock and we began just talking about everything. We discussed our family, our upbringing and how in prison we all wear these masks. That most guys always had to be hard and couldn't show weakness.

He looked at me. "But with you, for some reason... I can tell this to with no worry. Why is that?" he asked.

"Because you will beat me up, Two-soups," I said laughingly.

"I never told you it would be two soups to look at me. And you know I won't beat you up," he said. "Tell me why that is."

"Look, I'm no threat to you or your manhood. It's easy to open up to me because our positions are established. You don't have nothing to prove to me therefore it makes you comfortable to tell me things that you otherwise wouldn't. But that doesn't take nothing from you, it is actually a strength. And women love vulnerability in a guy," I told him.

He told me about this kitchen boss lady who was in a relationship with one of his locs; he had the opportunity to be with her but he didn't want everyone in his business. He didn't want to get busted for that. It felt really good to be trusted with that information but in prison you really don't want to know all this stuff because if they ever get busted you are going to be a suspect for telling. In this situation only he knew that I knew and I wasn't about to go bragging about it.

But a lot of guys opened up to me like this. I guess, in here, we all need that someone we can talk to about things. Prison is a horrible place and deprives us of the very thing that makes us human.

* * *

With the new job I was moved to 15 dorm. This dorm was mostly filled up with guys who worked days. Mostly they worked in the stainless-steel factory.

Because of my reputation I had no trouble fitting in, and I knew a few guys from the rec. yard or gym. I would play three-on-three B-ball, but I wasn't comfortable playing full court five-on-five yet.

There was a guy diagonally across from my cubicle named Jack. He was a Gangsta Disciple. He was light skinned, he wasn't all that attractive but he was funny and he flirted with me. I was still learning things, but a lesson right off the top—don't do anything with people unless you make sure they don't become possessive.

It started out innocently enough. Lying down in my bunk I could see him lying in his bunk and it started out as a show. It slowly progressed after rack time when other people were asleep.

I was able to do sexual things and not get any feelings attached. But some people weren't. I didn't want to be with him but in his mind, I was, and he was very jealous.

I was glad that Parole called me out to the office. "Come in, sit down Mr. Jones, You are being released on Mandatory Supervision Parole and we need to get the address that you plan to parole to," the unit parole officer told me.

I could not believe this. The day I'd been longing for since June 11, 1991. Would I really go home and wake up in my mom's house, my own bed and with no one telling me where to go and what to do? Dare I begin dreaming? Could I put down this mask I wore in here? Is this hope rising in my chest? He said mandatory so it had to happen.

I gave him my mother's address and phone number. Then a week later he called me back down and said that my mother's address was not approved because it was in a thousand yards of a school. Panic set in. "But this is my middle school." I complained. As if the fact that I went to school there would negate the requirement that I live a thousand yards from any place where children congregate.

"Do you have any other address that you can parole to?" he asked patiently.

I gave him both my grandparents' addresses and left. I was leaving in five days, so they were in a hurry to get this approved. I walked in to the parole office every day and asked him if he had heard back. Every day he told me no. "But no news is good news, right?" he said on the last day. That night I would be on the chain.

America, we need to take all those clichés and adages and throw them away. No news was bad news, as it turned out. We just need to stick to Murphy's law. I was in my cubicle at 10 p.m. I saw the boss man come in with the chain bags and list to tell people that they were on the chain. All my friends were in the doorway of their cubicles as the boss walked down the aisle, all awaiting my good news.

He stopped about five cubicles down. "Johnson, what's your TDC#? You are on the chain—pack your stuff." Then continued down towards me. I was so excited that it took me a minute to speak up when he passed by me without stopping. All my friends just looked at me. One enemy said loudly, "I knew you were lying."

"Hey, officer. Hey," walking after him, "Um, I'm supposed to be on the chain. I was in the parole office today and he said I'm leaving tonight."

The officer looked at his list and then back up to me. "Sorry, you are not on here."

My mind was racing. I couldn't imagine what had happened. The next morning, I waited until after 8 am and went to the parole office. I knocked on the door.

"Come in," a voice called.

"Excuse me, sir," I began.

"What are you still doing here?" he said and began pushing buttons on his computer.

"I'd like to know that also. They said I was not on the chain last night."

"Hmm," he said reading the screen. "Did you have some more cases in 1993?"

"Yes, but I went on bench warrant from prison and those three cases were a part of the original cases and I was given all my back time for them." I explained. I distinctly remember my attorney asking the judge on record and the judge stating "Defendant will receive all back time."

"Well, on here they have those cases beginning in Apr. 1993 which pushes your mandatory date back two years, to Sept. 1999."

"How can they steal two years flat time? They can't get away with this. It's not fair. It's not right. I got to go write my lawyer." Getting up to leave.

"Good luck, I hope you get it fixed."

I wrote my attorney and put it in the mailbox. That weekend my mom came to visit me.

"I can't believe they are doing this," she said and she pulled a newspaper article out of her pocket that she had cut out of the Dallas paper and folded it up in her back pocket to get past the guards.

I read it and it gave credit to parole for noticing that I was about to be let out too early and they fixed it. My attorney told the newspaper that it wasn't too early and that he'd be going to court to get this back time I was already given.

"I hope my lawyer hurries up. This was a big letdown," I said.

"Tell me about it. I was so excited; I had your room all ready and I was going to order a pizza and we were gonna watch all the old movies together," she said.

A mother's love. They should make it one of those Wonders of the World. My mom still loved me and she was excited that I was coming home. I wanted to go home so bad. This was one of the hardest visits, and then I had to go back in there, to prison. It was like turning myself in all over again. Sometimes I wanted to jump the fence and let them kill me. I hated the most how much I'd hurt my mom. In a way I thought being dead would stop her hurt. But another part of me thought it would hurt her worse.

We had developed a good relationship and I was honest about my gay relationships, although I didn't tell her how promiscuous I was. I explained to her about the wonderful gift Elijah gave me. She supported me because she knew that deep down, I wasn't a monster.

As I hugged her, I whispered to her, "I love you. Stay on that lawyers butt." Then I had to go back in here and play prison games.

*   *   *

I was still tenaciously overhauling my belief system and thought patterns. The tools that SOTP had taught me work very effectively when used over and over. You could make yourself stop liking chocolate and like liver instead. That's how much power we have within our brains. Before, I had always just *thought* whatever came to mind. What I had developed a taste for. That taste came over a period of years and with conditioning. Now, I could see some light, that maybe I could learn to control it rather than letting it control me. I was strongly motivated to do this for as long as it took, because I didn't want to be attracted to children. I didn't want to hurt them. Not anymore, not ever again.

I thought at the time that I had chosen children because I was not compatible to adults. I didn't know how to relate to an adult. During my offenses I saw myself as that little boy that didn't get to grow up normal, that didn't have close friends. Now, in prison, I was accepted by adult men. And not all of them through sex. A lot of guys were just friends and even sought out advice. I felt that I was perceived as an equal.

Yeah, I was still sexualizing things. That is unhealthy, both mentally and emotionally, for me, and I never stopped to consider if my actions harmed others. Until they did. I was thinking that we are all adults and if someone wanted to mess with a guy then that was their choice. I had an encounter with a guy and later on he began to avoid me. This really bothered me. My whole thing was about pleasing a guy so he would accept me. And now this guy wouldn't even look at me.

The dorms had a restroom section. On one side there were three toilets and a urinal trough. Across from them were about eight sinks and a mirror above each of them. One day this guy who was avoiding me was at the sink when I came in the restroom area. I approached him and asked him why he was acting differently towards me.

He looked at me and his look was conflicting as if he was struggling with some major issues. "DJ, what we did, well, that was my first time, and, uh, I feel bad, like guilty and every time I see you, I am reminded of it. I wish we never would have done that," he told me.

"Sorry," I said and walked to my bunk. I'd never considered that being someone's first gay experience could have an adverse reaction. I thought sex overrode negative feelings. That's how I'd started out, using sex to soothe me. But I saw that there was more going on here. At this time all I was able to internalize was how it affected me and I swore I would not do anything with anyone if it was their first time, because I didn't want to be the cause of them feeling anything negative towards me.

Everything is cumulative. All these things I was learning would become cohesive in the end. They had to.

*   *   *

August 1998

For the last eight months I had been in a relationship. I had flirted with 'Dre for a while. We had never been on the same dorm, and then he got moved to my dorm and we began to kick it. He asked me to be with only him. This stirred something in me. Here was someone who wanted only me. I liked that idea, and I committed to a monogamous relationship with him. I didn't know that I would leave in August.

We did everything together except work. He was in the fields and I was in the kitchen. But everything else, watching football, working out, playing basketball, we did together. When I was at Ramsey 2 a guy had showed me how to bring in cash money at visitation and I would get $20.00 bills from my mom and bring them back to buy a pack of tobacco from someone who was getting it brought in by a guard.

I did it again here at Pack 2 and gave the $20 to 'Dre to get us a pack of Buglers. We sold some but smoked a lot of them. We paid off the middle man and made a nice profit. The trick is to not put as much tobacco in each cigarette, so that we can make more cigarettes to sell. That was the game. We could get a hundred cigarettes out of a small pack of cigarettes. They sold for $1.00 apiece. It was a good turnover for $20.00.

Then came the day I was on the chain. I had been requesting to get back into SOTP and I was accepted in August 1998. This time I was sent to the Goree Unit.

GOREE UNIT

1998-1999

"No more victims."
-SOTP motto

I have read other books written by guys who have been in prison. Prisons in other states, prisons in other countries. And a few written by someone else with their account of their time in Texas prisons.

My story compared to theirs is quite different. At the time I entered prison an inmate sued Texas for a lot of issues. Ruiz vs The State of Texas. He won. A judge gave orders for the State to correct these issues or the Feds will step in and take over.

The State of Texas Prisons were in a transition state when I came in. The prison had lost the use of Building Tenders and put control of the prison into the hands of COs instead of other inmates. And that certainly helped change my experience. Or rather kept me safe. Also, it helped that I had the fortitude that I did, that I had developed from my childhood prison of abuse.

It's crazy how in the world I manipulated others to commit sex crimes. And in prison I manipulated others for survival and had sex for comfort. Prison is a conglomeration of a myriad of experiences.

Hardened criminals cliquing on someone for sitting in the wrong seat. Inmates paying protection, or joining a gang to avoid paying protection. Fighting at the smallest slight, but cleaning their cell and toilet daily.

I'm no match for these true con men, but I have maneuvered my way through this maze like a chameleon, picking up some things, resisting others. And survived. And on top of all that I learned the basics in life along the way. I made it with all my teeth.

There used to be a guy in county jail who yelled that all the time, "I did twenty years and I got all my teeth." I didn't know what that meant. I learned that it meant he survived without anyone knocking his teeth out. It meant survival.

Don't take from my story that prison, Texas or any other, is an okay place to be, because I didn't get beat up or killed. If I had been on close custody or even seg. I possibly would not have survived. In close custody and seg., it's the lowest custody levels. Inmates there have nothing to lose. It's a very dangerous, violent place. Rapes, fights, riots, stabbings, assault on officers, assaults all the time. It's horrible.

My experiences were a confluence of circumstances that don't happen all too often in here. It's an enigma. But again, I believe now that there was a Grand Choreographer ordering my steps unseen.

But on top of physical harm there is a more sinister sentiment that can be just as detrimental. And I told you before I have resisted this, but I began to see that it was deeper and more convoluted than I first understood. I could sense some part of it and I resisted it while at the same time ensconcing myself into another part of it. It was everywhere. And it was impossible to protect myself from it entirely.

Here I was getting rid of synaptic thought patterns that were harmful towards children, while at the same time developing unhealthy patterns that concerned sex and relationships with adults. That one was my choice. At that time, I couldn't or wouldn't have been able to break free from sex to soothe me, but I was determined that I would make sure that children were not involved. Period.

Prison takes so much from the people who live here, and even the people who work here. I don't believe that it has been by design, but it has developed, like I said earlier about the prison phrases and terms that are used, and over time it causes dehumanization. But I didn't realize what was happening to relationships in general. The way that we treat each other and the way we interact with bosses and the administration, nurses, doctors, teachers, and so on.

I believed at first that I was fitting into the masses, just so I might survive. That I was not giving my whole self over to it. I was staying in it but not a part of it. But it began to affect me. Just like a spy who becomes a double agent, I stopped seeing myself as above the masses and began to see myself as a part of it. I wasn't a spy. What I'm saying is that in the beginning I thought I was better than the masses because I was not a criminal, in the traditional sense, but that I had a sexual psychological problem. However, over time as I interacted with these people, I saw that we were more alike than not, it was just that the difference was in which crime we'd committed, and the motivation behind it.

I came into prison thinking that the bosses were the good guys and that I had to show them I was "not like these other guys." But they revealed themselves and they became the common enemy. At first, I did resist the assimilation into the masses, and the sentiment that came with it. But I learned that there are degrees to it. I stayed above part of it while still in it and took on some of the identity. Being on Pack 2, where no one knew about my crime, enabled me to settle into this identity. It was a dog-eat-dog environment. It was, "I give you one I want two back." We treated each other like this. Give? What's give? "Give me never got nothing," is a saying in here. And even in relationships it was, "I don't mind giving you yours but I want mine." This was how prison was. If you tried to be "normal" then you got run over, used and abused. We were oblivious to the belief patterns that we were developing. We lived in the moment. This was our reality and we were living in it.

*　　*　　*

Goree Unit, Huntsville, Texas. You can see it from I-45. When it was first built it was a women's prison, but now it was a men's. It was part dormitory and part cell blocks. The cell blocks were transient cells.

Everyone that came to prison went through the diagnostic tests and interviews at the Diagnostic unit (later renamed the Byrd unit) but some people were sent to Goree to finish the diagnostic process.

The SOTP was split between three units back in 1995. I had started at Ramsey 2, went to the Walls unit, and now I was going to the Goree unit. When parole took my 1997 mandatory discharge date, it was backed up to September 1999. I had one year to go through the program before I got out. Maybe less if my lawyer got the flat time back that parole had stolen from me. But either way, there was nothing that they could do—I would be discharged to finish out my sentence on parole.

The first thing I noticed when I got off the bus and into the unit was how quiet it was compared to the constant noise at Pack 2. And it felt like time was slower here because of it. As if noise made time go by faster. That was weird.

At UCC. there was a person from SOTP in there along with the usual: warden, chief of classification and someone from another department. I was told that I was put on this unit for the SOTP program and that having sexual relationships would not be tolerated. I was placed to work in the kitchen and that was it.

At the front of the unit there was a housing area that had four levels. Not four tiers as you see in the movies, but four floors. There was a door on ground level that entered into an alcove with two sets of stairs on each side. Beside each stair was a cell block. From the ground level there were two more levels going up and one level going down. The bottom level contained transient cells and lockup on one side and seg. and protective custody on the other side. It was rumored that David Ruiz was in PC here, the guy who sued TDCJ and won. He needed protection from inmates and bosses.

The level on the ground floor had transient cells on the left for men and transient cells on the right for women. Yes, real women. They had to stay somewhere while they were on medical chain to go to the hospital. The next level was more male transient, and the top level on both sides were the SOTP program and something new that SOTP was trying—a therapeutic community (TC). Which meant that since everyone who was in the program lived on the same wing, that therapy didn't stop when we left group. But we held each other accountable with TC rules and TDCJ rules. We had meetings on the wing where the therapists came over and spoke to us and we had inmates that were at the higher level in SOTP to monitor what we watched on TV. They actually had a large piece of cardboard and would cover the TV with it if there was a sex scene in a movie or something similar that might reinforce our deviant lifestyles.

Oh boy, yeah, I was not looking forward to this. My best friends, D and L, were here in the program. They had been successful in getting legislation to approve that prisoners could get castrated—voluntarily. That had passed in 1996 and they were getting all the details figured out, and the requirements.

"Ya'll are crazy. You got to change your beliefs," I told them. I also shared with them about my turning point and how I had been tenaciously reinforcing my new beliefs every time I had a thought towards children.

"Tenaciously, huh? I like that word," D said. Then gave me his usual spiel about combining the castration with corrective beliefs.

"Whatever. They may never have my nuts. But I am happy for you guys. You set out to do this and you have accomplished it. Amazing," I told them.

"Now I'm working on stopping TDCJ from being able to release information to the media about us or anyone," L said.

This was the first time that I had been in group and was actually serious about the work. I shared with my group about my turning point and I really participated in group. When I presented my paperwork, the therapist made a note of the internalization that I had done.

But, as always, I found ways to be sexually active. I worked in the kitchen and there were willing guys everywhere. Even on the wing there were guys who were looking and we found ways to do things.

In the T.C. if anyone broke a rule, we would hold them accountable by writing a "ticket" on them. The person who wrote a ticket and the person he wrote it for would sit at the table and "confront" them in front of everyone. The confronter would state, "Mr. Jones, I feel disrespected about your rule breaking," and would list the infractions. He would have to state feelings and thoughts, because this was to teach you how to communicate appropriately also. Then I would say, "You are right and I will get on top of this negative behavior by…" and list how I was going to get on top of it.

Then the therapist would ask everyone, "Family," because we were to consider ourselves a family. "Do you think Mr. Jones is sincere?" And mostly everyone would say "Yeah."

But if you said no, then you had to state why you didn't believe it.

Later on, on Friday afternoons, we would have what we called "Fun Fridays." We put on skits, someone would sing a song, recite a poem or whatever talent someone had. The idea was to learn to have fun with your "family."

Anytime we got up to address the "community" we had to say "Family, I'm Jones, and…"

Everything in the TC was geared toward teaching us how to be productive in a community; there were posters allowed in the day room walls and we had a creed, motto, and other things we said together. The creed was our goals. It was a list of things we were gonna have *no* more of. It contained something like: "No more manipulation, no more lying, no more blaming," and then ending with: "*No More Victims!*" which we yelled.

We called any of the guys who had no shame in their sucking up to the therapist a "Junior Therapist." I still believed that my only problem was with children and I was already fixing this. So, I was going through the motions in the TC. But I loved everything I could consume in therapy.

The SOTP still had a Treatment Team. This was not done in the TC but in one of the offices and several therapists would be in there to confront a person on something they had done. Sometimes it might have been a comment or action, and of course we had to go before the Treatment Team before we completed the program.

There were two weeks until I was discharged and I was sitting in the Treatment Team for my exit interview.

"Mr. Jones, I knew you at Ramsey 2 and I have to say that since you have been back this time there is a remarkable difference in you; I just hope that it truly is sincere."

"Mr. Jones, you know your offense cycle. You know your hotspot and what could cause a relapse. But you have stated, 'I won't relapse', and that concerns me. You have to admit that you *could* relapse and always be aware so that you do not."

Several others gave similar statements. Then the director Mr. Mable concluded with: "Mr. Jones, I knew you at the Walls unit, and there is progress documented," he began looking over my file, "Tell me something, are you still sexually active?"

They did not call this the hotseat for naught. Everyone was looking at me. I wanted to lie. I wanted to 'successfully complete' this program that I'd begun in 1992. I thought if I told the truth I wouldn't get that. But I felt that I needed to tell the truth. "Yes sir, I have been for the last year. I am trying to reinforce my compatibility with adults. I don't desire children anymore." Which, I thought, was the point.

"Mr. Jones, you can't change something while you are still doing it. You have irrational beliefs about sex. But I'm going to give you a successful completion. Use your tools and don't come back. Good luck, Mr. Jones," he told me.

In the meeting in the TC I was presented with a certificate, along with some other guys who had completed. But a week later I was taken on a van to Walls unit, where everyone is released from. My date was September 30, 1999, and it was September 29,1999.

WALLS UNIT

1999 - Going Home?

"You can't go home again."
-Thomas Wolfe

O n the Walls I was placed in a transient cell. Later that day I was called to the Parole office.

"Mr. Jones, you are being released tomorrow. You are going to the Wayback House in Dallas, a halfway house. Right now we are going to go over the paperwork and place an ankle monitor on you."

I did not know that this was abnormal. I had never left on parole before. But usually, you get your monitor at the halfway house. After we finished the paperwork, fingerprints, and so on, he told me, "Tonight at 1 a.m. you will be pulled out of your cell, so bring all your property with you. Internal Affairs of TDCJ will be driving you halfway to Dallas where another pair of IA will pick you up and drive you the rest of the way. There is a lot of media interest in you and we are trying to get you there without them plastering it all over the news."

"Okay, can someone call my mom because she is supposed to come down to pick me up." I had already sent home the things I wanted to keep. I wanted to walk out of Walls with nothing except the clothes they give me. I thought my mother would pick me up and I could go home. But it seemed that parole was not through playing with my life.

"We will contact her today. Okay? So don't worry," he told me.

Yeah right, don't worry. I couldn't even be released like a normal inmate. It had to be special. But I tried to stay focused. I was being released. I'd go to this halfway house and then get my mom's address approved.

At 1 a.m. my cell door opened. An officer yelled, "Jones, step out with all your property." All I had was my toothpaste and toothbrush and deodorant. I wasn't bringing anything else with me. I stepped out with this in my hand.

An officer yelled, "Where is your linen and blanket? You have to bring that out and place it in this buggy."

I kept telling myself, 'I'm going home. I'm going home." So, he can yell all he wants. I grabbed the linen and blanket and put it in the buggy and an officer escorted me to the Parole office and was given some clean clothes: 1979-style pants and a Multicolor dress shirt. "It's only temporary," was another thing we had been told in therapy. So, I kept telling myself this. My mom would bring me some clothes. It's okay. It's okay.

"Jones," an officer yelled once I was dressed. "TDC number."

"594835," I recited for the last time.

He looked at the picture and looked at me and said to the two IA officers, "Yep, it's him. He's all yours."

"This way, Jones," one of them said.

I followed them out of the parole office and we took a right and there was the front door.

"When you go out take a right down the stairs and we are parked in a white car with the State of Texas Seal on the door."

With no handcuffs I opened the door and walked outside. It was dark but there were street lights and the street was deserted, but had cars parked up and down it. I walked down the right stairs to the sidewalk to the car they had indicated, and waited for them to let me in. I was surprised when they told me to sit in the passenger seat in the front and one of them sat in the back.

On the way to the halfway point, they asked me questions about Goree unit. They wanted to know about dirty bosses.

"Sorry, I was in the SOTP program and the bosses didn't get close to us like that and I wouldn't know if they were anyway."

They eventually left it alone and we pulled into a gas station at the halfway point.

THE HALFWAY HOUSE

Twelve Whole Days

The same white car with the State of Texas seal on the door, and I was seated in the front again. It had to be policy. Not much on conversation except to ask how long I've been locked up and what I planned on eating first. Then I saw the green building on the Dallas skyline. It was close to 5 a.m. and it was lit up and then I saw Reunion Tower. Home. I knew Dallas hated me. But I loved Dallas. I missed my hometown. The Dallas skyline is beautiful at night.

The halfway house was on Stemmons Freeway and to get there you had to get off Central expressway and onto the service road. We were not on Central, we were on the I-45 and they took some back roads to circle around the halfway house and get on the service road.

In between a couple of buildings beside the halfway house we saw a lady and a camera man. The guy driving told me, "That's why we went this way, to avoid the media."

Then everything went quickly. He pulled into a hotel parking lot, but I knew it to be the Decker County jail. The old hotel had been made into a county jail years ago.

"Why are we here?" I asked.

"This is the halfway house, get out and go with that guy waiting for you," he told me.

There was a white man in blue jeans and a button up shirt walking towards the car, but I saw a guy in a suit by the entrance to the county jail and when I got out, I walked towards the suit dismissing the guy in blue jeans.

"Jones, this way," the blue-jeaned guy said. I turned towards him and followed him up about ten steps to a small booth. I heard a click and the gate popped open and we walked through a roundish-oval patio. The hotel was a highrise building but it had a wing shooting out from the left side and that was the halfway house. A wall of cinderblock encircled the patio that had given privacy to the patrons when it was a hotel. Rumor had it that Marilyn Monroe and the Beatles had stayed there. Over the cinderblock wall, as I followed the blue jeaned guy across the patio, I had a perfect view of the green building and the Reunion tower; it was like it was right there.

"Why did you go towards the jail when you got out of the car?" The blue jeaned guy asked me.

"I didn't know this," indicating the halfway house, "was here. I saw a guy in a suit and I thought he was there for me," I explained.

"That was an inmate in the work-release program, he was waiting to go to work. I'm John King, head of this parole division," he told me as we neared the building. I saw a double glass door and some people staring out at us. But Mr. King walked around to an enclosed stairway that went to the second level.

We walked up these stairs and entered the second floor. To the left and front there were offices. To the right there was a hallway with doors down the left-hand side and a line of tables on the right along the wall. I was ushered into one of the offices and although it was a small office, there were three desks. I counted ten people and three were white, the rest black (not including King and I).

Mr. King began talking: "This is Jones, everyone. Jones, these," and he pointed to six of the black people and said each of their names, "are your parole officers. This is Al, who owns the Wayback House, Lisa, his assistant, and Carol and Walter are case managers." Al, Lisa and Carol were white. Walter was black.

Al spoke up: "David, I bet you are happy to be out. And we will help you get situated. I know that this may seem overwhelming but just take it a moment at a time. Lisa, my assistant, is not usually a case manager but I assigned you to her since this is a special situation. You can talk to her, Carol or Walter if you have any questions or concerns. We will take care of the paperwork for the halfway house later after parole is finished," he explained. It was like he was treating me as if I were a human being.

"Mr. Jones," King was saying, "we, as your parole officers, have a job to do. Our boss from Austin is going to be here in any minute to talk to you. We anticipate a lot of media coverage and we recommend that you do not give them any interviews…"

"I don't want to talk to any media." I asserted.

"Good. Now between these six parole officers, you will be escorted everywhere that you need to go. One of us will check on you every two hours. You cannot leave the halfway house. But your family can visit you. Where is your property?"

"I have my toothpaste and toothbrush and deodorant here," pulling them out of my pocket, "I have already sent my other stuff home from the prison."

"I'm glad to see you pull that out of your pocket," parole officer (PO) number one said. "You wouldn't believe how many people don't bring that with them out of prison." She was in her mid-20s and was the lead PO (I don't remember their names so I will just refer to them as PO #1-6.)

A tall black man in a three-piece suit walked in the door. All the PO's straightened up in their seats and Mr. King stood to shake his hand. I guessed this was the parole big wig from Austin.

Pointing at me he asked Mr. King, "Is this him?"

"Yes, sir."

"Mr. Jones, I just drove up here from Austin so I could tell you how serious this is. There have been death threats against you and you have been all over the news. Our main concern is the children." He stood there looking down at me. He had one hand in his pocket while the other one he moved up and down to stress his points. "Myself, King, and the others, what we are going to be always asking ourselves is: 'What about the children,' 'What about the children.' So you got to walk a fine line or we will send you back. Remember, it's all about the children."

It was 5 a.m. in the morning and this guy had come from Austin to tell me this. I was being assigned six POs to escort me, and check on me every two hours. I'm sure that they have never done this in the history of parole. But I was still in shellshock and didn't quite realize what he was indicating. He was indicating that I was sitting here seething in some sort of monstrous evil desire and that I was going to attack the first child I saw. I can probably be glad that I didn't realize what he meant or they would have sent me back to prison right then and there. But I did understand a little so I did tell the room full of people, "Sir, something happened to me in prison and I had a turning point, and I don't want to hurt children or anyone anymore."

Again, his hand began moving up and down, "That's what we are thinking, 'What about the children?' We will be watching you, Mr. Jones."

Had this guy even heard what I said? I could see him practicing his speech all the way up from Austin. He never saw me as human but as a monster who couldn't change. But I didn't see what I was up against. I thought that now that I was free that I was entitled to that freedom. Maybe if I'd had a different perception, things would have turned out differently.

*   *   *

Later, Lisa invited me into her office; Carol was in there too.

"Now that all those parole people are gone, we will tell you what's really going on. There have been death threats against you. But the real reason that they are doing this to you—all the POs and checking up on you, the escorts—is to save face with the media. They get flak for letting you out early…"

"But this ain't early, it's mand—" I interrupted.

"We know, but the public doesn't know, so they lash out at Parole and Parole thinks if they do all this that that makes them look good. And did you get the feeling that he thought that you were just going to assault the first child you saw?"

"Yeah, that was scary. 'What about the children' makes me wonder about him," Carol said.

"So, this doesn't happen to everyone?" I joked.

"Nope, you are the first that I've seen treated this way. Our first infamous resident," Lisa said. "But that's why Al put me as your case manager, so I can make sure that no one tries to write you a BS case. Yeah, you can get write-ups here, but they will come to me first and I won't tell Parole if it's some minor petty case. Al don't like what they are doing to you, he thinks that it's BS. As far as it's up to us we will make sure they don't try any slick stuff to send you back to prison. But you will have to not give them a reason to either."

"Oh, I don't plan on it." I told them.

"We are going to put you in room one. It only has three other people in there and you make four. You should get along with these guys and they won't cause you any problems. We provide hygiene items and bedding. We can give you clothes to wear. Your family can bring you things: food, TV, clothes, and so on."

Lisa told me the meal times and other information. "Usually, residents have to pay 33% of their checks to us, but they won't let you get a job, so that don't apply to you. Residents who do not have a job are required to help out around the halfway house, doing different jobs. That does apply to you."

"Give me a list of the people who will visit you so I can put it out in the booth. What's the first thing you want to eat?" Carol asked.

"Pizza," I said.

They gave me bedding and hygiene products and I made up my bed. The other guys were older than me and they were nice. One guy had a big TV and a Nintendo 64 with a Super Mario Brothers game and he told me that I could play it anytime.

Finally, by myself. I went to the halfway house residents' phone and called my mother. She was excited and so was I. I told her where I was at. And she asked me what I wanted to eat. I wanted pizza very badly. But I didn't want anything to delay her coming so I told her what I wanted from Jack in the Box: a cheese burger, four tacos, curly fries and a chocolate shake. Jack in the Box has the best chocolate shakes, in my opinion. I told my mother that I was allowed my own TV and she had a small 13" TV with combo VCR slot. She brought this to me with the

VCR movies that we had watched growing up. *Urban Cowboy*, *9 to 5*, *The Coal Miner's Daughter*, *Back to the Future*, and she brought me some movies that I hadn't seen.

She also brought my grandmother and sister with her. There is a difference between hugging someone in a prison visitation room and out here in the free world. My grandmother's arms were like home. We sat out on the patio at one of the picnic tables, we talked, I ate and we just enjoyed the moment of being together, free.

I had asked my mother to bring me one other thing. A pack of cigarettes. She brought me one of my stepfather's packs. I had stopped smoking in '95 except for an illegal cig here and there. But I think that wanting to smoke had more to do with rebellion then being addicted. Like, the prison said I couldn't smoke and now that I was free I was going to smoke. We were allowed to smoke on the patio but not in our rooms.

My brother came to see me and he brought me a Discman and some CDs to listen to: Matchbox 20, Alanis Morissette, Counting Crows. At night I would sit on the patio alone with the head phones on and look up at the lit-up Dallas Skyline. I never felt freer than in those moments. It was like I was transported to somewhere far from prison or halfway houses, as Matchbox 20 sang "Push" and the Counting Crows sang "Mr. Jones and Me" and "Round Here." My girl Alanis belted out "You Oughtta Know."

There were a lot of things that I ought to have known, right then, but with my sense of freedom I felt entitled and as an entitled person, well, you couldn't tell me anything. What was wrong with me? Why couldn't I grasp the feeling of that hug from my grandmother and that moment at the picnic table and build off that, value that? Desire that above all else? But no. I was selfish and I wanted that control of my life back. (As if I ever had true control of it.)

This is another thing that prison will do to you. Don't get me wrong, *I* was selfish and I made the decisions to do what I did and I accepted responsibility for it. The thing about prison is that when you are there, you are essentially powerless. You are told when, where, and how to do something and at what time. Then the state hires unstable people who lord their sense of power over us. It's a strange macabre dance. But when I try, in prison, to take the reins of my life, I'm sure to get in a wreck.

And it goes back and forth. Not all officers usurp their authority, but enough do to sate the definition of insanity. And, we the inmates really believe that we are in control, at times, and this delusion is harmful. Just as harmful as any fantasy not based in reality. Because I got out under a false sense that I could manage my life, I fell flat on my face.

*   *   *

Every two hours some PO was checking on me. At the Goree unit, I got in with some guys who were working out, and I began working out, I ran that big rec. yard and took my turn at the reps. At the halfway house there was a "gym," and I would get there in the mornings to keep up with a workout.

The intercom barked: "David Jones, report to the office." So, I walked down to the office and Mr. King was there. "Where were you?" he barked.

"In the gym, working out," I told him.

"Oh, the one place we didn't look on the [surveillance] cameras," he said, chagrined. "Two of your POs are coming to take you to some appointments. Be ready," he instructed.

"Yes, sir."

Three came and picked me up. I sat in the back seat of the white car with the State Seal on the door. PO #1 was driving and she turned on the radio. Cash Money was on, Juvenile singing, "Back That Ass Up." #1 changed the channel real quick and looked at me in the rearview mirror saying, "Oh... you can't hear that."

"Really? I love BG Juvie and Lil Wayne. I jammed them in prison, what's the difference?" I told them. "Look, since you all are gonna be around me all the time, I want to get something straight. Okay?" I said. I explained to them about my turning point, and how much work I had been doing to change my thoughts and belief system. "I don't want to hurt anyone anymore. I promise you that."

And we pulled up to a red light and there were some kids on the side walk with their parents. And I looked the other way. I heard #1 say, "Wow, he won't even look at them. That's different from—" and she said some name. I assumed that she had been around this person and he'd ogled some children.

PO #3 looked at me and said, "You know what? When I read your file, I believed that you still wanted to reoffend, but being around you, I can sense a difference."

"What made you think that? What's in my file?" I queried.

"You told the person who interviewed you in prison that when you get out of prison that you want to work at McDonalds," he said.

"Wow, do you see what's wrong with the parole process? Do you know when I said that? I told parole that in *1993*. They interview you one time and never go back and update the file. So I've been judged by that one interview all this time? Amazing," I said, floored. "But I'll tell you all honestly, when I told them McDonalds, it wasn't with children in mind. It was because I know the job inside and out and the fact that they are always hiring. But, now? I would never seek a job where children frequent. I will not put myself in a high-risk environment."

After that, my PEs, Personal Escorts, changed towards me. We talked like equals. They treated me like a human. They brought me to the police station so I could register as a sex offender. They took me to the Probation office. Because back in '91, as a part of the plea bargain, I'd also received two deferred-adjudicated probation sentences of ten years. They ran concurrent with my prison sentence and I still had two years left on them.

So along with parole officers I had a probation officer. But I also had to go to the court and meet with some lady there. She was real nice and had a great sense of humor. Probation had a more intense SOTP that I was required to go to, and parole had an SOTP group that met at the halfway house.

The SOTP group for probation met in the same office in downtown Garland. The therapist there ordered me to have a penile plethysmograph test done, which he just so happened to administer. A PPG is similar to a polygraph test in that it measures a body's response. Though a PPG measures arousal to certain audio/video stimuli.

I objected to this vehemently. They wanted to show me pictures of children to see if I was aroused by them. The test showed pictures of male and female children to adults. The adults are naked, the children are in underwear or bathing suits. The audio is listening to rape stories. Both coercion and force, stories.

Do you see what is wrong with this picture? If I'd had these pictures, I would go back to prison but the therapists were showing them to me. But what is worse is the method. It's like taking a sober alcoholic or a rehabbed druggie and giving them their vice and saying "Does this still get you drunk or high?" It's ludicrous.

The therapist shared the results with me. "You showed arousal to teen males, elementary age males, adult males, and female teens."

"What? That's crazy. That test is wack and should be outlawed," I told them and we continued to argue about it. But there was a lot that he wasn't telling me.

"Mr. Jones, you are compartmentalizing and I want you to stop right now," he exclaimed, in a voice that I didn't want to give a rebuttal to.

I hadn't been to group with this guy yet and we were not seeing eye to eye. I didn't have a good feeling about this. Parole SOTP was a joke. There was *no* structured program. We sat around the table and talked. I was used to a confrontational setting. One where we presented paperwork.

* * *

One night I called my mom and asked her to find a pizza place close to the halfway house and she ordered a pizza. She called back and told me that it was on the way. She paid with a credit card over the phone. I waited by the gate for the delivery.

There were other guys hanging out on the patio. I sat and listened to them talk. I noticed this black guy looking at me. But didn't interpret it as a bad look. It was interest. He was cute, but until that moment I hadn't been interested in sex. But don't go to the press just yet, it's just that the freedom so overwhelmed me and I was giving it my full attention. But now his interest woke that up. I wanted to be wanted. He was an adult. Why not?

I shared my pizza with him and we sat on the patio and talked. He was thirty-one and his name was Martin. He knew my name from the news but I had to tell him that I went by DJ.

Over the next few days, we would sneak into his room and fool around. He could leave every day but I wasn't allowed to leave. The halfway house and Parole required that you go out every day until you found a job.

He left every day to go do that. The halfway house provided three bus vouchers a week to its resident.

Martin didn't have a serious crime so he was allowed to leave the halfway house to go to a store or fast-food restaurant frequently throughout his stay. I would give him money to go get me food or a pack of cigarettes, and he didn't mind doing that. Every time he looked at me it was like he was examining me, giving me his undivided attention. I didn't mind. It felt good to have someone like me that much.

"Tomorrow I gotta go back to this one place and they will let me know if I got the job," he told me as I lit my cigarette. We were on the patio. "I hope I got it so I can get money to buy me some clothes," he said looking down at the clothes the halfway house had provided for him.

"I like your clothes," I told him. It must have been two hours because Mr. King came in the front gate and called my name. I finished my cigarette as I walked towards him. "Who is that?" he asked.

"Oh, Martin? He's a resident here," I said, like you can take him or leave him. And we walked into the halfway house. He just asked his normal routine questions and I was free for another two hours. This could get old real fast.

VIOLATION

Back in County

"Go to Texas on vacation. Leave on probation. Go to prison on a violation."
-Common adage amongst inmates

The next day was October 12, 1999. I'd been out twelve days. I was in my room alone on my roommates Nintendo, fighting the Super Mario brothers' enemies. It was about 2 p.m. and Martin came in and said, "I got the job, I got to be there at 9 a.m. tomorrow."

"That's great. Let me finish this level and we will go smoke a cigarette." I paused the game when I finished, and as I walked by him, he reached out and caressed me. That changed my mood for a cigarette. He was sitting in a chair by one of those beds about eight to ten feet from the door. I stood in front of the door and pushed my sweat pants down. He watched me and then the door opened and hit me in the back, I quickly pulled up my sweats and turned to see Mr. King.

He didn't see anything, it was a smooth cover up, but he was suspicious.

"What's going on? Where do you live?" to Martin. Martin told him his room number. "Ge out of here, I'll talk to you later."

Turning back to me, "What were ya'll doing?"

"Talking. He said he got a job and we were headed outside to smoke," I explained.

"Jones, don't make me get you on one of these BS rules. Tell me the truth."

I remembered how it was in prison, usually a CO just wants you to tell him that he is right. I figured Mr. King was like that. So, I told him the truth. He put his hand on his forehead then ran it across.

"I've got to call my boss. Don't leave this room," he said to me.

"You're going to report this?" I exclaimed.

"Yeah, I got to," he told me.

"But you just said if I told you the truth that you wouldn't get me on a made-up rule violation." I was pleading with him.

"No, I said if you don't tell me that I would get you on something," and he left.

When he came back, he told me that his boss had told him to violate me. "But don't call your mom just yet."

"Why," bewildered.

"I'll let you know when you can call her."

I really needed that cigarette now. I went to the patio. Martin saw me and came over. 'What did you tell him," he asked.

'I told him what happened..." I began.

"Why did you do that? It was our word against his. Damn, man."

"I thought he was gonna let it go, he said he was gonna make up something if I didn't. Now he put a blue warrant out for me. I'm going back. You?"

"No, I'm not. I'm being wrote up for being in your room. That's all," he told me.

"That's real fair. Look man, I'm sorry, okay. But I need to be alone." My old friend fear was throwing a party along with dread inside my body. Twelve days. I lasted twelve days. Now I had to go back. I went to call my mom.

"David, how could you? Don't you want to stay out? Why couldn't you just wait?" she said. She was devastated.

"Mom, he's an adult. And guess what—they aren't arresting him—only me." As if getting her roused up on that would make it okay again. Like that injustice would override my inconsideration for her and what she was going through. She loved me and wanted me to be home. I kept hurting her and making bad decisions. But I couldn't see that at the time. I continued to blame others for my actions and play the victim. I was comfortable in this skin. This identity gave me a soap box and a cause to rally against. It sure was lonely up on this box with no one in the audience.

Two sheriff deputies came to arrest me. After I got off the phone, I packed up my belongings and brought them to Lisa's office. She assured me she would get it to my mother.

I told Lisa, "Thank you. I'm sorry."

"David, you are not at fault. They were waiting to get you on anything. They did not want you out here. We are not going to help them. They want us to write you up, but Al said that none of the staff have seen it and that we can't write up what we did not see," she told me.

"Thank you," I said.

It was like a cycle in my life. In my childhood I had abuse and rejection on my step-dad's side, and love and acceptance from my mother and her family. In prison, I created a world where I was "loved" and accepted and comforted. But the system, COs and rank always seemed against me. Then I fought against the sentiment and institutionalization. Now, I had Parole waiting to pounce on me and then the halfway house staff who were on my side.

I didn't know it but that is very destructive, very enabling to stay in victim stance. I needed to shake loose from that cycle and find some middle ground. But, alas, that was more than a decade away.

*   *   *

Lew Sterrett. Dallas County jail. I wanted to scream. How could I let myself come back here? In the holding cage there are seven collect call phones. But there was one that dispersed free calls. I got in the queue and waited my turn. When I got to the phone, I dialed my mom.

"Hello," she said.

"Mom, are you okay?"

"David, I don't want to talk. I'm hurting and I can't deal with this right now. I'll talk to you later."

I have never felt more alone than I did right then. I wanted to go be alone and cry but Dallas County stays full. There was no place to be alone.

*   *   *

A couple of days later I was informed that I was on the court list. I went down to the court house, sitting in holdover after holdover; it was an all-day affair. In the courtrooms in Dallas there is a door, either to the right or left and through that door is an alcove and a wall with a window that stops an inch from the bottom. There is a ledge and in the alcove is where a lawyer will stand. The bailiff gets the inmate from the holdover and he stands on the other side of the window to meet with his lawyer.

When the bailiff called my name, I went to this window and meet the Probation lady from the court. The nice and funny one. "What were you thinking? Well, I guess I know what you were thinking. But why?" she said in her humorous way.

"I really can't answer that," I told her.

"Well, I got bad news. You are on deferred adjudicated probation. When you violate that the judge can bring you back to court and 'adjudicate' your sentence that was deferred. I'm notifying you about this today. Jones, they can give you anywhere between 2-99 years."

"What, are you serious?" I asked, floored.

"Yes, quiet. They will have a hearing and you can't fight the case but you can provide evidence that you didn't break the rule and then your probation will be reinstated. Who is your lawyer?" she asked.

"Tom Pappas," I said.

*   *   *

Back in my tank I called my mother. She was talking to me again. "Mom, they are trying to use this as a violation of my probation also. I need you to call Tom for me. I've gotten a lot of requests to talk to the media but I turned them all down," I told her.

"Why? I think it's time that you told your side. They keep telling their side. Next time you talk to them," she told me.

But it didn't happen in county jail. The next day I was brought to my parole revocation hearing. My lawyer was there and he retracted my confession and put it back at "my word against his word." Martin testified for me and said we were just talking. My lawyer brought up the fact that I was arrested and Martin wasn't, that it couldn't be construed as that serious for one person and not another person.

But all these great points were to no avail. Parole answers to no one and they revoked my parole. And a week later I was back at the TDCJ Diagnostic unit. This was a record. Usually, you wait up to three months to go back to TDCJ. But they got a van and drove me down to the TDCJ a week after that hearing. Twelve days of freedom. Two weeks and then a personal escort back to prison. After the parole hearing, I was called back to the court. The same probation lady met me in the window. "Good news Jones. The prosecutor could not get any witnesses at the halfway house to testify against you so they dismissed the probation violation. You escaped a big one. Think first, well, think about this, next time. Good luck to you, Mr. Jones."

When they brought me in the back door of the Diagnostic unit, even those COs knew something unusual was happening. A female CO came up to me and said, "What did you do?" Thinking I was some famous serial killer, or something.

"Uh, I had sex with a consenting thirty-one-year-old adult," I told her. I was real cynical about this.

Wow, I couldn't believe it. I dodged a really big bullet. I was so grateful to Al and Lisa and the Wayback House staff. They helped me immensely.

DIAGNOSTIC - AGAIN

1999

B eing gone from the prison only a month, I still had to go through the diagnostic process, because technically I was coming back into the system anew. Parole violators kept the same TDCJ number but had to be screened and classified all over again. I stayed a couple of weeks at the Diagnostic unit and then went to Goree unit. The morning that Dallas County sent me back to prison in that van all the press was there to record it. Lew Sterrett has an underground parking area, where the cops bring the people they have arrested. When I came out the door to this underground area bright lights awaited me, all the local Dallas stations where there to report on my going back: Fox KDFW; KXAS NBC; KFAA ABC; KTVT CBS. And the Dallas Morning News. They let the media know just so they could look good. My family didn't know.

When I got to Goree the bosses and rank all knew me but they also knew why I came back because it was in the news.

"There's Jones. You just couldn't keep that pistol out of your hand, huh?" One of the COs said.

I was so humiliated. But they were not really judging me so much as ribbing me. When you looked at it it was kind of sadly funny. If we didn't laugh at some things, we'd probably go crazy. I could tell you a lot of stories to laugh at in here.

I was placed in transient status, like everyone who is just coming into the prison. I requested safe keeping at Diagnostic for my classification. But being over here I planned on asking everyone I knew if they could get me assigned to Goree unit.

During interviews I stopped by the library and asked the Librarian if I could get an address out of the Dallas Morning News. She allowed me in and handed me the newspaper. On the front page was an ongoing story about the Catholic priest scandal. The byline was Brooks Egerton. I read the article and it seemed that Brooks gave a fair objective story. So, I wrote down his name along with the paper's address.

When I got back to my cell, I wrote him a letter telling him that I would give him an exclusive interview as long as he promised to be fair and not slant the story against me. Mail generally takes three days to get to its destination, and I didn't know how these things went so I did not know what to expect.

The next week the captain called me out to the sergeant's desk in the main hallway.

"Jones, we have a fax here from the Dallas paper requesting an interview with you, and also a letter. Here," he said, handing me a letter.

I read the letter and it was from Brooks' boss, promising a fair interview and stating that it would be exclusive.

After I read the letter, I looked up at the captain and he said, "You can keep that letter. Do you want to give them an interview?"

"Yes, sir," I said.

"Sign here," he told me, pointing to a line on the paper in his hand.

*   *   *

A few days later I was called to the visitation room. Inmates are not allowed to have contact visits with non-family members so we visited through the glass. There was a mesh screen at the bottom so we could hear each other. He recorded it and I felt that it was a good interview. We followed up with a few letters and I was glad to tell my side of the story.

I was unsuccessful in being assigned to the Goree unit. As a part of the process, when they decide which unit they are sending us to, we are called down and stand in a line outside of a room. One at a time we go in and an employee will tell us our assigned unit. I was fourth in line. Anxiety coursed through me and I couldn't stay still. One guy came out and it had become a courtesy to tell everyone in line where you were going. But it sometimes causes more worry if the people in front of you are all saying they are going to a bad unit.

"Ferguson," the guy exiting said. And the next one went in.

"Beto," he said, coming out. The next one went in.

So far not so good in my opinion. "Wynn," the guy in front of me said as he came out. This gave me a glimmer of hope.

"Shut the door. What's your name?" the man asked as I entered the room.

"Jones, David, sir," I said, as if being respectful would win me any favors in a decision that had already been made. This guy was just the messenger.

"Let's see," he traced his finger down the paper in front of him. "Looks like you lucked out. Ramsey 2," he declared.

"But Ramsey 2 doesn't have safekeeping anymore, sir. I requested safekeeping." During the prison boom in the late '90's they removed S/K from all the old red-brick prisons, for security reasons. Everything they do they use the catch-all excuse of "security."

"Ramsey 2 is alright. It's where the GRAD program is."

"What is GRAD?" I asked. That didn't tell me anything.

"When a gang member leaves a gang and goes straight, we put them through a program to help them adjust, and on that unit, they will be protected," he explained.

"But I need to be on safekeeping." I pleaded.

"Just give it a try and if it don't work out you can request it again," he said.

That is always TDCJ's reasoning. You are adequately classified because *nothing* has happened to you. The inmate goes to them to prevent *something* happening. But they have to see blood before they will help you, if then. Maybe if the person is killed they have a meeting to discuss doing *anything*.

RAMSEY 2

1999 - 2000

R amsey 2. Wow, what a difference a few years make. The total atmosphere was different. I noticed some sergeants and lieutenants who'd been just COs when I'd last been here. Along with S/K the SOTP was gone. The place was transformed. I couldn't help but wonder what had made this environment so different now than it had been four years before.

I came to the conclusion that an environment consists of the majority of the people who make it up. When I'd been here before the majority had been homosexuals and sex offenders. Now there were hard men who used to be in a gang and had chosen to leave that lifestyle, for whatever reason. It seems that the aura of a place will mimic the people who are there. It had been full of deviants and gays. And what they'd collectively thought or allowed had been prevalent in the atmosphere. It had been such a force it had invaded upon the COs and rank, and had made this prison, at the time, very lenient, laidback, easy and a fun place to do your time.

Now, it wasn't lackadaisical. There was a tension in the air. Everyone seemed so serious. I guess that was how I would feel if I had gotten out of a gang and I didn't know who was going to be the one to stick a shiv in me. Prison is a very convoluted place.

I was placed on the wings with two-man cells. I requested at UCC for S/K, then to be housed in the dorms. But I was denied both requests.

It was football season and that made time go by fast. No one was trying to make anyone ride or pay protection. I didn't hide my "gayness" but I kept my case a secret. I'd find no sympathy here. I had a Muslim for a cellie who wanted to have sex on the down-low.

I met a guy that I liked on the rec. yard and we started kicking it. But he was exactly like me—a smotherer. And I was turned off by it. But I didn't break up because I didn't want to hurt his feelings. I was placed to work in the hoe squad, but one thing that stays the same is our medical records, so I was placed in the medical squad.

*   *   *

Y2K. Even in here it was a concern for the officials. It didn't mean nothing to us. We were doing time and we still would regardless of a computer glitch.

In prison there is not much we can do for New Years. Some guys make some hootch. Others rip up old newspapers to make confetti. We all watch *Rockin' New Years' Eve with Dick Clark*. We see our favorite singers and bands perform, then watch the ball drop.

But at 10 p.m. this New Year's Eve the officers started yelling, "Rack it up, rack it up."

"What?" an inmate yelled.

"Why?"—another.

"Hell no, get some rank, or we are gonna party like it's 1999."

The dayroom laughed. We'd all waited to see Prince perform tonight. But even after rank came, we had to rack up or they would gas us and we'd still have to rack up.

Usually, a group of inmates will choose the gas. But this night logic prevailed and we went to our cells peacefully. Once again, the reason fell on security. And security is never convenient. But if the computers went out and caused a blackout the prison wanted to have us contained so that we could not take advantage of the situation. We brought in the year 2000 in our cells.

*　　*　　*

February 6, 2000. The article Brooks wrote came out in the paper that day. He mailed me the section that the article was in and I received it a few days later. There were two articles concerning me. Overall, it wasn't bad. But I didn't want the inmates to read it. It totally exposed me. I went to the library and asked for the DMN with that date and I stole the section with my article in it. Now the worry was some inmates might have a subscription to the paper. But it was mailed and came several days later. Hopefully no one would make the connection.

The second article was about how the prosecutors let me get away with the "probation violation" in which they could have sentenced me to life in prison. I love it when a DA stumbles to save face.

But what I loved in the article was what Lt. Bill Wash said. He was the one who ran the investigation of my case in 1991.

"There is *no* evidence other than fondling in Mr. Jones' cases. All those allegations are just the parents trying to use leverage in the lawsuits," [against the place that I worked.]

I was glad he'd said this. Because—while it *doesn't* justify or excuse anything, what I did was horrible—it shows that I was not doing anything other than fondling. Some of the accusations were just horrible, and to think the parents put their children up to lie and say these things. And there were a couple of cases that I did not do and I was still charged with; my lawyer told me, "You got a good deal, don't rock the boat" back in 1991. So I didn't make an issue of it. And I passed a polygraph when asked about all those false allegations. Which is why I got this plea bargain that I did: "Fifteen years on all cases to run concurrently—if I told the truth about all I did."

*　　*　　*

I thought that I could prevent the whole unit from finding out about this article. I didn't want to be here on this unit, but once I got here and

I was not in any immediate danger, I got comfortable. So, I tried to keep it that way and remain here. I didn't want to have to go somewhere and start over again.

The down-low Muslim, my cellie. Sometimes I got the feeling that Muslims were just a religious gang. We fooled around a few times. But I didn't like the set-up at all. I don't know what it's called. Because I have to label it something so I can understand it. But when I'm outside my cell, and this is common with a lot of prisoners, gay or not, I am "DJ," I'm gay and it's like I'm *on*. But when I come to my cell, I want to relax, put my feet up and just be *off*. And be David. I don't want to have sex with the person that I live with, because you don't know when he will want it and then I may be too relaxed then have to perform and that takes energy. I expended all my energy outside the cell.

Years later, I saw a B-movie and the setting was in prison and one of the characters was gay and he got a new cellie and he told the cellie, "I don't eat where I shit." And finally I had something to say when the occasion arose. But for now, I just acted funny towards him in hopes that he would take a hint.

One day he started talking to me and he said, "What did you say you were in prison for?" Being cellies and sometimes fooling around overrode those etiquettes. I had made up something and I started in on that story and he lifted up the newspaper article.

"All my Muslim brothers read this and they told me that I can't be in a cell with you. They want me to beat you up. But I can tell them that I did if you take care of me."

"Look man, that ain't me," I tried.

"This picture looks like you." It was an old picture from 1991. The warden at Goree wouldn't let the reporter take a new picture.

"You don't think I got enough problems? And is that satisfying at all? Coercing someone to have sex with you. Let's get real, dude."

I already know what you are thinking. Ironies, seems like life is full of them. But life is also cumulative. And these lessons will come back and take root.

What I said made him realize what he was doing. "Yeah, I don't want that. You're right."

"So do you think the Muslims will get me?" I asked.

"Maybe, it depends."

"Hey, I'm about to go out here and file a LID. Will you write a statement that you overheard a group of people threatening to get me?"

"Yeah, I'll do that," he told me.

When the cell doors rolled open, my cellie and I went down the stairs to the hallway door.

"Where are ya'll goin'?" the hallway boss yelled.

"To the barbershop." My cellie answered.

Walking down the hall my cellie explained that that was the easiest way to get out and go talk to rank. We walked towards the barbershop; the sergeant's desk was right across from it. We saw Lt. Raines.

"It's Raines, he don't like paperwork." my cellie said.

"He made lieutenant? I remember him when he was CO," I said. "He used to kinda hunch over, but when he got sergeant, his chest came out a little. Now look at him standing straight with his chest poked out all in pride. He can't get no more rank or he will be all bent over backward," I told my cellie. We laughed. Then the lieutenant noticed us.

"Why are you talking in my *my* hallway?" He glared at us.

"Lieutenant I need to file an LID. I was in the paper and my cellie said he overheard a group of people threatening me."

"You know I'm gonna lock you up and write you a case, and you will be back out in a few days and then what? I'll go through all your property and…" he kept on spieling the company line to discourage me from causing him to earn his paycheck and fill out some paperwork.

"Ok, I still want to file." I said.

He grumbled and handed me a paper to fill out and handed my cellie a witness statement form. "Ya'll step in here and fill this out." He let us into the barbershop.

This lieutenant wanted to play games so I thought I'll cover my butt. I wrote on the paper that I brought to the attention of Lt. Raines that my life was in danger and that he threatened me himself, to go through my property, write me a disciplinary case, and that my LID would fail and I would get out and still be in danger from this original threat.

I slid my paper to him through the door and he grabbed it. About three minutes later he opened the barbershop door.

"Jones, come out here." Real polite. Extremely polite. He told my cellie to go on back to the cell. Then he went back behind the desk.

He had my incident form right in front of him, between us. Next to it was a blank form. His voice couldn't have been sweeter if he'd put honey on it.

"Mr. Jones. This isn't about me or what I want. No, it's about you, what you want. Let's say you re-write this and make it more about you and what you want, and let's rip up this other one, okay?" Picking up the old one and waiting for a nod. I nodded as I picked up the blank form. He ripped up the old one in half then quarters and put it into the trashcan. Smiling as he let me back into the barbershop.

He put so much pride in having rank, he couldn't turn in an LID with that in it. He feared looking bad to the higher rank. This time it had worked in my favor. That didn't work all the time. If you try to call someone's bluff it usually blows up in your face.

He brought me back to my cell and allowed me to pack my own property. Lockup transient cells were on one row of my wing. I got all my property in the cell and the door slammed shut. Once again I was back in lockup.

I saw UCC a few days later and they approved my LID and my request for S/K status, at unit level. They would send the file to Huntsville—state classification—to make it official or reject it. But usually they approved the unit's recommendation.

BARRY TELFORD UNIT

2000-2003

Twenty-four days. That's how long I waited on transient on Ramsey 2 unit until I caught the chain. From Ramsey 2 I was taken to the Walls unit where I spent the night. The next morning, I got on a crowded bus and was taken to Beto One unit. Telford unit is in New Boston, Texas, close to the Louisiana border. The bus from Walls to Beto didn't go to Telford, so I had to spend the night on a transient wing at Beto and get on another bus to Telford unit, the next morning.

A three-day affair, with no chance to shower. And it's three and a half hours from Beto to Telford, so I didn't eat breakfast or drink anything on the morning that I was on the chain. I hate being on the chain. There is no true rest. They tell you the night before that you are going on the chain and you have to pack your property and wait for the officer to inventory it. You try to go to sleep but your mind is running. When you finally get to sleep it's time to wake up and go sit in a holdover cage/room/cell and wait for the Blue Bird to come pick you up. Then to do this three days in a row. It's tiring.

There were only nine people on this bus heading to Telford. The bus could hold forty. This was a rare reprieve. It was still dark and cold but the boss turned on the heat and before long conversation filled the air.

"I just left Telford and they are on a thirty-day lockdown," one guy said.

"Thirty days? Why?" I exclaimed. I had never heard of being locked down for more than three days, a week tops. Was he serious?

"On 8 building they are stabbing each other. Mexicans against the blacks. They go on a thirty, come up then stab someone else, then another thirty. They are beating up bosses, too."

Why did I have to go to a unit like this, I wondered to myself. Survival games. It was like rolling the dice, you never knew what unit you would end up on.

"What's 8 building?" I asked.

"You ain't ever been on a unit like Telford?" he asked.

"No."

"They just built it in 1998 or so. But it's called a 2250 because that's how many inmates it holds. You got four different buildings labeled 3, 4, 7, and 8. 3 and 4 buildings are minimum custody. 7 building is medium custody and 8 building is close custody. Those guys are at the bottom, they have nothing to lose. Everyone has a shank over there. When we pulled up to the unit to the right is 12 building. It has AC but it's only Administrated Segregation. There are about six wings with single cells there. There is an 11 building but it's for lockup and transient. They are thinking about building some dorms, too."

I'd never been on a unit with so many inmates. It was crazy. How did they ever expect to have control?

Those guys kept talking but soon it was eerily quiet. Everyone had gone to sleep. I was lost in my thoughts. Well, I decided to join them.

The change of the engine noise as the transmission switched to a lower gear woke us up. Now I had a crick in my neck, a hazard of falling asleep on a bus with your head angled down, bending your neck.

The bus driver had got off the highway and was taking some back roads to get to the unit. Finally, the unit drew up on our left, and we saw through the chicken wire covering the bus windows. The employee parking lot, the admin. building, a tower, then different buildings that stood three stories high, and we could see that each bunk in each cell had a long rectangular window. Then we got to the back gate. After the back gate boss had inspected the bus, the bus pulled up through the gate and onto the prison grounds.

An officer stood at the door of the bus and unlocked our handcuffs. It felt good to be off that bus. We moved away from the bus and stretched and waited.

When an officer from the unit got there, he took his time laughing and joking with the bus officers. Then he started calling our names and once he was assured he had all of us he escorted us to medical. We gladly learned the unit was not on lockdown.

After medical had seen everyone, the boss escorted us to the building. I went to 3 building because that was where safekeeping was. They were taken to 4 building. On each building there was a committee room, and UCC went to each building to run committee for the people who lived on that building and the chain, who were waiting in the multipurpose room.

The unit was what I call an outside unit. It was similar in design to Briscoe unit where there were different buildings that were not connected. We had to go outside and walk to the other buildings. This unit had sidewalks that were fenced in, and a portico like a roof running overhead connected to the fences. The fences were our walls, and the sidewalks were a maze, except that you could see through them. But there were gates ever so often for containment purposes and security.

The boss escorted me to 3 building, and I got my property, mattress and linen and so on from the buggy and I was placed in the multipurpose room. I sat and waited in the multipurpose room and finally UCC came to the building. There was a sallyport in front of each pod, the outer door, coming from the hall, and the inner door leading to the pod, and the person working the picket controlled those doors. Inside the sallyport were two other doors. One led to a small office—the committee room. And the other to what is called a passive rec. yard. I entered the sallyport and into the committee room and saw the UCC. They were in a rush and quickly finished.

"Jones, initial here," he classification woman said.

"Jones, you have been sent here to be placed on safekeeping. Your job is utility. Any questions?" the warden asked.

"No."

"Next," the warden said again.

*   *   *

I went back to the multipurpose room and waited for a move slip. The officer at the desk turned the lights in the multipurpose room on and off from a control box at the desk, to get my attention. I went to the desk and he handed me a move slip.

"Sign here. You are going to A1-18B." I signed and he instructed an SSI to help me carry all my property. We went through the sallyport and through the other door to the pod.

I went toward one section. The door slid open. The SSI yelled up to the picket, "118." Inside the section was a dayroom, bigger than the ones on a red brick unit. There were two TVs, one on each side of the dayroom, with four benches facing each TV and tables spread out between the two sides. Anytime someone new entered everyone on S/K gawked and looked to see if it was someone that they knew or wanted to get to know. Several people came to grab my bags and mattress from the SSI and helped carry it to Three row.

I heard someone yell, "Maddog, you got you one." It turned out that "Maddog" was the name of my cellie, and someone was just playing with him, telling him he had someone gay for a cellie. I didn't let it bother me; it was just safekeeping banter. I hadn't been on S/K since January 1993.

The cell door was on a rail, but it could only be opened by the picket control. It had to be shut manually.

"The boss ain't paying attention, take your time and when you come out you can shut your door." One of the guys who helped me carry my things told me.

"Are you sure?" I asked, not certain about this advice.

"Look, she is already back asleep. You woke her up when you came in," he said, pointing to the picket. And sure enough I could see someone in the picket sitting in a chair with their head hanging down, just like I was on the bus.

"Where is the Rover?" I asked.

"Asleep in the bathroom," he said.

"Oh, okay, thank you," I said. I unpacked and made my bed. Then I grabbed my shower stuff and headed to the showers. I closed the cell door and then a yellow-skinned black guy came on the run. His face had pockmark scars and he had a muscular body.

"Oh, man," he said.

"What happened?" I ask.

"I'm your cellie. I was going to grab something out of the cell, but you already shut it." Not mad, just stating a fact.

"I'm sorry. I'm DJ," I told him.

"Maddog, uh, long story," he said at my bewildered look for such a strange name.

"I'm going to go shower," I said and turned to go. The shower had that half door that swings open. I finished and dried off and got dressed. There was a gap at the bottom of our cell door, about four inches, and I slid my dirty clothes and shower things into my cell and went to sit in the dayroom.

The guys came to talk to me and the "girls" to check me out, wondering if I was a threat and going to steal their boyfriend. Gays can spot another gay person even if he is not all decked out as a girl.

This unit didn't seem too bad at first. My job, utility, was not enforced. If I wanted to work, I reported to the desk boss at 6 p.m. and he put me on a list and at rack time, I stayed out and cleaned the pod. The rover didn't supervise, and the picket boss left the section doors open and went to sleep. They counted once and then turned in a "paper count" copied from the earlier count sheet for the rest of the night.

On safekeeping I soon learned that while there were a few people who came out to clean, there were twice as many coming out to meet up and hang out with their boyfriend or just for good old promiscuous sex.

I was still practicing and reinforcing my tools and new way of thinking. It had been four years and the impulsive thoughts were few and far between. The therapy works if you use it and actually do it. And when I get an impulsive thought about a child I have conditioned myself to feel disgusted about it. It's very powerful and I recommend this for anyone who wants to change *any* behavior.

I was still using sex, either masturbation or sex with someone else, to soothe and comfort myself, and to stave off loneliness. Although I still had a promiscuous streak, I wanted a relationship with a person. I don't believe that the problem with sex offenders is with children. I'm *not* saying that hurting a child is not a problem; I'm talking about trying to get to the root of the issue. Take a sex offender who acts out against a child, and take a person addicted to drugs. The issue is not the drugs or the child, those are just band aids to the real problem. They are what the individual chooses to use to soothe himself. But the real problem is, "What is making or causing him to feel a need to soothe himself?"

I had already fixed the issue of using a child to soothe myself. But why was I still needing sex and constant comfort, and distraction from reality? I didn't know. I didn't even know this distinction at the time. I thought I had recovered from my problem and now I was just as normal as everyone else, right?

Life is cumulative.

*   *   *

I got to Telford on March 7, 2000. I turned twenty-nine the next day, surrounded by strangers. I met a guy named Mike-Mike. He was a Crip who "caught out" from GP just to come to S/K to "marry" a punk. As relationships go it didn't last. Now he was considered to be on the market.

We started talking then began kicking it. He also had a relationship with a boss lady. And she was bringing him packs of Bugler tobacco. He was generous with it and sold the rest. I learned that when you are in the game you had to be generous or someone will snitch on you. He let me hold some packs. I cut a slit in my jacket in the lining of it on the inside and hid it there. I would roll up the "squares" and give them to whoever he told me to.

It was easy to go into his cell for a couple of hours. And we did this a few times. He had a lot of commissary because when you sell one cigarette for a dollar in commissary products, you amass a lot of it.

We had gotten pretty close during the first two weeks that I was there. One day the rover came in yelling, "Rack up. Rack up right now. Everybody. Rack up."

Everyone went to their cells and the Rover left. He came back with the remote control and turned off the TVs.

"Uh-oh, week one, day one," someone yelled out.

I asked my cellie what that meant, and he explained to me that when the unit went on lock down it was a four-week lockdown or thirty days. The administration would hand out a paper to each cell informing them they were on a lockdown and the schedule for the lockdown. The schedule was laid out by the week.

Week 1 – showers every other day. Johnies (a brown bag sack with a couple of sandwiches in it.)

Week 2 – showers every other day, Johnies.

Week 3 – showers every other day, Johnies, a hygiene and correspondence spend at commissary. One hot meal.

Week 4 – showers every other day. Johnnies, three hot meals.

And if our behavior was good, we would "come up" at the end of week 4.

"Sounds dismal," I said.

"You don't even know until you go through it."

"Why are we on lockdown, though?" I asked.

"We generally have two annual lockdowns a year to search our property for contraband. We have to pack our stuff and carry it to the rec. yard or gym for officers to search it and the field bosses search our cells, the dayroom and so on. But this could be a disciplinary lockdown and we won't know why until we know," Maddog said, logically.

"Hey everyone, look out your window," someone yelled over the run.

These rectangle windows were oblong and horizontal in the walls. There was a metal plate that had square openings punched out of the metal covering the windows. I don't know why they bothered since no one could fit through that skinny window. But if we lay on our beds, we could see the sidewalk that led to ¾ gate. We now saw a bunch of officers pushing a gurney with a sheet covering a body. Someone must have died and that was why we were in lockdown. But they'd come off our building. Who could have died on our building? It was all safe keeping.

The next day we got some of the story from a boss, and the whole story from an SSI they let out to work. The "grapevine," so to speak. An inmate who was on safekeeping and worked inside yard—mowing the grass of the prison grounds—while at work, placed a big rock in the windows that were in the stairwell on C pod 2 section. When he came home from work, he grabbed the rock and put it in a sock, and he used it as a weapon and beat this other person to death. Blood was everywhere, on the walls and up the ceiling. And it was a crime scene and could not be cleaned up. They could not recognize the person, he was so beat up. Then he told us that it was Rosie. I had met Rosie on the rec yard. He had been a small, skinny Hispanic homosexual. Very petite and effeminate. I couldn't believe that he was killed in such a brutal, violent way. We couldn't get a definite reason for "Why." Why did he kill Rosie? It was narrowed to two different reasons. 1.) He and Rosie had had sex and he'd contracted HIV from Rosie, who was HIV positive. 2.) He had a life sentence and was never getting out (that was a fact) and he figured he rather not do all that time and had killed someone to get the death penalty and die sooner. Only he knew. He may have shared the real reason to the courts, but it hasn't trickled down to us.

*   *   *

If you've never been to prison, here is a deterrent—shakedowns. There are two a year, but if one or two people do something wrong then the whole unit gets punished with a thirty-day lockdown. During the lockdown, officers go from building to building searching everything. Since this unit had over two thousand inmates it took close to thirty days to 'shakedown' each building.

On the day that your wing goes to shakedown, at 5 a.m. the rover will come in and go cell by cell waking you up and telling you to pack all your property and state issued items, except your mattress. After shift change at 6 a.m., the rover will come in and yell for us to pack up and be ready.

After 6:30 a.m., the field officers show up and they are just perpetually mad and they begin yelling and harassing those people who are not ready. They open our cell doors and we carry our bags of property—some people don't have many possessions and have it easy, some have four bags or even six bags—we have to carry our bags either to the rec. yard or to the gym. There is a row of tables set up with an officer at each table. We are then made to sit in a line in front of each table and when it's our turn we unpack our bags onto the table and the officer goes through everything, throwing away whatever he/she wants to throw away.

There is major contraband: drugs, shanks, tattoo guns, and items not allowed in TDCJ. Then there is nuisance contraband: rubber bands, paperclips, markers, just small things that do not pose a major security threat. The former gets you locked up, the latter are just thrown away, but a CO could write it up if he wants to.

People try to hide contraband, sneak it through, or find a way to get it back later. People will go to extremes to do this. Hide it in a mattress, in a commissary item, even in their anus. Guys even have pet rats and if the field bosses finds them, they stomp on them right in front of you. It's a cruel world.

Mike-Mike was in 20 cell, just two cells down from me. He made a line (a string made out of the thread in the elastic band of the state-issued boxer shorts.) and slid it under his door down to my door. I fished his line in and there was enough slack in it that we could tie a note on it and use the line like a pulley system. We call notes a kite. As in "I'm gonna shoot you a kite." It's on a string and everything, and sometimes you might "fly" the string to a cell further away than just two cells.

We wrote each other back and forth to pass the time and get to know each other better. He would cook some food and put it in an empty chip bag and tie the line around the top of the bag. I would pull it into my cell and I didn't have to rely on the Johnies. (Another deterrent—a peanut butter and jelly sandwich and a meat sandwich, dry, no condiments, and some raisins so you didn't get constipated.)

I got a kite from him one day asking if I would take his tobacco through shakedown for him.

"It's in my ramen soups and you can't even tell that it's in there. It's just that they know me and they might search my stuff hard. But you are new, they won't even look at your stuff," he wrote in the kite.

I told him no, that I had never been to a shakedown on this unit and I didn't feel comfortable doing it. He said he understood but it didn't stop him from shooting slugs at me. "You want to smoke it but you don't want to take the risks with the other part." Putting on the guilt trip.

The day came and we had to lug our bags all the way down to the gym. The bags were heavy and there was a lot of stop and go along the way, some people making two and three trips.

Finally, we got there and it was a long process. On our section there were about forty-three inmates, five short of capacity. There were five tables in the middle of the gym and each officer took their time. Mike-Mike got one of his friends to take his tobacco through and we all made it through with no major subtractions from our property. I felt sorry for the guys who lost their radios or hot pots. When we bought those items from the commissary, we had been issued a property paper for them. But some guys had bought theirs off the street and the officer would confiscate it if it wasn't legit.

Back in the cell my cellie and I were taking turns unpacking and getting back in our comfort zone. We still had to stay locked down until they searched the whole unit. I had just got to this unit and I didn't even know that you could be prepared for a lockdown, because I'd never heard of a thirty-day lockdown. But some guys keep a "lockdown" stash set aside, which consist of commissary food and books to read. I got lucky because Mike-Mike took care of me, but I planned to tell my mother about this so I could get a little extra money on my inmate trust fund and have me a stash.

Over the years I would give my mom a list of books and she would go to a bookstore and get those books and have the bookstore mail them to me. Every unit has a library and we can check out books to read from there, also. But library doesn't run during a lockdown, so I would have to start keeping some in a stash. Boredom is an inmate's worse enemy, and I've known a bored CO or two. It's not a pretty sight.

*   *   *

We were free! When a 'thirty day' is through and they call dayroom it's like getting released from prison. Prison itself is cruel and it takes mind manipulation to stay sane, and we all deny our reality to one degree or another. A lockdown drives the reality home: you are in prison—suffer! But being able to go to the dayroom and be distracted, and dumbed down by the drone of the TV—well, that is just gravy.

But wait, the picket boss was announcing a field trip to Six Flags: "Get ready for outside rec. Get ready for outside rec." Yeah, it was like that. Just to go out there and see people you hadn't seen in thirty days and get all the gossip, who broke up with who, and everything. A lot of us couldn't wait to play basketball. Releasing those endorphins is better than any drug.

I found out that you can listen to your radio in your cell and hear new music by your favorite artist, or any band, and that's good, but when you talk about it with others, "Man, did you hear that new one by Nelly, 'Country Grammar'?" And they've enjoyed it too, and then you sing a couple of lines together—it intensifies your feelings about the song, it gives the song a stronger connection and it validates you. It says, "I like this song, you like this song, we have something in common. I'm just as normal as you."

That is what the time felt like at outside rec. after that thirty-day punishment. We talked, we gossiped, we B-balled, we sang. We observed a moment of silence for Rosie. We are humans; we resisted, for a couple of hours, being a number.

*   *   *

I saw Mike-Mike talk to a black queen. Jealousy rose up in me. I waited until we were in the cell together to ask him about it.

"Oh, her. DJ, that's my 'wife'," he revealed.

"What about me?" I exclaimed.

"You aren't a girl, you're a gay boy," he said. "We have fun but I want a 'wife,' someone feminine. You can be our 'boy'."

"Your 'boy'? Three of us? No, Mike, no. I'm a one-on-one person, I don't do 'girls' or being in a 'family'," I told him as we lay in his bunk.

Some guys had a "wife" —a queen—and they had a 'boy' to make a 'family.' I wasn't down for that. I wanted it to be just me and him. I wanted to be the object of his attention and his desire. I don't share.

I got up and began to get dressed. He put his hand on my chin and lifted my face to look at him.

"DJ, I'm sorry. I see the hurt in your eyes. I didn't mean to hurt you. But look, she lives on a different pod, so while I'm here we can still kick it and I'll still look out for you on the cigarettes, okay?" he told me.

I nodded my head and relaxed a little. I wouldn't get him exclusively, but I settled with having him in a "kick it" type relationship.

"Who am I kidding," my low self-esteem popped up, "I couldn't have the type of guy that I like, no one wants me, no one has ever wanted me."

We are cruel to ourselves. "Look at you, just pitiful." This was my core belief, revealing itself during a bad time.

Those were my thoughts and they were a never-ending cycle of thought and belief patterns. And that proves Dr. Phil's adage once again: "You get what you believe that you deserve," (paraphrased). Why did I want something that was out of my league, so to speak? Why was I my own worst enemy? I was screaming deep in the forest, but just like the tree, there was no one there to hear me.

*   *   *

Appropriately, George Michael's song "Careless Whisper" came on. Mike had a home-, no, prison-made speaker, and when we heard that sax, we looked at each other. I'd already told him that this was my favorite song from the '80s. He stood up and grabbed his tube of toothpaste. I smiled. I grabbed a pen and stood up too.

In my mind the cell transformed and it was night and we were on a pier. I heard the water lapping against the pier and I saw the light from a ship out in the ocean. The tube of toothpaste and pen became microphones; we sang, moving around in the cell, but on the pier. He gave me my solo:

"Tonight, the music seems so loud..."

I don't think that I've ever sang it with more meaning, more emotion than I did in that moment. After the song was over, the cell appeared and we put down our "mics." He hugged me.

The radio station went to a commercial. He said, "Now if they would play my favorite song, it would be perfect."

But that's the problem. We have to depend on a radio station to play the songs we want to hear and are seldom satisfied. And they didn't play his song before we left the cell that day. His favorite was "What's Up" by 4 Non Blonds.

I liked the song, too. But over time this song became higher on my favorites list. I know that she is talking about being a woman in a man's world, and overcoming that "institution." But the lyrics fit being in a prison also. And instead of the "Brotherhood of Man", this world is made up of the mass incarceration of warehoused humans.

*   *   *

The officers work for four days, twelve hours a day, and they are off for four days. When you add it up you are only working six months out of the year. But there is an A card 1st shift and 2nd shift, and a B card 1st and 2nd shift. A total of four shifts, 6 a.m. – 6 p.m. and 6 p.m. – 6 a.m.

Mike's boss lady worked this card: A card 1st shift. And she was supposed to be making a drop of packs of tobacco to him. He'd already told me not to hang around him while she was working so she wouldn't know that Mike messed around with guys.

Later that day, under the guise of a "cell search," she entered Mike's cell and dropped off seven packs of Bugler and hid it in a box of detergent that was sold on commissary. Mike shot that box to his homeboy to hold for a few days, just in case somebody snitched. He gave me one pack and a $20 bill. I hid it in my jacket.

A couple of hours later six COs ran into our section. Their footsteps echoed in the stairwell and reverberated throughout the cell walls, and I went to my cell door and looked out. Those six officers ran by my cell and I heard them say over their radio, "Open 20 cell." Mike's cell. I heard that distinct noise of handcuffs being put on someone. And two officers took Mike down the stairs while the other four tossed his cell.

They found nothing; Mike had been too smart for them. But they were mad about being sent on a dry run and they locked up Mike anyway. I lay on my bed and watched out my window. After a few minutes I saw those officers walking Mike out of the building and down the sidewalk in handcuffs. I wanted him to know that I saw him and that he was not alone, so I yelled out my window: "Hey, what's going on?"

Mike turned his head and looked back. Message received.

*   *   *

They hadn't found anything and they would let him out in a week or so. They were just harassing him. But more than likely he wouldn't come back to this section. It was the first time that I had seen the results of a snitch. That ain't cool. To snitch on someone just because you are hating, or you have got in some trouble so you give up info on someone else to get out of it; whatever the reason, it's not acceptable, you could screw off someone's life by doing this, and then there is the boss lady. She could have been fired and wouldn't have been able to support herself or her family.

And before you say that they should not be doing wrong in the first place, I agree with you. But these people will get caught by themselves. Karma is real. What you sow you will reap. But to tell on someone for your own greedy purposes; no siree, Bob! Don't do it.

But the TDCJ rank love and exploit those who snitch. If a person wants to move in with a lover, they will snitch; if they get a case, they will snitch. Snitching is a better commodity than commissary and is spent with the rank to stimulate their economy of looking good to the higher rank. Do you want another irony? If a person snitches on an inmate, rank will believe you and go catch them. But if I tell on a boss for not doing his/her job properly or whatever, rank tells me to get lost. Oh, the double standard of prison!

And what does this teach the snitch? You don't have to take responsibility for your actions. And if you want something, just give up your neighbors. And the TDCJ's mission statement says: "… to promote positive change in offender behavior, reintegrate offenders into society…"

Join me as I sarcastically say, "Yeah, right."

*   *   *

The TDCJ's school system offers vocations, and I decided to sign up for a class: "Business Computer Information Systems." The class was for six hours a day and began at 5 a.m., but we actually had to meet in the gym at 4:30 and once everyone got there we were let out through A turnout and walked down through the back door to some sheet metal buildings. We entered a door into a huge room. At the front was the teacher's desk, then another desk for the inmate teacher's aide. All around the walls were small tables, a chair and a computer. There were student desks in the center of the room.

We had a nice teacher named Ms. E., a black woman, who wasn't afraid to work in a prison. The CO didn't stay in the room, but roamed between the three other vocation classes. I loved learning things. It's like I had been deprived, and my brain was soaking up new knowledge like a dry sponge in a sink of water. I became the best student in the class. Operating Windows became second nature to me. I made 100 on every test. Ms. E. never paid attention so I slipped the answers to the other guys but I told them to get some wrong, 'cause Ms. E. was not stupid.

I created comics with clip art. I made full jokes like brochures, and everyone loved my PowerPoint shows. I never knew that working on a computer could be so much fun. It got around to the other vocation teachers how good I was. And when they had problems with their computers, they began to call me instead of the teacher's aide.

*   *   *

Back on the section, other guys tried to get with me, but I wasn't feeling any of them until I saw JD. Talk about a pretty boy. He was cute and fine and he shot at me, so I thought he wanted me for me. It felt good to be wanted. I didn't know at this time that I was in a constant cycle of chasing waterfalls.

People behave according to their perception of reality. What was my POR? Dr. Phil explains it this way: (I'm paraphrasing my understanding of it, If I got it wrong that's on me not Dr. Phil), we all have a core belief of how we truly feel and/or think about ourselves deep down. We also project the image of how we wish to be seen or judged by others. I have lied to myself enough that I believe the image I project. The image that I want others to believe, I have been deceived by, and when that image is shattered by circumstances or events, my core belief about myself is there to tell me about myself: unworthy, unloved, rejected. "You're no good, do you really think you can have a guy like that?"

When everything is going the way I expect it to, I perceive that I'm in control. I believe that I am okay. This becomes my reality. But what is real is not necessarily true. I am behaving according to the image, and my POR is shifted to what I truly believe about myself at my core. This renders me to continue the cycle, and I begin to try to repair that image.

And that's more lies, because I'm telling myself, "If I can just do A, B, and C then all will be alright in DJ's world again." But is it, or is it just my perception that it will?

We all do this to an extent. How many times have you said: "If my husband/wife does such and such then I'll be so angry." You are already setting up the way to be angry. It's the same with me; "If I can do this, everything will be alright." I had to do whatever "this" was and I'd be happy. But if not, cue self-destructive behavior.

The biggest lie I was telling myself was that, "I am normal and everything I am going through is a part of life." But it was not a part of real life; I was generating these results because of what I believed that I deserved in my core belief, and my core belief was a mess. And this is what I meant when I say that the children, the drugs, and even the promiscuous sex were not the problem.

The problem was how I felt about myself at my core. If I could fix this, if I could change my perception of myself, then my perception of reality would be based on truth. It would be on a better foundation.

But right then, I was blind to any explanations that lay outside my POR and I perceived that this waterfall named JD really liked me. And so began a new phase that lowered my self-esteem even further, and my standards.

When I got with him, I fell fast. I garnered expectations for him, and when they weren't met, I questioned him. This led to big arguments, and causing scenes. I kept believing that we were in a loving, committed relationship, but his behavior showed otherwise. Even though my suspicions were true—he was only with me for commissary, and he was cheating on me—the way I handled it was not right and exacerbated the problem, and my mental health was taking a toll. In the Ferguson chapter, I questioned if living this lifestyle would hurt me later. The answer was a resounding *yes!*

A pretty boy like JD, who knows he's pretty, uses his looks to get with someone like me. He instinctively knew who had low self-esteem, and if that person went to commissary regularly, he would go after that person. And at first he played his role perfectly, but no one could keep up a pretense 24/7. And it's like a drug dealer, who gives a you a hit for free to get you hooked, then you end up stealing from your own mom to pay for that high again. This was year 2000, and they'd upped the game and I hadn't gotten the memo.

I kept thinking that if I could please him—sexually, monetarily, whatever—then he would love and accept me. It became my drive, my fight. My motivation. But essentially, I was paying someone to be with me. I told myself more lies: "As long as I get what I want I don't care." And throughout all the fighting and cheating I really believed I was getting what I wanted. After all, fighting, leaving and coming back—that was the definition of love. That was the definition my mother had showed me by example. (I had smaller cycles going on, but my life was one big cycle.)

After one big scenic fight where I yelled out embarrassing things, cussed him out, called him a bitch, told everyone that he gave up his ass to me. I sat down on one of the benches to stew. An older black man called my name.

"DJ," and I looked at him and he said, "What does that make you?"

"What?" I said.

"If he does all those things and he is all those names you called him, then what does that make you?"

But at the time I couldn't grasp the meaning of such a profound statement because it was outside my POR. Today, I still ponder the question that if I could have understood that then would that have saved me a lot of heartache?

I continued to go through this cycle with JD. Ups and downs, a scene of normality, well, our normal... and then JD ended up going to medium custody. He had a lot of cases, and after so many administration decided to demote him, give him a time out so to speak.

And for a while before he got moved to B-pod 1 section medium custody, he gave me all his attention, he was pouring it on. He was giving me that fix again so he would have me looking out for him over there. And yes, I did. I would give him care packs; I would fall out of place over there to go see him.

When his section would go to chow, I would hide by the gym just to see him for a few seconds and talk to him. Then one day I saw him walking with a gay boy. I went off and started yelling at both of them and I told that guy to stay away from my man. I knew how to cause a scene. People thought I was crazy, but no, I was just hurting.

Then as TDCJ usually does, they transferred JD to another unit and he was gone. We don't always know why someone gets shipped, but sometimes it happens suddenly. And once again, that one big cycle that was my life, another man had come and gone.

*   *   *

Packs of Buglers were sold quite regularly. Much later it was found out that the employee who was in charge of recreation and the craft shop had been letting inmates that were in the craft shop order supplies for their craft, but the "supplies" that came in the boxes were packs of Bugler. A lot of them.

At visitation I asked my mom for a $20 bill. My mom and younger sister came to visit often. My mother always wanted me to have things while I was in here, so she had no qualms about giving me a $20 bill.

The ID's that the TDCJ gave us at this time were hollow in the middle. I found this out through wear and tear; where it was sealed at the top came open. At visit I gave my ID to my mom and she took it to the bathroom and put the 20 in the opening. When she came back, she would slide it to me and I'd put my ID into my clear ID holder. And no one would see it when I was strip searched.

The boss who was doing the strip search that day was lazy and if no rank was around, he would not search us at all. When the visit ended, I went to the strip area and this other boss man came out of nowhere and right up to me and said, "Get out of 'em." (Indicating that I needed to strip.) I grabbed my ID holder and threw it on the floor. It was just an ID and a clear holder, no need to search something you can see clearly. But he bent over and picked up and picked it up pulled my ID out and saw the $20. "Get dressed and come with me."

In the lieutenant's office, the captain asked where I got cash money from.

"Your mother?" he offered.

"No, I was carrying it in for someone else," I said. I hoped he would believe it.

"Your mother is upfront and she confessed and she says that this wasn't the first time she has done it."

Oh Mom. My mother is not a criminal. She will tell the truth and try to take the blame. Not realizing that the TDCJ will accept her confession. Punish her and me too. The TDCJ is equal opportunity.

And she was removed from my contact visit list and for a whole year we visited through a glass, with a telephone to talk through instead of through a mesh screen. I was demoted to medium custody. But first, a few days later, I was brought to the major's office.

"Jones, I have two cases here for you. One, a soliciting case, and two, contraband, namely a $20 bill. These are serious offenses in a penal institution. However, they could disappear."

Here we go. The snitch game. That's where this was headed. He can solicit me to snitch, but I can't solicit someone to breach security. What kind of place was this?

"You let me know who my dirty officer is and these cases are gone."

"I don't know nothing about any boss and their hygiene habits. I don't deal with officers," I said.

"Then which inmate do you…"

"No, don't even go there. Two cases, you say? I'll see you in court."

And they slammed me. Restriction, took my good time, dropped my status level. And UCC placed me on medium custody. It was January 2001.

* * *

I know that you are tripping on my disregard for my mother. At the time I was too selfish to own up to what I'd done. My "need" to please men so I could be validated overrode everything else. You may say, "What man?" but look, there was always a man behind everything I did. Always in some capacity.

But to this day, now that I have a real POR, it plagues me, the things that I did to my mom. There are nights, when the distractions run out, and the books have been read, the puzzle completed, and there's nothing to stand between my past actions and my conscience, part of what torments me is the things I did to my mother.

There are three custody levels: minimum, medium and close. Everyone enters in as minimum, and your behavior (or getting caught for it) determines if you get demoted to medium or close custody.

Sometime in the last four years the TDCJ got smart (in this one area) and made being on medium or close custody an actual deterrent. There used to not be any difference between the custody levels except for which pod or wing you lived on.

Now, the policy is that a person on medium custody gets only two hours dayroom and one hour outside rec. per day. And close custody gets no dayroom, and one hour of outside rec. The rest of the day you are in your cell. In minimum you can stay in the dayroom all day and go to rec. as much as they call it.

Deterrents are necessary to put a stop to inmates breaking the rules. Or else it would be chaos. I had to do one year on medium but if I caught any case my year would start over.

This was my tenth year in prison. Another cycle, that was on a larger scale, started when I got punished for my crimes, then appeared again in 1993, and showed up again on medium custody. I felt convicted of how I had been living and I rededicated my life to the Lord.

There were a couple of Christians over there and we hung around and talked, and went to church when it was called. Although being stuck in the cell all day, you didn't have to be Christian or religious; when they called any 'open call' service, we all went to it. In that tiny chapel it was SRO.

Looking back, it seemed that the only churches that came to the prison to preach were mostly the 'prosperity gospel' preachers, the 'name it, claim it,' ones. But I still never distinguished between them and, say, the Baptist church that I grew up in. While some of that is on the church, a lot of it is on me. I was a mindless drone being led, and I didn't question it. I believed that church was church, and if one of those churches clapped, ran around "in the Spirit" and spoke in tongues, who was I to say the ones who didn't do this was either right or boring or wrong?

But the cycle in my life was I believed that I'd got saved at age nine, and that I "backslid" in my teens. Then when I was caught for my crimes, I "rededicated" my life to Jesus. Then when I didn't make parole, I "backslid" again. In 1993, I felt convicted so I went back to God. Each time that I went back to God, I would tell people, "I'm not gay anymore. I'm a Christian."

This is what I was taught: "Name it, claim it." Claim that you are not gay. Quote the verses in the Bible that condemn homosexuality. "Rebuke the devil and he will leave you alone." Just tell the homosexual spirit to leave you. You have authority over demons. (Luke 10:19) "Have someone cast that demon of homosexuality out of you." You can get saved but you have to get someone who is strong in the Spirit to cast that devil out of you.

"If you have faith the size of a mustard seed you can move that mountain out of your life." All you need is a little faith and you can be delivered. "Put on the Armor of God." The devil can't get you then.

Every time I went back to God, I lasted six months then I fell on my face. Every time I was told those same things listed above. And I did them all, with all my strength. Just like they told me to do. I read all the books by Hagin, Hagee, Copeland. But it never stuck. I was burning up with lust and needed the validation of a man on the inside, and I always fell flat on my face.

My church friends would always tell me after I fell, "If you just had faith the size of a mustard seed." They may have meant well. But what does that statement tell me? It tells me that I don't even have faith the size of a mustard seed. And the Bible says that in order to please God we must have faith. Abraham started this whole thing with faith. Faith pleases God. I didn't have any, that's what my strong Christian brothers were saying. That's what Copeland said.

If I don't have any faith, am I saved? I didn't realize it then but it was like they were teaching me that to overcome sin, be saved, delivered and all that, that I had to have an experience. They also taught that I could command God and He would do what I said. But none of these things worked. I kept going back and forth with God and my sin. I kept seeking this experience, this feeling, this authority. And I was blinded to the fact that I wasn't seeking the person of Jesus. I knew that in my lifestyle I was miserable, so I was seeking a feeling beyond that an experience that would transcend me higher.

Well, we can all thank God that He is higher and bigger than our paltry attempts to get our life right. He is Sovereign. There were times over the last ten years where, looking back, I could see God at work. He brought people in my life to impart His truth to me. God's voice is still and small, and He does not bombard you. He tells you his teaching, and I received it each time, but I didn't hear it. He first revealed to me that Jesus is God. And then the exchange that happened at the cross—He took my sins. He gave (clothed) me in his righteousness. Then He brought me to that guy Eli on the Walls unit. At just the right time.

Now you might say that it was a homosexual relationship, but I've learned that even while I was a sinner Christ died for me. God hates sin. He does not approve of it. But even us humans, if our child falls in the mud and gets hurt, we will get down in the mud to help them. God sent me Eli in the midst of my depravity to wake me up and give me a gift, the gift to come out of denial and see the truth of my actions and how my life was a destructive force, hurting people. And this motivated me to change. It was no coincidence that God sent me a guy name Eli, which was short for Elijah. The name Elijah, in Hebrew, means the Lord is God.

I stopped believing in coincidences long ago. There are two more truths that God "spoke" into my life in 2001. I received them but they didn't change my lifestyle at that time. "Receiving" requires a lot more and I wasn't there yet.

I met a Christian named David Cross. My first name, and the cross is the object of the gospel. I did not make the connections on these names until much later. God does have a sense of humor.

One day David Cross and I were discussing who can be saved. I told him everybody can get saved. He said that only the elect can. I brought up Bible verses to support my argument. "Whoever calls upon the Name of the Lord will be saved."

"Whoever <u>will</u>," he said.

"Yeah right, like I said." I replied. "For God so loved the world that He gave His only begotten Son that whosoever believes in Him shall not perish but have everlasting life."

"Whosoever <u>will</u>," he said patiently. "Not everyone <u>will</u>, DJ. Only those that the Father draws to Jesus."

We had these same debates all the time, and it would be years before I was convinced of the elect only being saved.

Being in my cell all day listening to music gets real old. I realized that radio stations don't program what they play with prisoners in mind. In the outside world no one listens to a radio all day long. You are in and out of your car, or listen for a while at home or the office. So every hour they repeat the top hit songs, and I got tired of hearing the same songs over and over.

I had the radio at the head of my bed and as I was lying on my back I reached over my head and moved the turner dial and I came across some guy preaching—Tony Evans, and it turned out that his church was in Dallas. After him another preacher came on, John MacArthur and *Grace to You*. There was something different about them and I could hear it in their voices, but more than that I felt drawn to listen to them. I still didn't know that there was a distinction in doctrine or in what is preached. I thought everyone was on the same team. I did not figure it out then either. But years later I realized that these two guys preached the truth of God's word.

The second truth that I received at this time happened at the end of my cycle, or may have been what ended it. One evening open-call church was called, and when they opened our cell doors everyone lined up at the door to go.

Church in prison. Anytime someone goes to church or refuses to 'go along with the crowd' and break the rules, there are always the nay-sayers putting them down.

"You didn't obey the rules in the world" or, "you didn't go to church in the world," are two common phrases that are said to us from the other men in white.

But we do go to church, and on medium custody everyone goes to church. And people wonder if anyone in prison sincerely gets saved. If I may answer for all the prisoners: "God we hope so!!" I mean Jesus said that He came for the sinners, and in here we are the majority.

We walked in single file, on the right side of the yellow line, down to the small chapel. It was packed but we found seats on the back row. I'd been back with God for several months, remaining abstinent, but I felt like I was standing on quicksand.

After we stood and sang along with the choir for a few songs we were seated again. The visitor tonight was a guy from a local church and he began to talk to us after the opening prayer. He said he had a praise report. This was good, right? Meant to encourage us and strengthen our faith. Who didn't want that? I needed that. Come on with it.

"Sixteen years ago, our refrigerator quit working. My son, who was five years old at the time, laid his hands on the fridge and rebuked the devil in Jesus' Name. My brothers, we still have the same fridge and it has still been working all these sixteen years. Stand up and give God the glory! Hallelujah!" he said.

Most everyone around me shot to their feet and clapped and yelled out praises to God. But I sat there frozen. I stared at the chair in front of me seeing nothing. I wanted to leave, to run. But in prison we become a true 'captive audience'. And I succumbed to the quicksand. I told God, "I'm through. I give up. If you let a kid 'heal' a fridge but I can't get rid of this sexual stronghold over my life, then I'm just through. I'm out."

I didn't know what exactly I was 'through' with, I just was done trying. That was the straw that broke the camel's back, and that camel might never get through the eye of the needle.

I went back to the instant comfort of my miserable promiscuous lifestyle.

*   *   *

Several days later I was called down to one building. An officer told me that I had a legal visit. I thought it strange that my lawyer would come visit me without writing me.

But when I got in there it wasn't my lawyer but an investigator for the Dallas District Attorney's office. As I sat down, I asked him where my lawyer was. His reply was "Oh, you have a lawyer?"

"Yes. I have a lawyer. Tom Pappas," I said.

"Well, I will notify him when I get back to Dallas. The DA sent me here to ask you some questions. But first I need to read you your rights." He read me my rights and then handed over a small blue card that had the Miranda rights printed on them. "Just initial this card, that states that I read these rights to you."

I should have gone with my gut. My gut said, "Don't initial anything. Demand your lawyer." But I knew that this could not be a good thing. I was curious about what they were up to. Why were my rights read to me? Demand a lawyer. Don't ever talk to these people without a lawyer. I went back and forth in my mind, looking at that blue card. Tom told me to never talk without him present. I'd read enough Grisham novels in the past ten years to know, beyond a shadow of a doubt, to *not* talk without my lawyer there.

But I couldn't go back to my cell without knowing what was going on. Without knowing what the Dallas DA was trying to do now. It would eat me up and stress me out. My curiosity won out so I initialed the blue card. But I wasn't going to talk. I would just listen. I handed him back the card.

"Mr. Jones, do you recognize this picture?" he pulled a picture out of his folder. And when I saw the picture, I knew that everything was ok

"Yes, I recognize it." It was one of the kids who'd attended childcare where I worked at. One of the liars, who'd said that I did things that I didn't.

"Can you tell me again the actions you conducted against this child?"

"Ask the DA, ask the Lt of Dallas Police, I took a lie detector test in 1991, about him and the others that made ridiculous claims about me. I passed the lie detector test, I never touched him. He was not my type."

"Not your type." He repeated. "Mr. Jones, Dallas has a new DA and he has promised these parents that he would look into these cases. It's best to get your side out in front."

"My side is that I never touched him. I was given a plea agreement to tell everything that I did. And I upheld my side of the deal. There are no other cases out there or in your folder. I was truthful, I proved it with the lie detector. I wish ya'll would leave me alone. I'm doing my time and I'm going to go home." I told him.

"But Mr. Jones…"

"I'm through with this interview." And I got up and reported to the officer.

*   *   *

As soon as I got back, I wrote my lawyer and told him about this visit. It took a couple of weeks but when he wrote me back, he again instructed me to never talk to them without him present.

He told me that a parent had gone to the new DA complaining that the old DA didn't do anything for them. The investigator was just digging around and that I shouldn't worry about it.

This calmed me down a little. I hated feeling so powerless. A couple weeks later I got a different letter that made me feel good. It was August 2001 and I received a letter from the Court Probation office informing me that I have successfully completed my deferred adjudicated probation. I had forgotten that the Probation had started in August 1991. It felt like an accomplishment. Even though I didn't really have to deal with it, being in prison. And I did dodge that bullet of almost getting more time. I could feel the tension release.

*   *   *

The radios that the commissary sold were encased in clear plastic; that way officers could see if we were hiding any contraband in them at a glance. A coax cable came out the back and screwed into a female coax receiver in the wall. This helped with reception. But if I moved my tuner to the end of the bandwidth, down by 88 I could get a TV station, NBC.

We got the officer to put the TV on NBC in the dayroom and I could stand at my door with my headphones on and watch TV and listen to what was going on. I watched Jay Leno and Conan O'Brien, every night. Even if the TV was off I would lie in my bed and listen to the shows.

I would always listen to it until I fell asleep. In the mornings when I woke up, I would hear the *Today Show* with Katie Couric on the radio. I'd change the channel and listen to the mix station.

But when I woke up that September morning, it didn't sound like the Today show. The somber voices, the reports. I knew right away that there had been a major incident. I turned over and put the headphones on. Katie was in the middle of her report:

"...two planes hitting the World Trade Towers. The president..."

I snatched my headphones off and ran to the cell door. The TVs were off and no one was moving. On medium custody pretty much everyone stays up all night and sleeps all morning. There are lazy bosses working but if you can get their attention sometimes they would roll your door. My cellie was dead asleep in a Thorazine coma. I began yelling.

"Hey picket. Picket. One section." The cinder blocks the prison is made of echoes and reverberates. She could hear me. I had a piece of cardboard that I stuck outside my cell door and waved it up and down to get her attention.

The intercom crackled, "What?" she said.

"Roll my door there's something happening." The door popped open and I put my shoes, shirt and pants on and ran down to the section door.

When she opened it, I ran around to the back and knocked on the bathroom door where the rover was asleep. "Who is it?" a male voice answered.

"Boss, the terrorists hit America. Come turn the TVs on." I said excitedly.

He opened the door and looked at me crazily. "C'mon, this is big." I told him.

He followed me into the section and turned on the TV with the remote. The image that appeared was of the first plane hitting a tower. Then the second one. Then they showed both buildings crumbling, imploding, in succession.

Our mouths hung open. Other guys started yelling for the boss to open their cell doors and let them watch too. After a few cycles of the news reports I slipped up to my cell and brushed my teeth and made a shot of coffee. Then I went back down to the dayroom.

Everyone was quiet. America had never been attacked before and now they'd taken over planes and flew them into the two towers in New York. I was astounded. I think we all were. And I think that this was one of those rare moments in prison when no one was concerned about their own trivial problems. We were all focused on New York, and we didn't know what to think.

They say that you always remember where you were and what you were doing when you hear breaking news.

There are a lot of artists in prison. And if you are really good you can get a job as a unit artist. If the warden wants a mural painted you paint it. Murals of the two towers went up. In the infirmary one artist painted an eagle looking at the New York skyline from a distance. The eagle had a tear in his eye because smoke was coming up where the two towers had been.

*　　*　　*

In prison life goes on. 9/11 came and went. And we were back to doing time. Finally, January 2002 came and I got called to UCC and was given my minimum custody status back. A whole year with no cases.

I got moved to C pod 2 section. This was where Rosie had been killed but they'd cleaned it up pretty good. I didn't see any blood. It was kind of eerie at first but no one else even thought about it and I soon put it out of my mind.

The guy who'd taught me how to bake on Ramsey 2 back in 1995 was over here on the section. He was at a table playing scrabble with a couple of other guys.

"DJ, put your things up and come sit down," he yelled when he saw me.

I put all my stuff in my cell and went out to the dayroom. "You know how to play scrabble?" he asked me.

"No, not really. I tried once but didn't score that good." I said.

"It don't matter, you'll be my partner," he said, hugging me. "It's good to see you. It's been, what, six years?"

"Yeah, 1995. Ramsey 2. You know Ramsey 2 is not the same? They got that ex-gang program over there and it's just not the same. So I came back to safekeeping," I explained to him.

Lil' Mike was still funny and soon had all of us cracking up at the table. I knew how to spell but I seemed to suck at scrabble. I ended up causing Lil' Mike to lose.

"It's alright. Take this to the cell with you. Go through it and write down all the two letter words." He handed me the 3rd Edition Scrabble dictionary.

"You want me to go through this?" I looked at him like he was crazy.

"Just skim each page until you see the two letter word. The first one is AA. Write all ninety-seven down and memorize them. It will help your game."

"You don't ask for much," I said, but I did as he told me and then one day he and I played scrabble by ourselves and he showed me how to play strategically. I pick up on things fast and soon we were winning against all partners.

*   *   *

I received a letter in the mail from Skip Hollandsworth, editor of *Texas Monthly* magazine. He said he read the *Dallas Morning News* article and wanted to do an article about me in *TM*.

I wrote him back and told him as long as he was fair and told my side of the story that I would do the interview. I mailed that to him and waited for his response. As I was waiting, I got a letter from my best friend who was also on Ramsey 2 with me, D. He was informing me that he'd finally gotten the castration surgery. He was the first one in Texas prison under the new law to have it done. He said that he now had control over his sexual urges.

I had always been against castration. I was a strong believer that you have to change your thoughts and belief system. I still believe that. I did that. I changed my beliefs and I have no desire for children. It worked.

But I was still spinning out in the cycle of promiscuous sex and masturbation. I didn't see a halt. I could not control my sexual urges to use sex as a soother. And when D said that he had control of his sexual urges, for the first time I considered getting castrated.

I wrote D back and told him my thoughts and about my continuous cycle. I also wrote to the SOTP Director at the Goree Unit and requested the surgery. I had been on the Telford unit for thirty-four months. In those thirty-four months we were placed on a thirty-day lockdown a total of thirteen times. That is over a year total of lockdowns. Not a very pleasant experience. Before I left the warden allowed my mother to have a pair of glasses mailed to me from an eyeglasses store. I didn't have to wear those state 'Buddy Holly' glasses anymore.

I was at the Goree unit by Jan 2003. I thought that they'd transferred me over there to go through the castration process. I was shocked and surprised to find out that I was brought over for a civil commitment assessment.

GOREE REPEAT

When I got to the Goree unit I was placed in transient status. The inmates that were potential candidates for civil commitment were brought to Goree about a year out from their possible parole or mandatory release. They would stay in transient on Goree for a month as they went through different interviews.

SOTP was still on Goree and if you were over there for the evaluation you also had to go to SOTP's introduction meeting. The head therapist, Mr. G., came in to tell us about the different parts of SOTP, individual therapy, group therapy, educational therapy and therapeutic community. When he brought up about the orchiectomy program (castration) it was clear that he did not approve of it.

I raised my hand and he called on me, "I wrote here a couple of months ago requesting to go through the orchiectomy process and I have not heard anything. Will you sign me up?"

"Why castration? It has nothing to do with rehabilitation," he said.

"I am still requesting this," I said.

"It's your body. Name?" I told him my name and TDCJ #. "Anyone else?"

"Hell, no. I'm not giving up my balls," A guy blurted out.

"What the hell, sign me up," a black guy said.

A few days later, I was brought to UCC and removed from safekeeping status after I signed a waiver that I would not hold TDCJ accountable if anything happened. I was assigned an SSI/Janitor job in the main hallway. Then later that afternoon I was moved up to the therapeutic community.

I was glad to be back on a small unit that felt good. No more thirty-day lockdowns. For some reason this unit was quiet. It didn't have that constant drone of fans, exhaust fans, TVs blaring, and loud yelling that is common in bigger units.

I met with my primary therapist, Mr. V. He explained to me that I had to go back through SOTP to get the castration surgery. In the meantime, I would be given a Lupron shot, which is chemical castration. It mimics the effects of an actual surgical castration. But before all that I would be brought down to John Sealy Hospital in Galveston, run by UTMB. Part of this hospital had been restructured as a prison and any time an inmate had to see a specialist for a medical condition he would be taken on medical chain. It's the same as regular chain; you get on a Blue Bird Bus and are driven to Galveston. I had to see Dr. William Winslade who was the head doctor over the orchiectomy program. He was also an attorney and he was responsible for the bill that made it possible for prisoners to be able to get castrated—voluntarily. He was a psychotherapist and he would evaluate me to see if I was mentally and emotionally stable to have such a surgery.

From Huntsville to Galveston on I-045. This ride brought back memories. We had always gone to Galveston every summer for vacations when I was younger. When you are in prison, locked away from everything familiar for years, and then one day you drive by familiar places, it evokes long-lost emotions. It's bittersweet, because being on a locked bus I could only see but not touch.

At the hospital I also had to have a physical examination. A doctor examined me and he pulled a string out of his pocket with different sized balls on it. From marble to golf ball size but oval instead of round; my eyes got big when he asked me to disrobe and lie on the table.

But, thank God, it turned out that those are testicle sizes. If I was approved for a bilateral orchiectomy then the process would be to remove each testicle and replace it with a prosthetic one. "That way you appear normal," he concluded the explanation. He compared and wrote something down on his chart.

After all my examinations we got on the bus and headed back to Goree. It was 5 p.m. and the I-45 is two-lane traffic and we caught Houston's rush hour, so the bus moved at a crawl. There was always a comedian on the bus who kept us entertained with impossible stories. Sometimes he would make fun of people in the cars around the bus. And yes, it's true, I finally saw it with my own eyes. Some woman will really flash a prison bus full of male inmates her bare breast. Good times.

*   *   *

I wrote Skip Hollandsworth at *TM* and told him of my unit reassignment and my decision to be castrated. At the end of the *DMN* article that came out in 2000, I was quoted as saying I wouldn't get castrated, that it's in the brain that we [SOs] need to be castrated.

A guy named Jim Atkinson wrote me back, he explained that he was a writer at large and that Skip Hollandsworth had asked him to do the story. Jim and I traded letters, he arranged to meet with me in the SOTP offices with the Director, Judy Johnson, present. He sat in group therapy with us. He kept this up for a whole year. And I felt that if anyone knew my story it was Jim.

In other news, a Senator's nephew had been in prison and he had been raped. The COs and rank had done nothing to protect him. The nephew wrote a letter to his family. He told them goodbye and that he couldn't live with himself anymore. He told them why. Then after he mailed it, he killed himself. His Senator uncle drew up a bill called The Prison Rape Elimination Act (PREA). It was bi-partisan and passed both House and Senate unanimously, and in about three days—a record. Just remember that if Congress wants to pass a law they can. Keywords being "wants to."

By May 2003 I was approved for the orchiectomy. I was brought to medical and given my first Lupron shot. "It should take two weeks to take effect," the nurse said, pulling the syringe out of my right buttock.

I played basketball all the time. For outside recreation we had a full court and we shot for captain. Then the two captains would pick a team; I would get picked at three or four. I didn't care as long as I got to play.

I was really good at defense. And I had a great set shot out to the left or right of the goal. When I was feeling really confident, I could knock down threes from downtown. I could run circles around my opponents and get back down to my team's goal and post up for the pass. I am so thankful for Marvin at Ramsey 2, who taught me. On days my self-esteem was low I was a bad player. I wish Marvin would've taught me how to stay confident.

During that day's game I was guarding a Hispanic guy who was a good offense player. He was one inch shorter than me and he could run. The captain who picked me told me, "Don't let him score." And I didn't. Not one score. And that was the problem. A "man" can't stand to be held in a B-ball game by a homosexual. He had too much pride. And he didn't get a score on me. Trouble.

As we were in the line coming off the rec. yard, he began whining to his homeboys, and he said something to me. I said something back. Then he was all up in my face, I said something else and he hit me. All I remember after that was picking him up and body slamming him. On the ground I held him down and asked if he was through. He said yes.

It all happened so fast I don't remember what happened. No boss saw it and we both got through the strip search coming back in without detection. There was a janitor closet for the hallway workers and I stepped there to check myself out. I had a couple scrapes on my hands and my head hurt from his initial punch. My coworker came in the closet and then the Hispanic came in and offered his hand.

"We good?" he asked me.

I shook his hand and said, "Yeah, we good man." And it was over.

*   *   *

In the gym there was a half court so we had to split up in teams of three and play. There was a chalk board in the gym and whoever got there first wrote their name on the board for captain and then next up. Three-on-three was fun and I played better at three-on-three.

Word got around that there was an opening for Janitor in the gym. The next day I went to the major's office and knocked on his door. Working in the hallway had its privileges; access to rank was one of them.

"Come in," the major yelled.

"Sir, the gym needs a janitor and I came by to ask you for the job," I told him.

He looked up at me and said, "You know that the gym janitor is also the chapel janitor?"

"Oh, uh, no I didn't know. But I just want to work the gym, uh, sir," I told him. I just wanted to play basketball… I mean, clean the gym, I didn't want to go anywhere near a church. I was so far removed from God, I couldn't go in the chapel—I might get struck with lightning.

"That's not an option. Either both or none, what's your decision?"

"Ok, I'll do both." I handed him my ID. He picked up the phone and called classification: "Assign Jones, 594835, to the gym/chapel job." And it was done.

* * *

At 7 a.m. the therapist entered our living area and a CO unlocked our cell doors. The therapist began telling us to wake up and report to the dayroom. Being in a Therapeutic Community, the schedule was changing, it seemed, all the time. Once we got to the dayroom, a therapist told us that we were going to have "family meetings" in the morning from here on out at 7:15 a.m. A Therapeutic Community is a "family."

"Alright," Mr. M. began the meeting. "Who is happy to be here?" he asked.

I raised my hand. Then noticed I was the only one. I got crazy side-eye looks from my family. They did not understand. Go through what I've been through then tell me you are not happy to be in a TC on Goree. Ever since I'd been in the TC, the last time I'd come away from it with an enriched experience. I had realized this after I was no longer in it.

Then as Mr. M. went along in his speech, he said something that was an "Aha!" moment. I have never forgotten it. He said, "Your crimes were not a one-time happening. A one-time event. No, your sex offenses are your lifestyle. You've got to change your lifestyle."

In all those years I had never heard it that way. This was deep. This had to do with thought patterns but on a bigger scale. I understood the criminal offense cycle real well, but he was referring not to a thought pattern as it pertains to an offense but to a thought pattern that is connected to your whole lifestyle. I was going to have to think on this and get more feedback.

My two best friends were there. D, who'd had the surgery, and L, who was also taking the Lupron shots and was waiting for the surgery. We all lived on the same wing and we hung out and talked just like old times. I explained to them about the constant offense cycle that I was in. I had previously shared with them about my turning point. So, when I discussed with them about being in a cycle they knew that I was referring to either sexually acting out with other men or masturbation, to soothe myself and seemingly "meet my needs." We all three had had the same therapist at Ramsey 2 and had learned the cycle very well. I enjoyed our deep discussions about our complex lives and our many issues.

I explained in an earlier chapter about the cycle and its stages. Being in what we termed a constant cycle is right after the *act* and its powerful feelings, I would automatically go straight to negative thoughts and feelings, and on through the cycle. At this time, I didn't know about that core belief of how I truly felt about myself. I thought those negative feelings only stemmed from the triggering event. But it was Mr. M. telling me about how my offenses were a lifestyle that planted the seed, but it wouldn't be for some years until I heard Dr. Phil talk one day about core beliefs and how a person truly feels about himself deep down. And I saw it again in a book called *Stranded in the Wilderness*, years later.

Apparently, since I had always felt this way deep down in my core, then I was always (in my perception of reality) needing to soothe myself and create this outer image that I was okay, that I was good. I had taken care of the issue with children, but sex with men and masturbation were still my drugs of choice. The answer was always in the cycle—"False Calm," that should have been my sign. But I was too pretentious to see it.

This lifestyle that I was living took so much energy, because I was always *on*, always at 1000 watts. And I believe that people can feel the energy that you put out. Some people have a good energy, but I'm sure that my energy was a conglomerate of negativity and sexual hunger and the need to be validated, and that sapped the people I was around. Years later, after I had settled all these issues in myself, I met this guy and I could feel his energy and it was like a woodpecker that kept pecking into my soul, saying, "Accept me, love me, validate me." He would talk nonstop, not realizing the energy he put out that was screaming for attention. I thought to myself that I must have put off this same vibe back when I was lost and I can just imagine how people felt around me, because I did not like this guy at all. His energy hurt. And for people who didn't have this insight, who didn't know what was pecking at their soul and just assumed that they didn't like this guy, they further ostracized him. "Don't you ever shut up?" "Get away from me." The very need for acceptance that our body puts out in some form of energy is the same source of our rejection, and we don't even know it, and we keep trying to obtain acceptance. I now see that I developed this by continuously trying to get my step-dad to love me. I developed this pattern from a young age and it was my driving force. "The hand you hold is the hand that holds you down." And I was holding my own hand. Talk about the definition of insanity. "Hello wall, will you please love me? Why won't you speak to me?"

But I didn't understand all of that in May 2003. I wish that I had, but instead I kept using sex. The day that led me to one of the best decisions in my life was May 14. I remember it clearly. I had gotten the Lupron shot on May 1. Being in that constant cycle, I was in my cell and I was getting ready to masturbate. When all of the sudden the urge just left. It was gone and in its place was a sense that I could control this. That nurse had told me that the Lupron shot would take two weeks to take effect, and she called that on the nose.

Then I thought, "If this shot mimics real castration and this can be permanent, then I'm going to tell them let's do the surgery right now." On the next in and out I sought out D and L and told them what had happened. D just shook his head and said, "That's what I've been telling you." L had gotten his shot after me so his hadn't taken effect.

"For the first time in my life that urge is gone and I feel like I can really control this from now on." I told them. "But there is something else. I'm not sure that I can articulate this but before [the shot] when my issues were all clamoring to be sorted out in my chest it felt like they were all clustered together, and I could not sort it out or make any sense of it. But an orgasm made it disappear…"

"Or they were just put in a box and ignored." D said. He knew.

"Exactly, but now without the testosterone [the Lupron shot tells the pituitary gland to not produce testosterone] to muddy things up, I feel that it's not a cluster anymore. I can take this issue and track it back to its unmet need, and meet that need in an appropriate manner," I shared with them.

It was like, now that the hormone testosterone wasn't there, all the things that I had intellectually learned in SOTP came flooding back and I could use those tools and apply them to what was going on the inside. I could begin to internalize these wonderful things that I had learned in SOTP.

Castration by itself will not cure a sex offender. It has to be paired with changing your thought patterns, belief systems—your whole lifestyle. Castration helped me immensely. I was like a car with no engine—no drive. Before if I saw an attractive person and I began to fantasize about him I would have that urge. And I never could stop once I had an urge; I had to give in to it. It was so overwhelming and compelling.

But now it was gone. And I noticed another thing: if someone was in my view and I began my fantasy of him (I hadn't stopped that pattern cycle yet), once the person was no longer in my line of sight I didn't think about him. There was no feeling of that urge to continue. And remember, in my explanation of the cycle: if you can stop the deviant fantasy, or any fantasy, that is more than half the battle. Another thing Mr. V. told us in group: 98% of our life was our sexual fantasy life. Now I could control this. Man, what relief, what freedom.

*   *   *

"Have you ever heard shoes squeak on a gym floor?" an older guy asked me. When I told him yes, he continued: "This is how you achieve that." He handed me a gallon jug of Hilite. It was a chemical for cleaning the floor after mixing it with water in a mop bucket. "You wanted the gym job, you better make sure our shoes squeak when we play ball. Otherwise, the floor will be slippery and someone will get hurt. This is the most important part of your job, gym janitor."

A lieutenant on shift had told him to train me in my new job and it seemed that mopping with Hilite was my priority; being a ball player I quite agreed. I needed the soles of my shoes to grip that concrete and make that squeaking sound as I shook my defender on the way to the goal for a lay-up. Steve Nash, eat your heart out.

The chaplain explained my other duties, which consisted of setting up the chapel microphones on Sunday and Wednesday night, for the visitors who came to preach. Also, I was to get glasses and a pitcher of water and tea from the ODR for them to drink. During the day I would help the chaplain with paperwork and putting out the pamphlets, books and tracts donated to the chapel.

Tuesdays were good days. I took care of the gym. But having to set up chapel on Sundays and Wednesdays was an inconvenience. This Wednesday night there was some premiere of a movie and on my wing we all planned to watch it. I decided that I would go to set up the chapel for service that night and get the pitcher of tea and water and ask somebody if they would take it all down after service was over.

But Someone Else had a different plan. As I left the chapel to go back to my wing to watch the movie I passed the couple who'd come to preach in the hallway, and I felt this weight in my heart and I sensed that I should go hear this preacher. I tried to ignore it because I wanted to watch the movie, but I recognized the conviction of the Holy Spirit. If you have never been in a church and heard the gospel, you may not understand. But this was one of the jobs that the Holy Spirit does; he convicts you and draws you to Jesus. Right now, Jesus was about to be preached in the chapel.

I kept walking toward my wing and had a dialogue with the Holy Spirit. "But Lord, I don't want to go in there. I want to watch this movie." I felt literally weighed down. When I got to the stairs I could not walk up. My legs were heavy.

I told the Holy Spirit, "Okay, I'll go but there'd better not be any fridges being healed." I turned and went back to the chapel. I found a seat on the third row. The man and his wife were from a local church which had a prison ministry. Tonight, he preached on the parable of the ten virgins. (Matt 25:1-13) I'm not going to go in to what he said, but what is important is what I got from it. What I heard was a warning: don't be foolish, thinking that I am saved and that I can keep on living my way. I didn't want to hear the words, "Depart from me; I never knew you."

Looking back, this was another time that God was speaking to me; telling me His truth. There was no denying that this was a weird encounter that could only be explained by the supernatural.

Again, I listened but I didn't *hear*. I didn't know how to wholly give myself over to Him. I still had too much of self that was leading me but I didn't know where I would end up. It seems I had only led myself to prison. When would I get off of this never-ending rollercoaster?

*   *   *

Days later I got a different message. I was called to the front where central control was. I was told to stand there and I could see a cop coming through the sallyport.

Even though I hadn't done anything wrong fear shot though my body and I needed to find a toilet soon. If you are ever constipated Fear is better at inducing a bowel movement than Ex-lax. The sallyport door rolled open and the cop and the captain walked out. The captain pointed at me.

"Are you David Wayne Jones?" the cop asked.

"Yes, sir." How could I be arrested when I was already in prison?

"I'm here to serve you with this subpoena. The state of Texas is suing you for civil commitment." He handed me the paper and he and the captain disappeared into the sallyport.

"What?" I said to no one. I stood there, flabbergasted. The lady in Central tapped on the window and made a shooing motion with her hand. I went back to the wing. L and D were at a table and I joined them and handed one of them the subpoena.

"Man, that sucks," said L.

"Oh, that's great. The state of Texas defends me from the state of Texas. How do they get away with this stuff?"

I was in a funk.

*   *   *

The next week, officers from Goree unit took me and a couple other inmates who had been subpoenaed also to the court in Conroe, which was about a thirty-minute ride in a state van.

Shackled, with a chain going from our handcuffs to our ankle cuffs we shuffled into the court room. There was a lady on the prosecutor's side standing up tall, joking and laughing with a man and a woman who were sitting down. When she saw me, she told the two people sitting down, "Look, who's this. Huh, who's this?" and she left them and walked over to me and put out her hand. I reached out with both hands, cuffed, and shook her hand.

"I'm Sally Milano with State Counsel for Offenders. I'll be representing you for your trial. Look," and she turned her head to indicate the man and woman she was talking to when I came in. "That's the prosecutors, they don't stand a chance. We got this." And she began laughing. It was contagious. And I felt a little hope.

At court, it was just a preliminary, sort of like an arraignment, getting everything on record. Sally gave me some papers with questions on it. "Fill these out, answer all the questions truthfully. I'll be by the Goree in a few days to talk with you some more. We will strategize and we'll get a game plan, okay? Sound good? Good, see ya later."

I shuffled back to the van after the other guys were finished and went back to Goree.

*   *   *

My mother had divorced her third husband, my second step-dad. It had been about a year. The weekend after that court date my mom came to visit. I told her about the civil commitment and my lawyer. It cast a somber feeling over the visit.

In a previous visit I'd told her about the Lupron and how I wanted to get castrated. She was against it at first but after I told her about how I had control for the very first time, she gave me her blessing on it.

Then Mom told me what she'd come to tell me. "Your sister and I went to see some movie and in the movie the girl ended up with the guy and she was happy. As I left, I was praying that God would let me find my guy, a good guy who will take care of me and I can be happy. Then coming out of one of the other movies guess who I saw?" She asked, all happy. I realized that she was 'man happy.' I knew that look.

"Sonny?" I guessed, but it could only be him.

"What, how did you know?" she said, not even upset that I'd answered right and she hadn't gotten to reveal it.

"Mom, it could only have been Sonny. He's the good guy and he is the one you should have married way back when. Remember that night in the Nova when I kept telling you to find my song on the radio, "New Kid in Town," and then he was there. He picked me up real high in the air? I think about it all the time. It should have been him. I'm so glad for you. Where is he?"

"In the car. Put him on your visiting list. Okay?"

"Yeah, I'll do it. I love you, Mom; I want you to be happy."

"Promise promise,"—her.

"Always always,"—me.

That was a quote from the movie *Stepmom* with Julia Roberts and Susan Sarandon. We hugged and I kissed her on her cheek. She was 5'3" I was 5'8½". The hardest part of the visit was to walk her to the door and not go out with her.

* * *

The lawyer Sally came back, like she'd said she would. I gave her my answers. We talked, I told her my concerns, she said that she would do everything she could to help me not get civilly committed.

"How many trials has SCFO won?" I asked.

"None; everyone they've sued for civil commitment has been committed by them. But I can tell that your case is different. I can win your case. I can tell that you have put a lot of work into changing."

State Counsel for Offenders is a division of the Texas Department of Criminal Justice. They defend a lot of inmates in a wide variety of cases. They are underpaid and overworked. Some of the lawyers care and some just collect a paycheck. Sally was one who cared.

Over the next few months Sally and her assistants would meet with me as we planned and strategized. We were set up to do depositions in August. But Sally showed up by herself. We went into the room where we usually met.

"Bad news David. Dallas County is about to bench warrant you to

Dallas. They have another charge against you. Your civil commitment has been postponed until after what happens with the case in Dallas," Sally told me.

"What charge? I have *no* other charges. I've been in prison. I don't have any other crimes out there," I exclaimed.

"I don't know what it is, but when you beat that, we will beat the civil commitment, okay?"

I really didn't know what this was. I knew that I'd told them everything and there was nothing to charge me with. The next week I went on bench warrant back to Dallas County Jail. Things were swiftly moving forward outside of my control. I felt like I was back on sand, slowly sinking. I didn't have anyone to rescue me.

MASS DELUSION

⊸•〰〰•⊸

> 'You're having delusions of grandeur again."
> -Leia – *Star Wars*

SOLUTION OR DELUSION?

Imagine, if you will, that you are a criminal. Drugs, robbery and the like is what's in your record. You don't want to steal, but you are addicted to drugs and an occasional robbery helps support your habit.

You have been in and out of county jail and even done a couple of two-year stints in the state penitentiary. But now you've got a twenty-year sentence, thanks to the third strike law, and they enhanced your felony. You enter a Texas prison and go to one of the units that have 2800 inmates. (Even if you went to a five-hundred-man unit the same theory applies.)

You think to yourself that you can finally get the help that you need. You have heard about all the rehabilitation services that TDCJ offers, when you were there before for those two two-year stints, but because you only had a two-year sentence you were not eligible due to waiting lists and you would not have been able to complete them.

You put in requests for as many classes and programs as you can take in a day. You are excited, motivated and you can't wait. While you wait for a response from your requests, you catch up with old friends who have been there since you last got out. You sit in the dayroom and catch up on old times. They remember how you used to conduct your hustle in the world and they hip you to the game that they've got going on right now in there. They have COs dropping off drugs and cell phones, and they are making money, real money not just commissary items. Your friends ask you to think about joining them—they want you on their team.

In your cell you struggle with your desires. You really just want to take these classes and get yourself better and stop living a destructive lifestyle, and you don't want to see the pain in your mother's eyes anymore, knowing that you caused it. But then there is that constant nagging thought, "Who are you kidding? This lifestyle is all you know. You can't change. You better join in and make that money, and you can get high for free. Stop thinking that you can do better."

The CO, who is working the wing, begins to pass out that day's mail. You do not get any letters from family but you get the response from your request for those classes:

"We're sorry, but you must wait until you are within five years of your discharge date, to even apply, then you will be on the waiting list, and can take classes/programs two years before your release date. Thank you for your inquiry."

All the hope that you had just deflates like air out of a tire. It's a big letdown. Wait, wait, wait. That is all you are told in this prison system that has nothing but time to do your time.

You reason in your mind, with the only reasoning that you have, that same criminal thinking pattern that has governed you your whole life: "I guess for lack of anything better to do, I'll join up with my old friends, make some money and get high. I wouldn't want them to think that I am a square."

You go to the dayroom; shake your homeboy's hand and he introduces you to the guys. He offers you a K-2 cigarette. You get high and forget all about your aspirations to change. Right then, a commercial comes on TV, something about littering and then they show that familiar sign every Texan knows: "Don't mess with Texas". Then, as you inhale deep, you think, "You're sure right!"

Welcome to mass incarceration. Now, not everyone gets involved in making money, or getting high, but when you get here and you see that you don't have to take classes, or cannot take classes, until the end of your sentence, you don't want to be ostracized by the people that you live around, so you join in with them. In whichever assimilation that may be—and it's never to change and obey the rules. "If you don't stand for something, you will fall for anything."

But with a criminal cycle of thought patterns, you are limited on what you can choose, and will more than likely go along to get along. Everyone wants to be accepted, it's a hard-wired need that is instilled deep down, influencing our choices

So you end up reinforcing these criminal thought patterns for eighteen *more* years, and for the last eighteen to twenty-four months of your sentence, you begin to learn a new way to think.

Which do you think will stick:

  a) The thought patterns that you used in your whole life(style) and for the last eighteen years in prison, or

  b) The new ones introduced to you during the last two years of your prison sentence?

Please help end mass incarceration, and reform prison, criminal justice and sentencing procedures and guidelines.

Resistance is not always futile.

WHAT SENTIMENT?

U gly, beautiful, fat, skinny, muscular-built, badly-built, fine, pretty—all these are labels. Survivor, victim, worthless, sex offender, criminal—all these are identities.

All these are just words at their most base form. And words can be very harmful. But we cling to these words as if our lives depend on it. And our identity surely does. We as a society define these words, and depending on what's trending right now determine what is "cool." But who determines this? The media, the stars, TV shows, movies, music, commercials and—in today's time—the internet.

They don't develop overnight. But they do get developed. And we are like the Borg, being assimilated. We are told what's hot and what's not. A commercial will use beautiful people to sell their product and this conveys the message that if we use this product, we too, will be beautiful.

Are we this shallow? Can we not think for ourselves? What does this say about our self-esteem? I have to have a Polo shirt because it's what is "in" right now.

This is the pressure we grow up in. And those who are deemed uncool we bully, we treat with disdain, we reject. And those we reject are alone and no one knows what they are thinking. Then when they act out in an unacceptable way, they are punished rather than asked: "How are you feeling? What are you thinking?" And when the irrational thought is identified maybe someone could help that person correct it before it becomes ensconced in their belief system.

But this didn't happen in my generation. And it's not happening right now. And right now, it has gotten to the point that people are saying, "Whatever you feel is alright, it's who you are," and then the government is giving them rights and making laws to enforce those rights. Now we have to call a guy a girl and vice-versa, and on top of that terms and words are being redefined for a class of people. They want to be called a "they" or "them" and not a "he" or "she".

Then religious groups are sued for not just their convictions but for viewpoints. Then these same people are forcing their viewpoints on everyone else. It has gotten so bad that even a comedian cannot make certain jokes lest they offend someone.

And I believe that these identities are what people are clinging to and when you start to infringe on people's identities they feel threatened and they lash out. But are these identities true? How can you define your identity off of feelings when feelings are not trustworthy? Feelings lie to us. Feelings stem from thoughts, and we think what we are told and it is now evident that we have been lied to by not just media, internet, and the TV but our family, friends, and the education system, and oh, yeah, the government.

Friends and family have been lied to so they in turn hand down these same lies. Our history books are wrong. If they lied to us about the Pilgrims, the Native Americans, who actually discovered America, and the big one, slavery, then what *did* they tell us that's true?

My mother taught me, inadvertently, not to show my true feelings to other family members, to keep it all quiet, distract myself from reality. At age five I had to grow up and be an adult. I took care of her. Then later on she wanted to be the mother again. And that's just one area. Her relationship with me. Her continually going back to her abuser. All this defined love and life to me.

No one knew what effect this had on me. No one knew what I was thinking or feeling. The Bible says that, "Evil is bound up in the heart of a child…" That's why the need to instruct, teach, and discipline a child is

+ 260 +

so important. Find out what they are thinking. Thinking causes feelings. If you can correct the thoughts, you will save them from a world of hurt.

There is a sentiment broadcast everywhere. The sentiment I received from my stepfather and his abuse, my mother and her worldview of how to deal with abuse, was that I was to blame, I was worthless. Then at the same time I had to fit into society. I had to be cool, I wanted the other people at school to accept me. This gave me a false self-esteem, a false feeling of worthiness. Because deep down I felt rejected by guys and accepted by the girls. Then girls became someone that I could manipulate to get my way because of the acceptance.

Just like Dr. Phil said: "In life, we generate the results that we believe that we deserve." I felt rejected by a man at home, so I felt I deserved that and it became my belief and then like a self-fulling prophecy. Keep in mind that's just one belief developed. And if this is the case in my life, can you see what happens in a society? Everyone grows up with all these different beliefs, and we all believe that *we* are normal. That *we've* got it right. That *we* have *the truth*.

But what happens when people's beliefs contradict each other and collide? The #MeToo movement believe that they are victims, and want all these rights and state that they are still affected by their victimization thirty years later. Then criminal advocates are stating "The prisoner was abused when he was young so let's be lenient." Then they are told that criminals don't get rights and that they can't use the fact that they were abused.

Those two views contradict each other. It's okay for #MeToo to say they were abused and have demanded rights and stricter laws that affect criminals years and decades later. But those criminals are told that they can't claim that. And must live in a prison where more abuse is poured out, where they are constantly told they are worthless and where they must be exposed to the identity of mass incarceration for years, reinforcing those criminal thought patterns; this is the sentiment.

And this is what's happening. And people wonder why crime still keeps happening. But they keep the same lawmakers in office making the same laws and this is another sentiment.

This is the epitome of the definition of insanity.

So if this is going on in one part of life, what is going on elsewhere?

Don't think that it's okay, because it's not. There is another sentiment in America and it's been passed down since the 1600s and 1700s. Some of it has been verbal but mostly it is unspoken. But it's been the most violent.

I'm talking of the sentiment of hate and racism that has permeated into all of America. America has been taught, told, and has felt the horrible urge to hate what is different. That it's okay to see some human beings as less than human. I read an article that books and TV and movies have so portrayed the black man as the boogeyman or bad guy, that it has aided that sentiment. But it's deeper than that. The founders of America were very wrong in this one thing: claiming that "*All* men are created equal," while at the same time *not* abolishing slavery.

And it's not just blacks and the racism towards them. People hate what is different from them. They don't tolerate other people when they are different. And that has caused a lot of violence and bloodshed in these supposedly United States.

If you want to know what a nation is like, go look in their prisons. It's a smaller version of the bigger world, but the lines are drawn in here and there is no pretense. Except, when you "free world" folks come to look into this human zoo, we are good chameleons and we are pros at seeming normal. But I've been here for thirty years and I'm telling you we are not. Something has to be done to reform the prisons. Pretty soon we will get out, to a neighborhood near you, and what sentiment do you want us to bring out with us?

There are all these commercials going on right now—"We are all in this together." But don't believe it. If so, we would not have been left to sit here and wait for Covid-19 to ravage the prison system. If so, mass incarceration, human warehousing, would never have existed. But they do exist. And we are labeled and identified and put into this box, this cage and left to fester.

We need to *squash the sentiment!* We need to do a lot of things but we've all got to pool together and squash it. I have been fighting against some part of this sentiment since I became aware of it. But I keep finding that it is deep and convoluted. I resist one part but ninety-nine other parts invade. In 1992 I remember my primary therapist asking me, "How do you see your self-esteem?" And I told her that I had a pretty good self-esteem. "Then she asked me "How, when you have sexually offended against others?" I learned from that exchange that I don't love or even like myself very much. That deep down I hate myself. And when a person hates themself, they can't treat others in a humane way. These two go together. The golden rule is "Do unto others as you would have it done unto you." But if I hate me, then woe to others. And this is the situation the world over.

The answer is *not* joining a group and adding stricter laws to criminals to just keep them locked up, or to exact revenge on them. The answer is *not* clinging to an identity that is self-defeating. The answer is first to love yourself, build morals and values and then examine your thoughts, beliefs and your feelings. Eliminate the lies and irrational beliefs. And most importantly ask your children how they are and what are they thinking, encourage them to express their feelings. And explain to them that sometimes our feelings lie to us.

The answer to squashing the sentiment is to do your part. We *are* all in this together and if I can see this from prison what does that say about you? Laws can be changed but how do you change the hearts of men?

The answer is to keep living as you keep learning. And stop compartmentalizing (I was told this so many times in therapy). That is dangerous.

I'm going to keep learning and living. I'll fall before I get to that finish line. But the falling doesn't define me. My past doesn't define me. My ability to be open and choose to change and not to harm anyone at all with words, thoughts, or deeds, this is what should define me. And this is the road that I'm on. Want to join me? C'mon. (By fall I do not mean reoffend.)

THAT IS SO BARBARIC

2003 - 2005

"It is our choices, Harry, that show what we truly are, far more than our abilities."
-Albus Dumbledore – *Harry Potter* Series

B ack to the Dallas County Jail. As soon as I got to the tank in the newly-built north tower, I put in a request to see the psychiatrist. In county you do not need any proof of medication history, you just tell the doctor what you want and they give it to you. Someone has to be benefitting from this besides the inmates. (Everything is about the money.)

Besides the antidepressants he recommended Klonipin for anxiety. I explained to him that I'd just started on Lupron shots and I was supposed to continue on them until the surgery. Without blinking he ordered it for a year. I was so glad. I wanted to keep the control over those sexual urges.

My attorney came to see me. He told me that this case that the prosecutors were charging me with was the same case that the investigator came to see me about in 2001, it was the same case on which I passed a polygraph back in 1991, and the 1991 DA and investigating lieutenant had been satisfied with and believed that I did not commit this and therefore did not charge me with it.

"But I have talked with the judge, and it's the same judge from 1991, he is very familiar with your case and he remembers the plea bargain and that you did not do this. He knows that this is just the DAs trying to keep you locked up. The DAs think that they look bad for you getting only a fifteen-year sentence and they want to keep you behind bars.

"They also indicted you on this in November 2001, and sat on it and did not notify you or me. Then they tell you almost two years later. David, this is BS and they know it. Just be patient and it will get thrown out. So how is your mom doing?"

And the wait was on. Hurry up and wait, it's like a rule that I have been forced to abide by since 1991. When was the 'hurry up' going to stop the 'wait' and give me some satisfaction?

Jim Atkinson came to interview me on this new development and took pictures of me for the magazine spread. He told me that he was waiting on me to actually have the surgery to publish the article in the magazine.

In county jail nothing happens. There is just the wait. The guys who can't afford bail must wait, and wait some more for their case to hit the docket. Cases are so backed up people are waiting two years to have their cases heard. Two years in this icebox human aquarium. The air conditioning is always on year-round and it is freezing. The outer wall that faces the picket is all glass. The officers in the picket can observe all six tanks that are in a semi-circle around the picket through the glass. We are like fish in an aquarium. All day long we stay in this one tank. One TV, single cells, the doors stay open all day and we can go to the dayroom when we wish.

The only time that we leave is for the gym or medical or court. Other than that, madness seeps in to our brains having to be captives in this glass zoo. The Dallas County Sheriff's Department staffs the jailers, and they have a goon squad called the Security Threat Team, STT. Any unruly inmate will find himself on the wrong side of this team. They don't talk, they eliminate the threat, and haul you off to solitary.

2003 turned into 2004. I was still here, no hearing. January turned into February and towards the end of February I was told that I was on the chain back to TDCJ, by a jailer.

"But I haven't been to court. This is a mistake." But once you are on a list for the chain, no amount of arguing will stop it.

The next morning a TDCJ Blue Bird came to pick up about forty people headed to the prison. We were taken to the Diagnostic unit and after being processed in and placed in a cell, I still didn't know why I was here. I had not been able to see anyone to ask.

It was a Friday; Monday would be March 1. Nothing would happen until Monday. The only thing that prison allowed me to bring with me was my Bible, and my radio and other paperwork and stuff. With nothing else to do I opened my Bible to read. I had a John MacArthur Study Bible; it came with study notes that made it seem like John MacArthur was in my cell helping me. I'd begun reading my Bible again since I'd been on Lupron. I wanted to see if God's word would get through to me now that the testosterone was gone.

An officer came to my cell door and told me that I had to go to the captain's office.

"Why?" I asked. Anytime a CO comes to get you and tell you that someone is calling for you, we, as inmates, always ask why. And even though we know that they would not know the reason, they are just the messenger, we always will ask why.

"The captain doesn't tell me why he does something, and I don't tell him why I do something. We like to keep it that way."

My cell door opened and I stepped out and the picket rolled it shut. In the hallway the rover gave me directions to the captain's office and when I knocked on the door, I heard a voice telling me to come in.

Inside I saw the captain, in uniform, two vertical bars in parallel on his collar. And there were two women, whom I knew. Judy Johnson the director of SOTP, and Ms. Engman, who used to be my primary therapist in 1996 back when I had my turning point.

"Hello, Jones, how are you doing?" Ms. Engman asked.

"I'm fine. I'm not sure why I am back at TDCJ. I haven't been to court yet." I explained.

"No one told you why you are here?" Ms. Johnson said, looking at Ms.

Engman, "It's a good thing we came; we almost didn't come. But your lawyer has filed a nunc pro tunc, and you are owed some time?"

"Yes, they erred when my time started. They started in 1993 and it was supposed to begin in 1991," I told them.

"Oh well, he got your time back and you are being released from prison and we brought you down here for you to get the castration surgery. You still want that surgery, right?"

"Most certainly, I've never been more sure about anything than I am about this."

"Well, good, the surgery is for Monday, March 1, and on Sunday you need to not eat all day, twenty-four hours before the surgery. Monday morning TDCJ will take you to the hospital and we will be there to see you in, give you support and we will see you after the surgery. Then you will be taken to Estelle unit to recuperate and then, although you are released from TDCJ you still have to go back to county jail until that case is resolved." Ms. Engman told me.

What kind of place was this prison, that in one moment they can deride, debilitate, and demean you, and in the next treat you like you matter, and that this is the next step in your life—a big step—truly meant something, and that I didn't have to do it alone. I believe that what Ms. Johnson and Ms. Engman did gave my decision validity and stopped any doubt that may have been seeping in. I am grateful to both of them for that.

Monday morning as I lay on a gurney being prepped for surgery, Ms. Engman informed me that *Texas Monthly* magazine had published my article in the issue that came out on the stands that day, March 1, 2004. She said she would purchase the magazine and read it to me after surgery.

The next thing I remember was coming awake in my room, and Ms. Engman was sitting there with the *Texas Monthly*. The TDCJ Transportation officer was in the room also.

"Jones, here, drink this. We can't leave until you take a piss, so drink up." Handing me a cup of Dr. Pepper.

Ms. Engman rolled her eyes, like she agreed with me: COs, what can you do? She pulled her chair close to my bed and began reading the article. (You may google this: *Texas Monthly* Magazine article, March 1, 2004 James Atkinson. Article name: "Your Friendly Neighborhood

Pedophile.")

"Hurry up Jones, drink some more," the CO yelled occasionally.

I drank and listened to her read the story. In the story he got a few facts wrong. Some I understand, he had to make it interesting: "Six officers swarmed the place of my employment to arrest me," when it was two plain clothes cops who came to arrest me. But mistakes like saying that I have a daughter when I have a son, didn't make sense to me.

The rest of the article was okay, but towards the end, as he reported that civil commitment proceedings had begun against me and then that the Dallas DAs were trying to put this bogus charge on me, that I was spiraling backwards as if all the hard work that I have done to rehabilitate myself could be undone by outward circumstances. As if I'd ever go back to wallow in the filth that I have cleaned myself of.

I'd like to clear something up. "*Read my word:* I do not care if I remain incarcerated for the rest of my life, or stay on civil commitment forever, even if they legalize pedophilia—know this, America. I will never, ever go back to that sickness, living that sick harmful lifestyle. You see, that change in my belief system is embedded in the new concrete foundation that I've built. It's not moved by outward events. This new lifestyle that I live is a permanent part of me. I don't want to go back, ever. I didn't change just to get out. I didn't give up my testicles as a game. No, that is my *new reality*, and I am living it."

"Jones, try to go to the restroom. See if you can piss," the CO said.

I went to the restroom and I pissed. The CO told the nurses and the doctor released me.

I thanked Ms. Engman for everything as I was being shackled up and I shuffled out to the van. The C.O. handed me a bag for vomiting and shut the door.

Immediately I felt nauseous as the van moved in and out of traffic. I lay down on the bench seat. About a mile away I quickly grabbed the bag and threw up about a pint of Dr. Pepper and bile.

I was glad when we got to Estelle. Estelle unit is in Huntsville out by Lovelady, TX. It was originally named Ellis 2 then changed to Estelle. It is considered a medical unit. It has a small hospital on the grounds and it also houses blind and deaf inmates. The regular part of the prison is redbrick, telephone pole style, two man cell. But I was placed into a room in the hospital.

While I was there the captain came to my room and told me that the media kept calling asking for interviews with me. The staff always tries to make you feel like it's not a good idea to give interviews. Not overtly, but by very delicately-placed words. They were in luck because I didn't feel like talking to anyone so I refused all media requests.

By the end of the week, I was processed for release from prison but I had to go back to county jail on a bench warrant. Dallas County came to pick me up, and about four others going back on bench warrant, and drove us to Dallas.

This time I was in the old Lew Sterrett aquarium. I was in an eight-man tank. Over the years Dallas had kept building county jails and no one had to sleep on the floor anymore. Again, I was bombarded with media requests. I agreed to talk to Brooks Egerton and Robert Tharpe of *Dallas Morning News*, and the local CBS and NBC news affiliates. When I talked with Brooks and Robert, they asked me to grant an interview with ABC. I relented and they came in with the cameras at the same time as my interview with *DMN*.

It was Monday March 8, 2004, my thirty-third birthday. The *DMN* came out on March 9 and I thought it was one of the better articles about me that captured my resolve to change.

Back to waiting for this hearing. My lawyer told me that the judge, who was on my side about this bogus case, was retiring in early '05 and that he wanted to hold off until then to hold this hearing.

All I could do was wait. The reporters for DMN allowed me to call them collect from county. I would call just to talk and it was like I was searching for info from them and they were searching for info from me.

In mid-December of 2004 I was brought to court for this hearing. I remembered a verse in the Psalms that states, "He confuses the counsel of the wicked." I prayed that God would confuse the DAs' counsel. To me the DAs were wicked, playing games with my life, trying to keep me in prison just so they could be reelected and look good to the public.

I believe that it is a travesty to have a position that you must be elected to when you are in charge of people's life or their death. Because you must continue to get convictions, for a DA, and hand down tough sentences, if you are a judge, if you want to stay elected. The focus is no longer on truth and innocence, but lies to make someone guilty and get a conviction. This has been my experience and I'll tell you more later on in this book, but for now this case, after twelve years (and two of those years they kept the indictment quiet), when I'd already satisfied the original investigator and DA that I didn't do it, was now being used to keep me locked up. I'm sure it was the Dallas DAs and other officials that were behind the push for civil commitment, when the law is clear that I didn't meet the requirements.

I had done nothing to earn this. I had not reoffended; I'd been in prison. And the one time that I was out I was sent back for having a sexual encounter with an adult. They couldn't be mad because I got fifteen years and did my time. In the legal world that's not only *not right*, it's unconstitutional malicious prosecution.

In the courtroom two DAs sat at their table as I entered and sat down at the table with my lawyer. He leaned over and said, "The top DA is sitting behind the DA's table. He came to influence the judge as to how important this case is. Especially in light of what the ADA did last month."

Last month I'd been brought to court, but it was a different court with a different judge. My lawyer had not been notified. The bailiff, doing her job, had asked me if I had an attorney or did I need the court to provide one. I told her of course I had a lawyer, and asked her why I'd been brought to this court. My case was in the 195th. She said that she would find out.

Later my lawyer explained that the ADA had snuck into the 195th court and on the clerk's computer reassigned the case to a different judge, a sterner judge. My judge was angry to say the least.

Now they were trying to stack the deck by bringing the head DA in here.

"All rise, the honorable Judge Nelms of the 195th District Court presiding."

"You may be seated," the judge said.

To the ADA: "I'm not sure why you brought your boss with you for a hearing such as this, but I won't be intimidated in my court."

The head DA stood up. "Sir, my presence here is to show you the gravity of the case against the defendant and I…"

"You are not needed, so either remain quiet or exit my courtroom." Then to the ADA: "Proceed with your opening but if it's already in your motion I don't need to hear it. Why don't you explain why you sat on the indictment for almost two years."

"Your honor, Mr. Jones was in prison and not out offending against children. So, while we were busy with the Texas 7 trials, we figured it didn't hurt anything to, uh, hold off on the trial for Jones." He stumbled on this excuse to the judge.

"Defense," the judge said.

"Your honor, it's our position that by withholding this indictment and not even notifying Mr. Jones, violates his rights. Mr. Jones will testify and…"

"We have witnesses to call your honor also," the ADA interrupted.

After all the witnesses had been called and rebutted, the prosecutors tried to say they had every right to bring this case after so many years, and after sitting on it for two years.

My attorney showed how we had a plea bargain agreement to tell the truth about everything I did. The old DA testified to this plea bargain and that he was satisfied that I did not commit the crime of this case.

The judge said he would have his response in two weeks. More waiting; Christmas came and went, then New Year. I waited. January 2, 3, 4. It had been more than two weeks, so I decided to call the reporters.

"Robert Tharpe," he answered.

"This is David Jones. I was wondering if you have heard anything from the courts?"

"Hi, David, you don't know? The judge dismissed the charges against you, you will be released today."

"For real? You mean it?" I asked.

"Yes, your lawyer hasn't told you?"

"No, not yet. Wow, I can't believe this."

"Do you have a comment, for the paper?"

"So, I'm ecstatic and excited to be getting out. I've done everything I can and more, to ensure that I won't hurt anyone anymore. Thank you, Robert and thank Brooks for me, okay?"

*   *   *

When the *nunc pro tunc* motion (Latin now for then) was granted, I was given the two years back time that was previously taken from me in 1997, and I was immediately eligible to be discharged on the mandatory release (flat time plus good time equals the whole sentence). TDCJ did discharge me but, of course, I went to county jail due to that case.

In January 2005, I still had a year and a half of time left on my sentence and I would be on parole for that year and a half. And in my experience of parole, I knew that they would not leave me to make my way to the halfway house. When they told me that day over the intercom to pack up, I made sure that I brought all my stuff with me. Because halfway houses are just another form of prison and I would need them.

Down on floor 2 of Lew Sterrett, where they process the inmates being released, my parole officer showed up and he brought with him the GPS box and the ankle monitor. After he connected the monitor to my ankle and activated the GPS on his laptop I asked him, "Where are the other six parole officers?" (He was not one of the POs from 1999.)

"I read in your file what they did in '99. That is not happening now. I am your primary parole officer. I'm Mr. G. My backup is Mr. W. I might be out sick or something and he would handle your case in that situation. Are you ready?"

"Oh, most certainly!" I told him.

"I'll go see if they can expedite your release."

Wow, I wasn't gonna know how to act. One PO—not that I have anything negative in mind, it's just that I was being treated like a regular parolee.

In his car on the way to the Wayback House, I asked him why I had to live at the halfway house. His reply was that it was the decision of the parole board, but that just like any parolee I could always submit an address to go to.

He told me that some things hadn't changed from 1999. I could not leave the halfway house; he would drive me to any appointment. I was *not* allowed to seek employment anywhere. I could have family visits but they would not be allowed to take me anywhere.

Basically, prison. You can be free but you can't do anything. So, I was only half a normal parolee. There were new staff at the halfway but a lot of the old ones remained. Lisa, Carol, Walter, Al of course, and I was able to thank Al and Lisa for helping me. Walter was assigned as my case manager this time. "Since it looks as if they lightened up this time."

"My goal is to make it past twelve days. Once I hit that twelve-day marker I know I will be alright," I quipped. They laughed.

"It's good to see that you didn't let them beat you up here," Lisa said, tapping the side of her head.

"I'm resilient if nothing else." I said.

In the upstairs office there was a house computer for residents to use to make resumes or whatever was needed. I had permission to use this. Downstairs they had a computer hooked up to a hand print reader. This they used for counts. At count times every resident had to go to the office and place their hand on the reader and it proved that we are actually on the premises. Once staff learned how good I was with computers I was being called all the time to fix it. The new staff came to like me once they saw that I did not have fangs and long talons and I was the handyman, once again, around the halfway house.

Another amenity provided by the halfway house was a fax machine. I used the computer to professionally type up a parole plan, with my mother's address on it. I explained that she lived out there in the country on five hundred acres of land and it was far away from any place where children might be. Once a week I faxed my plan to the Austin Board of Pardons and Parole.

There was a new case manager named Andrea. She had nothing to do with my case but she asked me into her office one day. I instantly had a crush on her. Dark reddish hair that went to the bottom of her neck, beautiful green eyes and a pretty face. And *zaftig*. (I've always wanted to use that word in a sentence.)

"You are nothing like the news portrayed you. And when I heard about the castration, I thought that it was so barbaric. Why did they do that to you?" she asked.

"Oh no, they didn't 'do' that, I volunteered for it and it's not as crass as it sounds. They only remove the testicles and put in prosthetics. I can still have sex, but I only shoot blanks. But for the first time in my life, I feel like I have control over the sexual urges. So I have not had sex or masturbated since the surgery March 1, 2004. Almost a year. I plan on going without sex, in any way, for as long as I can. I'm reinforcing

everything I learned in SOTP. I want it to be like second nature to me."
I also told her about my turning point and how I had been tenaciously
changing my thought patterns, belief systems—my whole lifestyle. "And
because of this the corresponding feeling that I get now at the thought
of a child is disgust, I can say with certainly that I will not reoffend."

We built a good friendship, in a place where the staff was not supposed
to be my friend. And to have these open conversations with a woman
was very refreshing. I really missed the companionship of a woman who
was not family.

She was a tea drinker, and she had this tea set that had different flavors
and kinds of tea and a round mesh metal strainer that you put the tea
leaves inside and placed it in the cup so that you could run hot water over
it. She turned me onto hot tea. But in the morning, I still had to have my
coffee.

My mother, grandmother and sister came to see me. They brought me
a 13" TV with a DVD player in the TV. Wow, technology. She brought
me an economy size of Folgers coffee and filters. The halfway house had
a coffee pot in the dining room for us to use. She brought me movies to
watch and clothes to wear. And a pack of cigarettes.

"Why won't they let you come home to my house?" she asked.

"I'm not sure. But I am going to put in a plan to go to your house."
I told her.

"You shouldn't smoke, David," my grandmother said. "It's bad for
you."

I will always be my grandma's little boy also. "I know, Granny, but I
don't inhale, and this is just my little rebellion against the prison system.
I'll get over it." I held her hand and kissed her cheek.

My sister was married and had had her second child by now. I was
proud of her. My mother had raised her better because, in my opinion,
she'd been a Christian and that had given her a better perspective.

Once a week they would come see me. Sonny came with my mom.
They were married now and she was happy. On Friday nights I would call
my mom and ask her to order me a pizza.

My brother and his wife came to visit. He brought me a Nintendo
Cube with a Super Mario Brothers Sunshine game. Also, a Madden
NFL game and a few others. My aunt would come and she would bring

Mexican food with her and we would eat it on the patio.

In county jail I'd become good friends with one of the chaplains that came every Sunday to talk with us, and he continued to visit me at the halfway house. I had a great support group.

One day in April I was called to Lisa's office. Her eyes were big, she said that Paul Ivey was here to see me from the parole board in Austin. But she didn't get the feeling that it was good news. I had faxed a parole plan once a week to Austin's parole office, requesting to be paroled to my mother's house. I couldn't fathom why else he would be here.

"If you do not want to go in alone Carol or I will go in with you." Lisa offered.

"Yeah, sure. I need some support." I said.

They both walked me to the prearranged office where I would meet Mr. Paul Ivey, of the Texas Board of Pardons and Parole.

"Mr. Jones, I'm Paul Ivey, Director of Parole. I'm here to figure out why you keep faxing me your parole plan. First of all, in your rules you're not allowed to use a fax machine…"

"Um, excuse me, Mr. Ivey, but we at the halfway house provide a fax service for the residents and it is a staff member and *not* Jones, who does the faxing." Lisa, bless her heart. I was glad they were in there with me.

"But why have you faxed me once a week?" he asked.

"Because you never answer. I ask my PO and he says that you have not responded to them." I said.

"Well, I have driven down here from Austin to answer you. The answer is *no*, Mr. Jones. You will stay at this halfway house until you ever have a civil commitment trial or you discharge your sentence or you violate. I have your file, which consists of two boxes, on my desk, and I am watching you real close," he said.

"But that's not fair. I have a place to parole to, no children are there. I have a support group, a job. It's perfect. You can't just hold me for civil commitment."

"I don't care what you think is fair or what you think that I can or can't do, Mr. Jones, I brought you your answer. And stop faxing me." He left the office.

Tears of frustration were in my eyes as I looked at Lisa and Carol in disbelief.

"I've never seen anything like this. I'll talk to Al and we will make sure that they don't violate you on some petty stuff. But you mind your P's and Q's, okay?" Lisa told me.

"Yeah, I learned my lesson," I told her. I left and called my mom.

PRISON AFTER PRISON

—⊶o◯∽◯o⊶—

Civil Commitment Trial, 2006

"What we obtain too cheap, we esteem too lightly; it is dearness only
that gives everything it's value."
-Thomas Paine

The GPS was always losing its signal. And it was always in the middle of the night. A staff person would wake me up saying that I had to go outside and walk around for fifteen minutes until the satellite acquired the signal again. A real annoyance.

But in May one day around 10:30 at night the GPS showed that I was ten miles away on 635 LBJ freeway, for 6 minutes and then back at the halfway house. The next day my parole officer came to ask me about this.

"It's news to me. I was in my room watching a movie at that time." I told him.

"I'll have to report it," he said, borrowing an office from the halfway house.

I went about my business. I was able to get in a three-on-three game of B-ball on the patio. Someone calling my name halted the game. I looked up and a staff member was escorting two sheriffs' deputies across the patio. My stomach fell and fear began eating up my insides.

The staff member pointed at me. "You Jones?" One of the deputies said. Out of my peripheral vision I saw Lisa, Carol and Walter and the other staff come out of the halfway house. It looked like a standoff, but outnumbered. I was hoping with the staff on my side that they would make these deputies leave. But it was an unfulfilled hope.

"Yes," I said.

"What's this about?" Lisa demanded.

"We have a blue warrant for his arrest." The deputy explained.

I told Lisa what the GPS had said. "Don't worry David, we will help you. We will call your mom and your attorney. You'll beat this." Lisa said as I was being put in handcuffs.

"Thank you, Lisa. Will you make sure my property is safe?"

"I'll pack it myself and put it in my office. You'll be out quickly."

"Don't forget your box," Carol yelled.

"He's not brining any box with him," the deputy said.

"No, his GPS box." Pointing on it sitting by the basketball goal pole. I could sit it down and be able to be up to twenty feet away from it.

"We still are not taking it with us." As they escorted me across the patio. Once we went twenty feet away the GPS box began beeping in Carol's hands. I guess my PO left after he called in the blue warrant. Probably felt guilty.

"Keep your head up David." Lisa called.

*   *   *

In the back seat of the cop car a deputy sat beside me. He had some paperwork that he was filling out and he began to ask me questions that he needed answers to for his paperwork.

"Full name and birth date," he asked.

"Ask my lawyer," I said with an attitude.

"C'mon, we are just doing our job; you don't have to take it out on us," he said.

I just looked out the window and ignored him. A myriad of emotions were coursing throughout my body. It just seemed that they were determined to keep me in jail. I felt like I'd been here all my life. I was mad at them, Parole and Paul Ivey, who I knew was behind this.

The driver got a call on his cell phone. When he hung up, he told his partner, "They want me to drive around for a while until all the media gets there."

"So, this is a show? They called the media and told them?" I asked him, even more angry.

"Ask my lawyer," the driver told me in response.

"Aw, that's cute. This is BS," I said and resumed my quiet fuming.

In the underground garage of Lew Sterrett all the local news was there and a photographer for *DMN*. The deputies were on either side of me escorting me and I remembered the last thing Lisa yelled at me. "Keep your head up." So, I kept my head up and showed them that they wouldn't beat me.

After staying in county jail a week the intercom crackled, "Jones, pack your stuff, pack your stuff you're going home."

Thank God. Same routine, Floor 2, release. Same PO came to put a new ankle monitor on me and activate the GPS.

"So, is this one going to malfunction?" I saw it was a newer model. But still the same size.

"No, it shouldn't," he said.

"Shouldn't, very comforting. My freedom hangs on an irrational supposition. Great." I was very cynical.

"I can do without the attitude," he said. "It was BS what they did and I don't approve, but they make those decisions and I have no say so okay. I couldn't even come tell you, I'm sorry. So, let's just clear the air, okay?" he told me.

"Yeah, okay, cool." And all the anger disappeared, at least toward him.

At the halfway house Lisa told me that the camera system had seen me go into my room a little after 10 p.m. on that night. And that is what made them pull the blue warrant, otherwise I would have gone back to prison.

On top of that, the DA's appeal concerning the judge dismissing that case against me has been successful, my attorney had filed another appeal to a higher court.

And due to that the Prosecutor for civil commitment decided to go ahead and have my trial. The SCFO came to Dallas for depositions. We met at the Dallas Parole office. I was looking for Sally but didn't see her.

"Where is Sally?" I asked the old lawyer who introduced himself to me.

"She no longer works at SCFO. I'll be taking over your case." All the confidence that Sally gave me to have a chance to beat this case was gone. Trepidation took its place.

After the depositions were over, Parole made arrangements to place me in a Houston halfway house for the time it would take to have the trial. Two staff members from the Dallas halfway house drove me to Houston Ben Reid halfway house and dropped me off at this compound. There was a fence with barbed wire around the compound. This was feeling more and more like a prison.

This was a big halfway house. They had several buildings for living quarters and everything else was outside. Well, you had to walk outside to go to the building for chow, visits, group therapy and to meet with your PO. I was placed in a building that housed Houston's Civilly Committed. We all shared our war stories.

A PO picked me up and drove me to the Conroe parole office. I was scheduled to meet with the State's expert witness; she had already evaluated me—if you call an hour interview a long enough evaluation to determine someone's behavioral abnormality status—back in 2003. Today's meeting was thirty minutes, and at the end she said, "I will still testify that you do have a behavioral abnormality."

My lawyer was in great back pain throughout the trial and he was retiring after my case. The morning of the first day of trial, the expert witness that Sally had obtained back in 2003 met with me on the sidewalk in front of the courthouse. We talked for maybe fifteen minutes. I remembered in 2003 when Sally told me about him: "He usually testifies for the prosecution, but he agreed to help us out."

After the fifteen minutes he told me, "I'll be testifying that you *do have* a behavioral abnormality."

"What? But you're my expert witness. What do you mean?" I pleaded with him.

"Mr. Jones, no one with any credibility will testify that you don't have one. It would end a career."

This is another contradiction in the civil commitment laws. Or rather a catch-22. No one will risk their job to say "He does not have a behavioral abnormality." Because if someone does reoffend then that looks bad for them.

I told my lawyer, who was not feeling good that day, what this expert witness had said. I asked him to get a delay or something. But he didn't. And that day my expert witness got on the stand and told the judge, jury and prosecutor that I do have a behavioral abnormality.

When I took the stand, I had my lawyer ask certain questions so that I may answer and tell the jury about my rehabilitation. But the prosecutor objected every time that I tried to explain and tell about my turning point, and the judge sustained her objections every time.

I have never gone through a trial, and I assumed that the SCFO had prepared everything to present in my favor. I announced this on the stand that I got castrated to ensure I would not reoffend.

"Objection,"

"Sustained."

You can't unhear that. But would this jury recognize this joke of a trial that was occurring? It was an all-white jury. Ex-sheriff, and the like. There was one old lady who was crying at what little I could get out.

It's like they only wanted to use my past against me and not let me explain how and what I've done to rehabilitate myself. In jury instructions they were not even allowed to know exactly what civil commitment consisted of.

Like this: "Lady and Gentleman of the jury, we are here to ask you to civilly commit the defendant David Jones, we can't tell you what civil commitment is but we still ask you to find him to meet the requirements. We will tell you all his past but he can't tell you anything positive, we will use highly inflamatory language such as "sexually violent predator (SVP)" but that's just to arouse your anger so you will commit him."

That pretty much sums up jury instructions. Then in closing arguments, the prosecutor said, "Mr. Jones is a convicted SVP, he says he was castrated but the defense did not put up any evidence to prove this. So, we have a lying, convicted SVP. It is now time for you to commit him."

My attorney was out that day, for a doctor's appointment, and his second didn't say anything memorable.

June 16, 2005 I was civilly committed. Was there ever any other outcome for a person like me? The story of my life. I believe that Dallas DAs, Parole, and this prosecutor, judge and maybe even SCFO, were in on this.

One thing the judge messed up on, although to date I have not been able to utilize it to bring me relief, is on my "Final Order and Judgment for Civil Commitment" there is a paragraph placed in the order that would transfer jurisdiction to Dallas County for the authority to prosecute any rule violations. The judge deleted this paragraph from my order. I didn't understand at this time the significance in this.

I was ordered to "Outpatient Civil Commitment," and in the same order I was ordered to live in a "Texas locked residential facility—namely a halfway house." Contradictions.

I was driven back to the Wayback house the next day.

*　　*　　*

Besides having a civil commitment case manager and going to group therapy twice a week, over a hundred new rules being added to my already heavily restricted liberty, nothing changed.

I was still on parole and he checked in with me weekly, but civil commitment has the driver's seat. Basically, civil commitment is further supervision and treatment after your prison sentence is over. Parole would just let CC have the lead, and take over therapy too.

Walter Brown was the halfway house case manager, Rachel Darling was the CC case manager, and Bill Bruner was my SOTP therapist. These three were my treatment team. During the first couple of months of my commitment, I had several one-on-one meetings with Mr. Bruner, taking tests and answering questions. And as a part of a civil commitment treatment plan, I was ordered to take a penile plethysmograph test. It's okay for the therapist to show you pictures of children half naked and have you listen to rape stories, but if I was to do this on my own, I'd go to prison.

"This gives us an idea of where you are at and what issues we need to work on." Bruner said.

My argument still stands: Why would you take an alcoholic who was sober for ten years and give him a beer to see if it could lead to a drinking problem?

Since 1996, I have been steadily renewing thought patterns, and not letting thoughts of children hang around in my mind. I've worked hard to retrain my patterns to not even go there, to not think it. I am, to borrow the term, sober from those thoughts. I was totally against being subjected to the images and stories.

But unless I wanted to go to prison for violating a Civ. Comm. rule, then I had to take this test. Mr. Bruner did not conduct these tests so they referred me to a group in Ft. Worth who did.

I knew I passed when I took it. But around August 10, 2005 at a one on one with Mr. Bruner he handed me the five page test report and results. On page 4 there was a chart that showed the measure of arousal to each age group and sex.

When the penis is flaccid and not aroused, the circumference at that state is the base measurement. Any arousal above that circumference is what is considered significant.

The only line indicated on this chart above the significant level was adult males.

That's right: *no arousal toward children. Only adults.*

Excuse me, I know you see this, dear reader. You've been following along and you are smart enough to realize the significance of this. Not even two months since the kangaroo court called the civil commitment trial of David Wayne Jones, where his lawyer let his own expert witness get on the stand and say that he had a behavioral abnormality that predisposed him to reoffend sexually against children with *no* volition in the matter, that he can't help himself, which resulted in the jury finding him to have a behavioral abnormality. A trial where the jury was only given information from his past and not a current true evaluation of who he is today. He is *not even aroused* by children anymore. So how can he reoffend against them?

Even by the legislation's definition of a behavioral abnormality, it does not and didn't fit me. I worked very hard to *not ever* hurt anyone ever again, and here is one of their tests that showed that I have achieved that reality, that result.

"So, you will inform all the right people and I will be taken off of civil commitment, right?" I asked Mr. Bruner.

"No, you have to go take a polygraph test to ensure that you did not fake the results of this test," he replied.

Eye roll.

I took the polygraph test. After the interview and the base questions to learn how my body acts during a lie, I was asked three questions:

Question:" Did you masturbate the night before the test?"

Answer: "No."

Result: NO DECEPTION DETECTED

Question: 'Did you do anything to manipulate the results of the PPG?"

Answer: "No."

Results: NO DECEPTION DETECTED.

Question: "Did you deviate your attention from the video or audio of the test in order to manipulate the results?"

Answer: "No."

Result: NO DECEPTION DETECTED

*   *   *

Back in Burners office I asked again for my immediate release.

"Mr. Jones, you cannot use this to gain release, this is used for the purpose of treatment only."

"But I'm not even aroused by children and I'm forced by the court to be civilly committed to a program that caters to guys who have a problem and can't stop raping kids. Obviously, that is not me, I have changed, I've done everything to make sure that I don't hurt anyone again. And I made that decision way before civil commitment was even thought of. I don't have a behavioral abnormality, and that is one of the two requirements. I'm also not a repeat offender so I don't meet either requirement."

But Mr. Bruner was not the judge. I told everyone my results but no one could see beyond their immediate jobs to see that I shouldn't be on civil commitment. Even SCFO. They sent me a copy of their appeal and I called them and told them I wanted them to place in the appeal the ground, "Ineffective assistance of Counsel." They told me that since that "counsel" was their colleague that they could not do it. I could not see past that and I kept insisting. They went to the judge and recused themselves as my attorneys due to the difference of opinion. The judge said he would appoint me a new attorney.

I was so angry, bitter and cynical that I could not grasp what I had just done. I only realized later that it was a big mistake. The court appointed me an attorney, a guy with his shingle out, and this lawyer did not consult with me at all, but after he wrote an appeal and sent it to the court, did he send me a copy of it. It contained one ground. That's it. The appeal court denied my appeal.

I stayed angry. I felt that I should not be on civil commitment. And I had the proof. This pushed me past my passive people pleasing, P's and Q's minding position, to present myself as a patient person. I got cynical and it showed up towards the people who were over me. Not towards the halfway house staff, just the civil commitment people. And I always felt that Walter Brown believed in me and in my rehabilitation.

I loved therapy itself, so my participation in the Civ. Comm. program was to reinforce the things that I had learned in the prison's SOTP. I loved the logic reasoning behind cognitive behavioral therapy. Mr. Bruner explained the difference between an impulsive thought (which everyone gets) and a deviant fantasy of a child (which sex offenders indulge in). We had to do journals to record when we got an impulse thought and when we either indulged and made it our own or describe how we dealt with it.

My impulse thoughts were few and far in between. That was due to all the hard work I continue to do, so I wouldn't have them. I presented paperwork and Mr. Bruner always said that I was steadily progressing in the monthly progress report.

Civ. Comm. had a rule that said I could not have any contact with any person unless they were approved by my tribunal treatment team. I couldn't visit with family or anyone until they met with Mr. Bruner to be approved. I was so angry at all these stupid rules. And how could I ever meet anyone as a friend or a girlfriend or boyfriend?"Hi," some person says to me.

"Oh, could you please call and get an appointment with Mr. Bruner, my sexually violent predator therapist, and get approved so we can be friends or lovers? I might even be sent back to jail for just talking to you to tell you this."

I joke, but it's that serious. Speaking of jokes have you ever noticed how the name "therapist" breaks down: "the rapist," I'm just saying.

*   *   *

My anger, the meds the psychiatrist gave me, the chemical imbalance from the castration surgery—I did not get to go to aftercare to learn how to adjust to that—did not make a very good combination.

I didn't always take my meds, because I would have slept 24/7. I violated rules, because they shouldn't apply to me. There was a guy that I was friends with and I was very attracted to him.

He was at the halfway house on probation. He had a drug problem and over time he had to piss in a cup. I would piss in an empty bottle and he would use my piss to pass his drug test. Some old man in my room figured out what I was doing and he told on me. I denied it, but it was considered an incident report. I was sanctioned with more duties around the halfway house.

I was working, helping out every department and enjoying it. I carried a couple of screwdrivers and a dull box cutter knife around in my pocket. I got these tools from a previous roommate and they aided me in my "job".

One day in Andrea's office we were just talking like friends. She was a great listener, one of the ones who looks you in the eye. I could have got lost in her eyes. But there was a guy who was on her case load. His name was Bob. Bob wasn't wound too tight; he had a sex case against a child. One day I was talking to Bob on the patio. I was one of the only residents who was nice to him, and he hung around me a lot. We were talking and I was always asking him questions to help him think out a plan, to be ready for anything, set goals.

"Bob, let's say that you are at the doctor's office and there is a child in the waiting room, what do you do?"

His answer frightened me: "That's why I bring this with me," he said, pulling out a Gameboy. "I let them play this."

"No, Bob, you leave, go to a place where there are plenty of adults and call someone to pick you up. You leave, Bob! Got that?"

His answer bothered me so much I told Andrea that day in her office. Bob didn't have a plan and he was dangerous. I didn't want him to reoffend. I believe that people need to be confronted so they can contrast what's real with their fantasy land.

Andrea thanked me and said she would notify his therapist. On her desk were three bus passes. The halfway house gave these free to residents so they could go look for jobs. Some residents would sell them to make a little money. The value for one bus pass was $2.50, but guys would sell them for a $1 apiece. Free money.

I asked Andrea could I have those three passes. She said no and left the room. Now being in prison for fourteen years, it was common to ask the officers for something, or to do something, that was not allowed. The officer would say "*No*," and turn his back. This was understood that he could say that he'd said no, and that we were on our own to do what we had asked, he didn't care but for his job's sake he'd said no.

When Andrea said no, and left the room, that's how I interpreted that, and I took the three bus passes. She never asked me about it, so that made me believe even more that she was cool about it.

Civ. Comm. would give us a different type of polygraph test. In Jan 2006 I was told that I had a "maintenance polygraph" coming up in the next couple of months. A maintenance polygraph will ask you a series of questions to check if you have broken any of Civ. Comm.'s hundreds of rules and requirements. And if you fail this—back to prison with a new felony for violating rules. (Even though we were in a locked residential facility.)

In my next one-on-one with Mr. Bruner I decided I would confess to him about the bus passes, so when I took the maintenance test, I would not show deception.

"Why did you take them, Mr. Jones?" he asked. I did not tell him about Andrea because I didn't want to implicate her, and she had gotten a job somewhere else by this time.

"I was going to sell them but my friend wanted them so I gave them to him." I gave them to the guy that I gave my piss to. I was enamored by his attention.

"Who is your friend?"

"The same guy who I was accused of giving my piss to." I said.

"Mr. Jones, do you know why you gave them to him?"

"He wanted them?" A question in my tone.

"You are an enabler. You enable him in his bad behavior and at the same time you enable him to like you. You, Mr. Jones, are an enabler."

I wasn't intending to get some insight into my behavior; I just wanted to pass the polygraph, so that was an added bonus. A side effect of confessing to a psychologist. But that insight helped me start questioning my motives as to *why* I do any type of behavior.

"I will inform Mr. Brown and Ms. Darling. I think that it shows growth and maturity that you confessed this. I'll let them assign a sanction."

When I got back to the halfway house, I reported to Mr. Brown's office. There were two computer-created pictures in his office, one on the front panel of his desk and one on the wall. I'd created both and given them to him, and he'd put them up.

He was always adamant that he was not our friend but our advocate. So, the sign on the desk was a clipart picture of a guy at a desk with his feet on the desk, and I'd inserted a lamp very similar to his. The caption read, "Walter Brown, your advocate." The second picture was a clipart of a guy at a desk talking to someone on the other side (similar to his office) and the caption that I made was a knock off of the UPS slogan at the time: "What can Brown do for you?"

I am very creative, but only having a standalone computer and no access to the internet I was limited with the clipart. But I'd think of people who I looked up to and create some touching scene and saying on paper and give it to them.

Now, he was shaking his head in disappointment. "Mr. Jones, I never thought that you would steal. I talked to Ms. Darling and we decided that you will pay the halfway house back for the cost of the passes. $2.50 x 3 is $7.50. Do you have that?"

I pulled out a five-dollar bill that I had. "This is all I got right now."

"I'll give you a receipt for that, with the understanding that you still owe us $2.50. Also, for one month you will not be allowed on the computer, unless Gwynn needs help with the handprint computer downstairs. Alright?"

"Yes, sir." I said. I mean they could have given me a felony. Not for theft—it was only non-promotional bus passes. But under civil commitment's hundreds of rules, a violation is a felony.

*   *   *

The rooms held three bunk beds which slept six people. I'd had several room changes over the last year and I was currently in a room with five other guys, one of whom was directly in opposition to me. I'd been in the local news and newspapers and everyone at the halfway house knew of me and knew my offenses. Most people were okay, some were indifferent. But this old black man exuded hatred for me. And I was uncomfortable. He'd sit on his bed and glare at me. If I moved any item in the room, even an inch, he'd grunt and grumble. It only worsened as time went on. It's the passive aggressive people that you have to worry about, because it's all going on in his thought process and since he's not voicing it there was no one to counter his thoughts with reason. There was an open bed in one of the rooms that I was in before and I got along with all of the guys in there. Having a TV/DVD and a Nintendo, I was a good roommate. The guys in this room were black and I was even attracted to a couple of them, but I was *not* having sex with anyone. For two reasons: 1. After castration I planned to go as long as I could without sex and masturbation, and I was coming up on two years of abstinence. 2. For me it was a felony to violate that rule.

I wanted to live comfortably. I wanted to be around people who seemed to like me. We played ball together, we played videogames together. If they were going to keep me in this place I felt entitled to live in peace.

I went to Mr. Brown on a Saturday. He was off Sundays and Mondays and on Tuesdays it was his late day. Part of Civ. Comm. rules state to report anything, to any member of your team, that may interfere with your treatment. This situation possibly could. I wasn't at the point to consider that living in a room with guys that I'm attracted to could interfere with my treatment. Okay they were adults, I wasn't going to have sex with them, and I shouldn't be on C/C and I had a right (at least in my mind) to live comfortably.

I had transference issues with older men. I either projected negative attributes onto them if they didn't like me (the old man roommate), kind of seeing them as my stepdad, or I transferred or projected a good type father-figure on to the ones I perceived weren't overtly against me. I had always seen Mr. Brown in the latter. He seemed to believe in me and in my rehabilitation. I felt comfortable going to him about a room change.

On that Saturday as I told him, he said that he would consider it over his off days. On Tuesday he came in around 2:30 pm. Common sense told me not to bombard him with it as soon as he got there. I had group therapy at 4:30 pm. I figured I'd go to his office at 3:30.

He had an open-door policy as long as the door was open. And I knocked and entered in and sat in the chair that was in front of his desk. He shared an office with the guy who replaced Andrea, Mr. Anderson. A tall bald black man, he was sitting at his desk doing paperwork. Mr. Brown was writing on some paper as I sat down, he glanced up then back down. I had sat my GPS monitor on his desk.

"What's up Jones?"

"I was just checking in with you about what I asked you on Saturday."

"I'm not going to approve that move," he kept writing.

"Why?"

"I think you have ulterior motives," he said, nonchalantly as if we were discussing the weather.

In my chest there was a tremble. A shift, like the bottom fell out of something that I had been building. My need to be legitimately validated, to be accepted by someone without me performing, to be believed in, was palpable. In my perception it made my rehabilitation more real if I had someone who believed in me that I was not friends with but he was an advocate. And I had this unmet, old need of just wanting, desiring, craving the approval of a father figure.

I didn't know that I had these transference issues projected onto Mr. Brown, but when he told me that he thought that I had ulterior motives, I had an emotional mental break down. I went off on him verbally. I do not remember everything that was said, but I remember some things.

"I thought you believed in me." I yelled. I looked at the pictures I had created and I tore them off the wall and the desk. "You say you are our advocate. You are just like Parole and Civil Commitment." I ripped the papers in half.

"Jones, calm down and go out on the patio and cool off." Mr. Brown said.

"I don't need to cool off. I need a room change. I'm reporting to you that I have a problem in my room and I don't feel comfortable. And you think that I have an ulterior motive. That's crazy. I'm not having sex with anyone, that's a felony remember? And if I wanted to have sex, I wouldn't need to be in the same room with them I would just do it. I only want to move because that old man's giving me problems."

He picked up the phone and dialed, and as he waited for whoever he was calling to pick up he said to me, "Do you want a room change? I got a room change for you. How about a cell number 4 at Lew Sterrett jail?

I felt betrayed. He was talking about sending me to jail? Really? That report said that I banged my GPS monitor on his desk. I don't remember doing that but may have lifted it and hit it against the desk to stress my words, but I didn't do it in a threatening way and it did not break.

I didn't notice but he said something into the phone and pushed the speaker button. Ms. Darling was who he'd called and she heard the rest of my ranting. A staff member came to the door and asked me if I was going to group therapy and I said "Yes, I'll be there in a moment."

Mr. Brown did not quit taunting me with slugs about sending me to jail. I was in extreme emotional pain, with the perceived betrayal and the reveal that he thought I had ulterior motives, then the chemical imbalance from the castration mixed with psychiatric medications, it all became too much. I couldn't deal with the turmoil of the pain and hurt that I was feeling and I pulled out the box cutter out of my back pocket and I told Mr. Brown, "Tell my mom I'm sorry, but I just can't do it anymore." And I slit up my forearm.

It only barely broke skin in a line going up from my wrist to elbow. A superficial cut, it was almost funny. Mr. Anderson grabbed my arms at the elbow and pinned my arms to my sides and told me to drop the box cutter. I did. My pain had left. I guess this is what happens with people who have a disorder to cut themselves and they say that it relieves the emotional pain.

I sat there until the two Dallas police officers showed up. He had called the police too. He wasn't even in the room, he had left 'to remove himself from the situation,' and I couldn't even look at him to accuse him of betrayal with my eyes.

"Mr. Jones, stand up. Do you have any sharp objects or needles on your person that could stick me?"

"I have a couple of screwdrivers in my back pocket, I am like a handyman around the halfway house," I told him.

"Turn around," he said. I did and he removed the screwdrivers and gave them to Mr. Anderson then he patted me down and placed handcuffs on me, then escorted me to his squad car.

I was driven to Parkland hospital psychiatric ward. I talked to a doctor and told him that I was not suicidal and that I was not thinking of hurting myself. He informed the Civ. Comm. that I could be released. While I was waiting in the holdover, there was a phone. I called my mother and this time she was on my side, because she believed not only in me, but that if they would have let me live at home with her none of this would have been an issue. She was angry with them.

I called Rachel Darling and told her I was released and I needed a ride back to the halfway house.

"Uh, Mr. Jones, I talked with Mr. Bruner and after a conference call with Mr. Brown, Mr. Bruner has terminated you from treatment. You refused to go to group tonight. And those are violations of your civil commitment order. We have issued an arrest warrant against you, so the police will come pick you up," she said.

"What? How can I go to group therapy from Parkland? Mr. Brown called the cops. I didn't refuse to go. And I was progressing in treatment. You can't do this to me. Now stop playing and call off the arrest."

"Sorry Mr. Jones, you violated these rules."

It was Feb 27, 2006. I lasted a year and a month out of jail and seven months on civil commitment. Back to Lew Sterrett

UNCONSTITUTIONAL

2006 - 2007

"They did it to me, they're gonna do it to you."
-Sandra Bullock, *The Net*

"This whole court room is out of order."
-*A Few Good Men*

I sat in county jail for a year and six months. I had a right to a speedy trial but it seemed more like the DAs had the right to get their case together, and failing that, to make up things just to get that conviction.

At first, I had four indictments, each one listing several different rule infractions from the whole seven months that I was on Civ. Comm. I asked my attorney, who was a Dallas public defender, since I couldn't afford an attorney, about this.

"I've already been sanctioned for these rule infractions, how can they bring this up and charge me with it?" I asked him.

"Don't worry, I'll check into this. I gotta tell you I've never seen a case like this. There is another public defender who had a case like this. I'll get her to work with me on this case. Okay."

He must have done something although it took until a few months into 2007 to get the indictments down to two. My charge was "civil commitment requirement" and one indictment read, in part:

"…intentionally and knowingly violate the requirements… to wit: by using and exhibiting a box cutter, and by refusing to attend sex offender group therapy, and by being discharged from his sex offender treatment program."

The other "…to wit: by stealing bus passes from the desk of Wayback House staff." Both indictments carried a paragraph which enhanced the 3rd degree felony to a 2nd degree felony which carried a sentence between two and twenty years.

I broke minor halfway house rules and they were enhancing this to a 2nd degree felony. Dallas was determined to lock me up and throw away the key. I got locked up at age nineteen. One day before I turned twenty. I've never been out. Free to do anything, nothing to get a felony for. I was thirty-seven at the time. That's almost the same amount of time as I was ever free, seventeen years of incarceration, looking at up to twenty more. I broke minor rules.

The DA offered a thirteen-year plea bargain. For breaking rules? No, thirteen years is not much different than that twenty, and as long as I pleaded not guilty and went to trial I could appeal. I told my lawyer, no deal.

Now it was a waiting game. I sat and waited. One day I got called to visit and my lawyer from my original case was there, the one who'd gotten that most recent bogus charge thrown out.

"Hey David, how are you doing?" he started.

"Not too good, man."

"Yeah, well, I got bad news. The higher appeal court has denied our last appeal, they said that the DA can prosecute you for the case even though they sat on the indictment for two years," he told me.

"But Tom, I didn't even do s___. Is anything going to ever go right for me?"

"I know, David, I have told them that they are creating a monster. But this brings us to what's next. Because I was your attorney in 1991 and I made the plea bargain with the then DA, then if you take this case to trial, I will be called on to testify for you at the trial and in that case, I can't also represent you. I have recused myself from your case and the judge will appoint you a public defender."

"Tom, you can't leave me too. You are giving the DA what they want. I don't want you to testify. Don't leave me with public defenders."

"I'm truly sorry. Good luck." He got up and left. I stayed in the visit booth on my side of the glass and hung up the phone and cried.

*   *   *

August 2007, my public defender filed pretrial motions. One of them was to dismiss on the fact that Dallas County does not have jurisdiction to prosecute me. All this stemmed from my order of Civ. Comm. out of Conroe, TX and on my order there was a paragraph that would have transferred jurisdiction to Dallas County to give them the ability to prosecute violations, but in my order it was deleted. The judge scratched it out by drawing lines through it, thus jurisdiction was never transferred to Dallas and the judge had to dismiss.

"Denied." Judge Fred Tinsley said. "Any other motions?"

"Your Honor, we request that the inflammatory language such as sexually violent predator be restricted from use and stricken from the indictments. Such language can inflame a jury (quote some case as a precedent) and evoke emotions averse to the Defendant."

"Denied," he denied all our pretrial motions. I might as well line up and let them just shoot me.

During the trial my attorney told me that it's my choice if I want to testify but once I step on the stand, I open up legal doors for the DA to bring up anything and everything from my past. He recommended that I don't testify. I went with his recommendation, which now I believe was a mistake. I only broke minor rules. But these cases were sitting on my shoulders like a mountain and to say that I wasn't thinking right is an understatement.

There was a psychologist and expert who testified for me. He interviewed me once for an hour and months later comes to the stand. And he messed up big time. He said that I reported to him that I was taking certain psych meds at the same time. I never told him that, he heard or wrote it down wrong.

I leaned over to my attorney and told him to get that clarified. He told me hold on. I wrote it on a piece of paper what he got wrong, but my lawyer never cleared it up. He said that then it was too late to do any good.

But the DA took advantage of it. She called witnesses that had the correct dates that I took each medicine and she made me out to be a liar.

Walter Brown got up there and lied.

Dr. Bruner got up there and lied. And broke confidentiality. Because Civ. Comm. pays his checks.

Rachel Darling got up there and lied.

The halfway house staff that were called only testified to things like "Did you go over the HWH rules with Jones?" "Yes." Al and Lisa couldn't save me this time.

In closing argument, the DA made it out that, "David Jones is a liar and SVP, stole bus passes and there is a bus stop right outside the HWH." She had a map on an easel, she pointed to a bus stop circled, then another spot that was circled on the map, on that bus route. "And down there is an elementary school, Mr. Jones was planning on escaping, taking the bus and reoffending."

Oh my gosh. No, she didn't. I got rid of those bus passes to a friend and I was not planning an escape. I'll never reoffend. I didn't lie. I didn't lie.

It seems like that DAs can't prosecute with the truth; they have to make up lies and stories and inflame the jury to get a conviction. If I was on that jury, I would have convicted me. I didn't refuse group therapy, I was in jail and I should not have been discharged from treatment, I was progressing in therapy, Bruner said so in the monthly progress report. I had already been sanctioned for the bus passes and paid two out of the three back with my word that I'd pay the other $2.50 when I got it. That left the box cutter. It was never a problem to exhibit it and use it in my job as a handyman around the HWH, but it became a problem when they needed another nail to put in my coffin.

In prison, in SOTP, Mr. M. had told us that our offenses were not an isolated incident but a lifestyle. This incident falls under that truism on a lesser scale. I was judged, and prosecuted out of context and in a complete lie. I was pressured into not getting on the stand to testify about my side of the story. I gave the DA all the rope she needed to hang me. There was a confluence of circumstances that led to my emotional breakdown, and in the end, I have done nothing that deserved a 2nd degree felony.

My attorney gave a pretty good closing argument. He had all my hundreds of rules stapled together and he held up that packet of papers and as he tried to tug on their sympathy, he laid out those papers one by one on the wooden rail that divided the jury seats from the court. He ran out of room. It was a scene worthy of a John Grisham book.

The jury deliberated less than an hour. They found me guilty on both indictments. My lawyer, once again, told me. "If you choose the jury to decide your punishment first, there is a holiday coming up, Labor Day, second the DA is going to bring in all your old victims to garner the pity and inflame the jury to give you a big sentence. I recommend you let the judge do the sentencing. He won't go too hard on you; this is your first violation."

Here's more rope to make sure it's enough to really hang me.

I agreed and the judge slammed me, I got the maximum sentence, twenty years. Yes, for breaking minor rules. Twenty years. Yeah, he won't go too hard.

Then the judge said, "We will have a victim impact statement."

Wait, what? Is the civil commitment requirement person going to get up there. Who did I victimize?

This has to be a joke. The guy whose case I was being charged with. The one that they indicted me with in 2001, that guy. I passed a polygraph test that I never touched him. I had not been convicted of his accusation. How is he a victim and how can he give an impact statement? He is not my victim and never was. But this was the DA's show from the beginning. I was only an observer. I was just watching what decisions they made for my life.

In the holdover cell, I said to God, "The Lord giveth and the Lord taketh away. Blessed be the name of the Lord." He was taking away a lot more than He was giving. I was numb inside; I couldn't feel twenty years. I had no idea where this road was headed and I didn't know how much longer I could stay on it.

*　　*　　*

A few weeks later I was brought back to court and met with another public defender, about the other case hanging over my head. He told me, "If you want to fight this, I will fight this all the way with you. It's up to you. But the DA has agreed to your original fifteen-year plea bargain from 1991 and you will get all the back time so it's time served. It's up to you."

"But I'm not guilty. Can I plead no contest?" I asked him. He went back to the DA and came back.

"She said no, a guilty plea for fifteen years' time served or trial," he said.

These were the thoughts that I had: I've been sitting in the jail for one and a half years; if I went to trial that could take another two years. I couldn't take that; I was already going stir crazy. If I took time served it would be admitting to something that I did not do. But what's one more case to my list of cases.

So, I decided to take the time served. "But I need you to make sure of one thing, okay? I told my lawyer.

"What's that David?"

"I want it on record from the judge that this fifteen-year sentence begins on 6/11/91. That is the date all my other cases began. Okay?"

"I'll make sure of it."

I believe the year and a half to two year wait for the trial is a tactic by the DA to wear a person down so that they will plead guilty. A copout just to get out of county jail.

We went before the judge, I pled guilty and he said I was sentenced to fifteen years with back time dated to June 11, 1991, which was official time served.

I was headed back to the TDCJ.

GIB LEWIS UNIT

2008 - 2009

"It does not do to dwell on dreams and forget to live. Remember that."
-Albus Dumbledore – *Harry Potter* Series

Before I went to prison, a lawyer from the Public Defender's office came to see me. He was an appeal lawyer and he laid out his plan. He seemed to grasp the situation pretty well. So I had a little hope that an appeal might overturn this twenty-year sentence.

January 2008, I went through the intake process and ended up being assigned to the Gib Lewis unit, down in Woodville, Texas. There was not a safekeeping on this unit, which I was fine with. I wasn't planning on telling anyone what I was there for. I had been writing to the SOTP department requesting to be placed in aftercare treatment at the Goree unit. D was still there in aftercare and I wanted to be over there on that Cadillac unit. Regardless of where I am and what is happening to me, I want to always be in therapy. Nothing will ever cause me to go back to wanting to hurt children. In 1996 I saw into the end results of what my offenses could do to a person. I stopped believing the lie that I was telling myself and I changed my thought patterns and belief system, by changing the terms I used to commit my crimes. I used fear hierarchy to pair with those sick fantasies. And these tools worked. I no longer desire a child. The thought disgusts me. So, I love therapy, to have the ability to talk things out instead of bottle it up and go it alone. That's insanity.

It had been four years since I was castrated. Four years since I had masturbated or had sex with anyone. I was still attracted to men and I made a decision that I would look for a relationship. Twenty years is a long time. I'd rather be in the company of a woman, but I was surrounded by men. I didn't want to be alone.

*   *   *

2008 turned into 2009. Shower crew, playing basketball at rec., and playing scrabble made my time go by fast. In March 2009 I went on medical chain to Goree unit and was seen by Dr. Winslade and Ms. Engman, who was Director of SOTP now. I explained to them all that I'd done, all that I'd been through and I asked them to have me reassigned to Goree in an aftercare treatment. I remember them agreeing to do just that, but I was on the chain headed back to Lewis unit. At first, I thought that this just took time and that I would soon be going to Goree. I could only hope that it happened soon. Then in June, a Hispanic inmate recognized me from Dallas County Jail. He said that he knew about my case and told me that he was going to get his wife to send the proof. He was gang related and I knew that I would not be safe anywhere on the unit.

I filed an OPI (offender protection investigation) with the administration with the intention of getting back on SK status. With my history, it was approved at the unit level-UCC, now I had to wait for State Classification to approve it.

I waited seventy-seven days on transient and was sent, finally, back to Telford Unit on Safe Keeping.

When I came to TDCJ in 1991 the prison was in that transition stage, going from inmate-run to officer-run. Now in 2008 and due to changes, such as PREA and stopping offenders from writing to other offenders, the prison was transforming into a different type of beast. The prison contracted with a phone company to put phones in our dayrooms so we could call our loved ones collect.

The TDCJ got a website and you could go on the website and look up an offender. It gave information such as name, TDCJ#, unit he's on, and all his charges. While you are on the phone with your loved one you can have them look up anyone that you wanted to know about and find out why they were in prison. And if you were being mistreated by officers you could have your family call up here to complain to the warden. It gave instant access to information, or informing on the bosses.

Those three actions were transitioning this prison into a daycare. It was crazy because the phones undermined the authority of the officer, a terrible reality in a prison institution. It did provide instant access to be able talk to a loved one; when before we would have to write a letter through snail mail and wait for a visit, now I could hear Mom's voice with a push of some buttons. Then there was the threat of other offenders finding out information about you that could put your life in jeopardy. That made the name "safe prison" more of an oxymoron than it was at first.

Prison advocates are lobbying for more and more rights for prisoners. And this is a controversial issue. There are pros and cons here. I believe in transparency and we need people to protect us from corrupt CO s who abuse their power and treat us prisoners in an abusive, inhumane way. And we should have certain rights, but too many and we, in an unrehabilitated, criminal mindset, start to feel entitled and we don't internalize the deterrent that a prison is supposed to be and we don't learn—we come back to prison.

When I came to prison it was *overstood* that you did not cuss a boss and you did not touch a boss. Today there is no respect for the COs. Offenders cuss the COs and they disobey them and then an officer has to call rank and backup to get this generation of inmates to mind. Most of the time the officer won't call it in because they don't want to look as if they can't control the wing or building that they are assigned to.

There is *no* more respect of inmates for other inmates, and no one is learning responsibility, because the deterrents or consequences are gone. And an inmate can snitch his way out of any trouble he gets into. It's

SOP here in Texas Prisons. Prison authorities are still using an archaic practice of punishing the majority for the sin of one or a few. In the old days if one inmate did something wrong it was common practice to put that wing on suspended activity (stay in our cells twenty-four hours), and the inmates would handle the inmate that did the wrong.

Now today this practice is still being used but we are not allowed to beat up another inmate (this is still a safe prison after all).

Back then the lieutenant knew what the fight was for. Today, that practice is used by the younger officers and rank who don't know how to use it and if we take care of the inmate who caused it, we get locked up and we lose out.

Back them "stuck out" meant just that. If you missed chow, commissary, work, your medical appointment, then you were stuck out which means you did not get to go. And sometimes that came with a disciplinary case. Now if you get stuck out officers will do what needs to be done to ensure you get fed, go to store, make it to work, or an appointment. The former taught responsibility, the later breeds pacifism and entitlement. And we are cons, we will see any opening and wedge in to "get what we got coming".

Previously I spoke of not being allowed to take vocation or therapeutic classes or programs until the last two years of your sentence, and mostly those programs are used as a condition of parole. If you go to SOTP for eighteen months we will parole you. The carrot and the stick procedure. If you take substance abuse for six months, we will grant you parole. This creates a situation of taking a class to get out of prison.

Therapeutic classes and programs don't work when they are mandatory. "How many psychologists does it take to change a light bulb?" goes the old joke. "One, but the light bulb has to really want to change." These programs must go back to a voluntary basis and should begin immediately when requested. Or otherwise, mass incarceration will assimilate more inmates into its collective.

Assaults on officers and officers assaulting offenders—both numbers are extremely off the charts in Texas prisons. In 2019 there were over seven thousand "use of force" incidents (where an officer has to put his hands on an inmate to force compliance to the rules.)

This is not a prison that deters you from coming back, it no longer teaches you responsibility, it doesn't encourage rehabilitation as long as they are giving it as a condition of your parole or only making it available in the last two years of sentence. The officers accrue sick time, then call in. The prisons are understaffed and overburdened. Other officers get rich with overtime and the black market.

The inmates do what they want, and have a little or no consequences for their actions. Cell phones, K-2 and tobacco are hot commodities on the black market. Inmates can have sexual relations with each other and with bosses and once you got something on a boss, they then have to provide whatever you request. And when the inmate gets caught, he just gives up a bigger fish and he returns to his comfort zone.

The morale amongst the officers is horrible. It all rolls down hill and then those on the bottom—the COs —take it out on us. We are deprived of our freedom and the ability to control our own lives and then we get an officer who just got yelled at by his superior, and he comes in and takes it out on us, the inmates.

And it's not so much the abuse, but it's a sentiment that tells us we are worthless and unredeemable. This is detrimental to a human being, especially one who is kept in prison away from family and loved ones. And to the ones who don't recognize that sentiment but are fed it all day long, it is devastating.

While the TDCJ says they are "promoting positive change in offender behavior to integrate offenders back into society," I, who have been here for the last thirty years, ask, "Where? Where and how are you doing this? You don't even know that you are a part of the collective and you are assimilated also."

What is the saying? "The inmates are running the asylum." It is the true definition of insanity. And it is not the answer. It is a delusion that stems from the top echelon of government. They think they are punishing crime and we think we are getting one over on the man. It's a cycle that never ends. And it's not even about rehabilitation or retribution—paying your debt to society. It's about justice, being "hard on crime so I can get reelected," and giving a sense of revenge to a victim on the news. A very few of the inmates sense the sentiment, resist it, and rise above. We work on bettering ourselves because we see ourselves as we are and we don't like it.

Being in here for thirty years I have a solution but I'll save it for the end. Hold on, we are almost there. Here is an article I wrote about the sentiment. (For other stories I wrote go to prisonjournalismproject.org and type my name in the search bar.)

SQUASH THE SENTIMENT

―――――⌐o⌐⌐o⌐―――――

"Conscience is the most sacred of all property."
-James Madison

"Labor to keep alive in your breast that little spark of celestial fire
called conscience."
-George Washington

"He who is void of virtuous attachments in his private life is, or
very soon will be, void of all regard for his country. There is seldom an
instance of a man guilty of betraying his country, who had not before
lost the feeling of moral obligations in his private connections."
-Sam Adams.

D allas, I'm sorry. And I apologize, too. For all the harm that I
caused, and the heartache to you. I grew up void of the virtue
and morals that could have made me a good neighbor, and I
have betrayed Dallas in the worst way.

And while in this institution called prison, I resisted the assimilation,
and when the crucible crushed me and I saw that I was void inside, I set

out on a journey of redemption and rehabilitation. This was not a hobby, but my new way of life—building a firm foundation of morals and those virtuous attachments.

Then, as I saw everything that is going on in the world, I began to realize that the assimilation that I've been resisting in here is out there too. I just didn't notice it until I was confined. But that sentiment is not confined. It has permeated every walk of life. Everyone is affected (infected?) to some degree. People that are assimilated don't realize that they are, until it is too late. But what is the sentiment? The most obvious is the hate, racism, and intolerance of people who are different. But there is more than this and it continues to feed us lies: "You have to be pretty, thin, and cool." "You have to style your clothes this way, your hair that way." We are influenced by the media: whom to hate, what to do with the people we hate, and what/who our identity is.

And feelings? Everything that we watch today endorses the living by our feelings. I believe that feelings are important. But feelings come and go, and your feelings can lie to you. Our thoughts cause our feelings and if I told you something that provoked a certain feeling and you act upon that feeling, because we have been told that "how you feel is okay,"—are we any better than the animals? Then, what if I tell you that what I told was a lie? Where does 'living by our feelings' take us? Where does it take us as an individual, or as a nation?

Have you ever seen a Star Trek episode when someone was being assimilated into the Borg? They are turned into half machines or computers that feed them their identity. Life imitates art, and well, look at us, we have that computer compacted and in our hand, and we get fed by it all day.

If we are in this together—truly together—we must squash the sentiment. But how, when it is so prevalent? In the book, *Best of Enemies* by Osha Gray Davidson, he asks the question: "Imagine the difficulty of listening to, and then accepting, a truth that overturns everything you believe about the world. And not merely that, but a truth that informs you that, 'The world is not what you think it is. And by the way, neither are you.' How many of us have the intellectual courage to consider, let alone accept, the truth when it demands so much?"

We, together, need to seek for the truth and let it envelope us, and to examine our feelings to see where they are coming from—a lie or the truth.

Ever since George Floyd, our nation has been in civil unrest, rioting and protesting for justice. And it is crazy that a person, any person, should have to fight for "justice" in America today. But maybe that was just that sentiment blinding me, and making me think that there was equality already.

Fighting for justice makes me think of Martin Luther King. It must have taken all his courage and strength to fight for equality and justice, in the 1960s, when that sentiment was even more obdurate. Oh, wait, it took his life.

The lawmakers promise to change laws, but I say, "What is the hold up?" Did you see what the US House did in *seven* days? They impeached Trump—the second time—*in seven days!* You see, our Congress is very powerful and if they *want* to, they can come together and change those laws—in seven days! But do they want to?

Even then, will the laws fix hate and racism? How can a written law fix something in a man's heart? My first exposure to racism was when I was little at the State Fair of Texas. My cousin and I were sitting in the grass playing and two African American kids called out to us and said, "You're a honky." I didn't know what that even was. Later that night I asked my grandfather and what he told me is the one true moral that I did grow up with and continue to live by:

"In the world some people hate others because they are different," he told me that night. "And they call each other names. But we don't do that in this family. We never say the N-word or the H-word."

Lawmakers, please change the laws. But for those laws to have an effect, we must pass this one sentiment to our children, and others around us: "Don't hate others because they are different." We must get this truth into the hearts of the human race and squash the sentiment, resist the assimilation, and remember: liberty, true liberty, is *not* doing what we want, but doing what we ought. Sam Adams said it best: "If you love wealth greater than liberty, the tranquility of servitude greater than the animating contest for freedom, go home from us in peace. We seek not your counsel, nor your arms."

"United we stand, divided we fall. Let us not split into factions which must destroy that union upon which our existence hangs."—Patrick Henry.

TELL YA ABOUT TELFORD

2009 - 2018

"Perseverance and spirit have done wonders in all ages."
-George Washington

"I always consider the settlement of America with reverence and wonder, as the opening of a grand scene and designed in Providence for the illumination of the ignorant, and the emancipation of the slavish part of mankind all over the earth."
-John Adams

Somewhere far away, or maybe close by, in another dimension in the spirit realm, there is a lake of fire. Jesus said that it was made for Lucifer and his fallen angels. And I wonder if Lucifer, Satan, that old serpent, the devil, does he ever go stand on the banks of that lake and peer into its fiery depths? Does he, deep down, know that this is where he will spend all of eternity? I can almost see him standing there.

I can see him come out of his reverie and nod his head as if he agrees with the twisted evil thought that had run through whatever angelic neural synapses that he uses to think with, and suddenly he takes off headed back to earth. He is determined to take as many humans with him as he can take to the lake of fire. And in the meantime, he wants to make a little hell on earth.

He materializes in front of a sign, in human form. As he reads the sign, he thinks to himself, "It's a start," And goes in to get a job. As he moves out of the way, we can read the sign: "The Department of Criminal Justice, Barry Telford unit."

(The devil is not omnipresent like God so he has to send the other fallen angels to accomplish his mission of lies and deception.) Due to a shortage of employees the prison system has lowered their hiring standards. And that is what made Lucifer qualify for the job; he could at least count to one third of a whole number.

"...woe to you on earth... for the devil has come down to you in great wrath because he knows that his time is short." (Rev 12:12)

There can only be opposition where there is something to oppose. Jesus said, "The Son of Man came to *seek* and to save the lost." (Luke 10:10)

And even the Pharisees grumbled, "...This man (Jesus) receives sinners and eats with them." (Luke 15:2) I don't know about you, but I do not know of a better place where you can find more lost sinners than a prison.

And in God's sovereignty, He had already set Christian men and women at the Telford unit, and not just among the staff, but amongst the inmates, too. There were angels, the holy ones, there as well, unaware. Well, we were unaware, not them.

If you want to find the devil, you may be surprised to find him in the church, but it makes sense he already has the unbelievers. He is trying to steal the seed (word of God) from believers so that believers will be deceived and not understand. (Matt 13:19)

Just remember that God is in control, and always was.

*   *   *

The morning I left Lewis unit I was taken to the Walls unit, where I spent the night. The next morning, I was on the chain again. I had to sit in a holdover at the back gate with the other people who were on the chain, at 4 a.m. in the morning. The boss at the back gate told us where we were headed as he checked us off to see if he had everyone.

"Jones, headed to Beto en route to Telford," he said going onto the next guy on the list.

State classification had reassigned me to Telford on safekeeping. I had to spend the night at Beto one unit and then I would go to Telford the next morning.

It's the little ironies that I love. I arrived on Telford on 9/11/09. I was on Telford the days of 9/11/01. Things like that I always notice and I like it when it occurs.

After UCC I waited in 3 building's multi-purpose room until I was assigned a cell. I was given a job as janitor on 7 building. When I was here last, safekeeping medium custody was on B pod 1 section. Now it was on 7 building, I wing, 2 and 3 section. The rest of 7 building is GP medium custody.

I was moved to B pod 2 section 27 cell. It was on One row which was good in that I didn't have to traverse the stairs, but it was bad because the day room with its noise was right outside my door. I had a good cellie who went by East Dallas for a nickname. Some people choose a nickname to let it be known where they are from. And East Dallas was a scrabble player. That was good because we could play during the thirty-day lockdowns.

There were still a lot of people here from 2003 when I'd left this unit, but there were a lot of new people too. Another reason I wanted to come back to safekeeping besides it being an easy environment to do your time in, I wouldn't have to sneak a relationship with someone. Although there were gang members on S/K, population gangs didn't take them seriously and there was no code to stop them from messing around. And I just wanted to settle down with one person and we could do our time. Together. I didn't consider flirting and getting attention from other guys as cheating.

I worked 7 building for about a week and then I was assigned to 3 building. I would rather have worked on the building that I lived on. In the janitor world there was a hierarchy. The top janitor was the Lobby Janitor and he kept all of that clean, and worked for the desk boss and building sergeant. He was also called the desk janitor, because his main job was to stand by the desk and watch the hallway leading up to ¾ gate, to watch for rank. He had to let the desk boss or sergeant know when rank was coming so that they could make sure everything looked good when they made it to the building. Or make sure everything was clean and in order when the rank came. The desk janitor's name was JR and he issued out cleaning equipment and supplies to each of us lowly janitors, who cleaned the pods.

This being safekeeping we wanted to "clean" the pod where our boyfriend lived, in order to spend the maximum amount of time with him. And to ensure he didn't cheat on us. It wasn't the boyfriend that you had to worry about; it was the queens. They would try to get your boyfriend just to do it and because they were tramps. It was treacherous times on safekeeping. The game kept changing every time I left S/K and it got worse.

I didn't have a boyfriend yet. In my maturity, I wanted to not jump into anything this time. I wanted to be sure that the person I got with really wanted me.

I was talking to a guy named Lil'C, who was "broke up" with a Hispanic queen. But it became evident that he was a playa. Their game was to pretend to break up while he would run game on an unsuspecting person and try to play them out of some commissary. And people whom I didn't even know would come tell me about him. There were a lot of haters on S/K.

I noticed another guy on the rec. yard. He was quiet and laid back. He always worked out every day. I played full court basketball every day, up to five games a day. But after the last game I would go over to the weight set and talk to him. I noticed my name, DJ, was tattooed on his right hand. He had other tats too. His name was Bonton which is what a section of South Dallas is known as familiarly. He was five years older than me, which put him at forty-three, and he was also a Pisces, being born on February 27.

I was attracted to the fact that he wasn't loud and an attention seeker. He knew how to do his time. He had smooth dark skin and wore his hair close to his head and sometimes he would rock a bald head. He looked good either way. I could sense a little pain in his chocolate brown eyes, but he was or seemed content. And he had a muscular body.

"Why do you have my name tattooed on your hand?" I asked touching his hand where my name was. And with that touch I felt that he was the guy for me, it was the chemistry.

"I used to deejay at a club," he said.

We would talk every day at rec. He lived on A pod and I lived on B pod. I would clean A pod on my four days at work. Like the bosses we worked four days on and four days off. I was assigned 1-1 card, which is first shift, first card. It was 6 a.m. – 6 p.m. He worked laundry 4 a.m. – 10 a.m. I caught up with him by chance one morning at breakfast (3:30 a.m.) and on the walk back to the building I asked if he wanted to be together.

"Bonton, I was wondering if you'd like to kick it?" I asked, a little nervous.

"You mean be together?" he said.

"Yes, just you and me. No one else. We don't need for nothing, just us," I elaborated.

"Yes, I'd like that," he said, walking by my side. And when we got to the front of three building, we hugged, right outside the front door. There was a blind spot and the desk boss couldn't see us.

I got a letter from D and he told me, in response to my letter, that Ms. Engman denied saying that she was going to place me in Aftercare on Goree when I had that meeting with her and Dr. Winslade. She further said that I had my chance and I came back to prison for breaking rules. So, since I wasn't going anywhere I settled into my life on Barry Telford.

The safekeeping environment has a myriad of characters living on it. Weird barely describes it. We all came from different walks of life and we'd all made decisions that had brought us here. You can tell, though, those guys who have had a hard and abused life. It's in their talk, and it's in their walk.

Over the years I have met other guys who have been abused in the past, and I see how restless and anxious they always are and I've seen cuts up and down their arms, I see how antisocial they are, how they cannot function in a group of people. I see the hurt and pain in their eyes. And the shame and guilt that drives them to make wrong choices that never satisfy but continue to hurt them. They are stuck in their own cycle of destructive thought patterns and belief systems. They believe that they deserve the life that they are living, and they don't know how to break out of that cycle. They don't know they are even in a cycle.

Restless, racing thoughts and rampant sex. These are the principles that guide them; they guided me for years. One of the thinking errors that I learned in SOTP was "Fragmentation." It's defined as extreme changes in my mental state occurring within short periods of time. There is a pattern of starting something, then changing my mind. I go with whatever I'm thinking about at the moment. "Forgetting" anything that might contradict my plan. Fragmentation is used to dismiss sentimentality and religion when they do not fit with current desires or plans.

This is restless racing thoughts, and it develops in children of abuse at a young age. I believe it stems from the thought or feeling of being unloved and that the abuse and neglect is their fault. And I had this dual love/unloved feeling going on. Love from Mom, unloved by this father figure in my life. Then when sex came in the mix, I started to equate being loved with having sex and pleasing others. My sex escapades became rampant.

I recognized this in some of the men who lived around me. In therapy they always preached, "Don't blame your crime on your childhood abuse." And I don't, not anymore. But I can see in these guys around me, they are still affected by the abuse that they suffered when they were young. The #MeToo movement claims that they too have been touched, fondled, molested, raped. People are coming out now for what happened to them thirty years ago. And I know that there is a difference between blaming a past for a present behavior, and having long term effects from being abused. I understand what it means to take responsibility for my choices and actions.

I am suggesting, though, in order to help us understand and get some insight into *this* pandemic, that people are people, we are human, and when we are brought up in a loving, stable family it sets us on a life course of virtue and morality. But when abuse of any kind interrupts the love and stability and security of a balanced family unit, that life course shoots off in another direction. True, not everyone turns to abuse, but people are affected by that abuse long term as evidenced by the #MeToo movement.

We need to address this issue, in the same way that America has addressed the COVID-19 pandemic: we're *all in this together*. But ex post facto laws do not help. We must begin in the family unit. Broadcast commercials for families and single parents to talk to their children, ask what they are thinking, and how they are feeling. To teach them to examine their feelings, to ask why. And does this line up with logic and true reason? An unchecked mind is a universe unto itself, bound by whatever rules it makes up, because there is no one there to counter it. Parents, please talk to your children, tell them it's not their fault.

When I would come across these men, I added this to my repertoire of tools that I used to ensure my rehabilitation. It reinforced all my empathy and my resolve to never go back. I would never again cause someone to be hurt and have it last a long time. Our actions have long term consequences and I did not want to be the person who affected someone for long periods of time.

In the movie, *Wonder*, one of the 'precepts' that was taught is: "Be kind because everyone is fighting a hard battle." Some of us have that battle on the outside, so be kind but also stop and ask someone "How are you? What are you thinking/feeling?" And don't just tell them to "be well," help them be well. Pay it forward.

The way to stop fragmentation and racing thoughts is, when you recognize that your thoughts are racing you have to yell, "*Stop!*" in your head. Or out loud, it doesn't matter. I had to keep yelling and trying to grab onto those elusive thoughts and think them. I had to slow down. And it's a process and it takes time but the reward is so precious.

* * *

2009 moved to 2010. I was moved to the same section as Bonton. Then a hater wrote to rank making up a lie and Bonton got moved to the next section. But we were on the same pod and that was better than being on separate pods. I wrote to the education department to take some classes. I was told that I wasn't eligible to take any education or vocation classes. I had taken two vocations in my previous time in TDCJ so now I could not take any classes. The only thing that I could take was the Cognitive Intervention Program (CIP). I told her that she had me at "cognitive."

This class taught the offense cycle module, the thinking errors, several other modules that helped you look at your problems from a different perspective. All these things were taught in the educational part of the SOTP, and I put my all in to the class to go over them again. It didn't hurt to reinforce the things I had previously learned. A new module was taught called "The Franklin Reality module." And it broke down a portion of the cycle that is not mentioned, belief windows and principles. And it's where I learned about the thought patterns and beliefs that we have and live by. This module teaches that if I have a bad principle on my belief window then this will not meet my needs over time. That was the question we continuously ask ourselves: "Will this meet my needs over time?" (WTMMNOT?) If not, we had to go find our bad principle and change it. And one of the laws this module taught is what opened my eyes and gave insight to what Mr. Bruner had told me about being an enabler: "If your self-worth is based on anything external you are in big trouble."

And that was exactly what my self-worth was based on, another person's love and acceptance of me. I needed that validation from someone else; when a guy would break up with me, I would be shattered. When Bonton and I would argue I would be devastated. But that in itself was a cycle pattern, and it seemed that I would nag him until he got mad and we would argue and then make up. Deep down I think I believed that that was how a relationship goes and I would subconsciously cause that to happen.

Knowing it and implementing it are two different things. But knowing or being aware is half the battle and it would be a while before I internalized this. At this time in 2010 I told the psychology department that I wanted off all psych medicines. I do not know what made me do that, but I got tired of taking meds, and they were not compatible with an active lifestyle.

About a month after I stopped, I actually felt great. I felt like I had been living in a dark cloud and now it was gone. I could think more clearly and I wondered why was I taking all that crap and putting it in my body.

At work all the janitors would show up at the desk fifteen minutes before 6 a.m. shift change. We would see day shift come in go to their assigned pods, and night shift leave. We had a Christian sergeant and the sarge was the last one to show up at the building. The janitors would sit on the floor of the lobby, backs against the wall, and wait on the sergeant.

When he entered the door, always laden with the folders of his sergeant's paperwork and his Bible too, he would see all of us and say, "Are you ready to start the day?" And he would begin praying. It wasn't TDCJ policy but it was his policy. It was totally against TDCJ policy, but none of us complained. He was a preacher and had a church and that's what people of God did. None of us janitors nor the desk boss were religious nor were we living right, but out of respect for the sergeant we all bowed our heads. He was not longwinded and once the prayer was over, he would mention certain areas to do detailed cleaning. The desk boss would open the closet that held all the mop buckets and the desk janitor would issue us the equipment and write our name and the number of the equipment that was issued to us. If I had broom #2, I was responsible for broom #2.

I would go to A pod to clean and I knew that if I wanted to sit down and hang out with Bonton later on then I had to work now. I always showed the boss that I was a hard worker. I learned what the higher rank would look for when they came to inspect for cleanliness, and I always had my pod clean.

I began to love the sense of accomplishment of doing a good job and the good report of the officers and the sergeant. I could carry on a Biblical conversation with the Sergeant, I knew scripture. And I didn't lie to him but he got the impression that I was a Christian. I kept my relationship a secret.

Bonton was, to an extent, what we call in here institutionalized. This was his third time down. He'd started his prison jaunts in the late '80s. Robbery and burglary of habitation. He used to be a Crip, he was stabbed on Beto unit in the '90s and was placed on safekeeping. This time he had a fifteen-year sentence for burglary/habitation, but it wasn't. He and his girlfriend lived together and got into a fight. She kicked him out, then he came back and went back in and she was still angry and called the police. He wasn't going to get any understanding from the police or DA. And as most people that are arrested for a crime and left to sit in jail because they can't post bail, when a deal is offered, they jump on it, not having the patience or even sometimes the fortitude to put up a defense and fight.

Bonton was a gentle person, which most older convicts become during the lull of false calm that comes with the prison environment at times. He also depended on the structured routine of the prison. It's a side effect of being institutionalized. We grew very close as we got to know each other. I told him my sordid past, and he accepted me still.

One morning reporting for work, as we all sat around waiting for our equipment JR, the desk janitor, was at the desk in conversation with the sergeant and desk boss. Then he left to go to the pod. Before I could ponder that oddity, the sergeant told us that JR had had a job change and then he pointed at me and said, "You, you're my new desk janitor and your job is to stand there," he pointed at a spot in front of the inmate barbershop, then to the window behind the desk, "and look out this window and let me know when rank is coming." Then he told the rest of the janitors what to clean on the pods.

What? Me, desk janitor? No, he had got the wrong person. I wanted to work the *pod* and spend time with Bonton. I didn't want to stay up here in the lobby all day with the bosses. I approached him.

"Uh, sergeant, can I talk to you?"

"What's up, Jones?" he said.

"Did you point at me to work up here...?" I started

"Get the equipment issued and park it right there, you are my new desk janitor," he said in a voice that brooked no argument.

I didn't argue, I just did what he said, and I was now the desk janitor. A job that I did not want. If I had to stay up here all day then I'd never get to spend time with Bonton. I didn't know how this was going to turn out.

The form for the equipment was similar to an excel grid. The column on the left was for the name of the inmate and then next to that was for their TDCJ number. There was a horizontal column going across the top with the items issued, broom, mop, etc. I filled out everyone's information in the slots and they all went to their pods.

The desk was to the left of the door in a horseshoe shape. The desk faced the lobby and to the left of the desk was the barbershop. It was a small room, with windows, and I stood with my back to one of the windows and I could see out the windows behind the desk all the way up the sidewalk to the ¾ gate.

Units like this that have buildings all separated from where the rank is, make for a poorly-run prison. This sergeant and desk boss weren't doing anything illegal that I could tell; they just wanted to be ready when rank came. But during the low activity they slept. Inmates had jobs, med appointments, school and places to go. When they left their pod, they had to go through the lobby to go to the ¾ gate to get to where we were supposed to be. The desk boss would also get calls from some department asking for them to send an inmate.

Chow and school were considered mass movement. A lot of activity, inmates coming and going. During those times I'd be cleaning. The lobby was easy to clean. The windows had blue painted frames with empty panes on the inside that collected dust, and needed to be wiped down. The floor was smooth concrete and collected dirt. I could sweep once then have the same amount of dirt when I swept a second time. If you used too much chemical in the mop water it left streaks on the floor. I would mop once with bleach water and then once again with plain hot water.

The sergeant told me that the sidewalk, fence line and the area right outside the building was the first thing rank would see when they came to a building. He told me to always make sure there was no trash out there. I would use a straw broom for the fence line and a deck brush for the sidewalk. I always made sure all these things were taken care of. As long as I was cleaning and continued to watch the hallway, I was okay. Because the lobby and front of the building had to be clean. I had talked to JR and he'd given me a few tips on how to get it all done.

Within a week I was filling out janitors' names and TDCJ numbers without them telling me. One day in the second week at the desk they were lined up for me to fill out the form.

"Tully," one janitor began.

"1684212," I said, and he looked at me in surprise. Then I did the next guy by memory and the desk boss did a double take. By the third inmate, they were all looking at me, like why do you know all our numbers.

"Hey, I got a good memory and I like to make sense of numbers,"

I explained. "Tully, your number 16 is the 8 twice, the 8 is 4 twice and 212 just flows but the 2 and 2 equals 4." It was also a kind of mnemonic thing. But my brain was always going fast. I learned fast and no offense but people were slow and I liked to get it done fast.

Something else became evident too. I memorized everyone on the building, that's 432 people. Not everyone's' number, but if the boss got a call for Smith on B pod, I could tell them his cell number and if they were at work, school or an appointment. It was almost eidetic.

I saw everyone as they left and they had to check in at the desk and I just remembered. It got to where the desk boss would ask me where someone was before he called the pod. Different bosses worked the building everyday with the exception of the desk sergeant. Until they were rotated every six months. But word got around about my memory, and just being the desk janitor had privileges. I could go to any pod or section and traffic and trade, which was getting commissary items from 1 section or pod and carrying them to another section or pod. It was weird because here were bosses liking me and calling on me, and letting me do what I wanted. Before, they were the enemy. This changed something in me. I liked to be called on to do something, and the fact that they were authority figures made it all the more fulfilling. The desk boss would get off the phone and say, "Jones, Ms. G. wants you on A pod."

And Ms. G. was a strict mean boss, always writing cases. But she loved me, and I don't mean in an inappropriate way, but it's like she trusted me over the other janitor assigned to her pod.

"Ms. G. you called for me?" I said.

"Yes, Jones, I want you to clean my restroom," she said, speaking of the restroom/closet where the rover hung out during the time they were not doing ins and outs or security checks.

In the officers' training they were told to never trust an inmate, that all inmates were conmen and that the long-term game was to either solicit the officer to bring in illegal items, or to desensitize them in hopes of laxing them on rules and to possibly escape.

But humans—you put a human over other humans and some of those humans will abuse that power, but there is always the equal and opposite reaction, and you get the CO who will sympathize with the inmate. With the COs on the card, when I worked 1-1, they liked me and even trusted me. This changed my perspective about officers and instead of having a mentality of it's us against them, I began to associate that if I can see things from their perspective, if I don't abuse their trust, if I can be needed by them and accomplish their needs then I just might be worthy and redeemable. I wanted to put into practice the new lifestyle that SOTP and the therapeutic community had taught me.

I had started out with the illusion that all the COs were on the side of good and wanted us to be rehabilitated. The illusion was shattered within the first several years. Then I saw that the COs were just here for a job; some were strict, mean and abusive in their authority, most were just lazy and indifferent, some did their jobs fairly, firmly and consistently. But living the lifestyle that I was living, which was totally against TDCJ rules, I was against the authority of what the bosses represented. They interfered with my comfort.

Now, I craved this new source of feeling I was needed. All the bosses called for me. Rank would call the building and tell the desk boss to tell me to have it ready for inspection by auditors or the warden. I felt that I had a purpose, not realizing that Someone Else was leading my steps for a different purpose.

Some desk bosses let me do their paperwork, and also I would tally the count and fill out that count sheet for them. I never counted inmates but the pods would turn in a pod count and the desk boss would have a rec. count, a janitor count, and a craft shop count. I would add all that up and tell them: call in this number for A, B, and C.

Even rank, if they were off on count began to call the desk boss and say, "Ask Jones where so and so is" and I would always know. With the rotation of sergeants and desk bosses, I got to know all of them and those sergeants would soon get promoted to lieutenant and the desk bosses would go up for the sergeant position. Then those lieutenants become captain and so on.

They all trusted me with their food or to make their coffee. Some officers, due to the fact that commissary was not open on weekends, would buy food and drink items and I would hold them in my locker. I would cook food spreads for them on the weekends. With the bosses who were rover or picket, since they were rotated so much, we had a rule that if two weeks went by and they didn't work over here on 3 building the commissary would be mine.

If they brought food from home they would leave something for me to "throw away." That was the code: "Jones, throw this away." Which meant, "I left you some food." In other words, these bosses treated me like a human.

But do not worry, I wasn't trying to escape or desensitize the bosses. I enjoyed having this reprieve from that sentiment that is so prevalent in prison. But for every action there is an equal and opposite reaction. The card I worked, 1-1, was also known as A card. Which meant that on my four days off it was B card. And those bosses did not like me, and they didn't like Bonton. And we had haters among the inmates. Anytime two people are together in here and don't need others, people get jealous and they hate.

They tell the bosses things about you; in my case they would tell them my charge and the bosses on B card did not like me due to that. The inmates didn't like me because I didn't need them. I never rubbed it in their face that I didn't need them, I never used my job as a way to lord it over them. I was surprisingly humble. But that stemmed from my fear of fighting. I didn't want to act all high and mighty. First, it just wasn't in my character, and second, this job, working with the bosses, people would blame me for everything. They would call me a snitch. But in my defense, I never snitched on anyone. I didn't even talk about anyone. When I was up there at that desk the last thing I wanted to talk about was the pod and the inmates that I lived around. Also, the bosses that I worked with were lazy, they didn't want to work, and if you told on someone and the bosses caught them, they would at the least have to write a case. My bosses didn't want extra work.

People went out of place all the time, from one pod to another to visit their boyfriends. I would block for them so they could get down to the other pod. But I was still the bad guy. Even though there was no proof, no one could say, "DJ got me in trouble," I was the one who had done everything. I was blamed. But that was just part of the job. When people actually thought about it, they knew the truth.

But it seemed like this was another cycle, or maybe it was the Dr. Phil rule that I generated this result because I believed that I deserved it. Maybe it was the world balancing things out. But just like when I was growing up and I had love from my mom and abuse from my step-dad, A card was my mom and B card was my step-dad.

Not being on the same section as Bonton became a strain. On my days off I would wait for him in the deep space, or he'd wait for me. If we'd been caught, we would have gotten a disciplinary. Some boss ladies would treat me with open hostility. Sometimes I didn't know if it was due to my case or because I was with a black man. Like they were jealous or something; I just got that vibe.

I lived in 2 section and Bonton was in 1 section. Inside the section there is a door that leads to the other section but it's only used in an emergency. It has a window in it and you can see in the section and talk to someone through the crack in the door jamb. But we were not allowed to be at this door and that rule was heavily enforced. Of course, I got cases for being at that door on B card.

One day a boss lady told me to pack up, that I was moving to 1 section. I was so happy, that would ease the strain of always trying to catch up and spend time together. But once I got over there and Bonton got home from work he was on the move list also he was going to 3 section. Administration was moving a lot of people around and this was one of those flukes.

Anytime a sergeant came to day shift from night shift, rank would assign them to 3 building. And they would tell them, "If you have any questions, just ask Jones." I was told that in the officers turnout meeting that they went to before shift, that I was brought up a lot.

This week we got a new sergeant. His name was Sgt A. The desk boss, Ms. W. and I, were worried about him at first because we didn't know him. But he ended up being the best sergeant that I ever had. His sense of humor was the best, and he and I would do crosswords or other logic problem puzzles together. At this time the janitors that were working the pods began to work all together. And it was a good squad. But they needed my pull to be able to make some money.

Commissary. In prison there are guys who run a gambling ring, parley's or pickems, and on Tuesday we would need to bring the jackpot from one pod to another, wherever the winner is. We charged 10% of the amount we moved. If it was $60.00 pot, we split $6.00 three ways. (Not every janitor was in on this). It was a hustle. Another hustle was on the commissary store day. There was such a madness on store day, everyone wanted to go first. But I sold spots in the line. Some were willing to pay $3.00, but when others didn't have much I'd give them a break.

Of course, the haters would write in and tell on me and the desk boss and the sergeant. But the person investigating would be one of my old sergeants who let me do the same thing. I'd be called to her office and the conversation would go like this:

"Jones, I have reports here that you are selling spots in the commissary line for $1.00. Is this true?" she'd ask.

"A dollar. They said a dollar? No ma'am, I do not sell spots for $1." I'd answer truthfully. And once she'd written in her report, "Allegations unsubstantiated," I'd tell her, "I charge $3.00."

She'd say. "I'm glad that you haven't lost your touch. But clean it up a little, okay? I'm tired of getting these snitch'o'grams."

It was 2011 and they moved all of the GP off of our building and brought back medium custody S/K. And sent a whole pod full of inmates (144) from S/K off of Alred unit. All of 3 building was now safekeeping. It was our building again.

On medium custody there was this old black man, and you can tell he was homeless in the world. But whenever he would come back from chow, he would grab trash out of the trash barrels outside of the buildings. It was sad. His cellie would complain to the sergeant and when his section went to chow the sergeant would tell me to grab an empty trash barrel. This was a fifty-gallon barrel that the unit used for trash. The sergeant would go into this guy's cell and get all the trash that this old man was collecting. It would fill this fifty-gallon barrel each week. It was old newspapers, empty food wrappers, it was nothing, it was trash. It was all this guy had. It broke my heart.

Then when he would get back and notice that his stuff was missing, he would come to the desk and report that someone had stolen his property. Tears would come to my eyes. The sergeant would make up a story, such as he'd had so much property that the property officer had had to come take it and get it sorted out.

On June 5 as I was playing basketball, I tried to save a ball that was going out of bounds, and as I fell, I put my left hand out to break my fall and I heard a pop. My wrist was swollen and out of place. Another player came to help me and when he saw my wrist, he yelled for Bonton. Bonton helped me stand up and walked me to the door to report it to the sergeant. This was B-card and when they saw us at the door, they first ignored us. But Bonton kicked the door until they opened it. The sergeant at first was mad until he saw my wrist. He took me to the infirmary.

I was sent with two officers in a van to the hospital in Galveston. A six-hour drive. I was gone for a week. When I got back, I came on the regular chain bus. The unit was on lockdown. All the departments came to talk to everyone on the chain. The safe prison sergeant called my name. She asked if I had Bonton's mother's phone number.

"Yeah, I do." I told her. "Why?" Suspicion clouded my eye. She was always trying to break up couples, and didn't like me or Bonton. I kept all Bonton's family information for him. I had always helped him write his mom and sister. He wasn't good at writing or spelling.

"We got a letter from his aunt that she's about to die and she didn't give a number," she told me. I began to cry and she said, "Why are you crying?"

"Because we don't just have a prison relationship. I care about him and I know he's hurting," I answered. I gave her the number, I had it memorized. This surprised her too.

"Sergeant will you move me to his section so I can be there for him?" I pleaded.

"No, I can't do that. Go back to the cage." I went back to the holdover cage until we got our move slips, but I couldn't stop thinking of Bonton dealing with this alone. I was still crying when the sergeant came over to the cage to call someone else's name. She had a perplexed look on her face and left.

When we got our move slips I noticed the cell, I was going to was on Bonton's section. I couldn't believe it. She had gone and done that; she had a heart after all. 3 building had already been to shakedown, but everyone was still in their cells until the thirty days were over and they'd completed shakedown for the whole unit.

The move boss pushed the buggy that had my mattress, property and linen, and since my arm was in a sling, I had to carry my stuff up the stairs one thing at a time. Being on lockdown there was no one out to help me, and my cell was on Two row, but I did have the bottom bunk.

After I finished putting my stuff in the cell, I ran up to Three row to Bonton's cell. He was asleep but I called his name, and as he came out of his sleep, at first there was confusion on his face, but as he registered that it was me, the look in his eyes made me fall deeper in love with him. It was the look of a hunger satisfied, of seeing someone after time apart, of I needed you and here you are.

He got off the top bunk and came to the door.

"Are you alright? I live in 38 cell, right underneath you, so we can talk through the vent." Our vent was connected and we could talk to each other. The downside was that five other cells could hear us too. This was our "cell phone" but it was on a party line.

"DJ, my mom…"

"I know, I gave the sergeant your mom's number so they should let you call soon. I'm here for you, okay? We will get through this," I told him.

They called him to make a phone call and he talked with his sister and they put the phone to his mother's ear and he told her that he loved her. When he told me this, I assured him that she heard him. I told him that God gives a Mom a special ear to always hear their child. It's called a mother's love.

Two days after we came off of lockdown Bonton was called to the chapel. He was told that his mother had passed away. When he left the chapel, he walked to the laundry and just sat down with his back against the wall outside the laundry. When he came back to the section, he told me that his mom was gone. I just hugged him and held him in that dayroom. It was B card also, but I did not care.

Most guys in prison are raised by single mothers with no father in sight. Our mothers are all we have in this world, who will never leave or give up on us. I couldn't imagine what he was going through. I know I have thought that if my mom ever died while I was in here that I would go crazy.

We bonded even closer through this. And he no longer wanted to have sex. I was fine with that, because I knew he loved me and I knew that I loved him. As time went on his pain became bearable and we were very close. But even before this, and afterwards, we had arguments. We didn't have a perfect relationship. I was insecure and out of that stemmed jealousy, and I always feared that someone else would take him away from me. It was irrational and there was no reason for me to be that way. But it caused a lot of arguments.

2011 moved into 2012. I believe that this was the year that Texas prisons began to become short on staff. More turnover, and the TDCJ began recruiting more strongly, and lowering their hiring standards. Telford unit had a training center for newly hired officers and once they finished their classroom training, they took them around to all the buildings. Then they would stick them with a boss who had been here for a while for on-the-job training, OJT.

When they came to 3 building, I would see old men and old women that had to come out of retirement to be able to live. I mean a little old lady like a grandmother. What was she going to do when a fight or a riot broke out? I would never let my grandmother work here. What is going on that people have to come out of retirement to be able to live and eat, and that a prison is their only option to work?

One day they placed three OJTs with the desk boss, which meant that they would be with him all day, learning on the job. Which meant I got a chance to talk to them and I could always get a feel for what type of boss they would be.

Ms. J. She was a beautiful young black woman. And she was an OJT. When I talked with her, she was always asking questions and she would look into your eyes as if she could tell if you were being honest. She wanted to know about the "girls" and what their "girl" name was and who their boyfriend was.

I told her all about me and Bonton and answered other questions that she asked. I knew then that she was going to be a "cool" boss. Because she seemed to like us, therefore, she wasn't coming into this job hating us.

COs have a sort of ranking system that shows seniority. When they first start working, they are a CO1, by the time they complete their OJT they are CO2s. Then every year after that they move up the hierarchy, which ends at CO5. A CO5 is a veteran and is placed in the jobs that need a veteran, such as being the desk boss.

After the OJTs of Ms. J.'s class began working by themselves, Ms. J. was assigned to 3 building a lot. Safekeeping is also an easy place to work for the officers. For the most part inmates on safekeeping do not cause a lot of problems. We are compliant and do what we are told. The prison administration would assign these new boots to work in safekeeping building at first to get accustomed to the job.

The buildings that had a desk were 3, 4, 7, and 8 building. And there were four CO5s who would alternate working each building. In 2012 a lot of younger CO2s and 3s began complaining about not being assigned to the desk. Administration then put all CO2s on the desk. There were six different ones alternating, and they would split the day, six hours each. Even I thought it was a bad idea because a desk boss has to be able to handle and contain a situation.

Sometimes the prison was so short of staff we didn't have a sergeant in the building. On those occasions it was just a new boot desk boss running the building. On 3 building I helped these officers know how to do their job. Pretty soon the rank would say, "Just ask Jones he will tell you what to do."

Ms. J. was placed on the desk. She had a husband who worked 7 building a lot. They liked to put men working a building with medium and close custody. As I said earlier, I could tell that Ms. J. was going to be a "cool" boss which meant that she wasn't going to be hard on us, always writing us up. I'm sure when TDCJ hires a boss they are not looking for "cool." They want fair, firm and consistent. I suppose that they want that because their administration lacks it in a big way.

On 3 building the desk boss would work the desk for six hours then switch with A pod picket for the final six hours. Ms. J. would, when she worked the pod, allow you to go in the cell with your boyfriend for an hour or so. She would open cell doors without a rover being in the section. The rover would also be a cool boss on those days. And there were times when Ms. J. would have to work with an uncool boss. On those days we all had to abide by the rules.

But in 2012 we entered an era where we usually had these new boots and they were still learning. When they were at the desk, I would make sure that they knew everything they were supposed to know. I liked being able to do whatever I wanted to do, but I had enough sense to teach them the correct way, because certain things had to get done in a day. But when these new boots were down on the pod they were "trained" in a whole different way.

Every inmate will push any boss to see how far they can get with them. And this administration was wrong to put two CO2s or 3s on the same wing, because the inmates would influence them as a whole, that certain behavior is okay. And the new boot won't know any better. It is like a reverse mob mentality. You hear of people participating in a mob riot and afterward they don't know why they did it. This was like that. When the TDCJ began experiencing staffing problems, call-in problems and the like, it hurt the prison the most, because things like this would happen. New boots were being influenced ("conditioned") by the inmates.

Telford unit became very corrupt at this time. Inmates will always take advantage of these situations. While some "cool" bosses might have allowed us to break a few rules, other ones become "dirty." Both hurt the system. But this type of thing can't happen if other factors would have (should have) been in operation. What I mean is that it's a slow fade, and the Texas State Prison System is at fault here. The morale, the way the bosses are treated, trained and placed in certain jobs is the biggest cause for Texas' staff shortages in their prisons.

This causes new hiring, fast training and the loss of veterans and you get new boots training new boots and sometimes inmates training new boots. But before Ms. B., Sgt. L. and Sgt. S. get mad at me I want to say that those three training officers/sergeants were exceptional in their training classes at Telford. But it's being short of staff and having an OJT be trained by a CO3 on the pods; that hurts the training. But overall, the prison system is at fault. Having a hundred units in one state is at fault. And lowering your hiring standards is a cause. The state needed a quantity of COs and they sacrificed quality.

The government and Texas has always tackled problems from the wrong end and thrown bad money after bad money. They are so involved that they can't see that is not working, yet they keep on doing the same thing expecting different results. We all know what that is called.

***

In 2010 my direct appeal for this violation case was denied. The Dallas Public Defender told me that was the end of the road and that they could no longer help me. They suggested I file an 11.07 writ of habeus corpus on my own. Which I did; however, I did not know the legal rules to file an 11.07 writ and I erred and my writ was denied.

I wrote lawyers, judges, senators, representatives, the Governor. I did not get a response from anyone but the representative of Bowie County. He said he agreed with me but that he did not know what bills he would bring to the legislation, which I interpreted as "if you give me enough money, I will help you." I didn't have any money. I wanted him to change civil commitment laws on the basis that they were unconstitutional. And he was supposed to uphold the Constitution. I suppose that I was naïve.

I began to write the media—magazines, newspapers, and news segments on the big networks. But I didn't get any answers from them. I had written to SCFO, and in 2012 SCFO, who had a high turnover rate in their staff also, had a new lady over their civil commitment division. She began to file motions on our behalf, to get us treatment, new trials and relief.

The state filed a motion to modify our Civ. Comm. orders to make it easier for DAs to prosecute violations of these orders, the court scheduled a hearing and although there were 175 men in prison for minor rule violations of their Civ. Comm. orders (which was half of the total men that were committed in 2012), they brought forty-five of us to Conroe for this hearing.

We all were brought on the chain bus from the unit that we were assigned, to the Walls unit. At the Walls unit we were placed on two big chain busses and brought to Conroe Court. We all had on foot shackles and handcuffs and we shuffled in and were made to sit in the spectator seats.

Judge S. was not the same judge who'd presided over my trial. This was a different judge but three times worse. Bias does not describe how much he was against us. Years later complaints would be made about him, and they had a court transcript when he told a defendant that he needed to be decapitated. He would be removed from Civ. Comm. court duties.

But in 2012 he had full authority to violate our civil rights. He had our SCFO lawyers—there were six of them there this July day—and four special prosecutors, to all sit in the jury box. He got a podium and stood in front of his desk and forced us to be in the audience.

"As I call your name, stand up and I will modify your order per the state's motion," he began.

"I object your honor," our SFCO lawyer said.

"Noted, now sit down," he told her.

"Your honor there is no due process, you are not giving our defendants a chance to talk with their attorney. I object to this hearing in the way that you are conducting it."

"Sit down and shut up or I will throw you out of my courtroom. That is your last warning," the judge replied.

Yeah, it went like that. He called each of our names and then told us he was modifying our orders. A few of us objected; one guy wouldn't shut up and he had the TDCJ officers take him out of the court room. When it was my turn, I spoke a sentence that I wanted on the record.

"Sir, I am not under the law, and it cannot retroactively be applied to me," I stated.

"Your order is being modified, sit down."

And besides our SCFO lawyers, no one cared. They did whatever they wanted and we were powerless. Our lawyer came to the Walls unit and spoke with all of us, and assured us that they would appeal.

We were all sent back to our units. Once the SCFO wrote the appeal they sent us a copy. It was a thick appeal, over a hundred pages. I read every word and I was excited because if we won, we would get out of prison. This appeal would give us relief from this unconstitutional law. We were told to be patient, that appeals take time.

A couple of months later, I got a letter from SCFO, one of the supervisors there. The letter said that the appeal filed by our lawyer is the last thing that SCFO would do for us on appeal, that the scope of SCFO's job is only to represent us at trial or Civ. Comm. proceedings but not to appeal modification hearings. Further, that we were no longer to write our lawyer about our case and to only write if it concerned things within the scope of our job.

I could not believe it. Somebody high up knew that she was about to get all of us freed and they put a stop to it. And they could put a stop to it because SCFO is a division of the Texas Department of Criminal Justice. They work for the State of Texas. I was, once again, being screwed without any grease.

Then we got the answer from the appeals court. It was short and simple. "We do not have jurisdiction to hear a modification appeal." They didn't deny merit or throw out our case, they just claimed that they do not have legal jurisdiction to hear an appeal.

And this is another flaw and civil rights violation because this gives the state, prosecutor, civil commitment office, and the judge freedom to do anything they want to us in a modification hearing and there is no one we can get help from. That's Texas jurisprudence for you.

But like Sandra Bullock said in the movie *The Net* from the '90s: "They did it to me and they are going to do it to you." All this is doing is setting a precedent for other Texans, other classes of people.

MOM

————————————⊰∘ᗡᘐ∘⊱————————————

My mom came to visit and I talked with her about all this. We didn't have the money to get an attorney. But my mother was having problems of her own. In 2010 she had had a mild stroke but it had caused a film to be over the brain. This slowed down her thinking process, she couldn't drive anymore because of it. She explained it to me like this: "My brain tells my arm to pick up that cup, but by the time the command gets there I'm doing something else."

"Oh, so that's why I don't have commissary money—because you told your hand to push send and you walked away from the computer," I said, teasing her. She could talk okay and think okay, it was just response time on body actions.

At the beginning of 2012 she told me that she had cirrhosis of the liver. She said the doctor had accused her of being an alcoholic, but my mom doesn't drink. They did all these tests and finally found out she had hepatitis C. She must have had it for years for her liver to look the way it did. I immediately volunteered to donate half of my liver. She said she would tell her doctor.

In this November visit, she revealed her thoughts: "David, no one has offered to donate half their liver except you. No one loves me, and you only volunteered to do it to get out of prison." She was crying, which caused me to cry.

"Mom, listen to me. If they allow me to give you half of my liver," I said, holding both her hands in mine, "they will take me to the hospital, take it out and sew me back up and send me straight back here to prison. I volunteered to give you my liver because I love you, I want you to live. You are the best mom in the world. I love you, okay?"

We both cried but I think I got it through to her. I wish she wouldn't feel unloved. But in the end the doctor decided to try out a new Hep-C medicine. It had a 95% cure rate.

*   *   *

AAAAAAAAAAAAAAAAAAAAAAAAAAAAAAH!!

Have you ever wanted to scream as loud as you can? Have you wanted to just ball up like a baby and cry and sob from your gut until you retch? Have you ever wanted to beat something into a bloody pulp?

Have you ever wanted to just go numb so you won't feel that pain anymore?

Yeah, it's like that but worse. How can I put into words how I feel when my heart has been wretched out, stomped on, cut into pieces and put back in?

On December 6, 2012, a Thursday evening, Bonton and I were in the dayroom and the officer came in to do an in and out and pass out mail at the same time. I had gotten moved to the same section as Bonton and we were able to spend time together, watch TV or cook and eat together. We always watched the Cowboys together, being diehard fans.

This evening Bonton went to Three row where his cell was and I was on One row. The boss came to my cell and handed me a letter. Well, a company named JPAY provides a service to prisoners' families and you can go to jpay.com and write a prisoner and hit send like an email. The mailroom prints it out on paper and sends it through the mail. It gets to us same day if it's sent early enough, but most of the time we get it the next day.

Underneath my name was the sender's name. I saw my mom's name and it was sent that day. I was glad to hear from her. But as I began to read it, it was very clear that it wasn't her that had written this. I decided that it was my step-dad, Sonny, and he told me that my mom had had some stroke again. That she was sitting on the couch holding a grandkid and she stopped talking and just smiled. He said he rushed her to the hospital and they were waiting to see what the doctor said.

I called Bonton and he knew something was wrong and came downstairs and I told him what the JPAY had said, and he just pulled me into an embrace and let me cry. The next day I was anxious for any news but I didn't get any mail.

Saturday at 8 a.m. I was called for a visit. When I got there, it was my brother and sister who'd come to see me. They told me what had happened.

"The doctor said it was a blood vessel that burst in her brain. They fixed it in surgery, but she is in a coma. She is on life support machines but when we left, she was taking more breaths than the machine and they were considering taking her off the machine because she was breathing on her own," my sister said.

"Well, that's good right? If she can breathe without it, it means she will come out of it," I said.

"Yeah, it's good. We all hope she comes to," my brother said.

They stayed the whole two hour visit and we talked and they told me what all was going on. When they left, I thanked them for coming and told them to keep me updated, to call the unit and they would tell me.

Sunday right at kickoff of the noon Cowboy game I was called to the desk. It was B card so I wasn't working. When I got to the desk the boss gave me a pass to the chapel. I thought that they would tell me that they took her off the machine and she'd have woken up.

My sister was on the phone: "David, they took her off the machine and she was still breathing, but she passed away this morning."

"No, I thought she was taking more breaths than the machine? No, how, why?"

I cried with her.

When I got off the phone the chaplain asked me if I wanted to pray. I looked at him with anger and said, "No, I've already prayed but God didn't listen. I'm through praying." And I walked out.

On my way back to 3 building it wasn't the cold weather that brought the tears to my eyes and blurred vision. I couldn't comprehend it, a million thoughts ran through my mind. The thing that I had always said would drive me crazy had happened. I remembered thinking "How does crazy come to you, do you snap or is it a process?" I couldn't live without my mother. She was my everything. She had always been there for me, even though I had hurt her so much. I didn't get to spend time with her before she passed. She was only fifty-nine.

Entering 3 building the desk boss was saying something about do I need some time alone. For security reasons the chaplain has to let the COs know so they can make sure that you don't harm yourself.

I kept walking to A pod. I told her that I was alright. When I got to my section Bonton was still watching the game. I sat down next to him and leaned into his arms and cried. Now it was his turn to hold me.

Years later I wrote this poem to her:

"Oh, Mom" by David Jones

1.
Why do dads disappear
and the ones that take their place treat you queer
year after year
there's no man to hold you dear
there is only drunk, yelling and fear.
2.
Why do moms love you e'er
they never leave but are always there
year after year
you give her tears
but with her there is only love, compassion, and tender care.
3.
A mother's love I will never understand.
but she got it from up above, straight from God's own hand
'Love is patient, love is kind... love does not insist on its own way."
Mom this describes the love that you've shown me every day
4.
I didn't know what I had in you, until you were gone.

I'm sorry, and I promise you that I won't be long
I gave myself to Jesus and he has sworn
To renew me on this rocky road full of thorns
5.
So save me a seat up in heaven, and to our Lord give a hail
I'll be there one day because his love never fails.

*   *   *

My four days off were over and I was glad to go back to work. Sgt. A. and Ms. W. were at the desk. When I told them about my mom they offered as many days off as I needed.

"No, I need to work to distract myself." I had to keep busy. I had done nothing but cry in my cell the last two days. Now I was numb and I didn't want to think, I didn't want to feel. I just wanted to keep busy.

Ms. J. came over to talk with the sergeant but when she saw me, she said, "Whoa, what's going on? I can tell something's wrong." I'm telling you, this woman looked us in our eyes, she saw that we're human. But although I was numb, pain was pouring out of my eyes. That is what she saw, and I suppose it affected my whole demeanor.

I told her those three words: "My mother died." And tears came to my eyes. But those three officers always treated me like a human, and they didn't condescend, they didn't give me fake platitudes. In this horrible place called prison, a place that I seem to have always been, and at such a time as this when I'd lost something so precious—a place where I'd been thrown away, and in this place where they weren't supposed to care.

They cared.

These people that I had worked with and had gotten to know and they knew me and my case but still liked me, still fed me, still looked out for me. We had violated the CO/inmate status quo. The lines had been blurred. Not in a bad way but in a human way. They cared.

How does something like this happen in this type of place? I can only conclude now that it was God. He takes care of His children. Yes, I was still mad at Him and I still was not talking to Him. But do you see His character? He is always gonna be good and true and faithful. In life things will happen, good things and bad things. People will love, hate, laugh, cry, live, die, commit crimes, or do good to other people. God does not always intervene because He gave Earth to Adam and when Adam chose to sin, he handed rule of Earth over to the enemy. It was a spiritual law. We make our choices. And when things go wrong, we want to blame someone else. God is an easy target.

I used to blame God for allowing my step-dad to do what he did to me and for letting me grow up and choose to hurt children. I blamed my step-dad too; everyone but me. And everyone right now is all clamoring for their rights: "My body my choice," "I feel this way and the US has to give me civil rights for this," "I have the right to vote, live, choose, marry, die, feel, do what I want, buy a gun, use my gun, say what I want, hate, love, have my own truth."

Then human government gives these rights to all these people, but when those rights clash, when life goes wrong because someone mistook liberty for doing what they wanted rather than doing what they ought, then fights, wars, riots, or protests break out and the world is what we have today.

God gave us choices and He even let us go our own way, but when something happens that causes us pain, we get mad at God. I do believe that although He may not stop hurt or pain or stop us from making bad choices, that He will redeem them and us. That is, once we respond to His knocking, he won't force us to come back to Him in the garden but He will knock, send people our way, speak to our hearts. And sometimes we don't hear him until the world has knocked us down. That's when He picks us up and cleans us off.

Lauren Daigle came out with a song called "You Say," and this song stayed at #1 on both Christian and pop radio for weeks. She mentions God only once. But in this song, she conveys the very thing that our hearts are crying for, to be held, strong, loved and to belong to someone who can handle it all. Because He says it.

*　　*　　*

But it would be years before I realized all this. Right then, I was mad, hurt, and grieving. And I have to point out that *not once* did I regress and think of a child. My new way of dealing with things were well grooved in my synaptic avenues. It was real. I wasn't going back. I could deal with life's worst—a mother's death—and I didn't try to soothe myself, or resort to old behaviors.

A friend told me, "Grieve. DJ, grieve. Pain is a part of the love you have for your mom. You have to go through it." Bonton and I hadn't had sex since his Mom had died. We had something real and it was even better without sex.

I still saw guys that were attractive and I fantasized about them. In early 2013 the prison shipped a lot of safekeeping off of the unit and once again made C pod a general population pod. Now A and B were S/K and C was GP. There were a lot more manly men on C pod, Crips and Bloods. I didn't like to have them on "our" building, but some of them were nice to look at.

* * *

We went on lockdown. At first, I was stuck in my cell. I hated not being able to go to work. I needed my distractions, and work gave me distraction.

One day Sgt. A. was off and the Christian sergeant was working the building this day, the one who had first assigned me to work the lobby. He came to my cell and I asked if I could come out and work.

"No, they don't want anybody out yet," he said.

"I'm mad at God, sir," I told him.

"Why? What's going on?" He settled into his spot. I knew that I had his attention.

"Well, my mom passed away in December and before that I prayed for God to heal her, but He didn't."

"How do you know that he didn't heal her?" he asked me.

"What do you mean? She died," I said, quite perplexed.

"Jones, healing is not indigenous to Earth. Let me ask you something. Was she happy or suffering on Earth?"

I thought about hepatitis C, the liver, her feeling like no one loved her, the stroke that made her a little slow. I thought of her feeling guilt for my life. Tears sprang to my eyes as I told him, "She was suffering."

"So, God brought her home so she wouldn't suffer anymore. In His house there is joy unspeakable that never ends. Change your perspective, son," he said.

And sometimes it's as simple as seeing things from a different perspective. I was looking at it from my point of view, a selfish point of view. But just like that I wasn't angry anymore. I knew that she was okay. She was better than okay. For the first time in a long time she was no longer hurting. I could only imagine.

As I contemplated all that after the sergeant left, I realized that my heart wasn't right. I thought, "I'm going to make sure that I get saved so I can go to heaven and see her."

I was a mess, though. How could I make sure I was saved? I came across a book by Donald Miller called *Searching for God Knows What*. I related to him right away. We were the same age, and we both grew up with only a mother. The difference is he was from Houston, Texas but I'm sure God overlooked that (LOL). (I don't understand the rivalry, I cheer all Texas teams, but everyone knows that the Cowboys are America's team.) In this book he denounced the false god that is widely taught today. But something happened to me that would change my perspective even more as I read this book. He was recounting the Genesis chapter 3 scene after Adam sinned and was hiding from God. The Bible says that "God was calling out, 'Adam, where are you?'"

"Adam said, 'Over here, I was hiding because I was naked.'"

"God asked him a very poignant question: 'Who told you that you were naked?'"

And when I read those words I heard in my heart, very plain and clear, God asked me, "Who told you that you were gay?"

This question floored me. I'd never considered it. Then I asked myself, "Who did tell me I was gay?" I didn't have an answer but I sensed that I was lied to about it. It seems as if I began feeling this way around twelve or thirteen and I just went with it because my body wouldn't lie to me. Would it? It had felt good, so I'd done it.

But now I believe that it is thoughts that cause feelings, so somewhere back then I began to think about it and I sexualized it and I told myself that this is how you get love, and it felt good. There was no one to ask me what I was thinking, and being gay had been so taboo among peers and society that I hadn't told anyone, and therefore, no one could counter these thoughts or feelings. Our country tells us in all the ads, and shows, and in pop music, to go with your feelings. I believe all that and all the dysfunction growing up contributed to these thoughts and I inferred from all that that I was gay. (Not all of it came from outside things.)

It is for you to decide if the things, events and upbringing led you to have certain thoughts and beliefs and feelings. And if you went along with those feelings and either chose to become a bank teller or a bank robber, then maybe we can say that our past does influence our future. And we can also say that if something can and does influence us to certain behavior, then we can also take a different look at our past and begin to see it in a different perspective and we can change present behavior and that will cause us to live in reality.

But just as Osha Gray Davidson asked in his book, *The Best of Enemies* when we find that truth informs us that neither we nor the world are what we think they are, "How many of us have the intellectual courage to consider, let alone accept, the truth when it demands so much?"

It is hard. But it is well worth the work. And I find this to be true about everything in life. We have all been lied to.

*   *   *

I told this to God after He told me that I wasn't gay: "God, okay, I agree with you. I'm not gay. It hasn't worked for me. But we have been here before. I still feel gay. And I'm going to keep on doing it until You take it away."

I left it at that. I wasn't going to tiptoe around, pretend to be delivered when I was still wanting men in a sexual way. That had never worked before. But I began to get up a little earlier and before I would go to work or start my day, I would read the Bible and pray.

In July, Bonton discharged his sentence. We had been together just a few months short of four years. And we were very close and I loved him. We were there for each other at very trying times in our lives, at the deaths of our moms. In the weeks before he left, we were even more inseparable.

Then the day came when he had to get on the chain bus to go to the unit he would be released from. It was B card and I hugged him goodbye anyway. I stayed in my cell and cried after he was gone. The same friend came and told me, "Grieve. DJ, grieve. Pain is a part of the love you have for him." A few words can really help at the right time.

*   *   *

2013 moved into 2014 and there were no changes. Every day was the same. In February I was coming back from chow and I was talking to the barber in prison sign language through the glass, and this being B card the desk boss wrote me a case for "refusing to go to A pod." Which was a lie because I lived on A pod and I did go, just not as fast as he wanted.

I had a Hispanic cellmate and he had a pet rat he'd caught as a baby and tamed her and trained her. The rat's name was Angel and it was fun to hold her and watch her do all the stuff he'd trained her to do. He even trained her to use the restroom in a certain place so it was always safe to hold her. There were lots of rats at Telford and we would have to place cardboard at the bottom of our cell door so we didn't get a late-night visitor. I had been woken up more than once with a strange rat crawling on me.

A lot of guys had pet rats and would even mate them and sell the babies. It got to where boss ladies before entering our cell for a cell search would ask, "Do you have a rat?" And if you said "Yes", then she wouldn't search your cell. Everybody answered "Yes," from then on.

The field officers made a sport of killing them if someone wrote a snitch-o-gram on us. But for the most part it was cool to have a pet rat as long as it was trained. I brought Angel to the desk one time to scare Ms. J. She screamed and ran into the bathroom. That was hilarious.

*   *   *

February 28, 2014. When I woke up, I felt different. I do not know how to describe it other than to say I did not feel gay anymore. It wasn't just a disgust for the behavior but also, I felt like something was missing. I was lighter in my chest.

The only conclusion that I came to was that God had answered my prayer. He took the desire away. I'm not saying that He took every thought, fantasy, and inkling away. But it was like I had a reprieve so that I would make the decision to stop. He gave me the strength to stop.

And I did stop the behavior. I quit having sex with men. I began telling people that I didn't mess around anymore.

*   *   *

Today is February 28, 2021. I have been writing this book since 2019. I do not believe in coincidences; that I would be writing about the day that I stopped being gay on the seven-year anniversary of that day. There is so much more to tell you about the last seven years but I shift forward here to say that I have not been with a man sexually in seven years. But I don't want you to think that it happened overnight.

No, it is not a coincidence that I write about that day on this day. Somehow God has caused it to be that I would get to this point of the story on the anniversary of it. A lot of Christians who witness or tell their testimony would have you believe that they had an experience and they were instantly delivered. The mainstream churches paint Christianity in such a way as to give you the illusion that once you come to Christ that you are saved and everything is going to be okay. Those churches teach the "prosperity gospel" or the "name it and claim it" gospel. Just like that guy that night talked about how his son "healed" the refrigerator sixteen years ago, in the chapel. It seems it's those churches who are the majority of the ministries that come into prison to preach to us. They get us all excited about an experience and when it comes time to stand on that faith, we find that it was made of sand and we fall. Maybe God does instantly deliver some people. But I believe that the majority of God's work is done through what is called progressive sanctification. Paul says to be transformed by renewing your mind. All those years, when I would go to God, I would fall away six months later. I was not seeking God but an experience. I would rebuke homosexuality or all sexual immorality away from me. I would get others to cast it out of me. But those "experiences" never addressed my identity, how I believed and thought about myself and others.

I'm not saying God can't instantly change that. But I don't believe that

He operates like that. It was over years and decades that I developed my thought/belief patterns and thus my identity. It was going to take some work to change it. I have learned that God is not an experience, he is not a feeling. He is not a place. Although I have experienced Him, I have felt His presence, and He seems to be in every place that I go. I always see Him in a kindness, or in a sunset, or in how the birds and ground squirrels do what God made them to do, outside my cell window.

So, when the casting out and rebuking didn't work, and I became broken enough to hear Him, he told me who I was. Then I told Him, "confessed," that I couldn't stop being who I thought I was. I agreed, "acknowledged," with Him that He was right and that He could take it away. As I continued to read the Bible and pray to Him, then he gave me the strength to resist sin, the outward behavior. Then over the last seven years this God has become my Lord and Master, but also my Heavenly Father. He did what the Bible calls progressive sanctification and Paul says it's renewing your mind. He began cleaning up my life. Teaching me His truth about Him and His Son Jesus and the Holy Spirit.

In east Texas there is a radio station called the Bott Radio Network and all they broadcast all day is preachers who teach the truth, and not the "name it claim it" trash. I will always be grateful to the Bott Radio Network. It was very hard to see God as a loving Father after my experiences with human fathers. But I had to actually read the Bible and renew my beliefs about Him, focusing on His attributes. When you *know* the truth, it really does set you free.

Over the last seven years, He helped me to stop cussing. I was no longer having sex with men, but I was flirting and verbally joking in gay humor. He convicted me of this and I began to stop that behavior. He has corrected so many wrong beliefs I had learned from all those prosperity preachers. I had always been taught to rebuke the devil off of my life, home, off of everything. I was taught to tell him he was a defeated foe and that I had power over him.

One day, I was praying to God before I went to work and as I always did in my prayer to God I would break off and start rebuking the devil and this day I sensed the Holy Spirit ask me, "What are you doing?" I don't know how to describe it. It wasn't an audible voice, but I sensed an offense in my spirit and it was directly related to my rebuking the enemy.

I answered Him, "I'm telling satan he is defeated, Lord." But again, I somehow knew that God answered and said, "You pray to me. I am your master. Don't talk to the liar." From then on, I never said a word to the enemy. Why talk to a liar? You know what they will say—a lie. But more than that I believe that there is a spiritual law here that holds if you speak to a person, you open a door for that person to come in and speak back. I refuse to listen to lies anymore.

The book of Jude says that, "Those people blaspheme (rebuke the glorious ones—verse 8) all that they do not understand and are destroyed…" (verse 10) The church is teaching to do this very thing. Teaching that we, mere humans, have been given power from Jesus to take on these fallen angels (glorious ones). But Jude says when we do this we are destroyed, because even demons, fallen angels, are supernatural and if we open that door, we let them come in and destroy us. Jesus said, "The thief comes to kill, steal, and destroy." (John 10:10) And in Matthew 28:18 and 19 Jesus says "All authority in heaven and earth has been given to Me [Jesus]. Go therefore and make disciples…"

We are not to go and fight demons but go and tell about the One who already defeated them. (Col 2:15 and 1 John 3:8) And he protects us from the evil one (John 17:15) but if we open the door then we allow that. God does not override our choices but when we realize and confess our mistakes, He redeems them. (Luke 22:31-34 and John 21:15-33) God is gentle, He won't force you, the enemy is the one who will violate your space and influence you to go away from God.

God also helped me forgive my step-dad, and others who have legitimately hurt me. And with that forgiveness given I was able to fully appreciate God's forgiveness of me. There is nothing like feeling clean on the inside. It has always felt good after a long hard day's work to take a hot shower and get clean. Or to dive into a pool on a hot summer day. But God, He can cleanse your soul.

In the Psalms it says "I have calmed and quieted my soul." (Ps 131:2, and in Ps 73:21,22,25) There is a comparison of our soul before salvation and after: "When my soul was embittered, when I was pricked in heart, I was brutish and ignorant; I was like a beast toward you." And verse 25 is our soul theme after salvation: "Whom have I in heaven but you? And there is nothing I desire on earth besides you." And this is what I experienced. My soul was not crying out for things to fill it anymore. I finally understood what Jesus meant when he told the lady at the well, "Whoever drinks the water (word, Holy Spirit) that I will give him will never thirst again." (John 4:14) I no longer thirst for anything else. I am fully sated by Him and yet I continued to desire Him. This is not based on feelings. God showed me an analogy of His salvation. It is just like a prisoner who committed a crime (sin), was brought to court and convicted (the Holy Spirit convicts us of sin) and we are sentenced (begin a new life with Jesus as Lord.) Then He showed me that after I came to prison, I had good days and bad days. Those bad days didn't change my conviction because I was still in prison. So why did I think that I was not saved just because of a lack of good feeling, or having a bad day. My salvation cannot be changed by something outside of me, when it didn't start outside of me. He said "Those who endure until the end will be saved." (Matt 24:13) We will suffer and have bad days but our perspective has changed and we no longer live for this world but we have a hope of eternal life through an intimate knowing relationship with Jesus. (C.f. Phil 2:29 and Col 1:27b)

And in this progressive sanctification we live this new life by faith. And John MacArthur teaches faith is not a mental activity but is a verb, an action. Which I interpreted to mean that because I know that sin has no more dominion over me then I will live as if that is true and the power of God rests upon me to help me choose not to sin. (C.f. Rom 6:14 and 2 Cor 12:9)

Galatians 2:20 breaks the Gospel down to two aspects: spiritual and physical. The spiritual is Jesus living in me: "It is not I but Christ in me." And what Jesus brings with Him is true for us—He defeated sin, Satan, and death.

The physical aspect is simple: "The life I now live in the flesh (physical) I live by faith in the Son of God who loved me and gave himself for me." I live by an action, faith, that knows I am dead to sin and alive to God. Would you eat feces? No. Why? Because you *know* you aren't supposed to, that it is not good. The same concept is in Romans chapter six. We know we are dead to sin, we consider ourselves dead to sin and we know and consider ourselves to be alive to God and now we present ourselves to Him, our new Lord. God never meant for us to have a new life of going back and forth between sin and serving Him. He is not a cruel God. He offers for us to turn back to Him in that relationship Adam and Eve had before the fall, before they knew that they were naked, and to depend on Him to tell us what is good and what is evil.

Do you remember at the beginning of this book I said that maybe God meant for us to *not* be dual in ourselves but to overcome that, overcome having to protect ourselves? To serve in singleness of mind and heart and be One with Him and by trusting Him? That is what He did in my life. John 17:23 says "I in them and you in me that they (us) may become perfectly one, so that the world may know that you sent me and loved them even as you have loved me." And I am no longer dual inside, or double-minded. As time went by and I spent time with Him in His word my mind has been renewed and my desires have taken on a different satisfaction. I am free of sexually immoral thoughts. I don't lust or fantasize about men. I see men who are attractive but there is no longer a cyclic pattern of thought that pulls in an attractive look and violates people's boundaries by imagining vile thoughts about them. I am free because He told me He made me to be, Free.

John MacArthur says there is a big distinction between the Truth of God's word and what is commonly preached in mainstream churches. And once you get a taste of his truth you are consumed by it and all you want is more. Those other churches led me out to the ravenous wolves and I was destroyed every time. But now all I want to know is God the Father and Jesus Christ whom He sent. I desire His truth. I am finally stable, sober-minded and see things from a true, eternal life perspective. I am in a fulfilling relationship with Jesus and am led by His Holy Spirit through his word.

I have to claim this: What is an "altar call, rededicating our life, and being in a backslidden state?" My brothers and sisters there are no such things. That is a revolving-door cycle that will bring you down a road to a place you do not want to go. It destroys you to go to an altar call, say a prayer, get saved, backslide, go back to church and rededicate your life to Him, all to do this over and over. My claim is if you are doing this, examine yourself to see if you are in the faith. Because when we go to Jesus and confess our sins, acknowledge that we can't, but He is true, right and He can, that He is the way to the Father, then He forgives us and causes us to overcome, (Ps 32:5 and 1Jn 5:5) we enter into a relationship with Him that never ends. There is no back and forth, being tossed to and fro. There is always being in His presence. "Fear not, little flock, for it is your Father's good pleasure to give you the kingdom." (Luke 12:32) He keeps us from falling.

"O Lord, who shall dwell in Your Holly Hill? He who... speaks the Truth in his heart." (Ps 15:1-2)

"Little Children, let no one deceive you." (1Jn 3:7)

DECRIMINALIZED

I n 2015 the Texas Legislature changed civil commitment laws. The hype in the newspapers quoted senators saying, "The whole program is a total failure," "We are going to bring civil commitment laws into constitutional compliance," and the like. I was so excited I couldn't wait until they did this, because if they said that it's a total failure and that it was not in constitutional compliance then they had to mean the two hundred guys being in prison for violating minor rules of Civ. Comm. It is our civil rights that had been violated. They had to let us out of prison. Right? Come on Texas Legislature.

Before they did this there was a tragedy at Telford unit on May 15, 2015. An officer was killed by an ad. seg. offender. I was at 3 desk when the call came over the radio by that officer's picket boss. "Help, an inmate is beating an officer. Come quick. Hurry." The scene was so horrible that this picket boss forgot radio etiquette.

A ranking officer then called over the radio to rack up the whole unit (put us in our locked cells). A feeling of somberness was felt over the whole unit. It was eerie. A few days later I was called out to clean up the lobby of 3 building. The director of TDCJ, Bryan Collier, was coming. I cleaned up everything then watched the sidewalk. When I saw them coming, I began mopping in front of the door with strong bleach. That way bleach is the first thing he would smell upon entering 3 building and think "clean," it was an old janitor's trick.

He walked right past me and went to the desk to meet the desk boss and sergeant. He had an entourage with him, some were rank at Telford and others were regional directors working under Mr. Collier. One of the regional directors nodded at me and said, "Sorry, don't mean to walk on your clean floor."

"It's alright, sir." I told him. They walked to each pod and left.

I sometimes wish I could talk to him and tell him how to make this a rehabilitating prison, but I would probably have to talk to Congress, because it just may take an Act of Congress to reform prison.

*   *   *

The decision from the Texas 84th Legislation was passed on 5/17/15. But I didn't hear about it until later. The three big changes were that the term "outpatient" was removed from the statutes, there were no longer a felony provision for violating minor rules (with the exception of tampering with GPS, contacting a victim, leaving the state, or not residing where instructed to), and all the committed would be moved to one Civ. Comm. facility and go through a tiered program that would allow you to work your way off of civil commitment. (Before in fifteen years no one had been released off of Civ. Comm. except through death, and maybe then.)

Then came the irony, if you will, worthy of the Alanis Morissette song. The savings clause made this new law to *not* be retroactive. Which meant Texas lawmakers were saying, "Yeah, we violated your rights, but we are not fixing it for you. We won't do it anymore." They left in prison the very ones harmed by the unconstitutional law in the first place. Which violates the equal protection clause and other civil liberty rights.

And this year, 2021, now makes six years since the crime that I was put back in prison for for twenty years, has been decriminalized. No longer a crime. And yet I sit here in prison being exposed to COVID-19. I have been set off from parole for the last thirteen years. I have received thirteen one-year set offs in a row. For the last seven years I have not had any disciplinary cases. And parole knows that when I get out, I will be going to another prison called the "Texas Civil Commitment Center" in Littlefield, Texas. But Texas must have its revenge and punish me for a crime that is no longer a crime. Even though the Constitution gives me a vested liberty interest in a Civ. Comm. program that will "treat" me and allow me to work my way off Civ. Comm. That is, if I even met the requirements for Civ. Comm., but I don't.

And some people say. "It's okay because you are a sex offender." But one of the Founding Fathers said this hard truth: "He that would make his own liberty secure must guard even his enemy from oppression; for if he violates this duty, he establishes a precedent that will reach even to himself." (Thomas Paine)

You see, because our State Legislators are smart, they didn't declare in writing that the old Civ. Comm. laws were unconstitutional, but just amended them, which leaves precedent in place. "They did it to me and they are gonna do it to you." (Sandra Bullock in *The Net*.)

*　　*　　*

I began a writing spree again. I wrote everyone involved. I got lawyers' addresses out of *Texas Monthly Magazine* and *D Magazine*'s super lawyers' layout. I wrote and begged for help. I did not even get a response. I wrote to the media again but not one wanted to write an article or do a report. I wouldn't get a response from them either. I kept telling myself, "Write a book and tell the whole story. Maybe it will help. And if not, it will possibly help others grow up and think and feel in a more appropriate way." But I kept putting it off.

In 2017 Telford unit began shipping to other units all of their ad. seg. inmates. All ad. seg. was in 12 building, in a single cell, and it was air conditioned. The unit decided to move safekeeping to 12 building. There were two majors on Telford who were over GP, and the other who was over ad. seg., with ad. seg. out of the way. This major was over B side of the Telford unit.

When I found out that I was going to 12 building I wrote a "job app resume" and gave it to a lieutenant who used to be my sergeant and she read it and couldn't stop laughing. I listed my skills as "watching out for rank, oh you are the rank, I mean I clean real good." My education as "yes, I got one of those." She brought it to the major and he had a good laugh. He hired me as his janitor on 12 building.

A major's janitor always makes sure the major is taken care of, addressing everything needed. I made his tea, got his food from the ODR, cleaned his office periodically, checked on him and asked if he needed anything. And still cleaned the 12 building hallway, offices, and so on.

It wasn't unusual for the major to call me into his office and say "Jones, do you like sleep?"

"No sir, never even heard of it."

"Good, after you finish your twelve-hour shift, get a crew together and go to 8 building and have it ready for the auditors tomorrow."

Which meant I handpicked people who would work hard and go get chemicals and floor stripper and deck brushes, squeegees, mops, and so on, and go to 8 building where close custody inmates were housed and clean up. This building was filthy. The inmates set mattresses and other state property on fire and it melted into the concrete. 8 building had three pods and three sections on each pod and we had to run the floor stripper in each one, on each of the three rows, squeegee it up, mop it up, and move to the next ones. Then I had to go back to my day job by 5:30 am. I would get my workers and myself food from the ODR and that motivated them to work for it.

In 12 building it is one long hallway that needs stripping, waxing, buffing and constant sweeping and mopping. We would strip and wax every six months; when someone would flood their cell all the janitors would come together to get it cleaned up.

The desk bosses and sergeants that I had on 3 building have now promoted to sergeants and lieutenants themselves. A couple had moved up to captain. I hung out in the lieutenants' office. I did the paperwork for some of them. I could sit in that office and feel at home; I never got the feeling that I was in the way. When they would have a shift spread, I would cook the food for them and of course, I ate very good.

Being on safekeeping, I could walk all over the unit and no boss would ask me what I was doing. I was highly trusted and I did not want to abuse that trust.

I had begun hanging out in the property room. The lady in the property room used to be my desk boss on 3 building so I would always help Ms. H. out when she needed it. My major moved to GP major and before he left, he called me into his office and told me I was now assigned to the property room.

He did this as a reward for my service to him. Property was a great job that required trust. I do not steal and I think that it is a real cowardice to steal from someone who is not there to defend his property. But the best part is Ms. H. had about nine filing cabinets that needed to be organized, filed, and old files placed in retention. I loved doing that because there is something very satisfying in getting all the paperwork in a sensible order and have it at hand when needed. There were over 2800 inmates on Telford unit and the property room has a folder for each one. My memory skills came in handy as I organized these files for Ms. H.

I would still hang out in the lieutenant's office after I got off work in the property room. I would still get the benefits of eating free world food. But here is another disclaimer: not every boss at Telford was lazy, or dirty. There were good officers who came to work every day and did their job fairly, firmly and consistently. And the dirty officer jeopardizes the good officer's life by doing what he/she does. If a person will bring one cigarette in, what won't they bring in? It puts inmates in jeopardy also, and demeans security in a place that has to be secure, and have legitimate authority over the inmates there.

*   *   *

In 2018 the Mike Barber ministry came and had a tent revival at Telford. I had written and typed up a two-page account of my testimony. Mike Barber, who never he lets an inmate get on stage, allowed me two minutes to briefly tell my testimony. (This testimony was later published in a Christian magazine called *Loaves and Fishes*, Issue 40. You can see it at lighthousepublishing.org)

After I gave my testimony an inmate who was on the inmate chapel ministry asked me why he hadn't seen me at church. Well, at Telford unit the safekeeping service was separate from the general population service and all of medium custody went to this service, and it was a place for boyfriends to meet up with their boyfriends. And most of the visitors who came to preach were of the "name it and claim it" group. So, it was fake doctrine preached to people who didn't want to change. I think Jesus said it like this: the blind leading the blind and they both fall into the pit. (Luke 6:39)

It was a crazy setting. But I began going to services. And the visitor preachers would always preach about homosexuality; the inmates would listen to them when they preached. I talked to the chaplain about this. And I was surprised by his answer. Basically, he told me that I only hear that every time because that is what is prevalent in the church. He was inured to safekeeping and didn't like the group. But I could understand that, seeing how they behaved. It's just that now that I was free from that lifestyle, I had a better sense of what would help reach people in that lifestyle. And it's not conversion therapy, not pointing a finger at their sin, and not judging them and telling them that they are going to hell.

But open arms of love, God's love, and preaching the gospel. The gospel is enough to save and deliver. The problem is not homosexuality, the problem is sin, the condition of the heart. Homosexuality is a symptom of the sinner's condition. Some people choose drugs, overeating, conning people, gossip, lying, and so on, to solve this condition of the heart, others choose same sex partners and believe that it's okay because they feel this way, always felt this way and want government rights to protect their feelings. I suggest we always felt that way because we were born in sin and in our developing years we picked up thoughts or behavior that became patterns and a belief system. And some people are abused into this belief system. I believe that it is that core belief which the Bible calls "being born a sinner," that we inherited, that causes us to find things to fill that void. And we gather things to ourselves that reinforce this belief and we are convinced that we are right and everyone else needs to calm down.

I further believe that the only one who can tell us who we are and whether we are naked or not is the one who created us. And this creator said that in order to enter His kingdom we must be born again (receive a new heart with a new core belief and our true identity).

I think about the court case where a gay couple sued a baker for refusing to bake a cake. I wish I could bake everyone a cake because my Bible says, "They will know you are my disciples if you love one another." (John 13:35) That is the creator talking. His love does no harm.

So, who told you that you are _____? (Fill in the blank)

PRICE DANIEL UNIT

2018 to the Present

"While I am in this world, I am resolved that no vexation shall
put me out of temper if I can possibly command myself. Even old
age, which is making strides towards me, shall not prevail to make me
peevish."
-Sam Adams

There is a solid satisfaction in one's having and being conscious that
he merits the good opinion of men of true discernment and real worth.
But to have a name among the weak and the wicked is shame and
reproach."
-Sam Adams

In December 2018, the TDCJ decided to start transferring safekeeping
off of Telford. I was sent to the Price Daniel unit. The Daniel unit is
built like the Gib Lewis unit, and is out in Snyder, Texas.
I was on Telford for almost ten years. That was the one of the hardest

things I had to do, leaving a unit where I had friends amongst the inmates and officers. My comfort zone was being snatched from under me. I could not have had it better in prison. As a major's janitor I worked five days a week on both A and B cards and a lot of B card officers had started to like me. It was like they couldn't remember why they didn't in the first place. I would work on weekends also, mainly to stay busy.

The morning that I was to get on the chain bus it was on B card so I didn't get to say bye to officers with whom I was really close. The people that I did go around and say bye to, I couldn't keep tears out of my eyes. What kind of place is prison where I could make friends, build trust and then be suddenly shipped to another unit, not getting closure, or getting to say goodbye. The opposite is to not make friends or get close to anyone. But that is not healthy; people need to be able to be social. In life there are many risks, and in prison it's a precarious thing to make friends. You can either turn your heart into stone and not feel or risk being hurt, or like me choose to be vulnerable. Life, I have learned, is full of a range of emotions and pain is a part of it. I finally know how to deal with it appropriately and not stuff it down or ignore it, or soothe it away.

Price Daniel unit was a 1300-man unit with good food and a nice chapel. Safekeeping was on J3 building and was on only one wing. Each building had three wings. The three wings on J3 are labeled G, H, and I. Safekeeping is on H wing. When I got there on December 13, 2018, there were about fifty-eight offenders on H-wing out of a possible eighty-four.

The problem was that on Daniel unit, safekeeping either works in the laundry or as a janitor on the one wing, H, that we lived on. We were not allowed to have good jobs such as I had on Telford.

When I went into UCC both wardens were in there, the chief of Classification and a maintenance employee. When the warden asked me if I had any questions, I told him that I was working for the major and property at the unit I'd just come from and could he give me a job similar to that?

"Right, now we'll put you as a janitor on your wing," he said.

They all seemed in a rush to get UCC over and that was all I could ask before I was led out. I found out later that on another unit in this region a boss lady had been raped by an inmate; they both worked in the kitchen. So because of that this unit didn't want to put any sex offenders in a job that would give them access to do that.

Being a janitor on just one wing is very monotonous and there are like ten janitors all on one shift. It is extremely difficult to go from major's janitor to wing janitor. And I wasn't being called on all the time. I wasn't needed. I tried to talk to a captain and before I could finish my question, he told me to get out of his face. Before, on Telford, I could go into a lieutenant's or captain's office and they wouldn't question my presence. This was going to take some adjustment.

Chapel services for Protestants were at noon on Saturday and 8 a.m. on Sunday, and visiting prison ministries would preach. They had an inmate band also. I introduced myself and told them about my testimony and inquired about getting on the ministry team. With anything that you join they want to watch you first and see whether your "on the wing behavior" lines up with what you say it is. I never missed a service and the Christian brothers on my wing gave me good reports and by November 2019 I was added to the chapel inmate ministry.

We took turns giving a sermon. We prepared it and turned it in on a form for approval. I had already been getting up before the congregation and giving encouragements to them or had led them in prayer. A couple of months after I was placed on the ministry, I prepared a sermon and gave it in January 2020. I used PowerPoint and I gave my testimony and taught the truth.

Most preachers are more charismatic than I prefer, but I gear what I teach to encourage people to stay grounded in the written word, and not be led by feelings. A lot of people are led by feelings and our feelings lie to us. Anybody can get up and say "Thus says the Lord," but if it is not backed up by the written word, be very leery.

Several years ago, Texas Legislation, in a bipartisan move, passed a law that allowed the southwestern Fort Worth seminary to place its seminary in one unit and to train inmate ministers. After they graduate, they are sent to all the units and they are called field ministers and they preach, minister, and teach classes.

We'd had five field ministers on Telford and I spent a lot of time with them. I learned a lot from them. When I got here to Daniel there were none. But eventually they started to send some and now there are six. One of them started coming to my wing twice a week to teach anyone who wanted to learn. At times there were two or three people in this "class" but I was the only one who stayed constant. Part of what he taught was how to interpret the Bible correctly, through hermeneutics.

I didn't even know there was such a thing. But it made sense, because some people, when they go to the Bible for answers, they read it on the surface, and the English language doesn't give the deep answers that the original language can give when understood. Many people pull one verse and claim it as a promise from God to them.

Hermeneutics taught me to find the understanding of the text that I was reading from the author's intent to the original audience. Determine the differences between now and then, to ask what the theological principle meant for them and if it was true for us, and that it would never change. And how did we apply that principle today. I learned that I couldn't be a surface reader, because the One who wrote the Bible is deep. I had to keep it in context and that it took a lot of observance and reflection.

The field minister began to teach me the basics of the Hebrew and Greek language. You don't have to learn the language to correctly interpret the Bible, but I wanted a basic understanding so that I could check somethings for myself. I was tired of being lied to, and a trust of men, especially men who preached the word of God, was hard to come by. I have high standards for preachers now, and if they start talking about things that I discern are not backed up by the written word then I do not have patience for that.

By the time we were to start learning Hebrew singular and plural words, well, the outside world had finally made it through that razor wire fence and affected us prisoners. It was April 2020 and the nation was shut down, and the prison began to enforce the same restrictions on us, as if we could social distance in here. Visitation and church were taken from us, a limit of how many people could be in the dayroom was enforced, masks and frequent hand washing was required.

In a place with nothing but time I suddenly had a lot more time. In April 2019 I had finally started writing this book, and now being forced into my cell a lot I put more time into it. I also began writing essays, stories and articles for Prison Journalism Project.org—a website that posts prisoners' writings. Just type my name in the search bar and you can see what I wrote about COVID-19 in prison, and other issues.

It is hard to do time, living and working on one wing and not leaving it except for chow, rec. and church. But in 2019 staff shortages hit even harder and this unit transferred about four hundred inmates and closed down a whole building because of not having enough staff to run it. Bosses from other units continue to come here on their days off to work overtime.

As I sat and watched the news and saw all the crazy things going on in the world today (pre-Covid) I began to think, "It's safer in prison." Now an invisible enemy was headed our way and the razor wire fence wasn't stopping it. No, because the ones guarding us would be bringing it in to us themselves. We couldn't expect TDCJ officials to have the same common sense that the NBA had and place their officers in a bubble or something. It was only inmates' lives at risk. Texas has the highest death rate for their prisons.

The officers and rank continue to yell at us to stay six feet apart and limit dayroom time, as they huddle up together and talk with no masks on. We live in a closed environment, we breathe the same air, there is no social distancing in prison. The prison pays millions in overtime to its officers rather than release inmates to parole. We are exposed to a virus every day. It is like they locked us in our cells and set the building on fire. It's like standing in the middle of the train tracks and getting hit by the train. It's just more of that sentiment that tells us that we are not worthy, that we are unredeemable.

Texas Prison has always run sans common sense: "If it makes sense don't do it," (TDCJ motto, unofficially official). But their response to Covid-19 is not even in the same dimension of common sense. The prison had standard operating procedures (SOP), and policies in place to ensure the security of this place, such as rotating bosses so an inmate couldn't get familiar and solicit them. But all this has been thrown out the window, due to Covid-19. We have had the same officers work on our building for months at a time before rotation. This is for tracking and limiting exposure. But in the meantime, it breeds not only familiarity but an inhumane treatment towards us by some officers, because SOP and policy are now made up as they go along. They hold us accountable for violating social distancing, or masks rules, while they violate it. They abuse the limited time in the dayroom, sometimes keeping people locked in their cells for three or four hours at a time. And the sentiment is prevalent and obdurate now more than ever.

And the tough-on-crime Texas government and lawmakers, they've decided to give the vaccine to the officers first and we will be last. The same captain that told me to get out of his face when I first got here was bragging the other day, "I had my two shots, I'm waiting for them to tell me I don't have to wear my mask anymore."

I couldn't keep quiet: "Sir, the vaccine lessens the chance of getting Covid-19 and its symptoms, but not from transmitting it."

He just looked at me and kept walking. I believe that the giving them the vaccine and not us first is one of the cruelest things Texas has done.

* * *

I continue to sit in this prison at the Daniel unit six years after my crime has been decriminalized. The environment that I live in on H wing safekeeping is a modern-day Sodom and Gomorrah. The guys and "girls" that live around me keep getting high, playing like kids and not acting like adults, engaging in sexual relationships, disrespecting the bosses and rejecting their authority.

That sounds like the old me. I see my old self in the people I live around, and I see it every day. But it has been a very cathartic experience. To sit around these humans and to truly understand why they do what they do, why they can't stop their patterns of behavior because they do not realize that they have conditioned themselves to patterns of thought and belief systems. That is a cycle that can be broken, but they have to want to.

This helped solidify in my mind and resolve to continue in the way that I am headed. I haven't had a disciplinary case in seven years and I haven't been in a sexual relationship with a man in seven years. I don't try to manipulate the system. I don't demand my way. I accept prison and take responsibility for my actions. I choose to live this new lifestyle of true freedom from the belief cycles that used to bind me up in destructive behavior.

I do want my freedom, but regardless if I get it, I will not ever go back to my old ways. Because, trying to avoid a cliché, I am free for the first time in my life even though I am still incarcerated. I turned fifty this year, so maybe this can be my jubilee year, who knows. But in the meantime, I keep doing time, and the people I'm around, well, some have noticed the difference in me and they ask me what it is. Then I tell them, because when they ask, they want to know.

It makes me ask, "When we *look* do we really *see*, or do we just take life as it comes?" For me, I choose to examine things to make sure I'm not being lied to. I know whose voice to listen to now, especially on important things like identity, emotion and what to believe. The name of being a Christian does not appeal to anyone because such a negative connotation has been put on that name. And all the divisions of Christianity have been clumped together, so much so that they can't tell. But I have found that there is only one truth in Christianity and it's His truth, correctly interpreted and applied.

When I was young, the big church after Sunday School was boring. And I always thought that this was how heaven was going to be. And I got the impression that we have to be really good and holier-than-thou. Now I realize that that's why the Christian religion is rejected. These two things that Jesus said, "They will know you are my disciples by your love for one another," and "Do unto others as you would have them do to you."

When I look around, in here, and out there, I see people getting high, shooting up schools and Walmarts, scamming people, and there is sexual immorality in every social order, from poverty to the POTUS. And it hit me, "How can we expect people to do good unto us, when we don't even treat ourselves well?" This is connected to love for one another, and our belief of what we think we deserve. When we continue in our cycle of self-worthlessness and believe that we deserve the bad, then we treat ourselves badly as well. This cycle won't be broken by adding ex post facto laws or keeping people in a prison long after their sentence is over. We as a nation must start in the family unit, pay attention to our children, guide them to question their feelings and not to take life as it comes, but to make sure they are not being lied to. And hate is a sentiment that is passed down, not necessarily in words but by behavior.

Maybe everyone needs to calm down and realize that although people are different, we need to look and see that we are so much alike. And if you want to treat others well, start believing, truly believing in your core belief that, first, you deserve it, and generate it for yourself and then you will treat others well also.

I have learned to stop running from the pain in life, to stop focusing on weakness. In the *Game of Thrones*, Tyrion, the dwarf, told Jon Snow to take your weakness and make it your strength. Carl Jung said, "What you resist, persists." In life, there is both pain and pleasure, and I cannot just try to pick out the pleasure and push the pain away by comforting and distracting myself.

I choose every day to live in reality. I accept both the good and bad emotions in life. Pain is inevitable, but misery is optional. I choose how I will respond to negative events in life; I'm not stuck in that rut of synaptic insanity-patterns anymore.

Pain makes you want to go find something to drown the pain with, but in the real world we have to be willing to let the waves of pain knock us down so that the pleasures of life can wash over us. The character of a man is revealed during times of trial and tribulation. The weak run to drugs, sex, and that kind of thing. The strong endure and enjoy the peace of life.

I am much happier living in the sobriety of reality. And now I know that it is a choice to live this way. Life truly is what you think and believe it is.

IN CONCLUSION

2021

"How strangely will the Tools of a tyrant pervert the plain meaning
of words!"
-Sam Adams

"He who trusts in his own mind is a fool but he who walks in
wisdom will be delivered."
-Proverbs 28:26

"In life, pain is inevitable but misery is optional."

On March 1, 2021 I received another one-year set off from parole.
That is fourteen in a row, and they all use the same excuse or
reason for denying me parole. Each time I got a set off they use
reason 1D:

"1D. The record indicates that the offender has repeatedly committed
criminal episodes that indicate a predisposition to commit criminal acts

upon release. Next review 02/2022."

That sounds like a cycle; don't they know I broke that cycle of behavior?

*　　*　　*

And a guy on my wing just tested positive for Covid-19. We are on our fourth quarantine lockdown. What is the definition of insanity again? I think TDCJ has changed their motto to "We just keep doing the same thing over and over and expect different results."

This cycle of insanity will just continue until they inoculate us or let us go. But this goes to show you how backward the Texas government is. They haven't done either.

The population of Texas prisons has decreased by twenty thousand over the last year, only because they are not receiving anyone from the county jails. When that floodgate opens Texas prisons will be in another mess. They have shut down about four prisons and the staff is still way short of par.

I believe that the Texas prison system could solve unemployment in Texas. But as an inmate I hear rumors that no one wants to work for the TDCJ. I hear commercials on the radio offering a hiring bonus. And that is sad for two reasons; first that they have to lure people in to work here, and second, I've known COs who get the bonus, "work" the required year, and then quit. During that year they call in "sick."

This is defeating the purpose, and it draws in people who are not equipped to work in a prison, and that compromises the security and aids in the mass incarceration assimilation.

And I don't want to be the type of person who sits back and complains, but doesn't offer a solution. Being here for thirty years gives me a certain experience that I can offer a solution.

I propose that the TDCJ release the offenders with drug problems, and technical parole violations. Did you know that when an illegal alien commits a crime that you, the tax payer, continue to pay for years, maybe decades? You pay for him to be in prison.

I am not against anyone coming to America, I mean let's face it., that is how America got started. Foreigners coming over and making this a nation, a country of (allegedly) no oppression. Then America gained a reputation for helping refugees and immigrants.

I totally get and understand people coming over here. But I believe that if you are an illegal alien and found to have committed a crime then America or the state where the crime was committed will give them a trial and if they're found guilty then America should deliver the offender to his/her home country's prison. It should be by treaty or international law that they do the time in their own country's prison. This will save tons of money.

Working in the major's office and with captains, lieutenants, sergeants and at the desk with the COs, I have seen how much paper is wasted in every office and every way. The prison needs to go to a paper free environment, as much as possible. But I am sure they can institute tablets for officers and inmates.

The prison wastes so much money in overtime due to being short of staff. But once the people with drug offenses, technical violators, and the illegal aliens are gone, that should shut down several more prisons. Texas has 102 prisons; the total population equals the same amount of all the Federal prisons in the US. Does anyone see a problem there?

After they shut a few more prisons there needs to be a major reform to sentencing guidelines and parole. Texas should retain between ten and twenty prisons and reform the prisons to really be about rehabilitation and corrections. Shortly after I got to prison thirty years ago, Texas took the word "corrections" out of its name.

We have become a nation that focuses on revenge and punishment. I'm not against punishment for crime—there has to be a deterrent. But mass incarceration in 102 prisons is not a deterrent. Texas prison is one big mess, a wreck just waiting to happen. They are only fanning the fire with the things they are doing now, before and during the pandemic. They aid in the problem and keep the cycle going.

There are hundreds of little things that they could do right now to save so much money, but they are so involved in the cycle they can't see that what they are doing is not helping, and it's costing taxpayers millions of dollars. The money saved should go to train COs to not just be security but to aid in the rehab process. Those ten to twenty prisons should be therapeutic communities, and during the offender's whole sentence he/she should be in a therapy program tailored for his/her crime. They should have different prisons for each type of crime. And with the sentence/parole reform, and the deterrent, and years of therapy, this should rehabilitate criminals a lot better, because it will be required to be in this program for the whole prison sentence, and because the masses are doing it no one will be ostracized for doing it and people just might change their thought and belief patterns, and perception of reality, and start to love themselves.

*   *   *

It is obvious that I didn't love myself, and in my core belief I believed I was no good, worthless and everything was my fault and I generated those results by my decision-making.

From the beginning I have said there is no excuse for hurting a child. And nothing could ever excuse it. I offered that there is a reason for it. Not that it justifies it, but it's a reason.

I grew up with a combination of love from my mom and rejection and hate from men. But I discovered something else. What I thought was love from my mother was not true love at all. She loved me in her way, but there was no discipline.

My first stepfather overtly abused me, and for years I thought he was my enemy. My mother seemed like an angel and a savior; all my positive emotions were wrapped in the mother-son relationship we had. But silent abuse I believe is worse.

Entered in my journal on 4/20/20 I wrote the following:

"SF (Stepfather) came as the devil and damaged me overtly.

Mom came as an angel but gave me silent abuse.

The silent abuse is the worst because you don't realize it until later and there are all my emotions involved. It's crazy."

*   *   *

As I daily continue to reflect and examine myself, I go deeper and have these insights. I had to be truthful with myself. I didn't grow up knowing true love and I didn't love myself. For years I held onto what I thought was a mother's love; it was my foundation, and now even that is gone.

This time, though, I didn't sink. I have been building a sure and true foundation built on truth and God's definition of love. The English language lacks the ability to convey this definition. We use the word "love" for everything, e.g. from "I love apple pie" to "I love Mom."

Love, true love, is a verb. It's an action. "It does no harm to its neighbor." And that love is how I act; it's how I treat others and it's how I treat myself. Because that golden rule is to love (do no harm) to your neighbor as you would love (do no harm) to yourself.

This is the sentiment that should be taught, overtly and silently, to our children, at home, in schools, in neighborhoods, and in prison. We must squash the other sentiment, the one that breeds hate and intolerance for people who are different.

I don't think anyone is asking us to embrace other peoples' lifestyles and beliefs, but to accept people as they are. To not attack people because they are different. If we like to watch Denzel Washington, Eddie Murphy, and Jackie Chan, Bruce Lee, Ellen or Sara Gilbert. Listen to J-Lo or Beyonce, John Pardi or Melissa Etheridge. If we read George R.R. Martin, Angie Thompson, Sister Souljah, Y.A. Gyas, or Kazuo Ishiguro. And if we eat Mexican, Indian, Chinese, or any other ethnic food. And we were entertained, laughing, learning, were transported and enjoyed the food, how can we so soon go out and hate the people that have given us these things?

By attacking anyone in that race you attack these people that we have grown to love. On the news recently in these attacks on Asians, a guy beat up a little Asian lady. Why didn't he attack someone like Jackie Chan? I think they know that Jackie Chan would get on that ass.

*   *   *

My whole point is that the reason behind *any* behavior is the same reason behind the crimes that I committed. We don't love ourselves, not truly. And we had to have obtained the definition of love that we do have from somewhere: our upbringing, peers, and media (social or other).

I am responsible for my decisions, clearly. But I wrote this book so that you may have a better understanding of how a child can grow up off track. But also, I want you to realize that we should never put them in a box and label them/us/me, as unworthy and unredeemable.

In America we help those in need and the ones in need are right here in your nation's prisons. We, in here, already believe that we are unworthy and a lost cause. We already hate ourselves—you see it in our actions against others and ourselves—it's how we got in here.

And then to spend ten, fifteen, twenty, thirty, fifty-plus years in here being told the same thing that we already believe about ourselves, only reinforces those bad beliefs, and then we get out and society expects no more crime? And all this time the TDCJ has been telling you that this is their mission statement:

The mission of the Texas Department of Criminal Justice is to provide public safety, promote positive change in offender behavior, integrate offenders into society and assist victims of crime.

*   *   *

As I look around with my thirty-year experience I do not see the positive change in offender behavior, I see them rewarding negative behavior. I have to still, today, resist the sentiment, and the assimilation. This is a never-ending cycle. I am fortunate to have seen it and to be able to avoid falling all-in. I consistently resist, examine, and remove any lie that has worked its way in. But I do this in accordance with the word of God and my savior Jesus. I no longer lean on *my* own understanding.

How much longer will you put up with prisons continuing in this insane cycle? Because if nothing else meets the definition of insanity it's the Texas Prison system. How much more tax money will you spend to support this prison system who issues out this sentiment, along with our TDCJ#. Taxpayers are paying for us to continue in the same thought and belief patterns and cycle that we came in with.

The rehabilitative services and programs in prison today are at best a band aid. They attack symptoms but not the root issue. It's like cutting a weed off at ground level but not getting to the root.

I have mentioned it several times in this book, the issue with molesting children, that while it is a problem, it was not the root problem. I, or more like, God, took care of that with the turning point He gave me that has changed that belief forever.

But that root problem was I didn't love myself. I had no idea what love was. My foundation was all sand, elusive and ambiguous. And everything I built on my foundation, that I thought was real, that I thought was true, never was around when I hit the bottom. I was living in a fantasy, made-up world.

I kept telling myself the lies. "This is love." "If I had this then I'll be accepted." "If only I can get his love, I will be alright." Over and over, ad nauseum.

Sam Adams said, "How strangely will the tools of a tyrant pervert the plain meaning of words!"

I had English words but I had wrong definitions. Have you ever woken up and wondered where your life has gone and how you got here? Yeah, it's like that.

I have quoted it before but it bears repeating:

"He who is void of virtuous attachments in private life is, or very soon will be, void of all regard for his country. There is seldom an instance of a man guilty of betraying his country, who had not before lost the feeling of moral obligations in his private connection."

*   *   *

Sam Adams said this in the 1700s. It's a truth that stands for all time. I had no moral obligations in my private life and I betrayed my country. And this is true with anyone who harms other people in any way, from a careless whisper to slander to gossip to face-to-face insults and the silent abuse wrapped in what seems to be a mother's love.

If it's true in one instance then it's true for all. We can't pick and choose who things apply to and who they don't. If it's good for the goose it's good for the gander. I'm not against the #MeToo movement, I believe people need to get their abuse out, I just don't think it needs to be ostentatious. It should be private. Because once you air it out and the movement gets going, I don't believe the truth can be found. Let the victims speak, and get it out. But you got to question motives for the ones who speak out to the media.

*   *   *

It all comes down to our core beliefs about ourselves, and how we saw those around us treat others, as we grew up. This is the common denominator. I hear on the news of drug use rising. The K-2 epidemic out there and in here. People like Whitney Houston, Prince and Michael Jackson and now DMX practically OD-ing. People are hurting on the inside and those people's core beliefs must be suffering. When I see people in here get high, I ask them, "Why do you hurt so bad?"

The people who don't harm others or themselves have a good self-esteem, a good sense of self-worth. They have a do-no-harm type of love for themselves. This is the truth in those two groups of people.

We must squash the sentiment and start portraying the sentiment of do-no-harm, of true agape love; it's the only way that people will stop hurting others and themselves. And when we really begin to love ourselves, then we can *look* and *see* that other people, while they are different, are really very much like us. And how can we hate when we know the struggles of our fellow human beings, who are just like us?

This is America, and we have always helped those who struggle. And if the Covid pandemic has taught us anything, it taught us that we are all in this together. Black, white, brown, yellow, and any other color; victim, LGBT and criminals, the virus has not discriminated. If it has hit any one race more than the other then that is ultimately the result of that sentiment.

It is time that we truly come together and get to the core of this. Let's love ourselves first, stop harming ourselves, then together we can stop harming others.

Let's begin a new thought pattern; when we see another person our first thought should be "How can I help? What can I do?" Our perception of ourselves and others and reality will be radically changed. It will make this world a better place to live in. Because if I help you and you help me, then both our needs will be met. There won't be any harm and we just might have some real joy that comes, apart from abuse, inside our hearts.

*   *   *

A last thought. It all started with a thought. A thought came in and was left unchecked. It was derived from my core belief. It became a pattern that persisted, it became the norm. A cycle of behavior developed. Moments of clarity would break through: why do I feel this way? Why do I keep doing this? These questions would surface but they were not enough to stop the cognitive loop that was on replay.

Only after a major event crushed me could I see that I was the one who was keeping myself in this unending cycle. And through much cognitive reconstruction I broke those destructive patterns and beliefs that kept me in a rut. I continue every day to reinforce my new core beliefs, examine myself, focus on the truth, squash the sentiment, resist assimilation, to love in action and I choose to remain living in reality.

David Jones
April 2021

ACKNOWLEDGEMENTS

In the words of Alanis Morisette, "Thank you, disillusionment." In order to be disillusioned, one must first have illusions. And I'm thankful to those potholes in the road of life that knocked me back to Living in Reality.

Of course, I thank my Lord and Savior Jesus, who is way more than a driving instructor. He led me down this road, made me hit every pothole and led me to know what true freedom really is.

Without the love and support from my family over the years, I would have stayed in a fantasy world. Thank you for your love and support.

It is places like Cadmus Publishing that helps incarcerated authors get their stories out, from A to Z they do it all, and they make it easy. In doing my research for self-publishing, I found that Cadmus offered it all for those of us behind bars. To the Cadmus Publishing staff, I thank you for doing all the hard work to get this book published. And Frank Reuter, my Author Liaison, I give special thanks, you answered all my (many) questions with patience and a professionalism that is rare in the world – at least in my world.

To the reader: I thank you also, because I trust that after you discover the truth of reality, you will have the courage to change your perception and in doing so, you will change the world – for the better.

www.ingramcontent.com/pod-product-compliance
Lightning Source LLC
Chambersburg PA
CBHW051846090426
42811CB00034B/2230/J